MAKING IT INTO A
TOP
COLLEGE

[
**10 STEPS TO
GAINING ADMISSION
TO SELECTIVE COLLEGES
AND UNIVERSITIES
2nd ed.**
]

Howard R. Greene, M.A., M.Ed.,
and Matthew W. Greene, Ph.D.

COLLINS
REFERENCE

ALSO BY HOWARD GREENE AND MATTHEW GREENE

The Hidden Ivies

Inside the Top Colleges

The Public Ivies

Making It into a Top Graduate School

Presenting Yourself Successfully to Colleges

HarperCollins books may be purchased for educational, business, or sales promotional use. For information please write: Special Markets Department, HarperCollins Publishers Inc., 10 East 53rd Street, New York, NY 10022.

SECOND EDITION

Designed by Jackie McKee

Library of Congress Cataloging-in-Publication Data

Greene, Howard, 1937–
    Making it into a top college : 10 steps to gaining admission to selective colleges and universities / Howard R. Greene and Matthew W. Greene. — 2nd ed.
        p. cm.
    At head of title on cover: Greenes' guides to educational planning
    ISBN 978-0-06-172673-6
    1. Universities and colleges—United States—Admission—Handbooks, manuals, etc. 2. College applications—United States—Handbooks, manuals, etc. I. Greene, Matthew W., 1968– II. Title. III. Title: Greenes' guides to educational planning.

    LB2351.2.G73 2009
    378.1'616—dc22   2008053189

09 10 11 12 13 ❖/RRD   10 9 8 7 6 5 4 3 2 1

CONTENTS

PREFACE]

We wrote our first book on planning for college admissions, and the sequence of steps that leads to successful admissions to selective colleges, in 1974. We have revised subsequent editions on the subject since then in order to keep the reader up to date on changes in admissions practices, testing, and requirements. This latest edition incorporates a number of these changes while adhering to the Ten Steps to College Admission, which have proven valuable to countless numbers of students. Over the years, we have witnessed monumental shifts in our social, economic, political, and international circumstances. America's educational system, from top to bottom, has reflected these changes. In the intervening years we have written additional books on the admissions process at the college and graduate levels, and on the experiences of students who have made it into the elite colleges and universities. In advising thousands of students for over forty years, we continue to find that the admissions process is both a science and an art. Those who have followed the ten steps described in detail here have achieved their goal of enrolling in a top college. At the same time, there are intangible, intuitive elements to the process that you must pay attention to as you move from step to step. Personal emotions, needs, and values—not just academic and physical features of a college—will play a significant role in your choosing the right college for you and completing the steps to influence the outcome.

It is time, once again, for us to assist ambitious, talented students like you who have set their sights on the top colleges by alerting you to the major changes occurring within these schools and how these are altering the admissions process today. The introductory chapter describes the major trends in our society which have directly affected our colleges and universities and what preparation is necessary for gaining acceptance to a selective institution. All of the key factors are discussed here, from the increasing competition due to more students graduating from high school and going on to college, to the rise in nontraditional students, the spiraling tuition costs and changes in financing an education, the marketing and recruiting by the colleges, the political and social tone of campuses, the technological revolution and its impact on the admission process and learning, the federal mandates that affect admission for learning disabled and physically challenged students, affirmative action for the socially and economically disadvantaged, safety on campus, and the role of athletic recruiting and community service in admissions.

Current Trends in College Admissions

As we write this at the beginning of 2009, a number of key trends continue to develop which we would like to mention briefly here. You will see that we explore them in more depth throughout the book. As we completely overhauled this version of *Making It into a Top College*, we were pleased to see that many of the trends that remain important today were discussed ten years ago in our first edition. We also remain firm in our belief that adhering to the principles and practices we outline in our Ten Steps is the surest way to ride out these trends successfully during the college admissions process.

1. Uncertainty and unpredictability have increased. The only sure thing about selective college admissions today is the lack of surety. As applicants and applications have risen, odds of admission have decreased, and applicants must be more careful than ever to balance their college lists appropriately, prepare

themselves academically to the best of their abilities, and present themselves in an outstanding manner.

2. The number of college-bound high school graduates is not going to decrease significantly in the coming decades. The number of high school graduates has increased from 2.5 million in 1996 to 3.3 million in 2008, according to the College Board and the Western Interstate Commission for Higher Education (WICHE). Over the next fifteen years, the number stays between 3 and 3.5 million. There is not going to be a precipitous drop in high school graduates, and college applicants, any time soon. The numbers will plateau over the next few years, but not decrease to the lows experienced during the early 1980s. There will be a diversification of the college applicant pool, with so-called non-traditional applicants, students of color, and first-generation college applicants becoming a larger percentage of the college pool.

3. Aggressive marketing and sophisticated enrollment-management efforts begun by the colleges to counter lower applicant pools two decades ago not only have not abated but have increased and intensified. These tactics have been facilitated by computer programs and the Internet. Selective colleges will continue to strive for a national applicant pool, to counteract the tendency of most high school students to attend college within a few hundred miles of home. Public universities will continue to ramp up requirements in order to reduce campus growth while enrolling those interested and qualified from within their state and from other states and abroad.

4. Interest in U.S. colleges and universities among international students will continue to grow. More international students, especially from India and China and other developing countries with more students able to afford an American education, will continue to apply. These students are and will be qualified and focused, challenging the best and brightest, let alone the average American high school graduate. And that graduate will need the advantages of a higher educational degree in the increasingly

knowledge-based economy of the future. For those who haven't read Thomas Friedman's most recent (2007) edition of *The World Is Flat*, we encourage you to tackle its section on education and the competition our young people will face as they move into the global working world.

5. The cost of a public or private education has risen tremendously. College cost increases have far outpaced the rate of inflation, and today the cost of a public or private university education comprises a much higher proportion of a family's income. The share of an average four-year degree covered by the need-based Pell Grant program has decreased markedly. Student loan debt has ballooned, with the average debt of a four-year-degree recipient climbing above $20,000. Apocryphal stories abound of students (and parents) borrowing $50,000, $80,000, $100,000, or more to pay for an elite private college education, scaring many families away from college, even though this is not the norm. Yet private lenders now represent the fastest-growing sector of the student loan market. With the recent chaos in the loan industry, student lending quickly followed the home lending market into a period of upheaval. Even colleges like Dartmouth, Harvard, Cornell, and Brown are sending signals of some bear market years to come, accompanied by hiring freezes, delays in campus construction projects, and challenges to their financial aid budgets. Still, stories of families' inability to borrow have been largely overplayed, in our opinion. There is still a lot of money available to help families afford college, in the form of federal and state need-based assistance (loans and grants) and need-based grants from colleges, including those like Princeton, North Carolina, and Amherst, which have increased the grant-aid and decreased or eliminated the loan debt of all or many of their aid recipients. Merit-based financial awards, or discounts, have also grown rapidly, so that academically talented students, if they are smart and apply to a broad range of public and private institutions near and far from home, can open up significant savings opportunities. Many colleges offer students in the top third or even fortieth percentile of that college applicant pool merit-based scholarships.

6. We have been writing for some time about a more hidden trend in
   higher education, which is the rise in the "gender gap," or the high
   proportion of female applicants and enrollees. Women now
   comprise some 59% of the college population in this country. The
   situation is more lopsided at many private liberal arts colleges and
   flagship public universities, with 60% to 65% female matricu-
   lants, and applicant pools that can be even more heavily imbal-
   anced. This trend raises any number of concerns. Sociologically,
   one worries about the abundance of highly educated young women
   and the decline of educated male peers. The trend is particularly
   pronounced among Hispanic and African American students. At
   colleges, neither men nor women seem to like an environment that
   tilts above 60% of one gender (single-sex institutions left out of
   this discussion). Socially, both genders tend to suffer. In terms of
   applications, the obvious dangers have been proven out. Colleges
   are giving preferential treatment to male applicants in some
   admission situations, even at highly selective institutions, where
   they need more men to enroll. Women are then being held to a
   higher standard and are finding themselves rejected or put on
   waiting lists while similarly or less qualified young men are admitted to balance out a class. This new "gender affirmative action"
   has turned the admissions world on its head in the course of one
   generation and holds true in many graduate programs, as well.
   The science, technology, engineering, and mathematics (STEM)
   fields seem to be the last holdout where men dominate the numbers, but one wonders how long that will remain the case.

7. It has become both easier and harder to apply to selective
   colleges. Students can now apply online through standardized
   application services like the Common Application and Universal
   College Application, or through colleges' own applications, yet
   they must often fill out numerous supplements and pay attention
   to pesky rules and requirements on a college-by-college basis.
   Thus, families must be well organized and pay attention to the
   fine print throughout the admissions process.

8. Standardized testing has become more and less important. There
   are more great colleges that have become test optional or flexible,

offering choices for students whose test scores are particularly out of sync with their courses and grades. However, at most of the selective colleges and universities, test scores are higher, and more important than ever in the admissions process. This is in part caused by the abundance of applications they are receiving, and the prevalence of high-range test scores compared to prior years.

9. Application strategies have proliferated, including Early Decision, Early Action, and Restrictive Early Action. Only a few high-profile schools have dropped their early plan (Harvard, Princeton, Virginia). Others have adapted theirs (Yale, Stanford). But overall, there are more colleges using one or more early-application options and most students we work with are doing something early, though often not binding Early Decision.

10. Waiting lists have also proliferated, as colleges attempt to assess students' level of interest and to manage overwhelming numbers of applications. For many students, the college admissions process is lasting longer than ever, well into the late spring and even summer after senior year. Your mantra should be never to give up and to see every year of high school as important for your college admissions success.

Note that portions of this trends discussion have been adapted from an article we wrote for DistrictAdministration *magazine, November 2008.*

The cornerstone of our approach to counseling is a belief that an intelligent and hard-working student will have a good chance of being accepted to one or more of the selective colleges listed later in this book. If you believe in yourself and are prepared to put in the effort, you will come through this competitive process successfully. Our task is to help you and your family support team by delineating the nature of the decision process and the procedures that will help you to apply to an appropriate group of colleges with the right credentials and the very best presentation.

The Educational Consulting Centers of Howard Greene and Associates have been advising families of a wide range of educational, economic, and geographic backgrounds since 1968. The information and strategies that we bring to the reader are based on our experience with thousands of candidates. College admissions officers, presidents, and deans have generously shared their expertise over the years to help us guide students wisely. Our continuous research and writing for the *Greenes' Guides to Educational Planning* requires us to keep our ear to the ground, so to speak, to be certain we are providing families with correct and timely information. *Making It into a Top College* is a comprehensive and accurate overview of the state of college admissions today and the means by which talented students can achieve their dream of taking their place in one of the outstanding colleges or universities.

Woven into the various chapters are information and guidance addressing the most frequently asked questions regarding admissions, fields of study, the nature of and differences between a liberal arts college and a university, and how to determine what is an appropriate institution for you.

Our hope is that you will learn two valuable lessons from this book: that there are many colleges and universities that provide a first-rate education, and that following a systematic approach to the admissions process will bring acceptance to one or more of these excellent institutions. As a further encouragement to take advantage of the advice we offer here, we share with you a letter from a parent whose son we advised in recent years was accepted to Harvard.

Your book is an invaluable reference in five distinct ways. First, high school counselors seem to have a much greater workload than in previous years. There is no possible way that even the best and most dedicated counselor would have the time to convey the amount of information that a student needs to be aware of not only in applying to college, but also in preparing himself to do so during all four years of high school. Second, there are very few counselors who have the expertise that you have so willingly shared with your readers. I consider myself a very well educated person, yet I found myself consistently amazed at the amount of foresight and preparation that is necessary today. Third, it is a sad fact that many superior and talented students are not admitted to colleges as they deserve, because their credentials are not presented in the most advantageous light. If they had only had the knowledge that you offer. Fourth, the number of students applying to selective institutions has increased dramatically and so therefore has the need for your guidance. Finally, you address the needs of all types of students applying to many different institutions of higher learning so that the book is an asset to all students planning to attend college.

ACKNOWLEDGMENTS

Over the many years of counseling thousands of young men and women about their futures, we have emphasized above all other factors the vital importance of choosing a life's work that is both pleasurable and rewarding. It is the people with whom one will interact and the opportunity to help them realize their accomplishments that has deep and lasting meaning. We have been fortunate, indeed, to spend our careers engaged with students who have the major portion of their lives ahead of them. Their dreams and ambitions, their hard work and persistence, bear fruit over time, as we have witnessed again and again. It is our good luck to be able to work closely with them over the course of their development into independent, contributing adults. Much of the material the reader will encounter in this book represents the voices of high school and college students who shared their personal aspirations, fears, doubts, and writing with us. They should know that their success in creating their own educational futures will serve as a guide for present high school students who face the daunting task of selecting and applying to colleges.

We also hold in high esteem the parents of the young people we have counseled. They have been assigned the ongoing task of providing unadulterated love, understanding, patience, and a leap of faith that their children will become the individuals they are meant to become. We are deeply grateful for their faith in us to help make the process of choosing a college more comprehensible. Parents' voices are also represented in this book through the many questions they asked and suggestions they offered as they participated in their son or daughter's college search.

We also wish to recognize the thousands of high school guidance counselors who carry an enormous responsibility in our complicated and stressful contemporary world. They have ever greater responsibilities for seeing to the well-being of the adolescents in their charge. Counseling for college admissions is only one of their numerous responsibilities. We have communicated with many guidance counselors who do their very best to assist students and parents in selecting appropriate colleges and understanding how to finance higher education. We are most hopeful that this book will provide them with a primer that may lighten their task.

Because of our professional experience, we understand the demanding nature of college admissions work. It is natural to view the admissions dean and his or her staff as the uncaring or insensitive gatekeepers to the college campus students strive to enter. To the contrary, the people who take on the role of selecting each year's freshmen class are committed to helping students make a successful transition from high school to college. A few days spent in an admissions office would make one aware of the long hours spent in reviewing candidates' applications with sensitivity and caring. The intensity of the deliberations in committee meetings to select those deemed most appropriate for entrance reflects their awareness of the responsibility they carry. Admissions officers put enormous physical and emotional energy into their job on behalf of both their college and the applicants each year. We appreciate their sharing of information and insights into the selection process with us.

INTRODUCTION]

The Changes in Our Society and Their Impact on Selective Admissions

Since the founding of the colonies well before America became an independent nation, education has directly reflected the values and beliefs of the majority of the population. While our educational system has grown into a superstructure unimaginable to earlier generations, this dynamic is everpresent. The sweeping changes that have occurred during our development into the most powerful and successful nation in the world have influenced the nature and purpose of our universities. The mission of most institutions and thus the content of the curriculum, the degrees offered, and the composition of the student bodies would be virtually unrecognizable to people who attended college prior to the 1960s, not to mention the pre–World War II era. Now that we have crossed the symbolic line into a new millennium, we can review the continuing shift in emphasis and challenges in our university system over the most recent decade.

These changes are having a significant impact on both the college selection process and the nature of the learning experience for any student today. Our population is shifting dramatically from a predominantly white middle-class citizenry to a multicultural and ethnic mix that within this century will mean that no one ethnic or racial group will represent a majority of the population. The greatest and most prolonged economic boom in recorded history, followed by significant financial turmoil, is creating complicated and conflicting effects: There are many more wealthy families who can afford to buy the best education at all levels at any price; at the same time, the divide between those who are accumulating wealth and those who are at or below the poverty level is growing wider and thus putting access to education out of reach for many families unless the colleges and the government come to their aid through scholarship assistance and tax benefits. As tuitions rise each year well beyond the rate of inflation in the economy as a whole, middle-income families are being squeezed at both ends, as they find it difficult to pay the full cost of a college education out of pocket but earn too much to qualify for need-based financial aid.

The alteration of our economic system, from a manufacturing and product-driven economy to a knowledge-based technological and professional service one, makes a high level of education imperative if one is to find a successful place in society. Post–high school training and degrees assume a critical role in career security, and therefore the competition for admissions is at an all-time high. Here is a statistic that reflects the trend affecting us: In 1977, the peak baby boom graduation year when our high schools were at an all-time high enrollment level, 50% of high school seniors continued on to college. In 2005, by contrast, 73% of high school graduates entered college. This figure does not account for the thousands of young adults who enroll in a degree program after working for one or more years or serving in the military. While the most selective colleges have felt the impact of greater application numbers each year, they have not increased the size of their undergraduate classes appreciably. Thus, the competition for admission has increased over the last several decades at a significant rate. The forecast for continued population growth in the coming decades adds fuel to the fire of competition and anxiety for families. The rise in technology as the ultimate tool for communication and business has accelerated the growth of the global economy. This dramatic shift to a knowledge-based economy has made advanced education even more important.

Intelligent students who, by virtue of their performance in high school, their talents, and their test scores, are qualified for the selective colleges and universities must recognize the greater obstacles to admission and the financing of their education, and develop a plan to surmount them. We hasten to reassure candidates that there are proven strategies for admission and for financing an education at the top colleges and universities. Out of many years of professional advisement, Howard and Matthew Greene and their associates have developed a system of guidance which has helped thousands enter the best educational institutions, and this system, brought up to date continuously to meet the changing conditions in admissions practices, will be effective in the new decade we have entered. Our resource materials and the files of successful applicants we have counseled have been put at the disposal of readers of this book to allow them to cope with the greater challenges they face.

Population Changes

A rapidly expanding, racially diverse population in the United States has brought greater expectations and demands for access to higher education among African Americans, Asian Americans, Hispanics, Native Americans, newly arrived immigrants, and poorer Americans of all backgrounds. According to the Western Interstate Commission for Higher Education (WICHE), virtually all the growth in the public high school graduating population between 2008 and 2015 will be in minority students. From 2004–05 to 2014–15, the number of white public high school graduates is expected to *decrease* by 11%, while that of Hispanic and Asian-American/Pacific Islander graduates is expected to *increase* by 54% and 32%, respectively. A great deal of this growth is expected in the crescent of sun-belt Southwestern and Southern states. As diverse population groups have gained a greater political voice and economic clout, they have stimulated the state and federal governments to ensure equal access to higher education. The response of the selective colleges has been to recruit aggressively non-traditional and disadvantaged candidates who qualify for admission. Affirmative action is in the throes of social and legal discussion and review, but nevertheless both public and private colleges and universities feel increasing pressure and desire to provide more spaces in entering classes for minorities and to assist in paying for their costly education. Since total enrollment in these selective schools has not increased, fewer first-year places are available for the so-called traditional or advantaged students, who now face stiffer competition among themselves. Whatever the eventual judicial renderings mean legally, most private selective institutions will continue to recruit these categories of non-traditional students and help subsidize all or most of their education. This is in keeping with their stated mission of broadening the learning experience of all undergraduates through exposure to a diverse student body. In many selective colleges, the proportion of the entering class consisting of first-generation college students equals the share of the class made up of legacies. Thus the selectivity of the top colleges will continue to grow, creating more challenges for some and furthering opportunities for others.

The Cost of Education

It is obvious to any family contemplating college for their children that the cost of tuition and residing on campus has skyrocketed over the past several decades. The present comprehensive cost of an education at a four-year public institution averages $14,333 for in-state students and $25,200 for out-of-state students per year, and $34,132 at a private college. The most selective of the colleges, by contrast, now average more than $40,000 for tuition, fees, room, and board. Although the annual rate of inflation in the 1990s and early years of the new century was the lowest since World War II, both public and private colleges raised their rates annually by significant percentage points. At one point public institutions were raising their tuition as much as 13% each year! By 2000, college costs had increased by 234% since the middle 1980s, while the median household income has risen only 83%. Between 1998 and 2008, tuition and fees at private colleges rose an average of 2.4% each year after taking into account inflation. This is a slightly less rapid increase compared to the preceding decade. At public four-year institutions, however, tuition and fees increased at a 4.2% average after-inflation rate, compared to 4.1% during the prior decade. As you will read in the chapter on financing education (Step Nine), the

top colleges have the highest sticker price but also the largest endowments and financial aid programs. For this reason, no qualified candidate should be deterred from applying to a high-priced institution.
Sensitive to the soaring costs, all of the top colleges have been limiting
their yearly increases to 5% or 6%. In a few instances, some of the
wealthiest schools are freezing their tuition or eliminating loans for all
or some students in order to remain competitive in the marketplace for
middle- and lower-income students. Approximately one-half of the students enrolled right now at these colleges are receiving financial aid
from the college, the federal government, and, possibly, outside private
organizations. The economic boom that ended in 2008 enabled all categories of colleges to raise substantial amounts of money from wealthy
alumni, companies, and foundations to ensure that they could attract
and retain top students of all socioeconomic categories. These gifts
were put into endowment funds for the purpose of dispensing scholarships to students. This is one of the key reasons we discuss the rich
endowments of the selective colleges. Thus, private four-year college
students get about $10,200 of grants and tax benefits and those at pub-
lic four-year institutions $3,700. So do not let the sampling of costs
listed on page 7 deter you from going forward with your goal of making
it into a top institution.

In spite of the good intentions of all major colleges, only a limited
number can actually practice "need-blind" admissions anymore.
("Need-blind" means that all candidates are considered in the admissions process regardless of financial need. Only at the end of the deliberations on their qualifications would the candidate's need be
considered.) Many colleges have acknowledged that they can no longer
abide by this practice, although they do their best to award aid coupled
with educational loans and work-study money to enable a student to
enroll. Many institutions now inform applicants who are placed on
wait-list status that they are unlikely to receive any financial assistance, so they should consider their other choices seriously. Some of
the richest colleges have recently changed their policy on awards by
eliminating or cutting back on the loan portion and adding more outright grants in order to reduce the growing debt of graduates. Princeton, Harvard, Yale, Dartmouth, and Stanford have been in the lead in
this more generous approach to financial assistance.

We recommend that a qualified candidate for a selective college research carefully which colleges have the larger endowment funds for aid and the more generous packages, so that the burden of paying for college does not become overwhelming. You will be pleasantly surprised, if you do your homework, at the number of outstanding colleges that promise to meet the full need of all admitted candidates. Changes in the factors that are used to determine financial need, starting with the Higher Education Amendment of 1993, which allows those applying for grants and loans to exclude as assets family ownership of a house, apartment, or farm, and continuing with the passage of the Higher Education Opportunity Act in 2008, have made more students eligible for aid. The individual colleges of means have made similar changes in their determination of need and thus more aid is now granted to more students. The federal government and individual states have continued their efforts to make higher education more accessible through such initiatives as education IRAs, specialized tuition payment and savings plans, SMART Grants and Academic Competitiveness Grants, and tax deductions and credits.

Merit-Based Awards

Over 80% of four-year colleges and universities offer scholarships to outstanding students irrespective of their need for financial aid. Their purpose is to attract highly talented academic students, athletes, artists, and student leaders to their campus, often luring them away from the most prestigious of the colleges where they might not qualify for any aid or would receive smaller awards. Only the Ivy League schools and a few other private liberal arts colleges hold to a policy of awarding scholarships only on the basis of need. One of the rapid developments on this front is the expansion of merit awards by public universities who also want to attract their fair share of outstanding students. It is no longer unusual for a top student to turn down an offer of admission from an elite private college in order to take advantage of a free education at a major public university. When conducting the search for worthy colleges, a strong student should be sure to check out the availability of academic and talent-based scholarships. More on this in Step Nine.

COMPARATIVE COSTS AT VARIOUS SELECTIVE UNIVERSITIES, 2007–2008

	OVERALL COSTS (Tuition, room, board, fees)	% FRESHMEN WHO RECEIVE NEED-BASED FINANCIAL AID
Amherst	45,652	51
Cornell	45,971	43
Dartmouth	48,180	46
Harvard	45,620	55
MIT	45,386	60
Penn	46,124	40
Pomona	47,845	51
Princeton	45,695	55
Rice	41,229	39
Stanford	47,212	44
U Michigan	18,637 (in-state)	41
U North Carolina	13,300 (in-state)	31
U Virginia	15,935 (in-state)	25
Vanderbilt	46,724	46
Washington U	48,884	39
Williams	47,530	52

THE HIGHER EDUCATION ESTABLISHMENT

According to the National Center for Education Statistics:

- Revenues for public and private two- and four-year institutions totaled almost $235 billion in 2004–05.
- The higher education system comprises some 4,250 public and private colleges and universities.
- Nearly 18 million students are enrolled.
- Some 3.4 million teachers, administrators, and support staff are employed.

Changes Within the Land of Academia

Educators who spend their careers tracking higher education have been highly critical of the quality of teaching at the undergraduate level. The large research, doctorate-granting institutions have especially come under fire for their emphasis on faculty research and publishing, and cultivation of graduate students. Undergraduates at the prestigious larger universities have voiced their disappointment at the poor teaching they have received and the inaccessibility of faculty for personal interaction and support. The growing cadre of graduate student teachers and part-time faculty, both of whom have little time for contact with students, has been one of the major cost containment trends but one that results in a negative learning experience for many students. As the criticism has become louder, many institutions have moved to rectify the situation on their campus.

Candidates for admission have the right to ask questions about what kind of teachers they will have, how accessible and committed to their students and classes they are, and what balance between teaching and research they are expected to maintain. Applicants should not be timid in demanding to know if their particular colleges of interest live up to their self-reported commitment to quality teaching and advising of undergraduates, and whether they rely on graduate students and adjunct faculty to run many of their courses. We found in our extensive interviewing of students at fifty of the elite colleges that this was one of the most important determiners of a positive or negative learning experience.

The Rapid Rise of Technology

It seems commonplace today to think of the computer, the Internet, and cyberspace as a presence in all of our lives. However, it was a mere blink of the historical eye when electronic technology went from being an unusual feature on college campuses to today, when one would be hard put to find a college that is not fully wired or wireless in the classroom and dormitory to make research, teaching, and interaction between student and teacher a natural extension of the traditional educational process. The contemporary high school student of excellence very likely has been using the latest technology for learning since elementary school days. He or she will know to investigate the state of technology on the campuses of potential interest and the ways in which technology serves the ultimate goals of education. It is hard to imagine that in so short a period we have come to take for granted the ability to "speak" with one another not at the drop of a hat, but with an e-mail, instant messaging, or social networking sites; or that we can research virtually every topic of interest via the Internet, or interact with teachers and specialists wherever they may be located. Students and faculty are no longer limited by physical space and campus resources in the pursuit of knowledge. Colleges and universities will continue to commit huge amounts of money to advance their technological capabilities to enhance the knowledge base of their students.

One element of this revolution is the ability it gives students to research colleges and complete the admissions process. In later steps we describe the ways in which you can carry out your search and make the application steps smoother and your presentation more impressive. The ability to locate financial aid sources and win a scholarship by using the Internet is also detailed. We provide a list of Web sites that will connect you with all of the major colleges in the country and with the financial aid search engines. Now a senior in high school can go to the College Board's Web site to register for the required entrance tests and even take real tests for practice. Most applications will be filed online. There is no excuse for a motivated student who is determined to gain admission to a selective college and find the means to pay for it not to be able to access the rich lode of valuable information. School guidance offices and local public libraries provide computers and Internet terminals to carry out research on colleges and scholarship sources for students without Web access at home.

The Growing Number of Selective College Applicants

High school students are targets of an enormous marketing effort by colleges of all sizes, types, and degrees of selectivity today. This practice is not new, but the change is in the accelerating volume of exquisite brochures, letters, YouTube videos, CDs, DVDs, and glamorous Web sites as vehicles to convince the potential consumer of the special virtue of each institution. The level of marketing has become as sophisticated as that of the for-profit sector of our economy. Senior admissions officers are more frequently given the title of "director of enrollment management"; teams of consultants are retained to assist colleges in getting their message out to targeted audiences and obtaining the highest possible yield— the percentage of admitted students who choose to enroll—in their admitted pool at the most efficient pricing or use of their scholarship funds. Why is this happening when there are so many more college-bound students today and when the number of applicants to the very selective colleges is at an all-time high? And why are there more high school graduates intent on getting a selective college degree today?

From the students' perspective, advanced education is essential for building a secure future and increasing a lifetime's earnings. Most smart young men and women are aware that the differential in job opportunities and earnings between those with a high school diploma and those with a college degree is increasing at a rapid pace. They are also aware that the better the college education they receive, the greater the opportunities will be. The best jobs and careers require more education and, in a majority of cases, post-college training in professional graduate schools. This, together with the sheer number of high school graduates, explains the surge in interest in the top colleges.

From the colleges' side of the equation, the top institutions are determined to maintain their reputation and position by becoming ever more selective to attract a broader and more diverse pool of candidates. The less well known institutions, in particular the private smaller colleges located across the country, are in a fight for survival as their prices make most families question the cost benefit of attending one of them. We will describe the dramatic increase in the use of Early Decision admission plans by a majority of the selective colleges to persuade more of the top students to commit to their institution, even as a few prominent colleges have dropped or modified their early-application programs. Whether a candidate should apply to a particular school on an Early Decision or Early Action plan has become an important strategic decision.

Public universities now enroll two-thirds of all full-time students working toward a four-year degree, a radical inversion of the ratio in the 1950s and 1960s. Many expanded their facilities, faculties, and programs in the years of the baby boomers to meet the demands for enrollment and the increasing desire of many students for specialized or professional training, particularly in business administration and science and technology. In the population downturn of the 1980s and early 1990s they were forced to reduce programs and find ways to manage their overhead. Thus they went on a campaign to encourage more students to enroll in order to retain their faculties and finance their extensive facilities, especially in the graduate fields where the siren of research and its resulting prestige lay. In order to attract the best students and build their reputation today, they have developed highly sophisticated marketing and academic programs, from the creation of honors colleges to merit-based scholarships and the recruitment of world-class scholars in many disciplines. Having a nationally ranked football or basketball team has become another means of attracting sports-minded students and more money from the state legislators who control the purse strings. Certainly this trend has created a very attractive opportunity for strong students, but you must understand both the advantages and the potential disadvantages of a large university setting and its rightness for you. The differences between the traditional liberal arts colleges and the more diversified universities are discussed in detail in Step One to help you decide which best suits your interests, personality, and needs.

Two particular groups who have been heavily targeted by top public and private colleges are students of color and international students. Recruiting students of color reflects the ongoing commitment to broadening the diversity of the campus population, both to open more windows of opportunity for learning and future leadership in the larger community, and to enhance the educational experience of all students residing on campus. The inclusion of international students also enhances the diversity of the community and adds to the perspectives that students will encounter in the classroom and dormitory. Today admissions officers are given specific assignments to fulfill these recruitment goals. They have devised all sorts of tools to reach these groups, which has resulted in larger numbers of applications. There are many more students of color and international students enrolled in the top colleges than there were a decade ago.

PC—the Political Correctness Issue

The dynamic of political correctness has become one of the most divisive issues on many campuses, and has attracted widespread attention in the media, especially since faculty and administrators have joined in an open battle for control of the curriculum that will be taught and the rules of behavior that will apply in the community.

On a number of campuses the divisiveness and tension among competing interest groups has led to administrative rules on personal conduct and speech that many students and teachers find objectionable. Most of the selective colleges have had to deal with verbal and physically threatening demands from many segments of their communities—demands for recognition by means of larger enrollment of students and hiring of faculty of a particular political or ideological persuasion or race, special-interest housing and programs, and formal academic departments focusing on a particular group or interest. The controversy, which is not likely to disappear as selective colleges continue their policy of increasing the diversity of their student bodies, centers on such sensitive subjects as racism, feminism, sexual preference, and cultural bias in the curriculum or in faculty assignment of reading and research topics. The backlash toward this from the right has been in the direction of a return to the Western Civilization core curriculum and a frequently heard emphasis on "traditional values" as the unifying theme of the entire education.

Although the "culture wars" have diminished somewhat in recent years, applicants should make themselves aware of the degree of PC activism at colleges of potential interest. They should consider their personal attitude toward the major issues causing tension and, in some cases, turbulence on campus. We have talked with significant numbers of undergraduates who are uncomfortable and therefore unhappy in their college because of the fragmentation of the community and because of the daily confrontations they have to deal with in the dormitory or classroom. This has led to a number of transfers to more subdued colleges in recent years. In our survey of students for *Inside the Top Colleges*, we learned that a significant percentage experienced discomfort over the intensity of the attitudes of some of their classmates. So, in your search for the right college, you should pay attention to the PC issue on each campus and the extent to which it might influence your comfort level as an undergraduate.

The political correctness wars, as some observers and participants refer to the debate over the recognition and rights of special groups on campuses, be they of a conservative or liberal bent, became heated enough to spur the former chief justice of the Supreme Court, William Rehnquist, to call for peaceful resolution in a speech on a university campus several years ago. Rehnquist opined that "the university educates but does not indoctrinate." But at some institutions, he said, "one senses there is an orthodoxy or sort of party line from which one departs at one's peril." According to the former chief justice, ideas one disagrees with should be met by argument, not suppression. Ideas do not constitute conduct that interferes with the rights of others. The clear implication is that when discussion over differences of opinion leads to verbal or physical abuse, this cannot be tolerated on campus any more than it can be elsewhere. We perceive a growing discussion on many campuses of the topics of civility, rational debate of issues, and the importance of values, ethics, and respectful thought and behavior within the curriculum.

Special Talents and Interests

The turmoil of the 1960s that greatly altered the tone of the college campus has also had a number of positive effects, including the greater flexibility of the curriculum and the broader cultural and socioeconomic composition of the student body. Today there is an active effort by the colleges to attract students who have a genuine concern for serving others through volunteerism in their community. Every top college's admissions committee looks for signs of service to others, especially since one of their stated goals is to turn out alumni who have a spirit of social responsibility and will use their education to improve the situation of the less fortunate. In the chapter on marketing your strengths, Step Eight, we describe the ways in which you can demonstrate your social values and work on behalf of others, as this has assumed an important role in the evaluation of a candidate. We do not encourage high school juniors and seniors to suddenly sign up for community service in the hope that this will impress an admissions committee. It is the individual who has participated in depth in a particular project over time and shown serious commitment who will win the hearts of the committee members. For those with a strong preference for service and volunteerism, many colleges have created programs in service learning as well as internships combining academic study with community work.

Leading colleges have also shown an increasing determination to attract and prepare more women for careers in the sciences. For all of the social changes that have occurred since the start of the women's movement and the emphasis on fairness in the workplace, women constitute only a small portion of science and engineering majors. Some of the top colleges have designed "women in science" programs to support talented female students through the rigors of an advanced science education. A student with a strong high school foundation in math, science, and computer science who is considering a career in any of the technology, medical, or engineering fields will find a welcoming audience at many of the top colleges today.

In an entirely different arena, the emphasis on equal rights and fairness of opportunity that led to such federal enactments as Title IX of the Higher Education Amendment Act in 1973 has changed the role of women's athletics on all campuses. Today women must be given access to the same level of teams, coaching, and facilities that men have enjoyed since the beginning of intercollegiate athletics. Successful lawsuits brought against some of the top colleges have propelled the development of competitive teams in more sports and the active recruitment of women athletes. As a consequence, a scholar-athlete who has a great edge in admission to top colleges can now be a woman. Observe any high school athletic program today and you will witness the extraordinary increase in the number and quality of girls' athletic teams and the number of participants. At the college level, female athletic participation has increased by 456% since the enactment of Title IX. We have encouraged many talented young women who fit the category of scholar-athlete to apply to the top colleges, and they have met with considerable success. Today over 160,000 women (43% of the total) compete in NCAA-sanctioned sports compared to some 60,000 (28%) a decade ago.

Male athletes should know that they, too, continue to have an advantage in a selective admission pool. We know from much experience that the strong athlete who is also a strong student has much better odds of being admitted than most other special categories of applicants. The strategies for taking advantage of this strength are detailed in a later chapter (Step Seven).

For a variety of social, cultural, and economic reasons, America's colleges have experienced an extraordinary shift in the ratio of men to women in their undergraduate populations. More female high school graduates are continuing their education directly after high school to meet a combination of social and educational goals. Many young men decide they would rather work or join the military either in place of or prior to enrolling in college. Since there are many jobs today for an individual with technical or electronic skills, which continues to mean mostly men, the choice of earning a good income immediately versus going into debt for a college diploma has persuaded many male high school graduates to choose the workplace. Within the major racial groups, more females are receiving high school diplomas and qualifying for college entrance. The gap is widening and is of concern to the educational world today. On many college campuses, especially the private residential colleges, women now outnumber men. This can make it more competitive for qualified women to gain admission, and it can also influence the social experience on campus. Thus, be sure to check out the ratio of men to women at the colleges you are most interested in and ask students to what extent this affects the social and intellectual life.

Crime on Campus

In recent years colleges and universities have had to become more conscious of the welfare of their students, and they have increased security measures. Campus crime has been on a steady rise in the past decade, since campuses are more readily accessible to outsiders and larger enrollments make it difficult to police the dormitories and other facilities. Parents are rightly concerned about the possibility of assaults, burglaries, rape, and even murders on campuses, big and small, across the nation. The world of the ivory tower where all is insulated from the problems of the real world is nonexistent. Students are frequently responsible for the assault of their fellow students as alcohol and drug abuse continues at a high level. Date rape, physical assault, and vandalism are directly linked to these chemical abuses, and college administrators seek solutions to this entrenched problem. Urban colleges are quite naturally prone to greater frequency of all categories of crime, which has led to larger security staff and measures to ensure student safety, from escort services to self-defense classes to all-in-one electronic ID and dormitory key cards. Those administrators who are not in denial about the problems of safety and protection of their young charges have increased the size and training of their security force. Ask about this when contacting or visiting a college. The street crimes reported daily in the media are also occurring inside the gates of the universities, and responsible institutions are working to prevent the worst sorts of criminal behavior.

As a result of a number of campus tragedies in recent years and the attention these brought, federal laws have been enacted that require college authorities to report annually the number and kinds of crimes committed on their campuses. Colleges and the courts are still working out the process and requirements of crime reporting. Students and parents have the right to see the report for any college under consideration. This information is available at any time, but is unlikely to be part of the glossy brochure or Web tour describing a college's special strengths, traditions, and student body. Three sites to check for campus and community crime statistics, in addition to each college's Web site, are: www .chronicle.com; www.ed.gov; and www.campussafety.org.

Another concern, as already mentioned, is the rise in heavy drinking on a majority of campuses, including the selective colleges. Numerous studies by research groups and governmental agencies all reflect the trend toward increased "binge drinking," which is defined as downing five drinks or more at one sitting. It is an intentional pun to state that it is sobering to learn that more students are binge drinking on a regular basis during the week and that women are engaging in binge drinking as frequently as men today. All reports confirm that drunkenness and heavy drug usage result in acts of vandalism, physical violence, rape attempts, and growing instances of death by overdosing or alcohol poisoning or accident. Parents must be reassured by strong evidence that professional campus security is enforcing the restrictions on drugs and drinking, and that administrative responsibility and active leadership for student behavior are in place to minimize the dangers to their children. We urge families to ask college officials during a visit or by correspondence what programs are in place to educate students to the dangers of substance abuse, and what measures are in place to minimize all forms of crime on campus. You will be surprised by the differing responses you will receive. On many campuses, for example, students who have been trained in peer mediation, drug and alcohol awareness, and leadership skills in high school or college are acting to implement peer mediation and conflict resolution programs, antiviolence campaigns, and substance and sex education programs. Many students are opting for "chemical-free" dorms and are working to reduce the abusive behavior of their peers. Ask about such programs if you are interested in assisting in this vital work.

The Trend Toward Useful Majors

Parents and students are understandably concerned about the benefits of a costly education—especially a traditional liberal arts education, which is what the great majority of highly selective colleges still emphasize—and whether it prepares a student for a secure career. Students in the main no longer view the four years of college as a time primarily to have fun and practice independence from family, because they understand that the greater advantage they take of the offerings, the greater the likelihood of landing a good job or gaining admission to a top graduate school.

At all of the selective colleges, half or more of the students are borrowing against their future through educational loans that they will have to pay off shortly after graduating. Parents and students need to ask, therefore, what an undergraduate should be studying during these competitive times. The claim of the prestigious liberal arts colleges is that the skills a student will acquire through their rigorous curricula will prepare him or her for a future career. Further, they espouse the virtues of gaining exposure to a wide range of studies, rather than a narrowly focused education, which will, in the long run, enable a graduate to adapt to all of the challenges of a constantly changing society. The statistics on the successful entrance into graduate schools and successful employment of liberal arts graduates is impressive. In our book *The Hidden Ivies,* we describe in detail the nature and advantages of an excellent liberal arts education. The more specialized institutions of higher education and the large universities, which are comprised of many specific career-directed programs, are attractive to those students who are convinced that their aptitudes, interests, and career goals are already formulated. Future engineers, technicians, businessmen and businesswomen, artistic performers, pharmacists, and so on, may well thrive in these special undergraduate studies. We can only caution high school students to take every opportunity to test their convictions through work, internships, and research into the nature of the intended career before they commit to a preprofessional or career program.

College applicants should take note of the increasing number of available majors with significant career promise, to determine what undergraduate concentration they will select and where the best programs are available. A significant trend in both the liberal arts colleges and the large universities is the creation of combined majors that fit with a potential future goal. These may include internships arranged by the colleges so that students may gain exposure to real workplaces; assistantships with faculty in an area of interest to provide deeper knowledge of the discipline and career opportunities; so-called service learning programs combining service to the public good with academic study and credit; and collaborative degree programs with major graduate schools, which are typically referred to as 3/2 degree programs. In researching your colleges, be sure to learn of opportunities in all of these areas.

The time-honored insistence on the part of the selective liberal arts colleges of avoiding any kind of "trade school" education has given way to a growing belief that an undergraduate education should continue to train the student in the intellectual skills critical to any field of endeavor but, increasingly, that it should also point him or her toward a feasible career. Liberal arts graduates have long been the staple of the law, medicine, and teaching professions. The rising dominance of science and technology in driving our economy has led all colleges of note to increase their academic programs, faculty, and facilities in these fields. As you read the literature provided by the colleges, you will see mention in every case of the career and placement service available to students. You should request information on the direction recent graduates have taken. What graduate schools have they enrolled in, what fields and what companies have they joined, and what kinds of companies interview on campus? In most cases we believe you will be reassured that the opportunities that await a graduate of any selective college are promising and diverse.

Students with Disabilities

For many years we have assisted men and women of good intellect and ambition who have some kind of a disability to succeed in meeting their college goals. Our hackles have been raised on more than a few occasions when a student has been advised that he or she would not be accepted to a selective college or university because of a physical or learning challenge. Nonsense! Since the enactment of the Americans with Disabilities Act (ADA), colleges cannot discriminate against qualified candidates on the basis of a known disability. In point of fact, a majority of top colleges have asked applicants for many years to describe a challenge they have overcome and how they learned or benefited from it. What competitive institution would not want as a member of their community an intelligent student who has demonstrated perseverance, persistence, hard work, and special talent in overcoming a major obstacle? We can recount stories of wonderful students who have compensated for a learning disability, blindness, deafness, cancer, or a physical deformity that they would not let stand in their way. We promise you that the great colleges and universities will take any of these factors into account with a positive attitude when considering candidates.

As you research the various schools, you will learn of the presence of special support services and trained staff that are there to assist all students. Note which accommodations are provided to make the experience work positively for you as an individual. Do not let anyone tell you that you will not be a successful candidate for a top college if you have performed well in a demanding high school curriculum. Be forthright in explaining to admissions committees what you will need to succeed in college, and look to make the right match with an appropriately challenging and supportive college. We can relate many admissions success stories of students who were encouraged by the counselors at the Educational Consulting Centers to share their history of a physical or learning disability and how they successfully coped with it.

Getting Ready

We have opened with this survey of some of the major changes in the selective colleges not to alarm you or to dissuade you from applying. Our goal is to alert you to what is happening in the halls of academe today so you are better prepared for what you will encounter. It is true that the top colleges are more in demand than ever, and therefore the chances of admission are not strong for students who are "on the margin." But who is a marginal applicant in today's world of admissions in the top colleges? The answer may well surprise you: It can be the high school's top academic graduate, or a high-ranking private school student, or it can be the all-around school leader, or the scholar-athlete, or the son or daughter of a long line of alumni from a particular college. It behooves applicants, therefore, to plan well their choice of colleges and their strategies for becoming outstanding candidates and, as we discuss in depth in *The Hidden Ivies,* to broaden their search to include some of the many colleges of excellence in addition to "the usual suspects."

To the uninitiated, who represent almost all applicants, this can be a daunting situation. What we have set out to accomplish is to educate our readers, to reassure them, and to instill in those who follow our Ten Steps the confidence that they will enroll in one of America's leading colleges or universities. To you high school students of talent with an outstanding record, we say there is every possibility you can win a place in a top college if you take the right steps throughout your high school years. But do not take anything for granted. The road to success is strewn with many obstacles, but with a critical eye, an open mind, the proper road map, and by making the right decisions, you can navigate your way to your chosen destination.

> To business that we love we rise betime,
> And go to 't with delight.
> —William Shakespeare

LET'S GET STARTED]

A Word About Our Ten-Step Plan

Since 1968 the professional team of the Educational Consulting Centers has used the concepts behind the Ten-Step Plan to help students make the transition from high school to college. As we have counseled scores of young men and women each year, we have studied the results of our approach to be certain that it continues to work successfully. We believe it accomplishes the goal of guiding motivated college-bound students to the right college. We have modified and added procedures and guideline materials continuously to keep in step with the changes in the colleges and the admissions process. You can rest assured that the program presented here is based on the latest trends and the strategies required to compete successfully for a place in a selective college or university. We are always sensitive to the individual qualities and abilities of applicants as we guide them through the complicated maze to the front gate of the campus. In no way have we ever attempted to fit the round student into a square hole strategic plan.

You will learn how to prepare yourself intelligently and skillfully for admission. However, it is you who must take command of the process and use the Ten-Step Plan to your advantage. All of the factors that go into the selection process are here for you to study and to use to position yourself accordingly. The worksheets and checklists can prove invaluable if you will employ them thoughtfully. Ultimately, it will be your hard work, your abilities, and your performance as a student that will gain you admission to a top college, and your preferences that will lead you to the right place.

Two Applicants Who Made It

Before you begin to acquaint yourself with the Ten-Step Plan, we would like to tell you about two different students recently admitted to top colleges who came to the Educational Consulting Centers filled with the normal anxieties about their prospects for admission. The young woman and man had much to commend them, but they were unfamiliar with the factors in the selection process and the essential steps they needed to take if they were to have a chance for acceptance. While they had different capabilities, interests, and backgrounds, they followed our recommendations with the Ten-Step Plan as their operational guideline.

Jennifer

Jennifer first visited us during the summer before her junior year. She and her parents were concerned that the small, semirural high school in Pennsylvania she attended was unknown to any of the top-tier colleges she hoped to attend. Further, while the family expressed their respect for the high school, they noted that the great majority of graduating seniors each year enrolled in local colleges. There were few applying to national-level institutions and fewer still getting accepted. Their first question, therefore, was whether a very strong student with many interests and talents could convince a selective college's admissions committee that she was well prepared for the academic rigor that she would face. Their ensuing questions had to do with the relative importance of academic course load, grades, testing, and any other factors that would persuade the admissions committee to select her over thousands of other qualified candidates. The answer from us was a reassurance that it was the quality of the student and her overall profile that could win the day, rather than the size and reputation of the high school.

After we reviewed all of the key factors in the selection process, we then challenged Jennifer to commit to taking on the work required to improve on them. Here is what she had to do to enhance her profile. Since Jennifer's high school graduated only 104 students each year and did not have a high recognition factor with top colleges across the country, she needed to distinguish herself academically by taking the most demanding courses her school could offer, and doing well in them. Thus, she enrolled in five Advanced Placement courses over her junior and senior years. All her other courses were honors-level. While there were moments of concern on her part that she could not meet the demands of this schedule with top grades, she persevered and succeeded by organizing her work schedule more efficiently and dropping several extracurricular activities that, in combination, took much of her time but were not especially rewarding to her. We recommended that her courses be well balanced by subject, that she not overload in any one area of study. The resulting combination of math, science, English, history, and language was an excellent foundation for any selective college.

The next issue was her average results on the PSAT and several SAT Subject Tests, taken in the sophomore year. Jennifer was concerned that substandard testing would automatically disqualify her for admission to the colleges whose admitted students had median scores on the SAT in the 1350 to 1450 (reading plus math) range. Jennifer was 200 points below this target at that time. "What should I do?" was her urgent question. From our years of experience we knew that outstanding test scores could be vital for an applicant from a small and less well known high school. We recommended, therefore, a two-part plan: first, that she begin a self-study program of reading intensively and working on vocabulary enrichment to ready herself for the March SAT, then, with her results in hand for review, undertake a test preparation course that emphasized frequent practice with simulated tests. Because her school courses were so enriched and demanding, she was positioned to take four SAT Subject Tests by using the May and June test dates as well as two Advanced Placement exams in May of her junior year. We could sense that Jennifer was an excellent performer in the classroom and that she worked hard to master the material in all of her courses. The Subject Tests would give her the vehicle to demonstrate both her ability and her intellectual commitment.

By the end of her junior year Jennifer had three SAT Subject and two Advanced Placement scores that were in the first decile for the top colleges. This gave her the confidence to continue her hard work and maintain her college goals. It was not surprising that her March SAT score improved but was still not in the desired range, since our counsel was that she make her grades and several activities the priorities for the year. We knew that she would have more time and energy to prepare for the SAT in October of her senior year.

With a strategic plan for courses and testing for the junior and senior years in place, we reviewed Jennifer's personal interests and talents. She expressed great enthusiasm for competitive sports, in particular horseback riding and cross-country skiing, and school and community service. She was very committed to her volunteer work with Pegasus, an organization that teaches disabled youngsters to ride both for pleasure and physical rehabilitation. We discussed the advantage of making a major commitment to these activities and eliminating a number of ancillary clubs and committees that did not matter as much to her and could prevent her from achieving the level of excellence, leadership, and satisfaction she desired. This would also give her those critical extra hours in the day to complete her demanding academic program. Jennifer and her parents were reassured to learn that what matters to the admissions committees is the nature of the activities a student engages in and the degree of talent and leadership demonstrated. A long list of activities on a résumé with little engagement will not impress them.

Although Jennifer, with the full support of her parents, had decided early on that she wanted to enroll in a top college and pursue studies in the life sciences for a possible career in medicine or research, she had no idea of the kind of institution that would suit her best. Because her high school was so small, the family was more comfortable with the idea of a small liberal arts college in the 1,500- to 2,000-student range. While we agreed that this was certainly a category that could work successfully for her, we encouraged Jennifer to also consider several of the top colleges in the middle-sized range. Our reasoning was that she was a socially mature, well-organized, and focused student who would take advantage of the resources of a small university. Together with Jennifer we developed a list of twelve top colleges in both categories for her to begin her research. The goal was to learn more about these schools, initially through reading their literature and visiting their Web sites, where she could gather considerable information on academic programs and resources, social life and activities, and specific requirements for admission. Then, during her spring break of junior year, she would plan to visit at least six of the twelve colleges in the two categories.

This was her assignment from us. We would then meet in the late spring to review her reactions to the colleges and her test results and grades to date to be sure our strategies were moving forward according to plan. Jennifer's initial visits included Amherst, Bowdoin, Williams, Dartmouth, Harvard, Princeton, and the University of Pennsylvania. Eventually she would decide to focus on the universities in the middle-sized range, which would include Dartmouth, Harvard, Tufts, Northwestern, Duke, Cornell, Washington University in St. Louis, and Northwestern. While Jennifer was very impressed with the environment and academic virtues of the small colleges, she recognized that she would prefer a somewhat bigger environment and a diversity of programs and students. She felt very good about her growing confidence that she was, in fact, ready for such an environment.

The next steps in the counseling process were the development of a final list of target colleges and consideration of an Early Decision application. When we met with Jennifer in the last week of August, we had a full picture of her academic and test performance for three high school years, and a clear indication that Duke was her first choice of college based on an overnight visit on campus, an interview with an admissions officer, and a meeting with a representative of the biology department who was engaged in research in genetic alteration, a field of interest that Jennifer was considering as her concentration. Having followed the earlier advice we had given her, Jennifer now had a profile that matched that of accepted applicants to Duke. Her SAT scores were all in the 700 range, she had either a four or five on three Advanced Placement tests, her grades were all A's and one B+ in outstanding courses, and she had won several awards for her leadership in volunteer work and sports. We felt that Jennifer was committed to Duke for the right reasons and that she could potentially help her candidacy by applying early. If there was any possibility that she was a borderline candidate who needed to build her credentials in the fall semester of senior year and thus ran the risk of early rejection, we would have dissuaded her from this strategy.

The remaining challenge was to present herself to the committee in the most meaningful way so that they would recognize both what she had accomplished and the ways in which she would enhance the Duke community. We advised Jennifer of the importance of her personal application. Again we challenged her to begin the process of writing about herself in response to the application questions with honesty, clarity, passion, and thoughtfulness. We knew that although she was a confident writer, she would need two or three serious efforts before she would have the final copy that she believed represented herself well. We also recommended that she create a personal résumé that would outline her many activities, awards, and recognitions, and her service to the community. With an Early Decision deadline in November, Jennifer would need to start this crucial step immediately. By the time she sent her application she had written a number of drafts in response to the questions Duke had asked her and she could say to herself, "I did the very best job I could and if I am not accepted to Duke, it was not for want of full effort."

Jennifer was offered admission to Duke on December 15. We share with you some of her presentation, which reveals both the quality of her writing and the things she did to make herself a successful candidate.

Responding to the question "Please write on a matter of importance to you. Any topic, and any form of written expression, is acceptable," Jennifer wrote the following:

> I am the complete embodiment of the "you throw like a girl" criticism. When I was little, I would watch my best friend play on her softball team but when asked to join, I always declined. I was

much happier spending the time at the stable horseback riding. Riding was my passion for ten years, so there was precious little time to develop my throwing arm anyway.

While I throw a ball like a girl, I do not always think like the stereotypical girl our prevailing culture perpetuates. Math and science have always been my favorite subjects. Application problems and their solution have long been my area of interest. I care deeply how science and math are used in the real world to solve problems and develop new methods of doing things that can benefit woman and mankind. Last spring, I was selected to attend the Economics for Leadership program, which is sponsored by the Foundation for Teaching Economics at Northwestern University. The focus of FTE was on integrating and comparing different aspects of economics and leadership. I participated in every aspect from selling and buying in a stock market environment to creating simulated communities where a balance of trade was essential for survival. In addition, I was faced with the question, "What did you learn in the last week about leadership?" To respond to this question I had to think about what I already knew about myself as a leader and what skills I needed to work on.

As a younger child I had been reluctant to view myself as a leader. That began to change at the summer camp I attended where I was voted to be a team leader. Once I got a taste of leadership, I became increasingly comfortable in this role. Throughout my high school years, I have made a major effort to be a leader in all aspects of my involvement in sports, community service, and the Hugh O'Brian Youth Leadership Program. This is now how I view myself and wish to assist my peers and younger students to grow into the roles they are fully capable of achieving.

I am aware that I will need to maintain my determination to follow my interests in the sciences and not let anyone deter me from my goal of becoming a scientist in the future. I have learned that I do not need to throw like a boy to achieve success in a field historically reserved for men. I understand that many women at Duke major in the sciences and enter graduate schools where they can prepare to become doctors and researchers. I hope to become a member of this community of scholars.

Asked "Why do you consider Duke a good match for you?" Jennifer responded in part:

> "Tenting with Internet Access." This concept epitomizes the balance between academics, athletics, and enthusiasm that I have been seeking in my college experience and which has worked well for me during high school. While the Duke student body is spirited enough to participate in Krzyzewskiville, they are also committed to their academics. It is not sinks and showers they need, but outdoor Internet hookups to continue to meet their academic challenges. Duke's student population—intellectual, involved, and ethnically diverse—is one of the major reasons why the university is a good match for me.
>
> My consideration for choosing Duke includes not only the quality of my four undergraduate years and classmates, but also my post-graduate goals. Duke will equip me to become a leader in my field by expanding my set of skills and enabling me to become involved in pharmaceutical research. With Research Triangle Park close by, I will definitely pursue an internship or a job at what *Fortune* magazine described as "the top place in the U.S. to do business." Duke offers a large number of exciting classes in the field of biology. I am most intrigued by the classes in genetics and cellular biology.
>
> With all that Duke offers its students, I would be very committed to giving back to the community. Having had such learning and service opportunities as the Hugh O'Brian Youth Leadership Program (Hoby) and the economic leadership summer program at Northwestern University, I feel that I can make a positive impact within the Duke community. I would hope to continue my commitment to disabled children through Pegasus or a similar organization.

Andrew

Andrew first visited one of the Centers' offices in the early fall of his junior year to begin sorting out the steps he would need to take to achieve his goals. He attended a large Midwestern suburban high school of 3,000 students which enjoyed a reputation for preparing its students well. Its size offered the advantage of a rich curriculum with many honors and Advanced Placement courses and many extracurricular programs. It also had the potential disadvantage that Andrew would be competing with his academically strong classmates for admission to the most selective colleges in which he had an interest. Further, Andrew's counselor was responsible for 500 advisees, which made it difficult to have ready access to him throughout the admission process, although he was very supportive of Andrew.

This is what Andrew wrote in response to the Centers' questionnaire prior to our first meeting:

> I feel I am an academically strong student who is motivated by desire for knowledge. My strengths are in the math/science/computer field, and I believe my weakness lies in the area of English. My teacher and counselor recommendations, coupled with my grades, indicate the strength of my academic performance.
>
> My personality reflects my ability to think and make decisions freely. I value my interests because I believe they will lead to my greatest happiness. I believe I have an obligation to use every minute to the fullest. To this extent, I spend a great amount of my time with computers and science. From the creation of the ice caps to the discovery of quarks, I want to learn about them all. I read with great interest, but sometimes reading cannot give me the fullest experience so I want to see things for myself. I talk with physicists and take courses like molecular biology. I climb a steaming volcano or see glaciers that form on top of mountains. I find the world around me is a fascinating place, and I try to enjoy it.

Both Andrew and his parents had high hopes that he would enroll in a university of academic excellence, one that was particularly outstanding in science and computer studies. They were in agreement that he would flourish in a middle-sized university in a suburban location with a diverse student body with eclectic interests. Andrew's father summed up the aspirations of most families these days: "Our main concern is finding a university that is attainable for Andrew and at the same time meets his desires."

It was evident that Andrew had analyzed himself thoughtfully in terms of his personality, interests, and goals. It was also clear from the rigorous courses he had taken in his first three years of high school and his performance in all of them so far that he was an outstanding student. The challenge, then, was to determine which of the top universities matched up with his particular academic interests in computers, physics, molecular biology, and biochemistry, in the environment he favored.

Andrew understood that the competition for admission to this particular group of schools would be intense. We reassured him that he had built an excellent foundation in his schoolwork and related activities which he could now build on, using the Ten-Step Plan. First we addressed the courses he would be selecting for the second term of his junior year, and for his senior year. By the time admissions committees would review his full dossier in his senior year, Andrew would demonstrate his overall academic ability and his commitment to his special interests with an academic program that consisted of Advanced Placement courses in chemistry, physics, calculus, computer science, and biology. He would also demonstrate his enjoyment of learning in other disciplines by taking honors or Advanced Placement courses in French, American history, economics, and literature. Andrew's grades were outstanding across the board for all of his high school years, again demonstrating his consistent commitment to learning. We indicated to him how significant a factor this was for admissions committees, since it was one of the best indicators of academic success at the college level.

The first round of admissions tests was of concern to Andrew. While his scores were well above the national average, they were not in the range for the top universities. By reviewing his strongest skills and course performance, we helped him focus on the particular SAT Subjects and AP exams he should prepare for. Given his exceptional motivation and energy, Andrew would make time during the junior year to study for the SAT in March. This would enable him to sit for more of the Subject Tests in May and June. He would also have the summer to study more intensively to retake any tests he needed to improve on in the fall of his senior year.

The next step to consider was how Andrew could differentiate himself from the thousands of other talented future scientists who would be in the same pool of applicants in the senior year. His involvement in school and community service activities was highly commendable, but we knew that he would be considered within the category of outstanding science concentrators and that it would not be sufficient to present a background of advanced math and science courses in high school only. Andrew sought out science programs for the summer that would add to his knowledge and skills and demonstrate his passion for scientific research. He thus enrolled in Brown University's Focus Program in Biotechnology for the summer after his junior year. He had also attended a Genetics Institute at a college in Maryland the previous summer. He took the initiative to learn of a research program at the Fermi National Accelerator Laboratory during the school year. His experiences in these programs were to serve as the high points of his presentation to all of the universities to which he applied.

The next step in the process was to help Andrew determine which of the many top universities best fit his criteria. After a number of campus visits, preceded by research, Andrew decided he would apply early to Princeton (this was just before Princeton dropped its Early Decision by plan). He felt that the size of the university, the tone of the campus, and, most important, the science departments and facilities were what he wanted. Because he had visited eight top schools, we were comfortable with this choice and encouraged him to proceed. By the time Andrew submitted his application he had excellent test scores, an A average through the end of his junior year, and a well-written set of personal statements that presented him in a clear and accurate light. His application was accompanied by a résumé of his science-related activities during the summers and school year. Andrew also wrote a thoughtful letter to the dean of the faculty, a renowned physicist, describing his interests in similar areas of research and his desire to study at Princeton. Here is one part of Andrew's response to Princeton's question regarding what particular skill, talent, or expertise he would choose to pursue:

> I envision myself intensely committed to the world of research. I have a desire to integrate the fields of computer science and physics that would enable me to develop an area of expertise in the field of scientific computing. The challenges posed by the realm of ubiquitous, interactive, networked computing are significant and exciting. I wish to pursue the development of emerging and unprecedented computer capabilities that have the potential to determine

whether scientific ideas can become a reality. How beneficial, informative, and cost effective it is to first simulate designs of complex experiments to determine their optimal conditions, potential
defects, or necessary changes! First exposed to the exciting, connected, and interdisciplinary environment of physics and super-
computers at the Fermi National Accelerator Laboratory, I watch
with wonder the advances made at the Princeton Plasma Physics
Laboratory and other national institutes for research. Through the
study of physics and computer science at a leading university like
Princeton I would develop the knowledge that would allow me to
play an essential role someday in discovering a new quark or determining whether a neutrino has mass.

The outcome for Andrew of a well-orchestrated admissions process
is instructive in a number of ways. He was deferred on his Early Decision application to Princeton, most likely because of the smaller number of admits the university was able to make due to an overenrollment
the previous year. While waiting to hear from Princeton, he revised his
essays and submitted applications to Harvard, Dartmouth, Stanford,
Brown, Northwestern, Cornell, Washington, and Tufts. There was good
consistency to this list; all of the schools fit the size, strength of programs in his field of interest, and balanced curriculum and social activities he wanted.

After the deferment from Princeton Andrew revisited several of the
campuses he had liked the most, with a more open mind. He now considered Stanford and Dartmouth his top two choices even though he
was still an active candidate for Princeton. In April Andrew received
letters of acceptance from all of the universities except Harvard,
Princeton, and Stanford, who placed him on their wait lists. By now
Andrew had determined he wanted to attend Stanford. This led to a
discussion of what steps he could take to make them aware of this fact
and how he could convince them to accept him. We recommended that
he write a personal letter to the dean of admissions at Stanford, stating
his commitment to enrolling if admitted and updating the dean on his
latest grades and achievements that were relevant. He had, for example, been selected for a Tandy Scholarship and been made the head of
two social service committees in his high school. His academic per-

formance continued to be excellent. We advised him to write to the dean at Harvard with a more neutral expression of continued interest, and commit to a place at Dartmouth. Andrew had decided that these were his top choices and so he removed himself from Princeton's waiting list. In May Andrew received a letter of acceptance from Stanford. He chose to attend Stanford, even after receiving a letter from Harvard during the summer offering him admission for the fall of the following year.

Andrew's experience provides several important lessons for the college-bound student. It is important to keep an open mind in determining which colleges are of greatest interest over time, and the popular phrase "It ain't over till it's over" is true. Andrew took advantage of the deferment from Princeton to consider more fully the other colleges that would meet his goals. By continuing to communicate with the deans regarding his accomplishments throughout senior year and maintaining his grades, Andrew was able to convince them that he merited a place in the new class. Choosing a class from a large and highly qualified pool of candidates is not an easy process for an admissions committee. It is also guesswork as to who is most interested in attending the institution. So all of the steps Andrew took paid off in the end. The ambitious student should note that each institution makes its own decision about a qualified applicant based on their overall pool of candidates and the particular interest and talent areas they are looking for to build a balanced class. There is more on this key principle in Step Seven: Find Your Place in the Class Pie Charts.

Jennifer and Andrew, by following the Ten-Step Plan, were both able to distinguish themselves from the thousands of other candidates through their hard work and their focus on the process. An important factor in their admissions was their understanding of the need to communicate to the colleges their individuality: that is, the assurance that they would make the most of the opportunities the universities would offer them and thus be significant assets to their respective campuses. By taking advantage of the Ten-Step Plan as Jennifer and Andrew did, you can gain admission to one or more of the selective colleges that are right for you. Doing this will require time and effort, but you will be a stronger person for it wherever you enroll. One of the great rewards the counselors of the Educational Consulting Centers enjoy each year is the sense of satisfaction and pride that students gain from the admissions experience. We believe this will be your final reward as well.

A Course in Admissions

The Ten-Step Plan is essentially a course in what is required to make it into a top college. It has been designed to cover admissions requirements, procedures, tests, essays, campus visits, interviews, applications, financial aid, and final enrollment in a logical sequence that demystifies the admissions process and reduces anxiety about getting accepted to college. By conceiving of this book as a course, you will fix your mind on the essential things to do progressively as you move steadily toward an achievable goal: acceptance by at least one selective college you really like—not a backup or a safety, but an institution to which you have chosen to apply because it suits your abilities, interests, and tastes.

It is our experience that when good students approach admissions the same way they approach a course in social studies or math, they stop wondering whether or not they will get into one or two particular colleges. Instead, they begin to see that surely they are going to get into a very good college, because they have earned their place by hard work and commitment. What they have to do is show the colleges who they are. The Ten-Step Plan is designed to help them do this.

The Selective Colleges

A selective college or university is defined as (1) one that receives many more applications than the limited size of its first-year class; (2) one whose majority of applicants are fully qualified on the basis of excellent course curriculum, grade point average, and admission test scores that place them minimally in the top quartile of college-bound students; and (3) one that can choose qualified candidates on the basis of special interests and talents that enhance the campus community. A selective college offers a higher quality of education than most institutions because of outstanding faculty, excellent facilities, capable students, and a tradition of the highest ideals and expectations for graduates. Being selective in no way means being exclusive. On the contrary, selective colleges actively seek to admit the broadest variety of applicants to achieve a balanced class that reflects the growing diversity of the nation. *Selective* means that each college is able to choose from a large pool of qualified applicants the students it seeks for its campus. This is possible because so many students believe that a limited number of the many four-year colleges offer the training and educational experience that promise a more rewarding life after graduation. This said, we have compiled the following lists of selective colleges and universities. The reader should be reassured by the length of the lists, as it represents the many choices available to ambitious students.

Relative Selectivity of the Selective Private Colleges and Universities

KEY

E = EXCEEDINGLY DEMANDING

V = VERY DEMANDING

D = DEMANDING

D American University

E Amherst College

D Bard College

V Barnard College

V Bates College

V Boston College

D Boston University

E Bowdoin College

V Brandeis University

E Brown University

V Bryn Mawr College

V Bucknell University

E California Institute of Technology

V Carleton College

V Carnegie Mellon University

D Case Western Reserve University

E University of Chicago

V Claremont McKenna College

V Colby College

E Colgate University

V Colorado College

E Columbia University

V Connecticut College

E Cornell University

E Dartmouth College

V Davidson College

Relative Selectivity of the
Selective Private Colleges and Universities (cont.)

D Denison University

D University of Denver

D DePauw University

D Dickinson College

E Duke University

D Elon University

V Emory University

D Fordham University

D Franklin and Marshall College

D Furman University

D The George Washington University

E Georgetown University

D Gettysburg College

V Grinnell College

V Hamilton College

D Hampshire College

E Harvard University

E Haverford College

V Harvey Mudd College

D Hobart and William Smith Colleges

D College of the Holy Cross

E The Johns Hopkins University

V Kenyon College

D Lafayette College

D Lawrence University

V Lehigh University

D Lewis and Clark College

D Loyola College (MD)

D Loyola Marymount University

D Macalester College

E Massachusetts Institute of Technology

D University of Miami

E Middlebury College

V Mount Holyoke College

D Muhlenberg College

V New York University

D Northeastern University

E Northwestern University

V University of Notre Dame

V Oberlin College

D Occidental College

E University of Pennsylvania

D Pitzer College

E Pomona College

E Princeton University

V Reed College

D Rensselaer Polytechnic Institute

V Rice University

V University of Richmond

V University of Rochester

D Rochester Institute of Technology

D St. Lawrence University

D St. Olaf College

D Sarah Lawrence College

D Scripps College

D Skidmore College

V Smith College

D University of the South (Sewanee)

V University of Southern California

D Southern Methodist University

E Stanford University

E Swarthmore College

D Syracuse University

V Trinity College (CT)

D Trinity University (TX)

V Tufts University

V Tulane University

D Union College

V Vanderbilt University

V Vassar College

V Villanova University

V Wake Forest University

V Washington and Lee University

V Washington University in St. Louis

V Wellesley College

E Wesleyan University

D Wheaton College (MA)

D Whitman College

D Willamette University

E Williams College

D Wittenberg University

D College of Wooster

D Worcester Polytechnic Institute

E Yale University

Relative Selectivity of the Selective Public Universities

D University of Arizona

E University of California, Berkeley

V University of California, Davis

V University of California, Irvine

E University of California, Los Angeles

D University of California, Riverside

V University of California, San Diego

V University of California, Santa Barbara

D University of California, Santa Cruz

D Clemson University

D University of Colorado, Boulder

D Colorado School of Mines

D University of Connecticut

D University of Delaware

V University of Florida

D Florida State University

D University of Georgia

V Georgia Institute of Technology

V University of Illinois, Urbana-Champaign

D Indiana University, Bloomington

D University of Iowa

D Iowa State University

D James Madison University

D University of Kansas

V University of Maryland, College Park

D University of Massachusetts, Amherst

D Miami University of Ohio

E University of Michigan, Ann Arbor

V Michigan State University

D University of Minnesota, Twin Cities

D University of Missouri, Columbia

V New College of Florida

D University of New Hampshire

V State University of New York, Binghamton

E University of North Carolina, Chapel Hill

D Ohio State University

D Ohio University

D University of Oregon

V Pennsylvania State University

D University of Pittsburgh

V Purdue University

D Rutgers, the State University of New Jersey

V St. Mary's College of Maryland

D University of South Carolina

V University of Texas, Austin

D Texas A&M University, College Station

D University of Vermont

E University of Virginia

D Virginia Polytechnic Institute and State University (Virginia Tech)

V University of Washington

D Washington State University

E College of William and Mary

V University of Wisconsin

Please note that these public institutions are considered Exceedingly Demanding, Very Demanding, or Demanding for in-state applications to the main
university campus in each system, or as noted. This does translate into a
similar level of selectivity for out-of-state applicants, although on a different
scale, since out-of-state admission is more difficult than in-state for these
public colleges and universities. The adoption of percentage admission
plans, whereby the universities must admit in-state applicants graduating,
for example, in the top 10% of their high school class, have made admission
of out-of-state candidates even more competitive in such states as California, Texas, and Florida. Merit-based HOPE scholarships for in-state students
have contributed to increases in selectivity in states like Georgia.

Because of its reputation for educational quality, a selective college attracts many more applicants than it can accept in a first-year class
limited to a certain number that has not increased over time. The most
selective, for example, now admit less than 15% of those who apply. It
is not all that many years ago that Harvard, as a prime example, admitted close to 50% of its applicants; now only 8% will be accepted.

We urge families not to despair when they hear of the competitive
nature of admissions today. A fact that is overlooked by students in
high school is the rise in the number of selective colleges available today. Over the past decade especially, more of the good-quality institutions have become outstanding academically. The competition for
places among well-prepared high school students, coupled with many
years of economic growth, has created an opportunity for many more
colleges to build larger endowments, to hire more outstanding faculty,
and to build first-rate facilities. They have also been able to increase
their financial aid awards to students of all backgrounds and talents
who deserve the opportunity to gain a top education. The counselors at
the Educational Consulting Centers are passionate in their belief that
there is a good selection of top colleges today that will serve a bright
student well. This was our major purpose in writing *The Hidden Ivies;*
we wanted to make certain that families knew of the many other outstanding colleges available besides the eight that comprise the Ivy
League. Even among the finest private high schools in the country, the
long-standing fixation on a small handful of traditional prestigious
colleges has given way to a focus on a larger number of top private

colleges and state universities that have attained selective status over time. These institutions are the beneficiaries of improved quality in high school academic preparation and higher standards in the honors courses. Better students attract stronger faculties, and alumni respond with more generous donations. All of this means that any student in the selective applicant pool, the upper 20% of each year's high school graduates, will be proud to attend any of the fifty or so most selective colleges.

Selective college applications are on a sharp increase for the foreseeable future for these reasons: (1) These colleges are held in high regard by graduate school admissions committees and employers; (2) more parents believe that degrees from the top colleges will ensure

---

THE MEANING OF IVY

Ivy was introduced into the American colonies by the British, who for centuries used it to cover the brick walls of English churches, homes, public buildings, and universities. Older colleges like Harvard, Princeton, Yale, Dartmouth, Brown, and Pennsylvania planted much ivy around their then new buildings and campus walls, and the practice was imitated by newer institutions. Ivy, over more than two centuries, has become a symbol of quality education and permanence, although merely decorating a building with this leafy climbing plant hardly suffices to make an institution academically excellent and therefore selective.

The phrase "the Ivies" or "the Ivy League" refers to a few of the oldest selective Eastern colleges. While some of the oldest colleges are located in the South, the Ivy League began as an athletic league of Northeastern institutions consisting of Brown, Columbia, Cornell, Dartmouth, Harvard, Pennsylvania, Princeton, and Yale. They formed the League in the 1950s with a common agreement on admission of athletes, athletic practice schedules, and rules to limit financial aid only to those who showed need. Athletic scholarships are forbidden under the rules of the League.

While ivy is associated in some minds with exclusivity and elitism, we know that it really connotes excellence and opportunity for outstanding students whoever they may be.

their children's success; (3) newly prosperous families can afford the high cost of private colleges and, at the same time, add to their own sense of accomplishment by sending their children to them; and (4) the U.S. is seeing increasing demand by international students from economically rising nations who want to take advantage of America's strong system of higher education.

FACULTY SALARIES AT SELECTIVE COLLEGES

One assurance of a quality education is the caliber of the faculty, which can be measured by their own education and training, and in part by the salaries they receive. At the most well-endowed colleges that put a premium on teaching and scholarship, the faculty are paid significantly higher salaries than are faculty at the schools in the less selective tiers. This information is not published in the colleges' brochures but is made public annually, and a smart shopper can ask to see the average salaries for all ranks of teachers. Here is a sampling of the average compensation for tenured professors at some of the most selective and highest-paying colleges in the academic year 2007–08. As a point of reference, the average salary nationally is $109,569 at the large public doctoral universities, $144,256 at private doctoral universities, and $83,560 at all baccalaureate institutions.

Harvard	184,800	NYU	162,400
Yale	165,100	Chicago	170,800
Princeton	172,200	Amherst	131,700
Stanford	173,700	Williams	126,400
Caltech	162,200	Pomona	129,100
Pennsylvania	163,300	Swarthmore	126,500
Columbia	162,500	Michigan	137,000
UNC–Chapel Hill	138,500	Virginia	132,700
Connecticut	127,500		

The Selective College Applicant

All selective colleges seek students with strong academic performances who have also demonstrated excellence in athletics, extracurricular activities, the arts, or community service. Knowing the level of performance and excellence the top colleges are used to seeing each year, we want you to have a realistic picture of what these standards are in today's world of competition.

What is a strong academic record? At least an A– average in the most demanding courses available at your school and combined SAT scores in the 1300 (or 1950) and above range, or 30 and above on the ACT. These are, with exceptions, the starting points for consideration at the highly selective colleges and universities. You probably know of students who were admitted to the top places with lower qualifications because of their outstanding athletic ability or other special traits, which we discuss in detail later. The number of such students who are successful in the competition is relatively small, a handful in the entering classes each year. Yet knowing that such a group exists should encourage any student with an abiding interest in a selective college and the willingness to work hard if admitted. The talented but lazy student should ask himself if he is willing to meet the constant academic demands if he were to be admitted or whether he is better served by enrolling in the next level of quality college. As we report in *Inside the Top Colleges*, a majority of the students we polled mentioned the high level of stress they experienced due to the amount of academic work required of them.

The best way to determine your prospects is not to make your own judgment regarding your chances for admission; instead, talk to a guidance counselor or coach or an artistic director and to the admissions officers at the colleges that interest you. There are levels of selectivity in any given institution. The colleges want to build a diverse and dynamic class that will take advantage of the many different programs on campus. You may be surprised by the encouragement you will get from colleges looking for just your kind of student. But be realistic and recognize that test scores and grades well below the colleges' standards will not impress the admissions committees.

Selective colleges look for hard evidence that you can do their academic work and that you have some absorbing nonacademic interest.

With the exception of the large public universities, they do not have any automatic cutoff level of grade point average, class rank, or test scores. If you have any interest at all in some of the colleges we have listed here, we suggest you follow up. Do not take yourself out of the running on the basis of hearsay, fear of embarrassment, or statistics that suggest you have to have a specified combined SAT to be admitted to a selective college.

If encouragement from your adviser is not forthcoming, seek confirmation from the colleges themselves and from the head of your special interest area that could bring you that extra attention you will need in the admissions committee's evaluation process. The worst that can happen is that you will be told your chances are poor, and so you will focus your efforts on other colleges that are more likely to admit you. Sometimes a top student fails to be admitted to one of the most selective colleges while another student with a less impressive academic profile is offered a place. We are never surprised by this because we know that all selective colleges, in seeking a broad diversity of student types, do not fill their class with only the brightest applicants. When a top student is not accepted, it is usually because of the nonacademic profile; in the judgment of the admissions staff, the student does not fit into the overall mix of the particular entering class in comparison to other outstanding candidates.

You can compare academic and test statistics of the first-year classes at a number of the top colleges and observe their similarity, but there is no meaningful way to quantify the nonacademic qualities of those admitted. Keep in mind that very strong students are admitted each year by some but not necessarily all of the top colleges. From our experience, we can attest to the truism that if the committee turned down the entire group of those accepted and instead admitted the next cohort of top applicants, their profiles would be just as strong. As we have already reassured you, there are a large number of colleges and universities of excellence available today, so any bright student can find his or her place with proper research and counsel.

Why Selective Colleges Want You

No one would be so foolish as to claim that the chances of being rejected by Stanford, with an applicant pool each year of 25,000 students, are not high when only 2,400 are accepted on average. But even the most selective colleges have urged us to communicate the fact that there are many good selective colleges and universities seeking students who follow the plan we have developed.

Selective colleges are quality educational institutions, which want quality undergraduates. You can demonstrate that you will be a quality undergraduate, and you can be a winner in the admittedly complicated and often baffling college admissions competition.

You have to believe in yourself, believe that you are unique. Admissions officers will come to recognize your uniqueness and see how you fit into their particular upcoming first-year class. So many applicants seem alike if they do not try to present themselves thoughtfully. We will show you how to create an impression of individuality that makes a selective college say, "We want this applicant."

The diversity of a balanced class of multiple talents, intellectual interests, experiences, and backgrounds creates "a catalytic effect," according to a former director of admissions at Dartmouth. Here is what Dartmouth notes on its Web site about its admissions criteria:

> Admission to Dartmouth is highly selective. The competition for admission is a function of both the number of applicants as well as their outstanding credentials. Each year, roughly 18,000 students apply for a first-year class of 1,075 students. A large and well-qualified applicant pool offers us the opportunity to enroll a first-year class that is broad in the variety of backgrounds, talents, and interests represented. Dartmouth seeks to enroll students who have established outstanding records of academic accomplishment and have made meaningful contributions to their schools and communities through their various pursuits.
>
> Our approach to the review of applications is thorough and thoughtful, recognizing that the mix of accomplishments, interests, and potential varies for each individual. In addition, the range of different opportunities and educational experiences of students necessitates an open-minded and flexible approach. There is no set formula or prescription for admission. Our understanding of the student's academic background is supplemented by essays, recommendations, and interviews, which provide insight into the applicant's curiosity, passion for ideas, and dedication to learning.

Yale describes its admission decision process this way:

> As it selects a freshman class of 1,300 from over 20,000 appli-
> cants each year, the Yale Admissions Committee is mindful of two
> questions: "Who is likely to make the most of Yale's resources?"
> and "Who will contribute most significantly to the Yale commu-
> nity?" These considerations require an evaluation of applicants
> that is more complex than simply looking for students with the
> highest GPAs or who are well rounded or who possess specialized
> talents. Given the large number of extremely able candidates who
> apply to Yale and the limited number of spaces in the freshman
> class, no simple profile of grades, scores, interests, and activities
> can assure a student admission to Yale. The admissions staff con-
> siders each application individually and tries to get as full a sense
> of the applicant as possible.
>
> Diversity within the student body is important, as well, and the
> Committee works very hard to select a class of able and contribut-
> ing individuals from as broad a range of backgrounds as possible.
> The ultimate goal is the creation of a well-rounded freshman class,
> one that includes not only generally accomplished students but
> also those of narrower focus whose achievements are judged ex-
> ceptional.

The concept of a balanced class works very much in your favor when you analyze the colleges and apply for admission to those that seem most suited to what you have to offer. We think of Joseph from a rural community in Maine, who wanted to attend an urban college outside New England. His personal statement on the application, following an interview on campus where he expressed the same desire, appealed to the admissions committee at Columbia. Although his academic record did not quite match up with that of the candidates from the large boarding schools and suburban high schools, he distinguished himself by taking four courses over his junior and senior years at the nearby state university in his intended field of interest, meteorology and physics. He was accepted in large part because of his uniqueness and his proven determination to gain the strongest academic foundation possible. Joseph might not have appealed as much to the top smaller colleges in small-town settings which did not offer this specialized field of study and had many more candidates like him.

To achieve a balanced class, the admissions officers travel extensively each fall to meet with and encourage students to apply who would otherwise not consider themselves qualified candidates. Roland, for example, whose widowed mother had limited financial means, was planning to commute from his small town to a larger metropolitan university that had an environmental studies program. A local newspaper report of his prize-winning air pollution research project caught the eye of a local Princeton alumnus, who notified the Princeton admissions office. A member of the staff encouraged him to apply to Princeton, which Roland had considered in the realm of the financially impossible. He was accepted and offered a full scholarship less his savings from summer jobs. The admissions committee saw in Roland not only a unique young man but also a student who would make full use of the exceptional resources Princeton had to offer someone with his interests.

Columbia University, which accepts fewer than one out of ten applicants, nonetheless is continually looking for unique students. Lizette is a marvelous example of how an ambitious and determined individual can take advantage of the many opportunities available to a disadvantaged student. In ninth grade she applied for and was accepted into A Better Chance, a national program that identifies outstanding disadvantaged students and places them in top independent schools. Lizette became an A Better Chance Scholar at Brooks School in Massachusetts. With the guidance of the counselors at Brooks, Lizette started her research on colleges during her junior year. After visiting Columbia and speaking with a number of undergraduates, she decided to enroll in the pre-college summer program at Barnard, the women's college of Columbia University. This experience gave her a taste of life in a large urban setting. The high academic standards, diversity of the student body, and opportunities for artistic and multicultural activities persuaded her to apply for early decision at Columbia. Lizette had wisely visited almost all of the Ivy colleges before she made this commitment. The university was impressed by Lizette's self-initiative on all counts: her applying to the A Better Chance program, making a major change in her life by attending a boarding school far from home, testing her preferences by enrolling in the pre-college program, and interviewing both the admissions officer and students of color at Columbia. She was admitted early and successfully completed her degree.

An Upbeat Approach

Applicants who approach college admissions with a "can do" attitude largely avoid the jitters that afflict many candidates in today's stressful atmosphere. A certain level of anxiety is inevitable, but can even be useful in pumping up the adrenaline as you begin the Ten-Step Plan. You will find as you proceed that your self-assurance will grow, and instead of asking, "Will I get in?" you will be thinking, "Which college will I choose when I am admitted to two or even three?" The belief that there is a place for you in at least two selective colleges will grow stronger as you proceed through the Ten-Step Plan.

When to Begin

The Ten Steps do not require a single time frame for completion. Most students begin the admissions process in the fall of their junior year, although we encourage earlier reading of this book to make sure all of the recommendations can be accomplished. This includes selection of high school courses, tests to be taken, activities to engage in, and use of summer time to enhance skills or to explore fields of interest. For a majority of students the process runs until the spring of senior year, but those who apply for Early Decision may be finished by December if they are admitted to their first-choice college.

How to Use This Book

This handbook should be used as a major part of your college preparatory program. It should be read in sections at the appropriate time in your admissions schedule, and then read again to be certain you understand the ways in which the steps can be adapted to your unique profile.

We suggest you read over the Contents, then read to the end of Step Three, underlining as you go, making notes of things you should do: Classify yourself; use the Internet and guidebooks to learn about colleges of potential interest; list those colleges you might apply to; note down admissions requirements; consider the advantages of applying for Early Decision or Action; answer the student questionnaire we provide; plan your demanding curriculum; and focus on those activities and talents that matter the most to you and that might also advance your chances for admission.

Read the succeeding steps in a sequence that fits your time schedule. Mark the calendar we present to include reading and reviewing relevant steps. Do the worksheets as you go along. They help you to keep your ideas, impressions, and information organized. Remember that every step and every worksheet has stood the test for many students who have succeeded in making it into a top college.

Your Syllabus: The Ten-Step Plan

The Ten-Step Plan is a course you are going to give yourself making it into a top college. This book is your text, and the Ten Steps we summarize are your syllabus.

Step One: Know the Selective Colleges and Their Admissions Requirements and Procedures

Amazingly, applicants will write in a personal statement on a college application that they plan to major, for example, in business when in fact the college has no undergraduate business program; or that they want to attend the particular institution because of its outstanding fine arts major, which does not exist. In Step One you are not asked to know all the colleges; you must know only those colleges you are considering as possibilities for your strengths and tastes. It is strongly recommended that you acquaint yourself with a dozen or even fifteen colleges of potential interest, visit as many as you can, and narrow your focus to eight or nine. Become very familiar with these from catalogues, videos, guidebooks, visits to their Web sites, and speaking with students and alumni. The more you know about the colleges, the sounder will be your choice of those to which you will apply.

In this step you will also learn why it is important to be thoroughly knowledgeable about admissions requirements and procedures. Such knowledge will help you to (1) clarify reasons to apply or not to apply to a particular college, (2) make your applications for admission and financial aid more complete and appealing, (3) discern the kinds of information that will be most useful to the admissions committee, and (4) determine courses to take in high school if you have not already committed yourself for a particular term. You might conclude that a fourth year of foreign language or mathematics would be more important than an elective in the arts or sociology, for example. Knowing how an admissions committee selects its first-year class is the beginning of your own education as you prepare for college.

Step Two: Determine Your Strengths

To reflect on who you are, to consider what you really want in life, and to know what you do best are fundamental factors in decisions you will be making to ensure acceptance to a selective college. We have prepared two questionnaires, one for you and the other for your parents, to help you in this quest for a clear vision of your strengths and priorities.

Step Three: Follow a Demanding Curriculum

All selective colleges have high academic expectations for their students, and the most important requirement they ask of applicants is that they undertake challenging courses during their college careers. You should know what the selective colleges consider to be the basic minimum of strong high school subjects. Such questions as how many honors or Advanced Placement courses need to be taken, how valuable it is to take a third or fourth year of different subjects, and what you can do to make up for required courses not taken will be answered in Step Three, which goes to the root of college admissions. You will learn what it means to go beyond your high school's basic requirements for a diploma in order to enter these selective colleges.

Step Four: Make Standardized Tests Work for You

In this step you approach the SAT and SAT Subject Tests, or the ACT, in a somewhat less tense mood than is usual, and you recognize that the SAT Subject Tests offer an opportunity to improve your academic profile. You first learn to appreciate why, despite the prevailing criticisms, admissions tests endure as a fundamental part of college admissions. Accepting the SAT or ACT as a given, you see how their importance varies from college to college. An increasing number of mostly small liberal arts colleges have even made submission of testing optional. You will discover how it is possible to improve your scores and what to do if a disability affects your testing performance. You will also learn to accept the level at which you test as only one indicator of your chances for admission to your favorite colleges. You will find out how to use the Subject Tests to bolster your candidacy. The value of preparing for them and pacing your test schedule can give you an edge over some students who take them all at once or at an inappropriate time.

Step Five: Excel Outside Class

Selective colleges are seeking well-rounded classes, not the well-rounded student. To be a member of a multitude of committees and clubs or to play several sports or to take part occasionally in theater productions will not make you a strong enough candidate in comparison to the editor-in-chief of an outstanding newspaper, the acclaimed varsity lacrosse or basketball player, or the student who gets the lead in plays regularly or conducts the school band and is in All-State band or orchestra. Even in senior year you can commit yourself to an endeavor that demonstrates your talent and commitment, and will thus add a special strength to the college community. You do not have to be an All-American to appeal to a selective college. You do have to go all out in some activity of your choice at school or in your community.

Step Six: Make the Most of Campus Visits and Interviews

Campus visits turn an abstraction into a reality. Visiting a variety of campuses, you will compare facilities, academic programs, and the social atmosphere. You will keep a valuable record of your impressions and be able to compare one college to another at the conclusion of your visits. In this step you will learn whom you should talk to and why it is important to stay overnight in a dorm before making a commitment to a college. You will rate the colleges you visit on a scale of 1 to 5, and use this rating to help you later decide to which colleges you will actually apply.

The subject of the personal interview is discussed, and you will learn why the interview is not necessarily an important factor in admissions decisions. You will also understand how to help yourself make a personal impression on those in the decision-making seat.

Step Seven: Find Your Place in the Class Pie Charts

Every selective college is made up of groups of students in such a way that you can construct pie charts that identify the different categories. By locating your position within such charts, you will learn where the competition is great and where it is less so, and where your special interests can help you to stand out. Finding your particular place in the chart of each college will allow you to adopt sensible application strategies. You will discover for yourself where you might have a better chance for admission to a selective college.

Step Eight: Present Yourself in the Best Light: Marketing Your Strengths and Writing Top Essays

In Step Eight you will see from examples how students have made extra effort to ensure recognition by admissions committees, faculty, and coaches. You can present yourself honestly and forthrightly to help the decision-makers understand what you have accomplished and why you merit a valuable place in the first-year class. Many students who have much to offer a college will lock their special talents and successes in a closet for fear of appearing boastful. You will learn why this is a mistake and why it cheats you of the opportunities you deserve.

Selective college applications ask students to write statements and essays that reveal aspects of their nature and of the life they lead in their school and community. Here is a critical opportunity to display your uniqueness. In Step Eight you will see how other students have shown admissions officers their feelings, accomplishments, and experiences in a way that reflects their character in a favorable light. You will learn which topics are appropriate and which are possibly not. You will learn to choose topics and to write an account that awakens the reader's interest. You will learn to respond to questions in brief, concise, meaningful terms. You will also learn what supplemental materials can help to highlight your strengths and appeal to the committees.

Step Nine: Plan Your Selective-College Finances

Knowing college costs and financial procedures, you can plan how to pay for the high tuitions charged by the selective colleges. Procedures are somewhat complex and will require time on the part of your family, not just yourself. You will learn how to undertake the process in the most efficient manner, what forms and information must be provided, what the procedures and programs are for applying for aid, and the best avenues for learning about the many sources of aid today. You will come to understand that you can consider applying to the top colleges and ignore their high costs if you are a strong candidate.

Step Ten: Enroll in the Right College for You

The final step in the plan for making it into a top college is enrolling in the right college for you, one where you will be happy and thus likely to succeed. Faced with two or more letters of acceptance in the spring of your senior year, you will have to choose the college that you feel will help you to do your best. In this step you will learn how to make that right choice. You will also understand what to do if you are wait-listed instead of admitted outright, or if you do not receive the financial aid you need in order to attend. Alternatives to enrolling in college immediately upon graduation and their advantages for your future are also discussed.

Profiting from the Admissions Process

The college admissions process has much to teach you. You will be learning how to make important decisions that bear on your future. You will learn a good deal about American higher education and the extraordinary opportunities it offers. You are going to be meeting educators who are interested in you and want to learn as much as they can about you. You will discover new things about yourself, positive qualities that will please you. It has long been our experience that students who apply to selective colleges enrich their lives as they prepare for those exciting years of collegiate life. The search for colleges that suit you, the essay writing, the campus visits, the interviews, and the engagement with other students should add up to a sense of genuine accomplishment, especially on that day when the colleges respond with their invitations to join their community. Treat the process seriously, remembering that this is one of your courses, but also enjoy the opportunity for new discoveries, and most of all, maintain a sense of humor.

STEP ONE

Know the Selective Colleges and
Their Admissions Requirements
and Procedures

A Strategic Start

Over the years, the selective admissions process has evolved to distribute thousands of outstanding high school graduates among a hundred or so of the country's top colleges. You can establish a strategic position in this process by learning how a number of selective colleges expect you to prepare yourself academically for their demanding work, and by knowing how particular colleges select their first-year classes from among many qualified applicants.

HISTORIC HIGH LEVELS OF U.S. HIGH SCHOOL GRADUATES
AND COLLEGE APPLICANTS

The total number of U.S. high school graduates is expected to remain near 3,330,000 in 2008, a record high, during the coming decade. College enrollment is expected to grow from 15,659,000 to 17,354,000 between 2008 and 2016.

(Chronicle of Higher Education)

To begin with, you will familiarize yourself with the admissions requirements of a number of selective colleges. Why so many when your chief interest may be in only two? A key feature of the Ten-Step Plan is that you will increase your chances of admission to a selective college of your choice by applying to a collection of schools where you believe your particular strengths give you a unique advantage. To do this, you will need to learn about a variety of selective colleges and their particular programs.

Begin with College Catalogues and Web Sites

You can acquaint yourself initially with a variety of colleges by looking over catalogues, viewbooks, Web sites, and other material available at your school, public library, or on the Internet. Send away or e-mail for information you cannot get otherwise. Selective colleges receive tens of thousands of inquiries each year! Colleges are anxious to help you learn about their institutions. As we will discuss, one of the major changes we have seen in the last two decades is the shift on the part of the colleges toward Internet-based marketing, information provision, communication with students and high schools, and even submission of applications. College Web sites and the Internet offer an easy, fast, and valuable means of gaining a great deal of insight on particular colleges and their admissions requirements.

The Class Profile

Every college publishes a profile of its freshman class, distributes this to alumni and guidance counselors, and, often, makes it available on their Web site. Useful data such as the number of applicants admitted by class rank, their GPA, advanced courses taken, test scores, extracurricular interests, and regions of the country can help you position yourself as a candidate for the colleges you are considering, and may lead you to add new schools to your list. Your guidance counselor should have such profiles, but if not, check the college's Web site, e-mail them to ask for a profile, or contact the local alumni representative.

INFORMATION SOURCES

If you cannot find a specific college catalogue or viewbook, visit the college's Web site, or write to the college to ask for one, by regular mail or by e-mail. Most often a college's Web site is "www.thecollegename.edu." Most colleges make their catalogues (or "bulletins") available in some form electronically. Your counselor is another source for this kind of information, but remember how busy counselors are, and do not be surprised if the counselor suggests you get this information on your own.

One of the effects of the increased interest in selective colleges is the occasional inability to keep up with the demand for costly printed materials. Viewbooks and brochures are cheaper to produce than thick course catalogues, but their information is often a summary, an overview, and they do not provide the kind of specifics you must have. Software programs or Web-based counseling resources in your school's resource room may or may not provide a thorough statement of requirements. When they do, print them out and add them to your notebook. DVDs and online videos often reveal institutional priorities in the most attractive light possible. Again, we have learned that the greatest and most comprehensive set of information on the colleges can be found on the Internet, where students can find not only admissions-related information, but also student-run newspapers, links to college clubs and organizations, e-mail addresses of professors and departments, virtual campus tours, and much more. Some of these come from independent sources, while other resources are offered by the colleges themselves.

The College's Requirements

As you read through the material, take particular note of the admissions requirements of colleges that interest you, and record the information in the notebook you should be keeping on your admissions procedures (this notebook can be a three-ring binder or a computer file). Or use our College Requirements Worksheet, a copy of which appears later in this chapter and in the Appendix.

THE IMPORTANCE OF A STRONG CURRICULUM

We are often asked by students, "How difficult a courseload should I take? Do those AP classes really matter?" We hear every day from college admissions officers that the number one factor they identify in making admissions decisions is the quality of a student's academic record. This includes both courses chosen and grades in them over time. So the answer to this question is that you should take the most challenging courseload you can manage without being overwhelmed or losing the ability to do the other major school and outside activities you enjoy. Try to challenge yourself in those areas in which you have innate strengths and the most interest. It is better to receive a B, for example, in an Advanced Placement (AP) or honors class than a straight A in a regular-level class, but avoid dropping into the C range. AP classes in particular show colleges that you are succeeding in rigorous courses that are standardized from school to school. And if you do well on AP tests in the spring, you can place out of introductory-level college classes and gain college course credits. So push yourself, particularly in your junior and senior years, but remember that you will have "AP college applications" as an additional hidden class on your schedule as a senior. Talk with your teachers and guidance counselor about particular classes you are interested in, and compare your curriculum and potential college major choices with the requirements and recommendations of colleges you are considering.

Relative Selectivity

Selective colleges' requirements can be rated in three broad categories: Exceedingly Demanding, Very Demanding, and Demanding. The table in the "Let's Get Started" chapter lists the selective colleges and their classifications. Be sure your research includes colleges in at least two and preferably three categories. Even though you may believe yourself highly qualified and a good candidate for Swarthmore, Stanford, Williams, Duke, or others that are Exceedingly Demanding, you can never be certain of admission to such colleges and should consider some Very Demanding and Demanding ones you would be happy to attend.

Or if you think that only a Demanding college will take you, you may be selling yourself short by not considering Very Demanding institutions as a possibility. You could be surprised to discover that a college you thought was beyond your reach would like to admit you for reasons you hadn't considered.

Preliminary Self-Classification

By going through various colleges' requirements in your notebook and comparing them with your curriculum and your performance to date, you can arrive at a preliminary classification of where you are in the selective college pool. You may already have had such a classification in mind, but now you are in a position to evaluate it realistically. This self-classification will help you establish admissions goals and work toward them systematically.

Let us look at the way two different students went about their preliminary self-classification.

Laura

Laura came to us in the spring of her junior year at a competitive mid-Atlantic boarding school. She had received PSAT scores of 63 verbal, 59 math, and 66 writing, scores that put her between the 81st and 94th percentile, and similar SAT-level scores. She was a varsity field hockey player with a strong curriculum that already included calculus, physics, and French 5. Her grades were good, but put her only in about the third decile of her class. Laura was looking for a highly selective college with a good field hockey program, but she was not sure she could compete on the Division I level. While she was initially set on Dartmouth, she needed to figure out if that goal was realistic. We walked her through this competitive Ivy's current statistics: median SATs in the 700 range on each section, 90% of the entering class in the top 5% to 10% of their high school class, students with a strong particular talent, and students with usually a few AP courses by senior fall. It became clear to Laura that Dartmouth, Princeton, and some other Exceedingly Demanding colleges would be too unrealistic a stretch for her. We encouraged her to set her goals for SATs in the mid-650s in October, to bring her grades up to a point where she was in about the top 15% of her class, and to stay with and a challenging curriculum in the fall of her senior year, including French 6, AP statistics, and advanced English. Laura would continue her discussions with field hockey coaches at the Division III level, and would be a prefect (leader) in her dorm the next year. She might continue to strive for a few Exceedingly Demanding colleges, but would see mostly Very Demanding schools as her targets, with one or two Demanding colleges as backups.

Laura was able to bring her grade average up almost ten points over the year, to receive "most improved" awards for varsity squash and varsity lacrosse, to generate interest from Division III coaches, to bring up her SATs modestly, but, more importantly, to score fours on the English Literature and French Language AP exams. She applied early decision to Middlebury, which had been recruiting her for hockey, and was deferred. She decided to continue to pursue this first-choice college, and to send out applications in the pattern she had initially identified. Eventually, she was rejected by two Exceedingly Demanding colleges, Dartmouth and Georgetown, and accepted at Middlebury (where she enrolled), Vanderbilt, Trinity, and Colby. She had classified herself almost perfectly, and had played to her strengths in athletics and academics (Middlebury liked her language skills and interest in foreign study). Had she applied early to Dartmouth and continued to focus on this unrealistic choice, she could have missed the opportunity to identify and gain admission to Middlebury.

Frank

Frank was in the winter of his junior year at a highly competitive private day school. Enrolled in a very strong curriculum, including fourth-year Spanish, AP U.S. history, physics, and advanced math, he was near the top of his class, with A/A− grades across the board. With PSATs of 63 verbal, 69 math, and 73 writing (all in the 90th percentile range), he had a good chance of going far in the National Merit Schol-

COLLEGE REQUIREMENTS WORKSHEET

Name of College _____

Level of selectivity
(Demanding,
Very Demanding,
Exceedingly
Demanding) _____

Units of high school
courses required
(1 unit = 1 year):

English _____

Mathematics _____

Science _____

Languages _____

History or

Social Studies _____

Electives advised _____

Total units required _____

Is SAT or ACT
required? _____

How many SAT
Subject Tests
required? _____

Tests recommended _____

Early Decision or
Early Action policy? _____

ED or EA deadlines _____

Notification dates _____

Regular admission
deadline _____

Notification dates _____

arship competition. He also had a chemistry SAT Subject Test score of 730. Frank wanted a highly challenging college where he could pursue math, science, and history, and he had an early interest in Dartmouth because of its combination of liberal arts and small business and engineering schools. Would this be a realistic choice for him? We discussed Frank's senior curriculum and determined that he would take four AP classes—Spanish, calculus, physics, and chemistry—along with two English electives (not his strength or interest). This program would clearly qualify him for a competitive science, math, or engineering program at an Exceedingly Demanding college, and it would be among the toughest programs for any student at his school. In terms of SATs, Frank knew he needed to get his section scores above 700 to make the most selective schools realistic. We encouraged him to work with a tutor, particularly on his verbal skills, and to focus on producing a strong set of at least three SAT Subject Tests. Given these goals, Frank would consider Exceedingly Demanding colleges as his tougher target schools, a few Very Demanding colleges as more reliable targets, and perhaps a Demanding college as a backup. His list included Dartmouth, Brown, Cornell, Johns Hopkins, MIT, Princeton, Tufts, Penn, Vanderbilt, and Washington.

Frank continued his strong academic performance, received a commendation from the National Merit competition, and put together SATs of 700 verbal, 740 math, and 670 writing, and SAT Subjects of 800 math level 2, 730 chemistry, and 720 physics. He continued his few key activities, which included tutoring children in math and running for varsity cross-country. Frank's interest in Dartmouth remained strong through his continued visiting of many campuses, and we felt that his record put him in a good position to apply. We noted that he would likely have a better chance at gaining admission to Dartmouth's math/science/engineering program, where he would stand out as a well-rounded and talented applicant, than he would at being accepted at MIT, for example, where he would compete with some of the strongest math and engineering applicants in the country, most of whom would have higher test scores than he had. Frank chose to apply Early Decision to Dartmouth and was accepted.

You and Your Guidance Counselor

Some counselors in large high schools have as many as 300 to 500 or more students to counsel, including those applying to selective colleges. Even in private schools, counselors may be pressed for time. If you find that your counselor is not being as helpful as you expect, give him or her a hand by putting in writing a brief résumé of your achievements, interests, colleges you are considering, and problems on your mind. Include your preliminary self-classification and ask the counselor to react at your next session. In fact, some schools have standard self-assessment and information forms that the guidance office distributes or makes available online during junior or senior year. Take these tools seriously as a way for you to help your guidance counselor help you through the admissions process. Is your self-evaluation on target or not? A constructive dialogue should ensue between you and your counselor which may cause you to reconsider your first judgments about yourself as a selective college candidate. Thereafter, keep your counselor informed with brief notes about your progress. Pass on your impressions of colleges you visit or your reactions to test scores.

If a counselor is to be helpful, he or she must know you. Fleeting visits with someone who counsels several hundred students are insufficient to establish a genuine understanding of who you are and what you aspire to be. By communicating in writing, you get the counselor's attention and make your file more personal. Knowing how motivated you are, the counselor will respond with more attention, because eventually he or she will bask in your reflected glory. Counselors take great pride in students who are admitted to selective colleges. While it is you who will decide what colleges you will apply to, your counselor will often have a broad knowledge of many colleges, as well as a sense of where past applicants from your school have been accepted or rejected. Such a perspective can help you to determine your relative chances of admission at various colleges.

In your notebook, keep a short diary of your meetings with your counselor and of notes you send. This will serve to show how constructive your relationship is, and it will let you see how frequently you are in contact. There is nothing to be gained by taking up more counseling time than you really need. Your demands will increase as you near application-filing time in your senior year. Then it will be important for you to make sure that your teachers send copies of their recommendations to the counselor as soon as possible. Remember that your counselor can be a strong advocate for you in the admissions process, representing you, your strengths, and your contributions to your school effectively to college admissions committees.

CHANGING SELECTIVITY

Times and trends change quickly in college admissions. Colleges that you or your parents or your older brother may have thought of as strong, but not overly competitive in admissions, may now have become much more demanding. For example, Bucknell University, rated by us as "Very Demanding," received 8,024 applications for a class of 960 freshmen in the fall of 2008. This represents well more than a doubling of their applicant pool since the 1990s. Only 2,395 candidates were admitted, and their middle 50% test scores were SAT Critical Reading 630–720, SAT Math 660–740, and ACT 28–32. We cannot emphasize enough how important it is to look at each college's current admissions statistics as you continue your self-assessment.

Requirements vs. Procedures

Requirements describe what a college expects you to accomplish as you prepare to go on to higher education. Procedures are the specific things you must do through high school, such as visiting colleges, being interviewed, and filling out applications for admission and financial aid.

You can begin learning different selective colleges' high school course requirements and standardized testing requirements at any point in your high school career. The earlier you do this, the more sure you will be that your academic work conforms to what several colleges expect. While the better high schools direct college-bound students toward a liberal arts– or science-oriented curriculum, it remains the obligation of the student to satisfy the requirements of colleges to which he or she applies.

Admissions officers complain about the following faults in applicants who disregard requirements:

- Improper investigation of the college
- Not reading material put out by the college
- Never questioning college officials during a visit to campus or at the student's high school, or by e-mail or telephone
- Not meeting minimum academic requirements
- Not explaining a gap or an inconsistency in their academic or school record

Meeting (or Exceeding) Requirements Is the Key

Of course, there is more to getting into college than meeting academic requirements, but how well you meet them will determine in part how desirable you are as an applicant. As we will see later, admissions officers use the first round of application readings solely to determine whether and how well the applicants have met the college's admissions requirements. Now is the time to study the requirements of those twelve to fifteen schools, and to tailor your curriculum and test schedule accordingly. At the most selective institutions, the absence of a required academic course or SAT Subject Test can be used to weed out candidates from so well-qualified a pool.

So make it your first priority to be sure you can meet the minimum requirements of several selective colleges. They are your initial step into a top college.

EXAMPLE OF ADMISSIONS REQUIREMENTS: DUKE UNIVERSITY

The selective colleges have in common a desire to see their applicants pursuing a strong and balanced curriculum through senior year. They usually require four years of English, three of math, three of natural sciences, three of the same foreign language, and three of history or social studies. However, they often like to see more, and these at an advanced level.

Duke University, for example, has noted, "Your secondary school record should include the best available and most challenging courses: four years of English and at least three years of mathematics, natural science, foreign language, and social studies. We also encourage you to enroll in advanced-level work in as many of these areas as possible."

If you meet or exceed these requirements and expectations, you will be qualifying for the more demanding colleges. What if you are a sophomore or a junior who is worried that you may not meet a college's expectations in a particular area?

We have seen students use a summer program, at a boarding school, college, or local high school, for example, to jump ahead in math, science, a foreign language, history, or English, so that they could study at a more advanced level. For example, students have attended a writing program in order to be prepared for senior AP English. Or, after completing chemistry in eleventh grade, they have taken a physics class over the summer to be ready for AP Physics as a senior. Students have studied abroad during their junior summer to gear up for an AP language course as a senior, or studied American history at a boarding school after sophomore year to qualify for AP U.S. History as a junior.

Admissions Procedures

To meet admissions *requirements,* you do academic work over a four-year span. Admissions *procedures* are intermittent and are followed typically from the fall of junior year until you are admitted. These are some of the major components:

1. Campus visits, including tours and group information sessions.
2. On-campus and/or alumni interviews (not obligatory for most colleges and sometimes not offered at all).
3. Applications, which include: the student's school transcripts, personal statements, and supplementary materials as appropriate.

4. Recommendations by teachers, counselors, heads of schools, alumni, and others as appropriate.
5. Your requests for official SAT, ACT, AP, TOEFL, and other score reports.
6. Financial aid applications if needed.
7. Letters of acceptance, deferral, wait-listing, or rejection from the colleges.
8. Letters of accepting or declining admission, and enrollment deposits from students.

Admissions procedures vary in some respects from college to college, as you will discover as you read materials from a number of them, but they vary within the eight categories listed. You may know these general procedures already, but what you have to know cold is what each college's procedures are, and particularly what their deadlines are for submitting applications. Each procedure is covered thoroughly in a later chapter. We have drawn up a four-year, month-by-month calendar showing how all these procedures fit into our Ten-Step timetable. You will find this at the end of the book, and you can refer to it regularly during your high school years and the college admissions process.

You need not at this point know all the details about what is listed on this schedule. As you go from step to step, these procedures will become clear. There is obviously a great responsibility imposed on you, the candidate, to follow the procedures. You must meet the schedules the colleges require of applicants, and the way to do this is by making a schedule for yourself and checking it regularly. This schedule will make your conferences with your counselor (and family discussions!) productive.

If you have already completed some of this schedule, such as taking the PSAT, revise the plan accordingly. In addition to the standard procedures, there are a couple of specific procedures that we will consider here.

APPLYING ONLINE: THE GROWTH OF E-APPLICATIONS

Colleges are making it easier than ever to download and submit applications online, either through their own Web sites or with the assistance of a variety of Internet services (see the Internet Resources list later in this chapter). Students have been responding with increasing interest to this fast and easy method of contacting colleges and sending in applications. The National Association for College Admission Counseling (NACAC) found that for the fall 2007 admission year, the four-year colleges and universities it surveyed across the country received an average of 68% of their applications online, up from 58% the year before. Colleges accepting fewer than half their applicants received an even higher percentage (80.6%) of their applications online. The growth of such standardized applications as the Common Application (commonapp .org) has also contributed to the increase and ease of online applications.

Students applying online should have done most of their application work (essay writing, gathering test scores, transcript information, activities lists, and so forth) before sitting down to do the application. They should carefully read the instructions, check all their work, contact the college with any questions, and print a copy of the application for themselves before hitting the "send" button. Students should expect colleges to confirm the receipt of their application fairly quickly.

And now on to financial aid: See our resource list for online financial aid and scholarship sites, and note that the main financial aid form, the FAFSA, can be completed online with the U.S. Department of Education.

Special Procedures—Early Decision

The Pros and Cons

Admission to selective colleges by Early Decision has developed as an advantage to the colleges and as a convenience to the right student. Early Decision means that you, the candidate, request a decision on your application in the fall, before the end of the first academic term of senior year. The conditions imposed upon you are two: You request Early Decision from only one institution, and you agree if admitted by

Early Decision to apply to no other institution thereafter. In short, you have been admitted and are de facto enrolled almost a year before you actually matriculate (enter the college). If you are not admitted early, your application may be deferred for final decision in March or early April. Recently, however, more colleges have been rejecting more inadmissible students at this early stage of the process. So we caution students not to take an Early Decision application decision lightly for many reasons.

Informally, we know from students that the number one reason they apply early is . . . to get it over with! But before you jump to the conclusion that Early Decision can put an end to all your worries, you should realize that there are as many potential disadvantages as advantages in taking this route. To begin with, only very strong candidates, those near the top of a particular college's applicant pool, should even consider Early Decision. You need high grades in a good curriculum, a breadth and depth of nonacademic interests and activities, SAT or ACT scores that would place you in the top 20% of those applying to that college (not the top 20% of your school class, the top 20% of all applicants), and all by the beginning of November of your senior year. If you are just below these criteria but have much to offer the college, you can possibly gain some attention and leverage by applying for Early Decision. You may be deferred, but you may also be favored among candidates admitted in April. Students are also urged to investigate enough colleges to be absolutely sure that the college from which they are asking an Early Decision is their true first choice and not a college they happen to know will accept them or one in which they are interested primarily because of its name and prestige. We have seen too many students jump at the chance for Early Decision from a college they are not happy to attend. Haste is the besetting evil of the Early Decision process.

The Early Decision Process

You should understand how colleges use Early Decision in an effort to enroll top students in their freshman classes before some other institution gets them. The great majority of colleges will not review and evaluate the large number of regular applicants' credentials until February through March. By that time, the admissions office has closed off applications, and so the committee knows how many applications are in and just how many admission letters can be sent out. Each applicant can be evaluated against the caliber of the total batch of applicants. However, very few colleges, only about eight to ten of the most selective, will see more than one out of two accepted applicants eventually enroll in the college. That is the college's yield rate, the rate at which accepted applicants accept offers of admission. That means that even some of the most selective colleges in the country must accept at least twice as many applicants as they expect to enroll. Without getting into the complicated computer modeling programs designed to simplify this forecasting process on the part of the college, suffice it to say that in an era of burgeoning applications from more and stronger students, colleges have been seeking ways to reduce their uncertainty. How can they enroll more of the best students, increase their yield numbers (because every Early Decision acceptance means almost a 100% yield for that student), and limit the overall number of acceptances they must send out to reach their enrollment goals in the spring? The answer is with Early Decision commitments. If 40% of a college's first-year class (a ballpark average for many of the selective colleges) is filled through Early Decision, then the college need only worry about the other 60% in the spring. Less uncertainty, less risk of over- or under-enrolling, and less work.

When applicants are judged for Early Decision, the admissions office has little idea what the total application pool for the year will look like. So the committee views the early applicant as only representative of the best of the lot. Such applicants must be deemed to rank between the top 10% and 20% of the class: the first-year college class, we again emphasize, not the secondary school class. The exception can be the outstanding athlete, class leader, or performing artist who is sought after by many colleges.

You can see that if Bowdoin, Middlebury, Colgate, and Penn can get top students in Early Decision, these are students Yale, Amherst, Dartmouth, Harvard, and other highly selective colleges will not take from them. Applicants, particularly those who rank very high in their classes, should recognize that not only are they competing among themselves for places in the freshman classes of the best selective colleges, but the best selective colleges are competing among themselves to enroll as many top students as possible. While the competition for admission is stiff, there is a limited number of highly qualified candidates to go around. The student's task is to determine where he or she will be most likely to be perceived as a top student in a particular college's applicant pool.

It pains Brown very much to lose a considerable number of those it admits, to Harvard, Yale, Stanford, and a few other colleges. It pains Amherst to know that students admitted to both Amherst and Princeton are more likely to enroll at Princeton. Early Decision is a kind of admissions aspirin to relieve selective college administration pain. In this sense, the applicant who is very strong is in the driver's seat. Like the U.S. Army recruiting poster of Uncle Sam pointing a finger, saying, "I want you!" Early Decision is saying, "This college wants you!" The question then boils down to: Do you want this college?

As the total number of selective college applications grows, so does the number of Early Decision applicants and the proportion of the classes at many selective colleges that are filled through Early Decision acceptances. Let no strong applicant rush to judgment without reflecting on all the implications.

Requirements for Early Decision

An interview? It used to be that an interview on campus at a first-choice college was not only encouraged, but often required. Over the last two decades, however, the place of the interview in college admissions has dramatically changed. While many colleges continue to encourage on-campus interviewing, few require it, some do not offer it, and most that do interview characterize these "discussions" as "non-evaluatory" and only "informational." We add that even "evaluatory" interviews have a less prominent place in the admissions decision today than do essays, recommendations, and extracurricular activities. Princeton, for example, no longer offers individual on-campus interviews, but rather makes group information sessions available. Yale continues to offer individual interviewing on campus, but utilizes trained Yale students to conduct most of these sessions. We will discuss later how the de-emphasizing of interviewing has focused more attention on an applicant's essay writing. Let us say here that Early Decision applicants should interview on campus, and with alumni, wherever possible, but they should see these interviews as informational opportunities to express their interest in the college, to give the interviewer more personal details about themselves and the reasons why they are applying or considering Early Decision, and to ask questions of the interviewer to gain a better understanding of the college and its application process.

Tests. SATs and two or three SAT Subject Tests, and/or the ACT, should be taken by June of junior year. If you feel that you will do better in your senior year, you can still apply early, but be certain to arrange to retake tests in your senior year. SATs are offered in October, and many colleges will also accept November scores for Early Decision applicants. This is cutting it close, however, and will not give you time to carefully consider your test scores and their bearing on your admission chances. Nevertheless, even if you are deferred on the early plan, you may very well be admitted by spring of senior year, having shown additional testing from test dates through the fall and even winter.

Teachers' recommendations. Usually two recommendations are required. Will teachers you already know give you very strong reports, or will you get better reports senior year, based on what you know about your teachers? Be careful that teachers do not send in boiler-plate recommendations—that is, one recommendation per student sent in duplicate copy to every college to which the student is applying. Early Decision applications are best supported by recommendations that focus on why a student is a strong applicant for a particular college.

Grades. Early Decision applications rest primarily on grades through a student's junior year. Are yours strong enough, or are you on a trajectory of improvement which would benefit from a full semester of senior year work? An often-heard refrain from college admissions offices when asked why a student was deferred is "We want to see how she will do through the fall and winter in her challenging curriculum."

DO I HAVE A BETTER CHANCE OF GAINING ADMISSION TO
A SELECTIVE COLLEGE IF I APPLY EARLY?

It is our continued opinion, based on discussions with college admissions officers, observations of the admissions process, and counseling sessions with students and families, that the average student has little advantage in applying early in terms of increased chances for admission. Colleges continue to accept only the best candidates as early applicants, and choose to defer or, increasingly, reject those students who do not clearly meet admissions requirements or standards. It is very much a case-by-case decision as to whether Early Action, Early Decision, or rolling admission is right for an individual student. Such factors as athletic recruiting or legacy status (particularly at the University of Pennsylvania, for example) may make it more logical for particular students to apply early. The two main questions every student considering an Early Decision commitment must pose and answer are: (1) Have I closely examined enough colleges, especially my potential ED school, to be confident that this is the right choice for me? (2) Is my record strong enough now to serve as the basis for an ED application, or do I need more time to show better grades and testing to my first-choice college?

Caveats

Don't try to beat the Early Decision system by secretly applying to another college if admitted by one through Early Decision. You can get burned when the college that first admitted you finds out and withdraws its offer of admission, and perhaps even contacts its peer institution, informing them of your lack of commitment.

Don't sell yourself short by being drawn into an Early Decision at a college that seems less exciting or less selective than one or two you hope to attend. You should give yourself every opportunity to apply to colleges that you truly want to attend.

Don't be so unrealistic that you apply Early Decision to a college that is entirely out of reach, meanwhile ignoring a great personal choice where your Early Decision commitment could make a difference.

Don't be drawn into the current Early Decision mania of feeling that you have to apply early somewhere, or you won't get in anywhere. Make the right choice for you, according to your preferences and strengths, and remember that while many colleges are filling close to half of their classes through Early Decision, that leaves more than half of their classes to be filled through Regular Decision in the spring. The statistics that make it seem as though you have a better chance if you apply early are often misleading, because the Early Decision pool of applicants is usually much stronger on average, with more special-status and self-selecting top candidates committing to their first choice. And if you want a college to carefully review your application for a specific reason, think about the fact that the colleges only have about a month and a half to get through those Early Decision applications, as opposed to three months or more in the spring. The last thing you want is for a college to make a rushed decision and reject you!

The Advantages of Early Decision

If you have a genuine, heartfelt first choice and are a very strong candidate, you put yourself in a very good position by declaring this in the form of an Early Decision application. Either you will be admitted then and there, or your name will be flagged as one to take a careful second look at later. The fact that you applied for Early Decision and did not make it is in your favor because of your commitment to the college. Be warned that this holds true only for the very best student, or close to the best. Ultimately every applicant is judged on his or her record.

Speaking of records, the colleges love the students they admit by Early Decision because of their great performance in college and thereafter. So colleges would like to take in more of them, and they would like the best students to apply early. So, to sum up: Apply for Early Decision only if you are among a college's best or most-desired students, and apply only to your very first choice of college.

EARLY DECISION/ACTION TRENDS

More and more students have been applying Early "Something" in recent years, reflecting national trends toward earlier commitment to colleges, and the development of Early Decision (ED) II plans. The National Association for College Admission Counseling (NACAC) reported that of colleges admitting fewer than half of applicants, 55.6% use ED plans and 22.2% use Early Action (EA) plans (some use both). In most of the years between 2000 and 2007, more than half of colleges with ED plans saw an increase in the number of ED applications received. During the same period, some two-thirds to three-quarters of EA colleges saw increases in EA applications. Some colleges, notably Harvard, Princeton, and Virginia, have dropped their early plans, to decrease pressure on students and ameliorate the skewing in the early pool toward wealthier students. Others, like Yale and Stanford, have taken a middle path with Restrictive Early Action, limiting students to one early application but not requiring an ED commitment from applicants. Most schools, however, show little interest in abandoning their early plans, and ED applications show no sign of diminishing.

Financial Aid and Early Decision

If you are applying for Early Decision and you will be requesting financial aid, you will have to fill out a "short version" of the financial aid form. When admitted Early Decision, you will, in most cases, learn right away what your aid package is—no waiting all winter to find out how you will fare. Another plus for Early Decision. Some concerns, however, are as follows, and will be discussed in more detail in Step Nine. While many selective colleges will provide students with all of the aid they require to cover their financial need, they will do so in varying combinations of loans (to be paid back), grants/ scholarships (not to be paid back), and work-study (sing for your supper). If a college to which you have been admitted Early Decision does not offer you enough aid to cover your expenses, this may be a legitimate reason for you to ask the college to release you from your Early Decision commitment. In general, however, committing Early

Decision removes some of the needy applicant's ability to compare aid packages from multiple colleges during the regular admissions process. The differences in loan/grant/work-study and need- and merit-based awards can be quite substantial, so if you think you will or may need financial aid, you should consider these issues carefully, talk with your parents, and even contact several financial aid offices at your major colleges of interest to discuss the ramifications of an Early Decision application.

Special Procedures—Early Decision II, Early Action, and Rolling Admissions

Early Decision II

A recent development, particularly among colleges of the second tier and those schools we term the Hidden Ivies, has been the expansion of Early Decision opportunities through the addition of EDII deadlines. For example, Vanderbilt University offers the applicant the option to apply EDI by November 1 (with a notification date of December 15), or EDII by January 15 (with a notification date of February 15). This compares to Vanderbilt's regular admissions deadline of January 15 (with a notification date of April 1). There are a number of strategic benefits and opportunities that EDII opens up. First, the applicant who wants to take the fall of senior year to research and visit more colleges before committing to a first choice can have the time to do so. Second, the applicant who needs the senior year fall to improve his or her grades and test scores can show a full semester's worth of work in a challenging curriculum and tests through November and December as part of an EDII application. Third, the applicant who has tried for Early Decision at an Exceedingly Demanding college during EDI, and who has been deferred or rejected and thus released from a binding commitment, may decide now to apply EDII to a second choice, Very Demanding college, for example. This opens up a world of possibilities for the creative student.

Carl, for example, was an international applicant who started the college search process late in the game. He had done a stint at an American boarding school which did not go very well, and had returned to a British school in his home country needing to improve his grades, regain confidence, and return to the United States to see many different kinds of college campuses. He prepared for and improved SATs through the fall of senior year while working hard in his courses, connecting to teachers, and carefully developing his application essays to address the reasons behind his change of schools, his recent resurgence, and his goals for college. Meanwhile, he engaged in conversations with golf coaches at a number of institutions, who were interested in his excellent performance on the links. We encouraged Carl to talk not only with golf coaches and admissions people at a number of campuses, but also to consider engineering-oriented academic programs, which fit his natural academic interests and abilities. In October, he was not ready to commit to a college, let alone send in a strong application. However, by December he had improved his record and had seen enough campuses and academic program materials to be able to identify a first choice. He applied EDII to Bucknell University's College of Engineering and was accepted.

A strong but not top student at a competitive private day school, Rebecca decided early on that she wanted a middle- to large-sized university in or near a city. With a strong record of community service and school involvement, she was an active, engaged student who would be an attractive applicant for many colleges. However, her SAT score of 1330, with SAT Subjects of 740, 700, and 720, and strong but not the best grades in a very good curriculum, meant she would be a marginal applicant at some of the most selective colleges. The child of a Penn alum, she had fallen in love with the university and wanted to do everything possible to gain admission. She knew that her grades and test scores would probably not improve substantially during senior year, and she was informed by Penn that for her legacy status to make a difference, she would need to apply for Early Decision by November. She did just that, but in the meantime worked with us to identify other appropriate college choices in case the outcome was not positive. She readied herself and her applications by the beginning of December, and identified a very good potential next choice. When she was deferred from Penn in December, she decided that Tufts University was in fact an excellent choice for her, and applied EDII by their January deadline, while sending out regular admission applications to a broader list of colleges. By February 1, she heard that she had been accepted to Tufts. She withdrew her other applications and looked forward to attending a very appropriate university, knowing that she had at least given Penn a try.

Early Action

Not to be confused with Early Decision is the Early Action process available at some selective colleges. Most schools, including Brown and Northwestern, have done away with Early Action in favor of the Early Decision commitment. However, MIT, Georgetown, Chicago, and Boston College, for example, still offer only Early Action or regular admissions options. Usually students apply for Early Action to colleges where they are reasonably sure of admission. Accepted early, they need file no other applications. In most cases in Early Action, you can be accepted, rejected, or deferred. Usually, you can apply to multiple EA schools. This is not the case with Restrictive Early Action (REA) as offered by Yale and Stanford. Most EA schools allow you to apply to one ED school at the same time, while others, like Georgetown and Boston College, do not. It is important to read the fine print in each college's application materials to see what they allow and prohibit in conjunction with their application plans.

WHAT DO I DO IF I'M DEFERRED FROM A COLLEGE THROUGH AN EARLY ACTION OR EARLY DECISION APPLICATION?

It is always a disappointment for a student to get a deferral letter from his or her first-choice college or university. The good news is, a deferral is not a rejection, and there is still a chance for admission later in the spring. While at the most selective colleges, only about 10% of those who are deferred can expect eventually to be admitted, the fact that a student applied early indicates to the admissions committee a strong commitment and interest on the part of the student. It is important to follow up on that initial approach to a college with continuing expression of intent and involvement through the spring (unless, of course, the student decides the school is no longer a first choice, and wants to take advantage of a second-round Early Decision plan offered by another school).

Strategies for students include: sending a letter to the director of admissions or another admissions officer whom you have met, indicating your continuing interest in the college, and bringing the committee up to date on any new developments in your life, such as activities, awards, and exciting spring classes (remember, you sent in your application in October or November, and a lot may have happened since then!); making sure that your school sends in new grades (colleges will look to see how you did through the fall and winter, and if you show improvement, that can reassure the committee); taking the SAT or SAT Subjects again (sometimes this can make a slight difference, especially if your test scores were below the college's average); and having alumni or additional on-campus interviews, if available.

A big difference between Early Action and Early Decision is that the Early Action candidate is not under obligation to discontinue all other applications. By the same token, the applicant does not become the same premier candidate for spring admission he or she becomes if deferred in Early Decision. Applying Early Action, without an actual commitment on the part of the candidate, in other words, has less impact on the college's assessment of a candidate's actual interest or likelihood of enrolling.

Applicants for Early Action run more of a risk than those for Early Decision because of the severe screening process, which is an effort to eliminate marginal candidates. We recommend against Early Action applications if there is a good chance of your not being admitted. Usually you can get an idea from the admissions office whether such an application is really welcome, but sometimes admissions offices will encourage many students to apply Early Action to increase their numbers and attract student attention.

Rolling Admissions

Rolling admission involves no commitment on the part of the student, but allows him or her to submit applications early and throughout the admissions process, and to receive a response from the college usually within one or two months. Many state universities, such as the University of

Michigan and the University of Colorado, and a few Demanding colleges use rolling admissions. We encourage students who are applying to a rolling admissions school to submit their applications early in the process, but when their record is strong enough to be the sound basis for an application, so that they are considered an interested and serious applicant. Often, applicants to the more selective private universities can take advantage of a rolling admissions option at a less selective but academically appropriate public university that can serve as a strong backup college.

WHAT IS THE DIFFERENCE BETWEEN EARLY ACTION, EARLY DECISION, ROLLING, AND REGULAR ADMISSIONS?

Many colleges and universities offer choices in admissions deadlines and commitments. With Early Decision and Early Action, students must apply by an earlier deadline (often November 1) than usual (often January 1). Some schools have second-round Early Decision (EDII) deadlines as well. In applying Early *Decision*, a student makes a commitment to attend the college or university if he or she is offered acceptance. With Early *Action,* a student may find out an admissions decision earlier than normal, but has no commitment to attend. With *rolling* admissions, a university accepts applications on a continual basis, often notifying students of a decision within a few weeks. Again, no commitment to attend is made by the student.

ADMISSION TO FIRST-CHOICE COLLEGES AND NUMBERS OF APPLICATIONS

According to UCLA's Higher Education Research Institute, some 80% of freshmen were admitted to and 66% are attending their first-choice college. Over 90% of students were in their first- or second-choice school, although this statistic does include students in nonselective institutions. Students using the Common Application average about four application submissions (though they might also apply to non–Common Application schools). About 33% apply to seven or more colleges, up from about 9% a decade ago. Anecdotally, we have seen students apply to fifteen or even twenty-five colleges, but we try to help students devise a list of eight to ten colleges. Some high schools, public and private, such as Stuyvesant in New York City and Choate Rosemary Hall in Wallingford, Connecticut, limit students' applications to seven or ten in total, for example.

Guidelines to Various Admissions Plans

Early Decision is a formal understanding between the student and the college that if admitted, the student plans to enroll.

- College will require a non-refundable deposit well before May 1.
- Student may apply to only one college under an Early Decision plan at any time, and may or may not be allowed to apply to other Early Action schools while the ED application is pending.
- College will respond to application for admission within a reasonable and clearly stated period of time after the deadline for receipt of Early Decision applications.
- College will respond to application for financial aid at or near the same time as an offer of admission is extended.
- If student is applying for aid, he or she will adhere to aid application deadlines established by the college.
- If accepted, student will enroll unless aid award is inadequate.
- Immediately upon acceptance of offer, student will withdraw all other applications.
- College will not offer special incentives (such as scholarships, special aid awards, or special housing opportunities) to encourage students to apply under an Early Decision plan.
- Some colleges offer more than one Early Decision deadline date or cycle, ranging from November 1 to February 15.
- Often the application or the acceptance form will request a student, parent, and/or counselor signature indicating an understanding of the Early Decision commitment.

Early Action permits a student to make application and receive a decision well before the spring of the senior year; however, the student is not committed to enroll at that particular college.

- College will respond to application for admission within a reasonable and clearly stated period of time after the deadline for receipt of Early Action applications.
- College may request a deposit prior to May 1, but must indicate in the offer of admission that it is fully refundable until May 1.
- Student may apply to more than one college under an Early Action plan, although this varies, and is under no obligation to attend if accepted.
- Student may apply to other colleges (possibly including filing one Early Decision application).

Restrictive Early Action (REA) allows an applicant to hear early from a top-choice college without a commitment to attend if admitted.

- College will review REA applications in advance of its regular decision deadline.
- College may prohibit student from applying to other EA or ED schools.
- Applications to public and foreign universities, typically under rolling admission, are allowed.
- Deposit not required until May 1.

Regular Decision is a term used to describe the application process in which the majority of candidates are required to complete their applications prior to a deadline and are notified of decisions within a time frame specified by the college.

- College will state a deadline for completion of applications and will respond to completed applications within a specified time period.
- College may request a deposit prior to May 1, but must indicate in the offer of admission that it is fully refundable until May 1.
- Student may apply to other colleges.

Rolling admission is the term used by colleges which review applications as they are received and offer decisions to students when review is completed.

- College might have no stated application deadline, but may indicate that applications will be reviewed only until the class is filled.
- After a stated date each year, the college will notify candidates of decisions within a reasonable and clearly stated period of time after completion of the application.
- College may request a deposit prior to May 1, but must indicate in the offer of admission that it is fully refundable until May 1.
- Student may apply to other colleges.

Selected Early Decision and/or Early Action Policies at the Ivies (and Some Other Elite Institutions) in 2008/2009

Brown University—Early Decision policy states that applicants may not apply to other non-binding Early Action programs.

University of Chicago—Early Action plan with no restrictions.

Columbia University—Binding Early Decision program. Applicants may apply to non-binding Early Action programs.

Cornell University—Binding Early Decision program. Applicants may apply to non-binding Early Action programs.

Dartmouth College—Binding Early Decision program. Applicants may apply to non-binding Early Action programs.

Duke University—Binding Early Decision program. Applicants may apply to non-binding Early Action programs.

Georgetown University—Early Action policy states that applicants may apply to other non-binding Early Action programs but not binding Early Decision programs.

Harvard University—No early application plan.

MIT—Early Action plan with no restrictions.

University of Pennsylvania—Binding Early Decision program. Applicants may apply to non-binding Early Action programs.

Princeton University—No early application plan.

Stanford University—Restrictive Early Action plan. Applicants may not apply to any other binding Early Decision or non-binding Early Action programs elsewhere, but may apply to public universities with rolling admission plans.

Yale University—Restrictive Early Action plan. Applicants may not apply to any other binding Early Decision or non-binding Early Action programs elsewhere, but may apply to public universities with rolling admission plans.

....

Please note: The information above is meant to guide you to Early Decision and Early Action policies at some major universities. These sometimes change annually. Please be sure to verify the information with each college to which you would like to apply.

....

CAN I APPLY TO MORE THAN ONE COLLEGE THROUGH AN EARLY DECISION OR EARLY ACTION PROGRAM?

It depends. Each college or university has its own specific Early Action (EA), Early Decision (ED), or rolling admission plan. Some, particularly Ivy League schools, state that no application to another school can be submitted if an application has been submitted to their school EA or ED. Other colleges allow students to submit an EA/ED application to them and to another school. But remember, even if one school allows an applicant to apply EA to them and to another school, that second school may prohibit the same practice. The rule of thumb is that, first, a student cannot submit two binding (ED) applications simultaneously; second, students should read each college's literature carefully to determine what each school allows; third, if accepted through an ED program, students must withdraw any applications to other schools.

Inside the Admissions Office

Far from being confined to back-room reading of applications, admissions officers canvass schools, talk to counselors, interview applicants, and meet with alumni committees who help conduct interviews. In this way, they become acquainted with thousands of secondary schools. These contacts are the admissions staff's way of keeping in touch and finding out what is happening in schools. "Quality dropping here," one may note of a particular high school, or, "This school is developing stronger candidates," or, "The students who enroll from this school always seem happy and successful."

Admissions officers spend time, too, on the phone and the Internet, answering questions candidly, even bluntly, if a counselor asks about a certain candidate's chances. The staff is approachable—by applicants, parents, counselors, or media—up to the time of the big crunch that begins in January, as applications are reviewed. Increasingly, admissions offices are busier earlier in the fall, as Early Decision applications and student inquiries rise in number.

One unfortunate trend in recent years has been the high turnover in both high school guidance and college admissions offices. Combined with the historically high levels of applicants and applications, this has led to a less personalized admissions process in many if not most instances. The links do not exist between many high schools and particular admissions offices or officers. Thus it is incumbent upon the individual to make his or her own case to the admissions committees.

PORTRAIT OF AN ADMISSIONS STAFF

An admissions office at any college consists of a small staff of professional educators, teachers, students, or administrators who like meeting families, talking to counselors, and helping the college choose freshman classes. "An individual who does not enjoy biography probably would not enjoy being an admissions officer," an assistant dean for admissions at Columbia School of Business once said, a statement that holds true for undergraduate admissions as well. Most colleges staff their admissions offices with their own alumni because of their knowledge of the college and loyalty to it, although, increasingly, young professionals are attracted to certain colleges for their specialized knowledge. At the senior level, admissions offices often have professionals skilled in the management of a large recruiting and marketing operation who work with other college offices to set admissions goals, strategies, and policies. As technology has improved, admissions offices have relied on information specialists and technology support staff to help them manage their growing databases, statistical models, and, sometimes, complicated admissions evaluation formulas.

How Applications Are Reviewed

There is no secret about what happens to applications. "We read every single application at least once," says every selective college admissions dean or director. While each admissions office handles the entire process differently, during the first reading two things happen: The most promising candidates are identified, and those who must be immediately rejected are also identified. The application in this second category gets a cursory second glance from another member of the staff, and unless the applicant is considered a possible candidate, it is filed and not reviewed again.

The few immediately identified as acceptable require confirmation by others on the staff and by the director, but they seldom take up much time. It is the big group of possible acceptances which will be pored over, discussed, and argued about. At the most selective colleges, between 5% and 10% of applicants are more or less instant admissions, and 10% to 20% more are instantly identified as not to be admitted, leaving thousands of folders for a small staff to consider (you can see how important it is that your application distinguish you favorably from the start!).

Special Rounds Considerations

During the winter, admissions offices consider candidates by categories known as *rounds*. There are minority rounds, alumni and faculty children rounds, athletic rounds, foreign student rounds, and miscellaneous rounds depending on applications (disabled students, for example). There are no geographical rounds as such, but the staff considers the advantage to the college of accepting students from parts of the country they want represented in the class balance. Regional representatives of the staff make pleas for top candidates from their territory. They win some arguments and lose others.

Special rounds, in effect, weight the chances of the applicant favorably against those who are not part of the round. Alumni children have a better chance of being admitted than non-alumni children, or an athlete may have a better chance than a non-athlete with higher academic qualifications. At the same time, there is competition within the rounds. Not all alumni children who apply are admitted, nor are all athletes, all minorities, or all of any group that is considered separately. Special rounds are covered in more detail in Step Seven.

Alumni play an active role in helping admissions committees identify candidates and interview them. Alumni trustees, fund-raisers, and benefactors sometimes put in a good word for an applicant, and this will have considerable weight in some application folders, and in others very little. In either case, candidates do well to understand that in the American college system, alumni support, financial or otherwise, is critical to the continuing excellence of the college.

Rating Systems

Each college has its own rating system, but few reveal its exact character. Rating systems exist for the convenience of admissions committees. Some may use a 1 to 5 scale, others a 9-point scale, others a 6-point continuum. There is really no way you can discover how you have been rated. Such information is confidential and is used only internally to classify candidates for committee discussion. You can drive yourself crazy by trying to determine your rating or position on the much-discussed "Academic Index," which is used mainly by Ivy League colleges to ensure that by such key criteria as GPA, SAT scores, and class rank, recruited athletes are within a certain range of a college's "average" student. It truly is of little importance to an applicant to know about these formulas, however widely they are used, or about rating systems. And there is very little you can do to alter a rating or ranking. What is important is to understand the criteria by which you will be most significantly evaluated, and to become familiar with the programs and emphases of various colleges in order to find an appropriate match. If you focus on four primary admissions criteria—a strong curriculum, consistently good academic performance in that curriculum over time, an impressive battery of standardized tests, and passionate commitment to a few key extracurricular interests—all of the other pieces will fall into place.

How Fair Is the Admissions Process?

In a word, very! Admissions staffs have been established as autonomous committees, which constitute a kind of high court beyond which there really are no appeals. Admissions committees are, by intent, relatively impervious to the influence of prestige, high office, and wealth in considering applicants. (At Princeton some years ago, the admissions office received a call from the White House about a candidate, but even this failed to improve the candidate's chances!) There are so-called "development cases" at colleges, which may involve a very wealthy donor's son or daughter, and these are handled with care by the colleges, but we can tell you from experience that no amount of money can guarantee a place in a college's class. In fact, those colleges that are the most selective, and have the most endowment available for financial aid, are the most able to practice need-blind or virtually need-blind admission, and to avoid the undue impact of financial or status influences in the admissions process.

A well-meaning party attempting to influence the committee on your behalf may end up feeling rebuffed or even insulted if his or her recommendation does not result in your admission to that college, and sometimes such contacts from "somebody we know at the college" can have the effect of treading on the turf of the admissions committee, leading them to wonder, "If she is such a strong applicant, why does she need to ask an influential person who barely knows her to interfere on her behalf?" We would hope to spare you and your admirers this sort of embarrassment. (Of course, the attempted influence we are talking about here is quite different from letters of recommendation from teachers, counselors, coaches, employers, and others who know you well, which do carry weight with admissions committees in the proper course of the admissions process.)

As a result of the colleges' emphasis on the fairness of the selective admissions process, the top colleges are open to all who qualify by virtue of their own efforts. You who follow the Ten-Step Plan can feel confident that your application will receive the same consideration as any other. The selective admissions process is fair to all, and neither influence nor manipulation can subvert it.

The Five P's

We have over time asked many admissions deans and directors what they felt was important in the admissions process, and what they would advise prospective students to concentrate on. It is remarkable how consistent their reactions have been, across many different colleges and over a long period of time. Whether in survey form, through personal discussion, or by way of open-ended questions, admissions officers have made clear what they are looking for from applicants, and how they would advise them to proceed through high school and the admissions process. We would encourage readers to consider our detailed comments from admissions officers in *The Hidden Ivies,* to which we refer only briefly here, for more perspective on what matters in admissions.

We often talk about the "Five P's" of college admissions as a shorthand means for students to understand the most important ways in which they can prepare for entry into a selective college. One can also look at the Five P's from the perspective of what admissions officers are looking for. The top three factors in selective college admissions are overwhelmingly:

1. Program: Colleges encourage students to challenge themselves, to take risks, to pursue intellectual strengths and interests, and to stretch their minds. They look for a demanding curriculum, including some honors and Advanced Placement–level (or equivalent) course work, a program that is balanced, but also includes focus in one or two key areas. They admire students' willingness and ability to push themselves, to seek out more learning through summer programs and independent studies, for example, and to go beyond minimal requirements.

2. Performance: Colleges look for consistently strong success in a student's high school program. They question bumps in the road, but look positively upon improvement over time. A student's most recent grades matter most.

3. Preparation: Most colleges look for a strong complement of standardized tests to help compare applicants with different profiles from different school systems. Strong SATs, SAT Subject Tests (at least two or three of them), ACTs, APs, and other tests help to show the colleges that you have learned content in your curriculum. A good battery of tests supports your course grades. Knowing a college's requirements means in part knowing which standardized tests, if any, they require or strongly recommend.

Beyond these three factors is an essential cluster of elements that colleges look at in evaluating individual candidates. Without these, you are just a number. These aspects of your background and application make you come alive:

4. Passion: Colleges look for your commitment to one or more key activities or interests. They may be extracurricular school activities, like a sport, club, or student government office; outside-of-school involvements, like a religious youth group or a job; summer plans, like traveling or interning for a government official; or activities that you are committed to year-round, in and out of school. These are your passions, those areas you are truly excited about and involved in, committed to and rewarded for,

knowledgeable about and interested in continuing in college. They define who you are.

5. Presentation: Here is how colleges learn what is important to you and how you present yourself. See more on this in Step Eight, but let us say here that colleges consistently emphasize the importance of a student's writing in the application itself in helping them to evaluate the candidate. Strong essays, combined with supplementary materials, positive recommendations, perhaps an interview on campus or with an alumnus, and so forth let the applicant stand out among thousands of other talented candidates.

LOOKING FOR ELIGIBLE BACHELORS

Hey, guys! Although according to the census there are roughly the same number of college-age males in the population as females, the U.S. Department of Education reports that college-enrolled women outnumbered men by a significant number. The number of women enrolling in college has grown much faster than the number of men over the past three decades, and is projected to continue to do so in the future. Women represent 57% of applicants and accepted students, and 55% of enrolled college students. The National Association for College Admission Counseling (NACAC) reports that private colleges are seeing 59% of their applications from women, versus 54% at public colleges.

Know the Colleges

Avoid the Cluster Effect

The richness and variety of our colleges are often overlooked by applicants who have their hearts set on one or two particular schools. We want you to consider colleges of different levels of selectivity, in different parts of the country, and differing in such characteristics as size, academic programs, lifestyles, and traditions. In doing this, you will have an advantage over many applicants, who fail to diversify their applications sufficiently to avoid rejection by all of the colleges, a phenomenon known in admissions circles as the cluster effect. The cluster effect is fatal to the chances of many applicants, but can be countered by keeping an open mind, "suspending disbelief" about colleges you may not know very much about, and expanding your horizons.

Among clusters that have been identified in admissions studies is Stanford, Berkeley, Pomona, Reed, California Institute of Technology, and Rice University in the West. Another cluster is this group of women's colleges: Wellesley, Smith, Bryn Mawr, Mount Holyoke, and Barnard. Another cluster in the East consists of Middlebury, Bowdoin, Colby, and Colgate, while many competitive students find themselves saying "I'm only applying to the Ivies." But the Western colleges do not want to enroll mostly qualified upper-middle-class students from their region, nor do the women's colleges want to enroll mostly upper-middle-class women from the Eastern suburbs. As we have pointed out, all colleges seek a diverse body of undergraduates—students of all economic and social levels, of varied racial origins, from different parts of the country.

David, for example, a solid student in a strong suburban high school in Connecticut, was a competitive swimmer. Looking for a small, academically challenging liberal arts college that would allow him to continue swimming at a competitive level, David began the admissions process by looking mainly at that group of liberal arts colleges in the East which have strong Division III swim programs, as well as a few Division I programs. With SATs in the 1200s and solid B+ grades, David knew it would be difficult to gain entry to some of the Eastern schools, particularly since so many strong students from his high school would be applying to the same places. We encouraged David to add a few different choices to his list, and to take a trip to California, where he found himself very impressed with Claremont McKenna, which had a strong swim program that saw him as a potential recruit. Examining his choices, he applied to and was accepted by Claremont. Comparing the quality of the academic program there to his other potential options closer to home, he chose to stretch himself and enrolled at Claremont.

We find that the students who are least happy with their eventual college choice are those who have refused to acknowledge changes in the admissions environment and realities on individual college campuses. They have not fully evaluated either the particular school or schools they are most interested in, or those schools that could be very good fits, because of preconceptions, name, or other reasons. Students who have a difficult time with the admissions process, and who are often unhappy in senior spring or as entering college freshmen, often persisted in applying only to colleges they knew, colleges where they thought they would feel comfortable and at home. The fact is that their images of these colleges were often incomplete. Today's selective college campuses are more geographically, ethnically, academically, internationally, and socially diverse than ever before. Apparently the changed composition of many American campuses has escaped the notice of many bright young people and their parents.

Research on admissions has shown a widespread tendency of applicants to cluster their applications among similar institutions, rather than to shrewdly calculate the probabilities of acceptance and scatter their applications in what we call an acceptance pattern.

Richard, for example, was a strong student at a competitive private high school in Connecticut. From an international family, he had spent three years building a strong Advanced Placement course record and testing package at his American boarding school. Unaware of the dangers of clustering his applications among the most competitive schools on the East Coast, he applied to most of the Ivies, MIT, and Boston University as a backup. While he was undeniably a very good applicant, he was competing against many others with similar profiles and accomplishments. He was rejected by all of the schools except BU, where he enrolled. David turned out to be quite happy with BU. He excelled there in a challenging academic program, and decided to stay. He regretted, however, that he had not looked beyond the East and at some other smaller, more selective colleges and universities that would have been more similar to the Ivy environments he was seeking.

Jacob, on the other hand, was a bright, creative student in a large public high school in Michigan. He had every opportunity to attend his state university with its honors program, but decided he wanted a smaller college environment. Instead of applying only to colleges near home, he looked east and west. He found a perfect fit for his writing and creative talents at Swàrthmore, and was accepted through Early Decision admission. No doubt he was competing against fewer students with his profile and interests who were also from the upper Midwest. In this case, geography worked in his favor.

Applicants chance a great deal by clustering their choices among colleges, one or more of which might turn them down simply because their folders are indistinguishable from many others. In these situations, some candidates are accepted almost arbitrarily. It is too risky a way to choose the colleges where you will apply. An acceptance pattern is one that includes at least one college where you know you will be accepted. Often, this requires that you broaden your geographical boundaries, correct misconceptions about the state of competition to get into the selective colleges today, and go against conventional wisdom about particular institutions.

Why do so many students cluster their applications? Because of family pressure, peer pressure, and preconceived ideas about where they should go to college. A willingness to pioneer a bit, to go outside the circle of institutions you feel you belong in, will not only create an acceptance pattern in your applications, it will broaden you. You will be a freer person for breaking the bonds of custom.

Do consider those Exceedingly Demanding or Very Demanding colleges that may fit with your instinct to stay closer to home, which you know about and like for one reason or another, and which you feel might admit you. But also consider other wonderful colleges that are comparable academically, socially, environmentally, and so on, but which may be farther away, less demanding to gain entry to, and searching for applicants with your particular qualities.

In doing this, you will be going against the grain of common applicant practice, and you will be positioning yourself for enhanced acceptance chances. You will also be doing what many experienced college advisers urge their students to do. These counselors make a point of getting to know a wide range of colleges around the country so that they can counsel their students on how to develop an acceptance pattern in their applications. The more flexible you are, and the more information you give your counselor, the more he or she will be able to help you to identify appropriate colleges of varying degrees of selectivity in different geographical areas.

LONDON CALLING

Are you looking for something different, something overseas, and something prestigious and traditional at the same time? Many students have helped to create an acceptance pattern by looking abroad, primarily in the U.K. Such universities as St. Andrew's and Edinburgh in Scotland have a long history of attracting strong American applicants. So do some Canadian universities, such as McGill in Montreal. Recently, such top institutions as Oxford and Cambridge in England have expressed their desire to attract highly talented American students, those with strongly developed academic interests and a high degree of Advanced Placement preparation. Want a university older than Harvard with a comparable reputation and record of achievement? These may be appropriate for you to consider, but start early, because application deadlines are earlier and the process different from that in the U.S. For more information, visit UCAS, the U.K.'s common application service's Web site, at http://www.ucas.ac.uk.

Discovering Colleges

The former director of admissions of Dartmouth College has suggested that in considering where to apply, all selective college applicants should "use both chemistry and intellect to make the right choice of colleges." There is, he observes, a "match factor" to take into account when the student decides that a college may be the right place for him or her. This is a sensible approach to take, considering the kind of competition applicants to Dartmouth and other Exceedingly Demanding colleges face. "Be broad-ranging in choosing your list of colleges," the former admissions director urges. This is especially important today, when application numbers are up so dramatically, as are the actual numbers of highly qualified candidates.

If students do their research ahead of time, they will not be surprised when they get their decisions. Read the literature and ask very specific questions. Take advantage of receptions, school visits, interviews, and all contact with students and alumni.

—Admissions officer, Pomona College

SIGNIFICANT INCREASE IN APPLICATIONS AT THE TOP COLLEGES

Take a look at this initial data on admissions for fall 2008 at some of the Exceedingly Demanding colleges and universities.

College	Applications	Increase from Prior Year
Harvard	27,728	+19%
Chicago	12,277	+18
Amherst	7,800	+17
Northwestern	25,000	+14
Dartmouth	15,593	+10
Williams	7,064	+9
Cornell	32,655	+8
MIT	13,350	+7
Princeton	20,118	+6
Duke	20,250	+5
Columbia	22,249	+4
Virginia	18,776	+4
Stanford	24,564	+3
Pennsylvania	22,641	+2

Source: The *New York Times,* 1/17/08.

We realize that no selective college applicant begins the admissions process without some preconceptions. From your parents, teachers, peers, and from older students, you have heard about colleges. Some may be only names to you in the sports world; others may be part of your community. Some may be prestigious names you recognize from the media, from your parents' sweatshirts, or from buzz around school. You have probably browsed the career and guidance center at school looking at college brochures in a random way, playing with the software that helps identify colleges according to size, location, academic programs, and the like. You may have glanced at mail from colleges which has already come your way, or surfed across college Web sites. You may already have your heart set on one or two places.

Now you are going to struggle with "the match factor," putting together a set of tangible reasons for considering any college and your gut feeling about the place—the chemistry that attracts you to it, "the vibe" that many students talk about experiencing when they step onto "the right campus." The procedure that may take weeks of investigation, off and on, should produce a personal list of up to fifteen colleges of varying attractiveness, a list you will reduce when the time comes to visit campuses. Today, students are visiting and applying to more colleges, in an attempt to improve their acceptance pattern and gain entry into one or more selective colleges. We do not advise students to feel they have to visit every college in the book, or apply to every top college. We find that visiting perhaps five to ten colleges of varying sizes, personalities, and locations will help you to understand your preferences and narrow your list of possibilities. Applying to about eight colleges, if you have done your homework and balanced your list, is usually sufficient to create an appropriate acceptance pattern. It is a paradox that the stronger the applicant, and the more demanding the colleges to which he or she is applying, the more rather than the fewer colleges he or she needs to apply to, due to the impossibility of counting on an acceptance to the most selective schools and the increasing unpredictability of the selective college admissions process.

INDEPENDENT SCHOOL VARIETY

It has been years since private schools channeled their graduates to a handful of Ivy colleges. A recent summary of graduating classes from 2006 to 2008 at Phillips Exeter Academy shows that the school sent about 10% of its 1,000-plus graduates on to state universities. The largest single group choosing one college was 88— they went to Harvard; 22% in total went to the eight Ivy League institutions. The vast majority of these classes went to selective colleges, but it would be difficult to establish a pattern showing that this school prepares its students for any particular place.

One reason why private school graduates now attend such a variety of colleges is that these schools counsel their students to explore widely for admissions opportunities. It is striking to observe that Exeter, one of the most prestigious private schools, sent its students off to almost 200 different institutions during this time period. Other private schools show a similar pattern.

Part of the explanation for this diversity of college placement, beyond the diversity of preferences of students at these schools, lies in the flip-flop that has taken place at the top colleges in terms of the high school background of their entrants. At Princeton and Dartmouth, for example, about 60% of students graduated from public high schools, and only 40% from independent and parochial schools. This is a reversal from the situation several decades ago, when some 65% of students at these colleges had graduated from private schools. While private school graduates now constitute a smaller percentage of selective college classes than in the past, they still take up a disproportionate number of places, given that only 2% to 3% of college-bound high school graduates in the U.S. graduate from nonsectarian private schools.

Sources of Information

Even without visiting a campus, you can develop considerable information about a college from several general sources: people in your community, the public library, the shelves of larger bookstores, your school college and career resource center, and the Internet. People in your community may be your parents and relatives, family friends, counselors, teachers and coaches, college undergraduates, and alumni of the colleges.

With your list of fifteen colleges, let's say, you immediately eliminate the sense of being overwhelmed by the entire directory of over 2,000 four-year colleges and universities in the country. It will be helpful to draw up a list of characteristics such as size of enrollment, cost, special facilities, academic programs, extracurricular activities, and positive and negative qualities as you see them. You will soon develop a chart that is easily consulted, and this will allow you to make tentative judgments—"Not for me," "Possible," "I will apply."

We want your list to be far-ranging, to include places you had never thought of before, places that don't fit your original predilections. You say you want a small college. Look at some larger places, too. They will probably confirm your conviction, making it more convincing. Or you may decide that a bigger college offers courses not found at a smaller one; Harvard offers several thousand, to take the extreme case. Alternately, you may think you want the biggest, most urban environment you can find after your suburban high school experience in a school of 1,500 students. But do you know what a small college campus of 1,800 students is really like? Perhaps you will be drawn to the community, security, talented peer group, and faculty interaction available at a small-town liberal arts college. And, of course, there are many variations of colleges in between.

Using your notebook, you can gather such information under the headings of a number of colleges, being careful to put down the source, in this way:

COLUMBIA UNIVERSITY

*"Greatly improved undergraduate experience
since the rebellions of the 1960s."*
—Peter Flatley, Columbia grad

*"New York is a great place to study international relations.
I used the UN like a lab."*
—Katherine Miller, Columbia grad

19,117 applicants to Columbia College, 3,465 to Engineering.
—Viewbook

Judo-karate facilities.
—Catalogue

*"Columbia's faculty of stars actually spends much
time with undergraduates. I loved it!"*
—Stanley Chow, Columbia grad

"At Columbia, New York is the campus.
What a cosmopolitan experience!"
—Helena Ryan, Columbia grad

93% in top 10% of high school class.
—Web site

Photocopies of vital information, articles, statistics, and your own reflections collected into your notebook become permanent fact sheets for quick reference when you visit colleges.

ATTEND A COLLEGE FAIR

Your counselor will probably make arrangements for juniors and seniors to attend a college fair in your area. These are usually held during the fall in a number of regions in each state. Thousands of students, counselors, and parents may show up at one fair, to mingle with admissions officers and other college officials at booths and tables.

You have no obligation to attend a college fair, and it will have no impact on your chance of getting into a selective college. Still, we think it will reveal to you the intensity of the competition among institutions for applicants, and the breadth of opportunity for specialized training.

Some fairs are held on college campuses, others at high schools, some in civic auditoriums or hotel conference centers. You will probably come home with more brochures than you will ever read, but with a much better sense of the diverse college opportunities available to you.

The shelves of your local bookstore, your school guidance office, and your library will usually be filled with guidebooks and other sources of information on colleges. Doing some browsing there will show you what is available. The online bookstores also provide a wealth of references to consider. Several major guide series, including those from Barron's,

Peterson's, Princeton Review, Kaplan, Fiske, and the College Board, offer a wide array of resource materials, often in an annualized format. Rather than list every available book or guide on the market, we are providing the reader with a list of Internet-based resources. We believe this will be more useful and, even considering the ever-changing nature of the World Wide Web, more current as a starting point for the college applicant.

The Web really is the place to start and continue your college search. Information is plentiful, to the point of being overwhelming, but is often the most current and comprehensive material available on particular colleges, trends, and aspects of the admissions process. And searches on the Web can direct you toward additional information available from the colleges and other organizations. Such search engines as Google, Yahoo!, MSN, and AOL are good places to start. Note that some Web sites require colleges to pay a fee to be listed, and that our listing of sites here is not an endorsement of their products or services.

Individual college home pages typically found at "www.collegename .edu" are an excellent source of current information. The sites offer virtual tours, and an easy way to begin research on each school. They are the places to find information on colleges' departments, programs, clubs, admissions requirements and procedures, coaches, and faculty. Students can request information; e-mail professors, students, coaches, and admissions officers; and even download and submit applications.

Below is an introductory list of useful Web sites for you to consider. Given the nature of the Internet, some of the addresses here may have changed, and new sites may have been developed that will be particularly helpful in different areas. We encourage interested readers to visit us at www.greenesguides.com to find updated admissions-related information and links, and to give us suggestions for other good sites to add to our list. In any event, here are some places to start:

Internet Resources: Essential Tools
for the College-Bound Student

General

ACT	act.org
All About College	allaboutcollege.com
Campus Outreach Services	campusoutreachservices.com
Campus Tours Online	campustours.com
Chronicle of Higher Education	chronicle.com
College Board	collegeboard.com
College Bound: Issues and Trends	collegeboundnews.com
College Preview Tours	college-preview.com
College Prowler	collegeprowler.com
College View	collegeview.com
College Week Live	collegeweeklive.com
Colleges That Change Lives	ctcl.org
Collegiate Choice Walking Tours	collegiatechoice.com
Collegiate Way Residential Colleges	collegiateway.org
Education Conservancy	educationconservancy.org
Education Trust	collegeresults.org
Education Week	edweek.org
Educational Testing Service	ets.org
Greenes' Guides	greenesguides.com
Institute for Higher Education Policy Rankings Clearinghouse	ihep.org
Kaplan	kaplan.com
National Association for College Admission Counseling	nacacnet.org
National Center for Education Statistics	nces.ed.gov/collegenavigator
National Center for Fair and Open Testing	fairtest.org
National Survey of Student Engagement	nsse.iub.edu
Number2 Free Test Prep	number2.com

Peterson's	petersons.com
Princeton Review	review.com
Ten Steps to College with the Greenes on PBS	pbs.org/tenstepstocollege
Unigo	unigo.com
U.S. News & World Report	usnews.com/sections/education
U101 College Search	u101.com
Youniversity Online Tours	youniversity.tv

Online Applications and Research

Common Application	commonapp.org
Embark	embark.com
Naviance	naviance.com
Universal College Application	universalcollegeapp.com
Xap	xap.com

Financial Aid and Scholarships

CSS/Financial Aid PROFILE	profileonline.collegeboard.com
FAFSA Online	fafsa.ed.gov
FastWeb	fastweb.com
Federal Student Aid Guide	studentaid.ed.gov
FedMoney.org	fedmoney.org
FinAid	finaid.org
Fox College Funding	foxcollegefunding.com
National Association of Student Financial Aid Administrators	nasfaa.org
National Merit Scholarship Corporation	nationalmerit.org
Nelnet Education Planning and Financing	nelnet.com
Paying for College with the Greenes on PBS	pbs.org/payingforcollege
SallieMae	salliemae.com
Savingforcollege	savingforcollege.com

Multicultural and First-Generation College Resources

A Better Chance	abetterchance.org
American Council on Education's College Is Possible	acenet.edu *and* knowhow2go.com
Association of Black Admissions and Financial Aid Officers of the Ivy League and Sister Schools	abaschools.org
AVID	avidonline.org
Black Collegian	black-collegian.com
College Fund/UNCF	uncf.org
Hispanic Association of Colleges and Universities	hacu.net
Historically Black Colleges and Universities and National Association for Equal Opportunity	nafeo.org
Journal of Blacks in Higher Education	jbhe.com
NAACP	naacp.org
Pathways to College Network	pathwaystocollege.net
QuestBridge	questbridge.org

For Athletes

Future Athletes	futureathletes.com
Ivy League Sports	ivyleaguesports.com
National Association of Collegiate Directors of Athletics	nacda.cstv.com
National Collegiate Athletic Association	ncaa.org
National Scouting Report	nsr-inc.com

For the Learning Disabled and Those with Special Needs

Americans with Disabilities Act	ada.gov
Attention Deficit Disorder Association	add.org
Children and Adults with Attention Deficit/Hyperactivity Disorder	chadd.org
Council for Exceptional Children	cec.sped.org
Hoagies' Gifted Education Page	hoagiesgifted.com
Learning Disabilities Association of America	ldanatl.org

LD Online	ldonline.org
National Center for Learning Disabilities	ncld.org
Smart Kids with Learning Disabilities	smartkidswithld.org

For International Students and Study Abroad

American Institute for Foreign Study	aifs.org
Canada School Finder	schoolfinder.com
Council on International Educational Exchange	ciee.org
eduPass	edupass.org
Institute for International Education	iie.org
NAFSA: Association of International Educators	nafsa.org
U.K. Universities and Colleges Admissions Service	ucas.ac.uk
U.S. Government Visa Information	unitedstatesvisas.gov

The Attributes of the Colleges

To expand the information about each college on your list, you should include in your notebook any special programs or facilities the college singles out in its literature. Bowdoin College, for example, touts its purchase of land on the ocean and its development of coastal studies and environmental sciences majors, with student opportunities to conduct hands-on research on the Atlantic. If this fits with your interests and talents, it is just the kind of rare program that might make the difference for you in deciding on a first-choice college. On a campus visit, an applicant who expressed a desire to know more about the coastal programs would be sent by the admissions officer to a campus representative. This could even lead to a faculty recommendation for admission.

What does the college say about itself in its brochures and on its Web site? Dartmouth College's emphasis on its Women in Science Program sends a clear message to female applicants who have talents in the sciences. These young women should make a note to tell the admissions committee of their potential plans to go on to graduate study in medicine or engineering, for example, and their interest in opportunities at Dartmouth to engage in scientific research with faculty mentors. Obviously, their applications will be viewed with considerable favor, but only if their transcript, testing, and extracurricular activities back up their expressed interest in this or another program area.

HOW TO E-MAIL COLLEGES FOR INFORMATION

E-mail is a great way to contact colleges and to stay in touch with them through the admissions process. E-mail should go to the admissions office, and you can find the right address in guidebooks or on the college's Web site. You can address the e-mail to the director of admissions, or just to the admissions office. Ask them to send you current informational materials and an application, and to put you on their mailing list. Tell them your high school and class, and, if you want, mention any particular academic or extracurricular interests that you also want information about.

As you go through the admissions process, you may find it convenient to e-mail the financial aid office, student representatives, coaches, and faculty members as well, to get information or ask particular questions. Some colleges have "prospective applicant" forms to fill out online, as well as regular blogs, IM chat opportunities, and even a presence on Second Life or virtual college fairs.

What is your special interest? English literature? You will see that Lafayette College boasts of being the first American college to teach this subject. Expression of a genuine interest in Shakespeare or in any English author will elicit a warm response during a campus visit. Are you especially interested in foreign affairs and international relations? Princeton's Woodrow Wilson School and the university's requirement that all seniors complete a major thesis project involving original research, through which you could focus on an international issue of particular concern, might be just the program you are looking for. Make sure on your visit to campus and in a group information session to mention your interest and your potential goals, ask questions to learn more about the Wilson school and the political science/government major at Princeton, and visit the particular departments, buildings, and libraries where you would study.

We hope it will be self-evident that your interest in what a college has to offer must be genuine. Your attention must be drawn by some attribute that answers your personal need. Just to strike up a conversation on some new laboratory or performing arts or athletic center you have read about is not going to help you. Colleges have long experience in assessing the sincerity of applicants' statements, and will look to your record for evidence of consistent and multilevel commitment to the areas in which you have expressed interest. It is not worth trying to be something or someone you are not, just to impress a college that might not be right for you in the first place. It is far better to pursue your passions and strengths, and to look for colleges that offer programs that match your preferences.

It may take considerable investigation to find a college that has a facility, a discipline, a program, or an activity ideally suited to your needs. You may have to give a little here to gain a little there. Perhaps you wanted a larger university in the city, but have found that some of the best undergraduate majors in philosophy are found in some of the smaller liberal arts colleges, such as Swarthmore. A little digging will help you begin to identify the particular schools, and the particular programs, that best fit you.

Know the Trends

Do you realize that business and economics are two of the most popular majors today, and that some departments in the humanities, such as comparative literature or classics, are desperately seeking to keep their enrollments up? One response might be "If business is such a popular major, and I want to be in business someday, I'll major in business, too." For a selective college applicant with strengths in the humanities, however, the response should be "I don't want to get lost among all those vaguely defined business majors, and my math grades don't show a lot of strength for economics, and since I love French and English literature, I ought to look for colleges with programs in comparative literature which might be looking to attract applicants like me." Another trend is the growth in engineering majors graduating from college and eventually going on to the top business schools. Engineering majors are valued for their quantitative, technical, and problem-solving skills. An applicant with strength in math, physics, and computer science should consider applying to engineering programs within the selective universities. Princeton, for example, reserves a portion of its class for engineers, who are considered separately from liberal arts applicants, and Swarthmore actively advertises itself as the only top liberal arts college with an engineering program.

There is also renewed interest in selective colleges training elementary and high school teachers, in addition to college-level faculty. Prospective teachers should keep this in mind as they build their lists and make plans for college visits. There will be a desperate need for qualified teachers in America over the next decades, and bright, well-educated graduates will write their own ticket in the elementary and secondary teaching market. These and other professional and educational trends are certainly relevant for today's college applicant, and you may want to ask colleges about where their graduates go in terms of careers and graduate education, which has become increasingly important in today's marketplace. You may want to talk with your parents and with professionals in fields of interest to you, to ask what insiders believe to be the future of their industry.

COMMUNITY SERVICE OPPORTUNITIES

A wonderful trend in education in America has been the growth and encouragement of community service opportunities and involvement. Many high schools, public and private, have built into their curriculum a community service requirement, and we have found that many students have gone far above and beyond these requirements in pursuing their interest in helping others. More good news: many colleges actively facilitate student volunteer service and internship programs and make attempts to link with their surrounding communities. Here is another chance for talented students with backgrounds and interests in service to find a program match. Some examples of colleges with a tradition of and commitment to community service? Brown University, in Providence; Trinity College, in Hartford; Bates College, in Lewiston, Maine; Davidson, in North Carolina; and many, many more!

One key trend that no one can ignore is the rise of technology in the classroom and the workplace. Today's "i-generation" or computer/

digital native student, raised on the Internet with early access to computers, may take for granted the role of computers and the information superhighway in education, communication, and business. However, it remains an unfortunate fact that many students have not had access to computer training and the use of the Internet, with its vast informational and networking resources. Most selective colleges will help needy students purchase computers for schoolwork, and many high schools have improved their technological sophistication and student access to the Web on campus in recent years. It behooves all students, not just those with a major interest in computer science, to prepare themselves to integrate computer technology and the Internet into their educational and personal lives. They will find on entering college campuses that dorms, classrooms, and libraries are wired or wireless for easy and instant access to the World Wide Web, and that professors and peers will expect neat, polished, revised, and laser-printed papers as the classroom standard. Faculty will assign research on the Internet, expect complicated information searches in the electronic library system, and hold office hours and distribute homework and the class syllabus online. Students will register for classes by computer, study faculty course evaluations in the university's or independent databases, and communicate with their neighbors down the hall by e-mail. Let the uninitiated beware, but not be afraid. Today's college campuses have built-in technical support staff and computer instructors to help you get up to speed and stay in the fast lane. Nevertheless, if you are computer shy, the time to start learning about word processing, search engines, and instant messaging is sooner rather than later.

Public College Options

Generally speaking, only a small number of public universities or their satellite institutions can be called Exceedingly Demanding. Yet they present a problem to the mediocre student, who may be shut out of a place because it is reserved either for a high-paying out-of-state applicant or a high-performing in-state candidate. A small state school like Vermont enrolls half its students from out-of-state because these students pay considerably more in tuition than Vermont residents. The same dynamic holds true across the United States, with the so-called flagship campuses of the state university systems actively seeking to enroll talented, higher-paying out-of-state candidates, and with the state legislatures being more or less restrictive on the overall proportion of out-of-state students allowed to enroll. The interest of the state legislatures is to ensure that the leading public institutions in the state are serving the state taxpayers. Since these taxpayers foot the bill for most of their public universities' operating costs, they gain preferred entry requirements and subsidized tuition costs. States differ in the percentage of out-of-state students they will allow in their leading universities, with competitive schools like the University of North Carolina and the University of California at Berkeley enrolling 18% and less than 10% out-of-state students, respectively.

What should be clear, then, is that out-of-state applicants to schools like Virginia, North Carolina, Michigan, Wisconsin, and those in the California system should expect to be treated differently and more harshly than in-state applicants. They should also be aware of the ramifications of studying in an environment where between 50% and 95% of the students are from the same state. Additionally, in evaluating all candidates, not just those from out of state, the larger public universities are more quantitative in their approach. That is, they focus primarily on GPA, SATs (or ACTs), and class rank in making their more formulaic admissions decisions. An applicant who is weak in one of these areas, or whose case would benefit from a closer, more personal reading of application essays and teacher recommendations, will generally, but not always, have more trouble getting a second look from a larger public university.

Can a general trend in public university admissions be discerned nationally? Well, most state systems report more applications, in part due to demographics, and probably also because their tuitions are anywhere from half to one-quarter as much as those of the private colleges. What this means to applicants is that some state systems are no longer the fallback safeties they used to be for mediocre students. In fact, a number of highly selective private college admissions officers and presidents have stated in recent years that some of their toughest competition for top applicants is coming from the first-rate state universities, which offer extensive resources, tuition bargains, exciting social campuses, and, increasingly, *honors* or *residential* college programs to attract the best and the brightest students by creating a "school within a school" model. High schools should take heart that this situation can spur students to better academic work, in order to qualify for their own or other states' top public campuses.

Even rejection by a state university may be offset by an applicant's attendance at a community college and a later transfer into the state university system, providing the student has met the minimum standards for admission. Many states have agreements whereby students who perform at a certain level in the junior or community college system, or on a less competitive state university campus, are guaranteed admission and transfer of academic credits into the state's more selective programs. For many talented students, it makes sense to consider the public universities as additional options when applying to college. For more information on public universities, see our book *The Public Ivies*.

Comparing Colleges and Paring the List

You probably cannot visit twelve or fifteen colleges, so you are going to make some fundamental decisions about attractive institutions that you must disregard. A small Midwestern college like Oberlin looks awfully attractive to a New Yorker interested in majoring in art and performing in the college orchestra, but Wesleyan is so much nearer home that Oberlin may have to be stricken from the list of considerations, at least for an initial visit (remember our discussion of creating an acceptance pattern—if you visit and like Wesleyan, or Vassar, perhaps you might apply to Oberlin, and visit it if you can, or interview with an alum in your area and, if you are accepted, take the time to spend a day there in the spring).

In *The Hidden Ivies*, we discuss extensively the criteria by which you can evaluate a top college, and those characteristics that make an Ivy an Ivy. Here we introduce some initial guidelines. You can compare colleges in a number of ways, such as:

- Relative competitive admissions chances
- Academic offerings
- Facilities
- Location
- Size

- Size of endowment relative to the undergraduate student body
- Financial aid offerings
- Extracurricular and athletic programs
- Social environment
- Access to faculty
- Faculty/student ratio
- Cost
- Tradition

You may ask what the presence of graduate students adds to an undergraduate experience. Climate can be a factor in deciding to exclude a place that may be too hot or too cold for you. You may include a college just because of some unique quality—Outing Club and freshman trip programs at Dartmouth and Middlebury appeal to those who like to hike, climb, canoe, mountain bike, and camp. Or you may exclude a college with fraternities and sororities. The prospect of working in the local community after graduation attracts some students to an institution like Stanford University, located in a high-tech area. The emphasis on spirituality and social service may put a college like Wake Forest on your list.

THINKING OF GRADUATE SCHOOL

The bachelor's degree, B.A. or B.S., has become increasingly commonplace. According to the 1990 census, 13.1% of the adult population had one, and 7.2% had a graduate or professional degree. By itself, the B.A./B.S. no longer guarantees entry to a career. Not only engineers, doctors, lawyers, and educators must do graduate work to enter their professions: virtually all future professional specialists will need advanced training. Planning their undergraduate training with this prospect in mind is critical. More and more undergraduates are considering postgraduate training, at least sometime in the future, in order to provide for their long-term job security.

- U.S. Department of Education data from 1995–96 show that 406,301 master's degrees, 44,652 doctoral degrees, and 76,734 professional degrees were earned in that year. Those numbers increased in 2005–06 to 594,065 master's, 56,067 doctoral, and 87,655 professional degrees.

• 43,440 of the professional degrees were law degrees. 15,455 were medical degrees.

• 146,400 of the master's degrees were in business, management, and marketing.

• The largest numbers of doctorates were earned in engineering (7,396), education (7,584), and the health professions (7,128).

It is therefore not too early to be thinking of graduate school when you apply to a selective college. You will not be alone. Among the top colleges, it is not uncommon to find from 50% to 70% of graduates pursuing an advanced degree within five years of graduation!

Excellent college work at a strong institution is the fundamental qualification for acceptance by a good graduate school. Attending a selective college can be a help, but not a guarantee for acceptance by highly selective graduate programs at institutions like Harvard Law School, Cornell Medical School, Tuck School of Business at Dartmouth, and Stanford or Berkeley's engineering divisions. What counts is not just the name of one's undergraduate college, but one's grade point average, strong curriculum, faculty recommendations, and track record of research, writing, and internships. We like to talk about the "top third" strategy with students: find the right college, do well, and graduate in the top third of your class, and you will find many good graduate options available to you. Some of the Hidden Ivies, such as Reed, Carleton, and Bryn Mawr, have incredible records of graduate admission to medical, science, and Ph.D. programs.

And do not forget the chemical factor that the former admissions director at Dartmouth mentioned. Include in your list those colleges that "feel right" for you and take note of those that make you uncomfortable. The emotional response is important and you need not apologize for it, whether the "preppy" look of students pictured in a brochure turned you off, or the description of the warm fellowship on campus moved you. You still may want to visit a campus that gets a low rating from you, and the visit may change your mind. Try to visit a few different types of schools to see some contrast. Just let the chemistry work and trust your feelings.

What you are doing is learning about your own tastes, preferences, and possibilities, and at the same time making decisions on your own. You are in the driver's seat. It is not selective colleges deciding about you, but you deciding about them. And do not think that because the number of applicants to many of these colleges is increasing, they do not need you. Even the most selective college loves to see its applications increase. So you can take momentary satisfaction in deciding not to consider MIT because by comparison to Cal Tech it is too big for your taste.

Enjoy this search for places you would like to visit and consider seriously how you would like to spend your years at each of them. The ones that appeal to you most are the ones you will visit. That we will cover in more detail in Step Six.

PROTECTION FOR THE DISABLED

Applicants with physical or learning disabilities are legally protected from discrimination by federal law. The Rehabilitation Act of 1973, the Americans with Disabilities Act (ADA) of 1990 and the ADA Amendments Act of 2008 prohibit discrimination against disabled applicants to any college receiving federal monies. Laws like the Individuals with Disabilities Education Act (IDEA) further protect the rights of those with special needs.

Disabled applicants may want to query colleges about their programs and facilities. Most but not all campuses have someone responsible for coordinating special-student services. Knowing in advance what to expect, the disabled applicant can avoid disappointment and, as has often been the case, actually enhance his or her chances for admission by informing the college of his or her motivation and ability to overcome significant obstacles. There has been great progress in the area of disabilities support services on most college campuses and we encourage you to explore the general resources we list in our Internet Resources list on pages 102–105 as well as individual college learning support resources.

Awareness and discussion of learning disabilities and attention disorders in particular have increased through the 1990s. In response to student and parent concerns, and legal enforcement of colleges' responsibilities to assist students with legitimate learning needs, colleges have developed a wide array of academic and other support services, from the availability of individual specialists to the establishment of comprehensive learning support programs and centers. Again, we encourage disabled students to examine closely the available support services on campus, to have learning evaluations updated during their junior or senior year to comply with college requirements, and to discuss the appropriateness of their sharing evaluation materials with college learning support programs as part of the application process. We have found that this is often a student's best strategy, allowing them not to excuse poor academic or standardized testing performance, but rather to explain inconsistencies in their record and their relative strengths and weaknesses. Students can ask themselves about what they are comfortable sharing personally with colleges, and choose to write directly about their experiences and overcoming challenges resulting from a learning disability or attention deficit disorder, for example. We have found that most colleges react positively to such forthright discussions, which reflect personal self-knowledge and maturity. And in our opinion, if a college were to react negatively to such a disclosure, it probably was not the right place for that student anyway!

Step One Checklist

✓Begin to use your notebook, a computer folder, and our checklists on college admissions to record key information.

✓Consult a variety of catalogues, viewbooks, and Web sites of colleges that may interest you; list their admissions requirements in your notebook.

✓Plan the remainder of your high school academic program, and possibly your summers, to make sure you will meet, if not exceed, the requirements of potential college choices.

✓Stay committed to your key extracurricular passions and look for opportunities to develop them to the next level and to achieve leadership positions. Be willing to drop those activities that no longer interest you and that may be taking up too much time.

✓Give yourself a preliminary self-classification, estimating how well qualified you think you are to apply to colleges with requirements that are Exceedingly Demanding, Very Demanding, and Demanding.

✓Give your counselor a brief summary of the colleges that interest you. Include your preliminary self-classification and your list of interests. You can use the questionnaires and worksheets included in this book if your counselor does not use a particular school form.

✓Draw up a schedule of your plans for tests, campus visits, and applications.

✓Continue your research into a variety of selective colleges by reading published material and by talking with teachers, alumni, and undergraduates you know.

✓Consider selective colleges with a wide variety of characteristics, to develop an acceptance pattern among the schools that interest you. Remember the "chemistry factor," and consider colleges you feel good about.

✓Note facilities or programs of special interest to you at these colleges and follow up on these features later on during your campus visits and in your applications.

✓Ask teachers and your college adviser about new trends in higher education and find out what opportunities these present at different selective colleges, where your interests might match a particular college's needs.

✓Draw up a list of about fifteen selective colleges you may visit, taking care not to cluster your list. It is hard not to hear the drumbeat call to the most prestigious colleges you know, but be careful to avoid "bunching" with your classmates at the usual suspects.

✓Begin comparing the colleges' attributes and gradually revising your list.

✓Discuss with your college counselor and with the appropriate admissions offices the advisability of the various Early Decision and Early Action plans.

STEP TWO:
Determine Your Strengths

]

Making a Choice

Choosing a college is really one of your first major decisions in life. The process involves discovering, among possibly 100 or more places you have never seen and know little about, a handful where you think you will be happy and productive for your undergraduate years. What is more, you are asked to prepare yourself at one of these colleges not for four years, but for the rest of your life. You are, in effect, laying the foundation on which you will build your career and your life's work. The quality of that foundation rests on identifying your personal and academic strengths.

The former president of one of the Ivy League colleges once stated, "The first requirement of being genuinely well educated is to have the capacity of being useful." He did not mean merely successful in a pragmatic way. Admissions committees of selective colleges seek to enroll students who will be useful to themselves, their fellow students, the college, and ultimately to society at large. A social conscience, a commitment to serving the larger good, and leadership in one's profession are indicators of the well-educated graduate today.

But how do selective colleges identify such students? In reality, admissions officers look for applicants who identify themselves as useful. These are the students who know their strengths, and are therefore likely to be motivated and directed by them.

Contrast these two self-assessments to make the point:

Ricky, a student in a competitive high school near Richmond, Virginia, wrote the following statement on the student questionnaire for the Educational Consulting Centers prior to his first visit in the winter of his junior year:

> I would like a career in journalism and communications. I have had this idea ever since my uncle visited us from California a few years ago. He is the city editor of a daily paper in a small city, but he made me feel that the whole community depended on his work. For example, he described how his paper handled a racial zoning problem and avoided a potential racial confrontation. My uncle suggested that I read a daily paper and study lots of American history. My 700 score on the History Subject Test is one result that should help me realize my goal of getting into a top college. As I indicated elsewhere, I am in the top 12% of my class. I have tried to make my writing for the *Scripture,* our school paper, an influence in the school community. My articles on drug abuse were reprinted in our two weekly papers. Perhaps some students are avoiding using drugs because of these articles. I am hopeful that I will be elected editor of the paper in my senior year. My grades and SAT scores are good enough for Chapel Hill, according to my counselor. This university appeals to me because of its strong history department, and because it is a large university in a high-tech area where things are changing. I believe I can acquire the background a good newspaperman needs—although I might wind up in radio or TV—at such a great university as North Carolina. I would like suggestions for other comparable colleges I ought to apply to in case I don't make Chapel Hill.

Jacqueline, a junior in a private day school, concluded her questionnaire for the Consulting Centers this way:

> I am a typical all-around person. I believe a person must make a contribution in life, so I take part in as many school activities as possible. My best sport is tennis—I am number six on the team and play doubles in matches with other schools. I also play field hockey (JV) and basketball. As a member of the Student Council I am responsible for advising on Robert's Rules of Order. In my church I attend Youth Group meetings monthly and have helped

Asian refugees moving into the community. I am not sure yet just
what college to apply to. It will depend on how much I can bring up
my SAT scores next year—I know I am really not an 1100-level
student. I hope you can help me decide what colleges I should
consider and how to raise my test scores.

Ricky clearly had a handle on himself, and indeed enrolled at the
University of North Carolina. Jacqueline was less mature at the time,
more concerned about all her involvements than her future. As college
admissions became a reality in her mind, she learned to concentrate her
energies during her senior year, spending much of her free time at the
local hospital. Doing that suggested the possibility of the health fields.
She also learned to accept the fact that she needed to put focused time
into preparing for the SAT if she were to bring her scores up to the
range expected by the selective colleges. We helped her to recognize
that her strength was her ability to relate to people and assist them in
their needs. This led to a search for universities that offered strong
programs in psychology and human development, fields of study that
could lead her to a graduate degree in counseling, teaching, human
resources, or the health professions. We also redesigned her senior
curriculum to include Advanced Placement psychology and biology in
her program. By December of her senior year, Jacqueline had raised
her SAT scores 150 points through concentrated practice over the summer and fall, and had visited six college campuses. She eventually
settled on the University of Pennsylvania, a highly selective school that
she had little knowledge of at the beginning of her college search and
for which she was initially unprepared.

Academic Strengths

Academic strengths are easily recognized and quantified by grades,
class rank, and test scores. These are reinforced by teachers' comments, and here is where you can turn weaknesses into strengths. The
natural tendency is to read over those comments that praise your work
and merely glance at those that criticize it. But it is critical comment
that can teach you to overcome bad habits and force you to master material you find difficult or unpleasant to learn. So your procedure
should be first to note your obvious strengths, from grades, test scores,

and comments. These will be apparent to an admissions committee, too, and so you should continue efforts to keep these strengths. But you should also reflect on your teachers' criticisms for clues to ways to improve your record. Awareness of your academic strengths will give you confidence to accept criticism and act on it.

Extracurricular Strengths

Identifying obvious talents such as athletic achievement, election to class office, or success on the school newspaper or in the drama club is a simple matter. However, you should be careful not to confuse mere involvement with strength. Participation in itself is not a noted strength. Admissions committees are unimpressed by laundry lists of activities in school or in your community. Rarely does any student excel in six different areas. Even in athletics today, the demands of a single sport make it difficult for a good athlete to be outstanding in several sports. The modern school athlete is expected to train in the off-season for skill and strength development. Summer training camps are an increasing part of the preparation for the next season. They have also become a showcase for college coaches to observe potential varsity players for their teams.

What colleges look for are standouts: 20% of a typical class at Williams College, for example, had been distinguished athletes, some 30% achieved distinction in music and other performing arts, 18% had been heads of a service organization, and several hundred had been either the heads of their student government or debate captain, or editor in chief of the school newspaper or literary magazine or yearbook. By identifying one or two of your strengths, you clarify your extracurricular goals and assure yourself of the possibility of becoming an accepted student.

Your Student Questionnaire

To help you discover more about your abilities, we created a questionnaire that has proved to be of great value as students embark on the Ten-Step Plan to college admissions (see below). In it, you are asked to examine your academic performance and personal qualities, and to rate the features of colleges (size, geographical location, environment, and so on) according to your preferences. We encourage students to put a large question mark next to any criteria they are uncertain about so that we can address this in our first meeting. What matters here is that they now know these are important factors for them to consider in choosing a college.

Reflect on the questions, and jot your answers in your notebook. The questionnaire is intended to take time and thought as you fill it out. Some points you have probably been thinking about already; others you may be reflecting on for the first time. For instance, let us say you live in New England and are thinking of applying to Cornell or Berkeley, both of which your mother attended, or Dartmouth, where your father went, as well as Vanderbilt, which you have heard great things about. The first question asks you to check your priorities of locations. Already you have to think about which of these colleges you would prefer, and to deal with such thoughts as, "Will Mom be offended if I do not put her schools as my possible first choice?"

Knowing your strengths and preferences is a matter of looking at palpable records—your school performance, test scores, and extracurricular accomplishments—as well as your preferred tastes. Your school records are a known quantity up to this point, but do you know if you prefer a small, medium, or large college? Or a college that is within a university with graduate schools? Do you think you will do better in an urban setting, or a small-town or suburban environment? At first you may say a university, because it is supposedly more stimulating. But then you visit Amherst or Pomona or Bowdoin and wonder what could be more stimulating for you than these selective small colleges.

Filling out the questionnaire can reveal your individual strengths as well as your needs, and help you concentrate your efforts where they will be most rewarding and useful. As you know your personal powers better, they will serve you better, not just in getting into college, but in all that you will do in your life.

Answering the Student Questionnaire

Let's take a look at the questions, to start you thinking about them before you actually fill out the worksheet.

Student Questionnaire

1. What type of college do you see yourself in? Please review the following characteristics and review your current priorities before checking the appropriate line. You may wish to discuss your answers with your parents or counselor prior to completing the questionnaire.

Geographic Location Please number choices from (1), most desirable, to (5), least desirable:

Northeast ___ Mid Atlantic ___ Midwest ___ South ___ West ___
Doesn't Matter ___

Setting: Urban ___ Suburban ___ Rural ___ Doesn't Matter ___

Size: Very Small (under 1,000 undergraduates) ___ Small (1,000–3,500) ___
Medium (3,500–6,000) ___ Large (6,000–15,000) ___
Very Large (15,000–35,000) ___

College (undergraduates only) ___ or **University** (undergraduates, graduate
and professional students) ___ Doesn't Matter ___

Coeducational ___ or **Single-Sex** ___ Doesn't Matter ___

Atmosphere? Conservative ___ Traditional ___ Middle-of-the-Road ___
Liberal ___ Alternative ___

What characteristics would you like to incorporate? _____
What characteristics would you like to avoid? _____
How important a consideration is institutional prestige? _____

2. Intended major(s) _____
Possible majors if undecided _____
How intensive an academic workload do you want? _____
Academic interests apart from your intended major _____
_____

3. List the courses you are currently taking and your approximate
grades _____

4. Tests taken to date and scores:

PSAT (10th Grade):   CR _____ M _____ WR _____

PSAT (11th Grade):   CR _____ M _____ WR _____

SAT: (Date) _____   CR _____ M _____ WR _____

SAT: (Date) _____   CR _____ M _____ WR _____

SAT Subject Tests: M1 ___ M2 ___ LIT ___ BIO ___ CHEM ___ PHYSICS ___
W. HIST ___ US HIST ___ Other ___ Other ___

ACT PLAN: COMP ___ ENG ___ MA ___ READ ___ SCI ___

ACT: COMP ___ ENG ___ MA ___ READ ___ SCI ___ WR ___

AP (Subjects, Scores): _____ _____ _____ _____ _____

5. Please list your most important extracurricular pursuits. Specify years of involvement and positions of leadership or responsibility, and indicate which ones are most important to you.

	YEARS	FRESH	SOPH	JUNIOR	SENIOR
School Activities					
School Sports					
Outside Activities					
Work and Summer Activities					
Hobbies and Interests					
Awards (academic and others)					

6. Are there any colleges in which you are particularly interested at this time? Please name them and tell us why. _____

_____

Have you ruled out any colleges? Please name them and tell us why.

_____

_____

7. Will you need financial aid? _____ Do you want a part-time job? _____

8. How would you assess yourself as a student? What do you consider your academic strengths and weaknesses? Do you think your transcript and teacher/counselor reports accurately reflect your academic abilities?

_____

_____

9. Tell us anything about yourself that would help us understand you better—your personality, values, background, interests, aspirations, other significant people in your life, etc. Please give as thoughtful a response as possible. Use additional space if necessary.

_____

_____

Questions 1 and 2

You may already have a clear vision of the kind of college you would like to attend. But perhaps you have not given much thought to second and third choices. We want you to reflect on them because there are so many good college opportunities in different sections of the country.

For instance, let us say you live in the East and you visited Amherst and found it most appealing. You believe you have only a 50–50 chance for admission based on your academic and activity profile, so you are also considering Wesleyan, Hamilton, Bates, Vassar, and Colby. We might ask you to consider similar colleges of excellence such as Carleton and Grinnell in the Midwest and Pomona in California.

You may still end up putting Amherst as your first preference, but you will have a second and third choice after considering other places.

Characteristics you prefer might be a strong college spirit, proximity to ski slopes or the ocean, opportunities for political action, a diverse student population, or social service programs supported by the college.

Characteristics you might like to avoid could be a heavy emphasis on fraternity/sorority life, a strong orientation toward sports competition, fundamentalist religions on campus, a place known for frequent drug and/or alcohol usage, extreme weather conditions, limited course selection or large lecture halls, or total isolation (see more in Step Ten on positive and negative reactions to colleges).

We ask how important is institutional prestige, to make you think about the real reasons you are interested in certain colleges. Granted admission to Harvard and Princeton, 75% of applicants will accept Harvard, 60% Princeton. Most of those turning down Princeton's offer will go to Harvard for the added prestige even if they might favor the environment and size of Princeton. As competitive for admission as the Ivy colleges are, only slightly over half of those offered a place will elect to enroll. Many students will choose a college they have been admitted to for its prestige more than for its appropriateness. This is what we refer to in *Inside the Top Colleges* as the "halo effect." We only ask you to consider the key ingredients you will need to succeed as a college student and where you are most likely to find them. It may or may not be the most prestigious of the many top colleges in America.

Our own feeling is that the reason why any institution enjoys prestige is that it has exceptional qualities and resources that add up to an exceptional education. But merely having a prestigious undergraduate degree will not in and of itself guarantee self-fulfillment, a strong academic performance, admission to graduate school, or the best job. Today it is all about outstanding performance in one of the many top colleges. The colleges in *The Hidden Ivies* demonstrate the value of a successful experience in the right college for you, by the extraordinary rate of acceptance for students into top graduate schools of all kinds, and employment with prestigious companies.

How intensive an academic workload and grading system do you want? The question is related somewhat to the prestige issue. Prestigious colleges expect hard work from their highly competitive students, and, grade inflation notwithstanding, their professors are loath to give out too many A's these days without excellent performance. Let us say you are used to getting A's in high school. Are you prepared to settle for B's in a college with an intensive workload? Or would you be more comfortable in a very good college where your hard work will enable you to excel? To answer this question you have to know how you respond to challenge, for make no mistake, college is in many ways unlike secondary school. In a literature course you will read one or more novels a week. Science courses call for labs that will take up several afternoons a week. Whatever your field of study, you will be expected to complete research and writing projects at a significant level of thought and content. If you are taking Advanced Placement courses in high school, for example, then you have a fairly good idea of what awaits you in college studies. Can you say to yourself, "I enjoy this degree of challenging work and would look forward to doing more of the same in college?" If the answer is yes, then you are an appropriate candidate for one of the prestigious colleges.

Imagine yourself already in college. How will you spend your time? What will you major in? What courses will you take not related to your major? What sports will you play, or what will be your extracurricular activities? Some students know that they want to become doctors, and they major in biology or chemistry. Others plan to go to law school and decide to major in history or government or political science. Business-oriented students think of economics as a possible major. Future journalists or writers think of English or communications as the appropriate concentration. Future educators choose the academic subject they like the most and take related courses in education that will prepare them to teach.

Probably as many or more students heading to college are not sure what direction their education will take. They may have favorite subjects, but no idea of what their future studies should be. This uncertainty is quite normal, and the questionnaire is not intended to push you into a premature commitment. It merely asks you to indicate potential interests. You are going to college to acquire knowledge you do not have at present. How does a person fix on subjects he knows nothing about? By listing interests and reviewing college literature to see what the course offerings are. You can also get an idea of what it means to major in a specific field by looking at the description of departmental requirements in the college catalogues or Web sites.

Most important, remember that admissions committees expect that students enrolling in their colleges want to explore a range of courses and special programs in order to determine what they like best. They anticipate that most undergraduates will change their intended major one or more times before they settle on the field that brings them the greatest satisfaction. No college asks enrolled first-year students to declare what their major will be. You will major, or concentrate, in one particular field or combination of fields during your last two years. Exceptions are obvious, such as engineering or business or arts majors who enroll in the specialized colleges within a university or technical institute at the time of their entrance. You do need to take a number of prerequisites in your first two years to concentrate in a major in your later years. It is very common for a student to enroll in a college with the goal of majoring in French, for example, and ultimately minor in the language while majoring in a subject like art history. The examples we could provide are endless, so feel confident that you will find your favorite field of study once you are enrolled and explore across the college curriculum. In putting down now what you think you might pursue academically, you are not casting your thoughts in concrete; you are simply making it easier to look at potential colleges from an academic view.

What else will you do in college besides study? Have fun, of course, make new friends, join special interest clubs, sororities or fraternities, or societies and community service groups, and go to parties. But how about going out for the campus paper, the radio station, or the dramatic society, running for the honor council or student government, or playing on one of the many club-level or intramural sports teams? When you look into your potential colleges of interest, check out the activities offered to be certain you will find a home in one or several areas that matter to you. In college you will have many more free hours of discretionary time, since you only attend classes for two or three hours per day. We believe it is important to engage in some organization that will bring you pleasure, facilitate your making friends easily, and help you organize your day with a proper balance between work and play.

Your participation in athletics will, quite naturally, depend on your abilities and passion for a particular sport. Varsity high school players may not be college varsity material, but they can still engage in intramural or club sports. Many students take up new sports in college for the first time: rowing, squash, rugby, water polo. You may decide to take advantage of the fitness center for intense exercise, or join one of the many special-interest clubs like mountain biking, hiking, mountain climbing, and so on. But we urge you not to make the choice of which colleges to consider solely on the basis of their athletic programs. Remember that only a small percentage of high school athletes will actually get to play at the varsity level in college. You will want the college you enroll in to have many of the other activities and academic programs that matter to you.

As you begin to envision your campus life, you will see that there is a temptation to spread yourself too thin because of the richness of opportunities that await you. Now is a good time to begin thinking about the best use of your college time for enjoyment and self-development. Overdoing extracurricular activities and sports can not only weaken academic performance, but lead to frustration as well as possible exhaustion and poor grades!

Questions 3–6

These are purely factual, to help an adviser guide you in your choice of colleges to which you will apply. For instance, knowing where your parents went to college is to know that your chances of admission as a child of an alumnus (referred to as a "legacy" by the admissions committees) are greater than the chances of most other applicants to those particular colleges. If you have a parent on a college faculty, you know that you have a stronger possibility of admission and the tuition will be significantly less, since this is the policy of most colleges and universities. If you are a first-generation college-bound student, this is an important attribute for your counselor and colleges to know about.

It helps your counselor to know what kinds of colleges you are considering and which you are not interested in initially. This leads to a more directed discussion of your preferences on a number of criteria and helps in suggesting other similar colleges.

Your current courses and grades, and your standardized test scores to date, will help you and your counselor to consider which selective colleges will be realistic or potential reaches, targets, and safeties. Going over your current curriculum will help you to plan your curriculum for the remainder of high school. Detailing your school, outside work, and summer activities will help to show you where you are spending your time, where your passions are, and where you might need to focus.

Question 7

If you will need financial aid or a part-time job, some colleges are less likely to admit you, while others that are more well-endowed practice "need-blind" admissions. You can increase your chances for the necessary scholarships by concentrating on those top colleges that award substantial grants (rather than loans that must be repaid) and work-study aid, and those that have generous merit awards for special-talent students. You may be influenced by the location of the college in terms of job opportunities off-campus.

Question 8

This question asks you to evaluate your academic performance, to interpret your transcript to yourself, and to explain any unusual circumstances or unfairness you have experienced that affects your overall academic profile. You will help yourself immensely by explaining that a downturn in grades for a particular term was due to an illness or accident that kept you out of school; or that you were placed in an inappropriate level of a course that you were not prepared for; or that the teacher was new and inexperienced, or perhaps just plain mean.

A willingness to acknowledge any weakness is in itself a strength and will be a step on the road to academic improvement. It can also help determine that certain colleges might not be the right place for you due to their stringent course requirements, which will show up a chronic weakness, while a comparably demanding college will give the flexibility you need to be successful. You may have to respond on an application or in an interview with a staff member or alumni interviewer to this question, so be prepared for it and be honest in your response. Remember that no one is expected to be perfect or nearly so in all areas of study.

Question 9

We ask you to conclude the questionnaire with a warm-up for the all-important personal statements you must write on your applications. You can count on the more selective colleges' asking you the most thoughtful questions in order to help them in sorting out the multitude of qualified candidates. However the questions are phrased, the bottom line is that the committees hope to know you better. Who are you? How would you describe yourself to a sympathetic stranger like an admissions officer? This is an opportunity to express how you see yourself. Here is a thoughtful and honest response to this question from a high school junior that helped us to counsel her to the right colleges and also turned into the general theme of her personal application essay:

> I feel in personality I am somewhat of an extrovert—enjoying others' company. I am also acutely aware of and I hope in tune with others' feelings and inevitably I am the communal shoulder to cry on! In the context of my aspirations I'm not quite sure where I'm going but I'm certain of one thing: Whatever I do I want it to be the best I can do. I am desperate, one could say provocatively, to be a success.

Another student wrote:

> I come from a Chinese background. English is my mother tongue. I think a smaller college would be more suitable for me because I am not used to a liberal school, where no one cares about what you do. I am not aggressive. I tend to be more passive about things. That is part of the reason why I think a smaller university would be better; there is a more personal touch.

Can you sense the different personalities of these two students as they have expressed them in their reflections?

Your Parents' Role

Your parents play an important part in the admissions process. They are concerned that you attend a college where you will have a happy, successful, and, of course, safe four years that prepare you for the future of your choice. We hope that they will be visiting most of the colleges you are considering with you. Their emotional and financial support is critical for most students. We have found that college admissions is a family affair, and when students and parents collaborate in harmony, the experience is enhanced and the results are a great success.

The Parents' Questionnaire is a stimulus to encourage your parents to discuss your admissions program with each other privately, so that they will have reflected on their concerns and expectations honestly, and will then share them with you. In most instances we find that the future applicant and parents have pretty similar goals in mind and have the same issues that need to be addressed. Parents, no less than their son or daughter, need to understand the dynamics of selective college admissions. We have found that their meetings with counselors are more satisfying if they have thought about matters raised in the Parents' Questionnaire. We suggest that each parent answer the questionnaire separately and that they then compare their responses before showing them to anyone. Often there is information that is important to share with the counselor without embarrassing their child in a meeting.

From your point of view, the questionnaire is a good way to involve parents in the admissions process. A parent may react strongly or over-anxiously when taken by surprise or when dealing with misinformation about admissions criteria and the process. A student may produce a set of objectives for herself that come as a complete surprise to her parents, who then become reactive and refuse to listen to the reasoning behind her ideas. For all of their subjectivity and natural worry, parents do tend to know their child best and can offer important information and insight into the choosing of the right college model. At the least, let them be heard and then have an open discussion of what matters most to them and to you.

Parents' Questionnaire

1. Please comment on your son or daughter's relative strengths and weaknesses as a student. Include your perspective on the student's motivation, self-discipline, energy level, organization, independence, creativity, level of confidence, etc.

2. How would you describe your son or daughter's personality and values? Please comment on leadership ability, maturity, concern for others, social and/or community interests, etc.

3. What is his or her greatest achievement? In what sense is he or she special? In what area does he or she "shine"?

4. Please indicate any family, medical, psychological, or testing background which we should be aware of in order to effectively counsel you in the college selection process. Are there any adverse conditions your son or daughter has had to overcome to achieve a level of competence currently attained?

5. What characteristics are you especially interested in finding in a college or university? You might want to comment on the type, size, atmosphere, facilities, location, academic reputation, or institutional prestige.

6. List the names of any colleges or universities to which you would encourage your son or daughter to apply.

7. If you wish to add anything not covered above, please feel free to elaborate.

Example of Parents' Response

1. Kevin has demonstrated a sense of responsibility, independence, and self-discipline in handling homework. He manages his time by himself and, although he sometimes procrastinates, on the whole he structures his studying so that he does not have to cram at the last minute. His teachers have commented positively about his maturity in the classroom. He writes well and does well in his presentation of creative research papers. In math, he tends to rush and make careless errors; and he has trouble linking logical math sequences. On the other hand, he has demonstrated a talent for foreign languages and sciences.

2. Kevin is mature for his age and thoughtful in his interpersonal relationships. He is, however, very hard on himself and frequently sets unrealistically high standards. He is not exceptionally energetic or ambitious. Although he often assumes a natural leadership position, he is reluctant to run for class office.

3. Kevin would probably consider his baseball accomplishments as being his greatest achievement. He was forced to overcome a number of disappointments and fear during his many years playing baseball. In our admittedly subjective eyes he is special because of his kindness and good humor. And he is special not just as a son, but as a friend.

4. Kevin has always performed better in the classroom and on papers than on standardized testing. His school performance has consistently exceeded his showing on this kind of measure of aptitude. We are looking into an individual assessment to uncover the reason for this.

5. We would be interested in a college with a high academic reputation and institutional prestige. Presumably there is a basis in fact for a school's reputation and we believe that graduating from a highly regarded college can only help one's career. However, we are also aware that the college must be appropriate for Kevin's record and abilities. We hope to identify

colleges that offer not only a reasonable chance of gaining admittance, but an atmosphere—personality if you will—that will be pleasing to Kevin. A liberal arts versus a highly math/engineering oriented institution would seem to be more suitable to Kevin; also, at this time, he thinks he would be more comfortable in a smaller, rural environment.

6. I am a Cornell graduate and Kevin has expressed an interest in pursuing a career in veterinary medicine. Cornell has an excellent veterinary program that would allow Kevin to take many liberal arts courses. My husband graduated from Dartmouth and would be pleased if Kevin were to apply there—but he would not encourage him to apply simply because it's his alma mater; that is, there is no arm twisting.

7. When reviewing our responses to the questionnaire, please keep in mind that Kevin is only beginning his 10th-grade year—opinions and views, his and ours, can change dramatically in the next two years. We feel he has lots of growth ahead of him.

Overestimating and Underestimating Yourself

Many of us have a tendency to over- or underestimate ourselves. Some typical overestimations arise from a natural instinct to forgive ourselves for little faults that we think do not matter. Jeremy, for example, writes brilliant papers but fills them with spelling errors he could easily correct by reading through carefully what he has written or using his spellcheck on his computer. He gets a B or B+ instead of an A, which his thought and content merit, but dismisses this as meaningless because he has read that some great thinkers and writers never could spell. He almost views this weakness as a sign of his unique talent and expects others to someday edit his writing.

Many a student who has exceptional mathematical reasoning ability has little patience for the details of problem-solving or demonstrating for teachers the steps he or she has taken to arrive at the correct answer. In both cases this can be viewed either as laziness or arrogance by teachers, who want to see a student succeed by making the most of his natural talents.

If your academic performance has suffered because of this tendency, you may not be qualified for admission into some of the most competitive colleges. Even more important in the long run, though, the habit of overestimating your capacities blurs your own vision of yourself and impairs your ability to change and improve.

The habit of underestimating yourself may arise from some prior criticism. A music teacher puts you in the back of the chorus and suggests that you sing softly, and you conclude that you have no ear for music. This then becomes a prominent part of your self-description. The first time a coach criticizes you for a poor play, you may think you will never turn into an important member of the team, and question your moves on the playing field.

In assessing both your strengths and your weaknesses, then, it is important to be clear-eyed and avoid the pitfalls of over- or under-estimating your abilities. An admissions officer is always impressed by a candidate's self-awareness and willingness to reveal genuine limitations without self-deprecation, the latter being a more elegant word for selling yourself short. We grow, in large part, by confronting our weaknesses or bad habits and determining to conquer them or at least not to let them overtake our strengths. Don't be surprised to open a selective college's application and read a question that asks you to describe your weakest point and how you have worked to correct it.

As you learn more about specific colleges, Step Two will help you focus on those schools where your strengths will be best developed. We urge you to look at your responses to the questionnaire often. Confer with teachers, counselors, your activity directors, and your parents to see whether you have got yourself "right," whether you can see yourself as others see you.

The Confidence of Strength

When you know where your strengths lie, there lies, too, the basis for self-confidence. Selective colleges are training students for future leadership roles in their chosen fields of endeavor. A leader must be confident in his or her ability to lead, whether it is in scholarship, a collaborative laboratory project, a business, the government, law, or community volunteerism. Discovering what you are good at will make you feel proud of it, and will strengthen the way you go about the admissions process and thus your chances for acceptance.

Step Two Checklist

✓See the Student Questionnaire as a guide to your feelings about colleges you are considering. Change your answers in your notebook over time as you get to know more about yourself and your priorities.

✓Involve your parents by having them fill out the Parents' Questionnaire. This will make their meetings with your counselor more productive and will open up a healthy dialogue between you and your parents so there are no misunderstandings of your (and their) preferences.

✓Look for overestimations and underestimations of your strengths. As the admissions process unfolds, you should find your academic performance improving as your study habits become more effective. Nonacademic strengths will grow through focusing on what you do best. Listen to what people who know you well say about you to discover strong points in your character that you might not be aware of.

✓Think of being on a voyage of discovery where you find the person you truly are, for the purpose of choosing the right college for yourself and then making the best case for your acceptance to the admissions committee in your senior year.

STEP THREE:
Follow a Demanding Curriculum

]

Your Academic Record Comes First

Above all else in the admissions process, selective colleges want to enroll students who are able to successfully undertake advanced-level academics. Yes, they want their students to have other capabilities, as musicians, artists, writers, campus leaders, athletes, and as young adults who contribute to the dynamic life of the campus and the local community. But first and foremost, colleges exist to educate, and selective colleges conduct their educational enterprise at high levels of excellence. This is why admissions officers quickly turn to your academic program and performance when you send in your full application. They are under an obligation to the faculty of their institution to bring strong students with genuine intellectual curiosity and excitement into their classrooms.

All of our research and communications with the top colleges confirms that the foremost factor in considering candidates is the academic transcript, which simply is a track record of your courses and grades over the four years of high school. Here is the high school curriculum that the selective colleges recommend and that successful candidates follow, with some personalized variations:

English language and literature	4 years
Mathematics	3–4 years
Laboratory sciences	3–4 years

Foreign languages or Latin	3–4 years
History & social studies	3–4 years
Arts electives	2–3 years

It is not enough merely to complete your high school's requirements for a diploma. As many of these courses as possible should be at the honors level, beginning in the 10th grade. Highly competitive students take six honors-level or Advanced Placement (or similar level) courses over their junior and senior years. Of all the factors considered by the admissions committees, the quality of the high school program is the single best indicator of who is prepared intellectually and attitudinally to cope with the academic demands of a top college. Those students who perform well in high school are the most likely to perform well at the next level. Equally important to you is the fact that you will be well prepared to cope with the courses you will study in college.

The Academic Criteria

Admissions officers judge your academic record on your curriculum, your honors-level or Advanced Placement courses, any advanced or enriched courses taken elsewhere during the summer or after school, your grades, and your SAT Subject Test scores. Write down these factors in your notebook and use them as a reminder as you prepare for college admission. You may spot a missing subject from the outline above that you can complete in your senior year or over the summer before the senior year. Remember that your academic record is distinct from your SAT scores, whose significance is discussed in Step Four.

Your Curriculum

Use a page in your notebook to list your subjects year by year. Better still, ask your school counselor for an unofficial copy of your transcript to date. This will show all of the courses you have taken, the final grades, and the units of credit you have accumulated. Even if you are a senior reading this book, you should review the courses you have taken, so as to look at them in the same way an admissions committee will consider them. If you see that your overall program has not conformed to the traditional liberal arts curriculum we list below, you should take note of this fact and discuss with your counselor how you will explain this to the admissions committees in your applications or interviews. It is not uncommon for talented students to plan a program of study that emphasizes their special interests. If you are a junior, you have ample time to reconfigure your program to meet all of the requirements. If there are gaps, some colleges may not consider you a qualified candidate, while others may allow you to fill in such gaps in college, so long as you explain the reasons behind your curricular choices in high school.

We list here the curriculum that is the surest road to admission to the top colleges. Some deviation from this scheme is permissible, as we shall describe. But this is the model to follow if you are aiming for a highly selective college.

The Ideal High School Curriculum

9TH GRADE
English
Biology (laboratory course)
History (ancient or European)
Mathematics (algebra or plane geometry)
Language (1st or 2nd year for those who had
   a 7/8th-grade course)

10TH GRADE
English
Chemistry (laboratory course)
Mathematics (plane geometry or algebra II)
Language (2nd or 3rd year)
Social science (history, economics,
   psychology, etc.)
Elective (art, music, drama, computer
   science, etc.)

11TH GRADE   English
Physics (laboratory course)
Mathematics (algebra II or precalculus)
Language (3rd or 4th year)
Language (1st year for certain students)
U.S. History (regular or Advanced Placement)
Elective (computer science recommended)

12TH GRADE   English
Mathematics (precalculus, calculus,
   or probability and statistics)
Language (4th year or 5th year)
Language (2nd year for certain students)
Science (Advanced Placement biology, physics,
   or chemistry if science-oriented)
Social science (Advanced Placement U.S. or
   world history, economics, or psychology, if
   liberal arts–oriented)
Advanced music, art, drama, computer
   science, etc.

This curriculum does not include other possible electives. Admissions officers recognize that students like to pursue their special interests in high school, so such courses as economics, psychology, anthropology, drawing, architecture, drama, photography, and computer science that appear on the academic transcript are respected, particularly if you are praised in a teacher's recommendation for work in a subject that absorbs you. We like to encourage students to demonstrate their interests to the admissions committees by their choice of elective courses and particular advanced-level core subjects. This is one of the ways in which you can distinguish yourself before the committee.

A few suggestions we can offer as you plan your curriculum: Stay within the outline we have just described. You do not have to take advanced-level courses in all of these subjects. It is best to stretch yourself (a favorite phrase of top-college admissions officers) in those fields where you are strong and have serious interest. The senior year provides you with the opportunity to "make a statement" to the committee by electing to take the most advanced courses your high school offers in the areas of your expressed interest and potential major in college. For example, if you plan to apply to top colleges as an engineering or science concentrator, then you must take the honors or advanced-level courses in mathematics and sciences. If you indicate a goal of becoming an international studies major, you should follow the strongest language, history, and economics program available to you. You get the point, but if you are uncertain of the ideal program related to your intended studies, check with any admissions office, and a counselor will assist you.

Honors Courses

Some high schools label upper-level courses "honors" or "accelerated," while others call them "college-level" courses. Selective independent schools and public high schools may offer the same courses without designating them as honors level. Admissions committees usually are aware that these schools make heavy demands on their students regardless of their class-naming conventions, and so they give their candidates credit for the academic intensity of their studies. Some schools offer few or no AP courses. In some cases their own courses are even more rigorous, and students will still take and excel on the AP exams in May. The International Baccalaureate and British A-Level programs are also highly regarded as demanding curricula.

One of the chief reasons why some students fail to be accepted into top colleges is that they have not been willing to risk the challenge of courses on the "fast track." Many of the admissions officers we communicate with specifically note that they want applicants who are risk-takers, students willing to find out just how well they can perform in the advanced courses.

Those who take risks will be given credit even when their grades are not perfect. Furthermore, willingness to follow a demanding curriculum puts you in a position to attain high scores on the Subject Tests and Advanced Placement tests. We emphasize this point to prevent the discouragement from a natural tendency to compare yourself with those who do better academically than you do. Accepting the level at which you perform is a sign of maturity and individuality that admissions officers admire, when they are convinced that you have made a wholehearted commitment to a challenging program. Rest assured that students who intentionally develop a light course load for their high school years in order to achieve top grades will be immediately found out by selective college admissions officers, who have years of experience in evaluating transcripts.

Assessing Your Academic Competition

The rising number of applications to selective colleges is intensifying the competition for places in the first-year class, especially at the top colleges listed in this book. This general state of affairs will only increase anxiety if you fail to look closely at the way academic accomplishment is distributed among the admitted class each year. We encourage you with a reminder that only some fifty colleges and universities are so selective that they can admit less than 50% of their applicant pool. The very most selective colleges are the ones you hear the stories about most frequently. Yes, there is a small group of colleges that accepts less than 20% of those whose apply. But this represents a handful within a large group of top-rate institutions.

At the Ivy League colleges, some of the Hidden Ivies and schools traditionally known as the Little Ivies (Amherst, Williams, Wesleyan, Bowdoin, and Swarthmore, for example), Stanford, MIT, Cal Tech, and others, 90% of the accepted candidates ranked in the first decile of their high school class. When only 10% or less with lower academic standing are admitted, it is clear that the first consideration of the admissions committees is given to academic achievement. Those admitted who are an exception to this rule possess outstanding talents within a wide range of categories, or they make it through the rigorous screening of the special categories of alumni children, athletes, disadvantaged students, and others we describe in Step Seven, on finding your place in the pie chart.

We find it instructive to explain to students the significance of the "yield factor" in the admissions process. Take a cluster of top colleges and you will read that the percentage of students in the first or second decile admitted is the same. This holds true for the average of their SAT or ACT scores. What you are not aware of is that each of these colleges has to admit a certain percentage of applicants to reach their target for the first-year class. Thus Harvard and a few other universities admit less than 10% of those who apply, while the other top schools will admit 15% to 20%. These statistical differences can affect your chances for acceptance to one of the top colleges. You should also recognize that the range of test scores can have a wider variance at particular selective colleges even though the average is about the same as for other peer institutions.

The message, then, is a reiteration of what admissions deans and directors will tell you: Work your hardest to create a strong academic record in a challenging curriculum. If you have done your best in school and you are not number one to five in your class, do not despair. You will find that many top colleges look for students like you. Your task is to identify those colleges that appear to offer you the better opportunities for admission.

What Admissions Officers Are Looking For

We asked a number of experienced admissions directors to indicate the order of importance the high school curriculum plays in their choosing from among a large group of candidates. Here is a sampling of responses:

Bowdoin College: "The admissions process is a transcript-heavy selection process."

Bryn Mawr College: "One of the main sets of questions the committee asks in its evaluation of candidates is, 'Has the student challenged herself in the most academically demanding program available to her? Has her performance in it distinguished her from her peers? Has the student made the best use of the resources available to her? Has she been recognized for exceptional academic promise and do her teachers and school recognize her intellectual creativity?'"

Carleton College: "A student's academic record, both the nature of the courses and grades, and demonstrated intellectual interests are clearly important in admissions decisions."

Colgate University: "Like most of our peer institutions, the number one criterion for admission is a strong high school transcript. If we had only one document to use in our selection process, it would be the transcript. It is the most revealing document in an applicant's file—it records a student's academic achievement, ambition (seen in course selection), and upturn of success, advancement, and universality of interests over three to four years of high school."

Middlebury College: "The top criteria in admissions are as follows: the quality of the work done in high school is #1. The standard measurements of ability are #2. But the quality of the person is a must."

University of Virginia: "Your academic program is very important to us; we need to see you challenging yourself in the classroom. In general this means that you should take one of the toughest (if not the toughest) academic programs offered by your high school. In other words, if the toughest program normally taken by a college-bound senior at your school consists of four AP courses plus another honors-level academic solid, such a schedule would look good to us. On the other hand, if the best program for a senior at your school is two honors-level courses plus three academic solids that would look good to us, too. Because terrific students come to us from many different kinds of schools, we try to evaluate an applicant's academic program within the context of his or her school."

Vanderbilt University: "A key admissions factor is a proven record of academic success in a challenging high school curriculum; consistency of performance at the highest level, academically and in extracurricular activities, or an upward trend in performance indicating growing ability and maturity; and an indication of interest in and special abilities to make a difference."

Wellesley College: "The Board of Admission seeks students who have intellectual curiosity, the ability to think, to ask questions, and to grapple with answers. Wellesley looks for students who are excited about learning which comes through in the review of her academic record, her recommendations from teachers, and what she writes about herself in her application."

You, as a selective college applicant, should be capable of taking honors courses. How early in high school you start taking them and how many you can cope with successfully is something your counselor and teachers can help you discover.

Is there any honors course that counts more in admissions than another? No. Any intensive courses that stretch your mind will be recognized for their intellectual value and as an indicator of your academic capacity. Many selective college applicants enrich their minds in courses taken outside their schools as well, through summer enrichment programs or evening classes that are available in virtually every region of the country. Is this essential to being accepted? The answer is no if you have selected the best program of study your high school can offer and you have met the level of requirements described here.

Be aware, too, that some schools have neither the budget nor the enrollment to support an extensive honors program. This presents you with an opportunity to reach beyond the walls of your high school to take enriched courses at other institutions. The ability to pursue further study by long-distance learning over the Internet is another option, one that offers flexibility for the high school student. Admissions committees are impressed by these signs of outreach by the intellectually curious and energetic student.

You can feel comfortable calling or e-mailing the admissions office at any top college of interest to you to discuss your curriculum and their view of what constitutes a competitive program of study. Admissions people can advise you whether some enrichment programs that you have researched and are considering would strengthen your candidacy. While admissions committees make allowances for limited choices of advanced study in your particular school, you should push yourself to take as many honors or Advanced Placement courses as are available to you. But be sure to strike a workable balance between a demanding program and your ability to perform well in it.

Advanced Placement Courses

One of the dramatic changes in the content of our secondary school curriculum is the emergence of the Advanced Placement extra program, which is developed and directed by the College Board. The AP program was an initiative in the 1960s to enhance the level and rigor of the major subjects taught in the high schools by introducing courses designed by college faculty in cooperation with high school teachers. In 1967, some 18,000 students undertook one or more AP courses and sat for 54,000 exams. In 1999, by contrast, 700,000 students took more than a million AP exams. In 2008, 1.6 million students took 2.7 million exams at 17,000 high schools! For all the public dialogue on the decline in quality of our secondary educational system, the number of highly trained teachers eager to teach so many motivated students an AP subject is encouraging. The rising popularity of the AP program also reflects the rise in competition for admission to the top colleges: More students are taking a more rigorous academic program and more are applying to the selective colleges. Some 15% of the class of 2007 earned at least one AP score of 3 or higher on the 5-point scale, and about a quarter of students took at least one AP exam during high school.

All AP courses are considered the equal of an introductory college course in the particular subject. Available to high school juniors and seniors, and occasionally to a very advanced freshman or sophomore, there are thirty-seven AP courses and exams from which to choose.

Each AP course offered in every school follows the same syllabus and uses the same texts and supplemental materials, although some teachers may teach the class in a slightly different manner and add materials of their own. The courses prepare you for the AP tests, although you are not required to take them unless your particular school has a policy that you must. One can also take an AP exam without having taken the AP class. The tests are graded on a scale of 5 (the highest) to 1. Almost every college grants a college credit to a student who scores a 5 or a 4 (and sometimes a 3) on the exam. Not only does a good score help your chances in the admissions evaluation, it also lets you waive a required course in the subject once you are enrolled in college. If a student's score is disappointing, by the way, it does not have to be reported to the colleges to which he or she has applied.

A frequent question we are asked by both students and parents is whether there is recognition by the admissions committees of the demands and potentially lower grades in an AP course. The answer is yes. Note the comments of the admissions officers we cited earlier. A transcript that shows several AP courses and strong exam results indicates the ability, motivation, and preparedness of an applicant, which the committees focus on in their determinations. If you can do well in one or more AP courses, you will be considered among the more qualified applicants. You should attempt courses in those subject areas that interest you and that fit with your intended field of study in college. Colleges will look for this connection when they review your application. We also encourage students to send an impressive research paper or artistic piece they have created as a requirement for their AP course. More on this in Step Eight on presenting yourself to the admissions committee.

Here is the College Board's official list of Advanced Placement courses:

Art History

Biology

Calculus AB

Calculus BC

Chemistry

Chinese Language and Culture

Comparative Government and Politics

Computer Science

Economics (Macro)

Economics (Micro)

English Language and Composition

English Literature and Composition

Environmental Science

European History

French Language

German Language

Human Geography

Italian Language and Culture

Japanese Language and Culture

Latin (Vergil)

Music Theory

Physics B

Physics C: Electricity and Magnetism

Physics C: Mechanics

Psychology

Spanish Language

Spanish Literature

Statistics

Studio Art: Drawing Portfolio

Studio Art: 2-D Design Portfolio

Studio Art: 3-D Design Portfolio

U.S. Government and Politics

U.S. History

World History

Note: Computer Science AB, French Literature, and Latin Literature were offered in 2008–09 for the last time.

Concentrating in Your Specialty

There is a limit to the amount of work even the best students can do. In which subjects should you take honors or an AP course? The decision is easier if you know what your academic plans are for your college years. Are you going to prepare to be an engineer, lawyer, scientist, doctor, journalist, teacher, or technologist? Your answer should determine your high school junior and especially your senior year advanced course selection. For example, history is for future lawyers, media professionals, politicians, economists, businesspeople, educators, and those going into public service or international relations careers. Art, music, literature, languages, and psychology are some of the key subjects for the future writer, creative artist, or arts manager.

A combination of Advanced Placement and honors courses in these subjects will strengthen your record. It is all right to drop electives that will take away critical study time from your advanced courses. Another frequently asked question concerns the number of AP courses you should have on your transcript. There is not an absolute formula to give you here. The admissions committees will not have a minimum number of honors and AP courses that you should have taken; they will review what subjects you take, how they relate to your stated interests on your application and in interviews, and how well you perform in advanced course work, and they will look to see how you have taken advantage of opportunities for honors-or AP-level work at your high school.

The Significance of Grades

Grades have been shown to be the single most important predictor of academic success in college. The many national studies on the transition from high school to college and the factors that account for positive or negative retention, and the self-studies of hundreds of colleges and universities confirm the primary role that a strong academic foundation, in combination with good grades, plays in a successful college experience. The more A's and B's you have in your record, the more positive attention admissions committees will pay to your application. A few aberrant C's will not automatically exclude you from consideration, but you will have to explain the reasons behind the lower grades to the committees. We reassure you that you will find them to be reasonable in their understanding. Many admissions applications, in fact, ask students to explain any performance that is inconsistent with the larger academic record. It is not uncommon for a strong student to experience a downturn in grades due to an illness or injury or a change of schools due to a family move, and so on. We all know that sometimes a particular subject is unfathomable, or that a disconnect with the instructor's style of teaching the course makes it difficult to learn the material. Being honest and forthcoming in taking responsibility for any inconsistency will only earn you the respect of the committee.

Some applicants with mixed grades will be accepted to selective colleges because of their considerable talent in other fields. We refer here not only to the star athletes, but also to the dancers or actors or student leaders who have dedicated thousands of hours to their passion, thus demonstrating their drive and discipline that will be converted to their academic studies in college. As more and more students who "have it all" apply to the top colleges, the competition will grow more severe. We see each year that fewer allowances are made for candidates with unimpressive academic performances and fewer are admitted.

Once again, no discussion of grades is meaningful without an evaluation of the intensity of courses you take. Selective college applicants must force themselves to discover their true academic capabilities by achieving good grades in a demanding curriculum. Far from spoiling your record by getting grades in honors courses that are lower than those of students in regular courses, you provide admissions officers with clear evidence of your academic potential and attitude toward your studies.

Your Subject Test Scores

We will discuss the College Board's SAT Subject Tests in Step Four, but here we want to relate them to your academic record. As a general rule, you should take three SAT Subjects where you are most confident as soon as possible after completing courses in the test subjects. You may take as many different SAT Subject Tests as you are ready for and are capable of handling, but you need only submit a maximum of two or three to the top colleges. A significant innovation for the benefit of today's college-bound students is the new Score Choice policy of the College Board. You now have control over which SAT and Subject Test scores you will ultimately submit to your colleges. There is no risk in trying all Subject Tests in which you have a possibility of achieving a good score. The very selective colleges are impressed when they review a candidate's file and note that he or she has submitted four or five different Subject Tests with strong scores. This serves as ample validation of the *preparation,* academic ability, and drive of the student.

The chances of achieving three good test scores are excellent, provided you take the tests in challenging courses in which you have good grades, and particularly if the tests are taken soon after completing the course. The SAT Subject Tests examine you in subjects you have studied. In this regard, they differ from the SAT, which is more of a test of your reasoning, critical reading, writing, and analytical thinking abilities. You can prepare in a more focused manner for the Subject Tests and thus improve your scores to a considerable extent if you are willing to dedicate yourself to the time it will take. Most important, remember that the Subject Tests were developed in order to allow students of all backgrounds of schooling to demonstrate their knowledge base and ability to learn.

Compare Your Record with Selective College Requirements

If you will take a moment to glance at what you wrote down in Step One under the academic requirements of a number of selective colleges, you can begin to compare these with your actual academic work. Using the four criteria of curriculum, honors and AP courses, grades, and SAT and Subject Test scores, you will be able in the case of each college to answer the simple question: "Am I meeting their academic requirements?" When the answer is no, it will be for a specific reason. Perhaps you have not taken any Subject Tests yet; perhaps your grades are too low or your course load too weak for you to compete for a place in the most competitive colleges.

This procedure is a moment of truth for you, one that allows you to take your academic bearings to enable you to steer a better course toward your ultimate objective, namely entrance and then graduation from a strong college that you enjoy.

In the notebook where you have listed your curriculum, put an H after every course taken, or that you plan to take, on the honors or AP level. How many H's are there? Ideally, they are a majority of your courses over the last three years of high school. This is one of the first exercises we at the Educational Consulting Centers perform when we review a student's transcript in anticipation of meeting and making recommendations for appropriate colleges. It is a rough rule to follow, but a workable one: The more H's you have on your record, the closer you come to acceptance to a top college.

In her notebook under Step One, Louisa, a junior in a strong New York suburban high school, put down in this way the requirements for admission to the colleges she was considering:

School Subject	Colleges & Years Required
English	Stanford, Yale, and all others, 4 years
Math	Stanford 4, Yale 4, Amherst 4, others 3
Language	Stanford 3–4, Yale 3–4, Amherst 3–4, others 3
Sciences (lab)	Stanford 3, Yale 3, Amherst 3, others 2–3
History	2 years at all colleges
Electives	Flexible at all colleges
Level of courses	Stanford, Yale, Amherst, emphasize honors and APs

Louisa's notebook under Step Four showed that she had taken honors French II her sophomore year and had a good score on the Subject Test in the June testing. She was taking honors French III now in her junior year and intended to take Advanced Placement French in her senior year. When her adviser told her she was a marginal candidate for Stanford and Yale due to the severe competition, she got permission to double up in Spanish I and II in her senior year, since languages were her strong interest and future major. She also decided to take the risk of Advanced Placement Math, in which she would have to work hard to do well. Then she asked her parents if they would allow her to go to France for the summer on the Experiment in International Living, a well-established student exchange program that includes a home stay with a native family. Her objectives: to gain fluency in French and a new experience. As an unintended benefit to her summer abroad, Louisa wrote a delightful college essay entitled "What Driver's Ed Never Taught Me," which described the nightmare of learning to drive a stick shift car in the hills of northern France with a French instructor.

After considerable reflection while away, Louisa decided that she did not want to attend a large university or to be very far from home. So instead of applying to Stanford as she had planned, she applied to Amherst, which admitted her on the strength of her academic program, evidence that she would take advantage of the strong language departments at the college, and her broadening experience. Her SAT Subject Test scores improved in her senior year thanks to a good deal of study in August when she returned from her travel program.

We can cite many cases of bright students we have counseled who learned to stretch themselves intellectually by taking as many of the top courses their school offered as they could handle successfully. This foundation enabled them to perform better on the entrance tests, be they the SAT or the ACT program. You can view an enriched high school curriculum as a form of insurance on several counts: (1) The better your grades, the better you will perform on tests; (2) the admissions committees will consider you more favorably even if you do not achieve high test scores; and (3) you will be better prepared to handle the academic load at a selective college.

Benefit from Enrichment Programs

Admissions committees react very favorably to students who have taken advantage of any of the rich variety of summer enrichment programs available today. Almost all of the top colleges include a form of the question "How did you spend last summer and what do you feel you accomplished and learned from the experience?" We counsel students to consider using the summer prior to their senior year in a productive way that accomplishes the goals of personal and intellectual growth, confirmation of their intended field of study in college, and exposure to new people and environments. This may sound overly ambitious, but it is very possible to achieve. In our many years of guiding students on ways to enrich their backgrounds and grow as individuals, we have witnessed the virtual explosion of programs available to students in all areas of talent and interest, from academic to artistic, athletic to environmental to social action.

Andrew, whom we described earlier and who is now enrolled in Stanford, was eager to use the summers following both his sophomore and junior years of high school to explore in depth his scientific interests. After a discussion with him, we recommended Brown University's Focus Program since it would enable him to experience firsthand scientific research under the guidance of a professor. The course he took was called Techniques in Biotechnology. This experience accomplished all of Andrew's goals: He learned what it is like to live on a college campus, he made many new friends from all corners of the country, he gained social independence and maturity, and he confirmed his passion for the life sciences and hands-on research. Further, he came away with a glowing report from his professor and mentor, which gave him the confidence to continue his dream of enrolling in a top university to study science and computer science, with the idea of joining the two disciplines for advanced research. Here is the summary his professor wrote at the end of the summer, which the colleges eventually read:

> Andrew is the best example I have seen of a student taking full advantage of the opportunity provided in this course. He is a "natural" in the lab; imaginative, creative, skilled in technique, and highly motivated. Rather than choosing an established independent project, Andrew researched and developed his own independent laboratory project. It was original, extremely well planned, and it worked!
>
> In his oral presentation on recombinant HIV vaccine, Andrew did an outstanding job of both researching his topic and of successfully explaining the complex background material to his classmates. All aspects of Andrew's performance in Techniques in Biotechnology were outstanding.

The next winter Andrew, with the help of his high school science teachers, researched internship opportunities in university and research institutes. He secured an internship at the Fermi National Accelerator Laboratory, where he had unique exposure to very advanced experimentation in the physical sciences.

The admissions committees at the highly selective colleges to which Andrew applied were impressed by his initiative in stretching the boundaries of his knowledge in his areas of interest. It was clear to the committees that he was the type of young man who would profit from the great educational resources of their universities. There is no doubt that his summer experiences played a positive role in his acceptance to Stanford, Harvard, Cornell, Northwestern, Dartmouth, and Washington University.

When Martha, another outstanding public high school student, came to the Educational Consulting Centers, we discussed summer enrichment programs that would let her explore new interests. She had a strong school curriculum in place that included a combination of honors and Advanced Placement courses in the five core academic areas. What she hoped to gain from a summer program was broader exposure to new subjects that would lead to greater self-awareness. After a careful reading of several options we recommended, Martha chose to attend the Harvard University Summer School. Here is what she wrote on her college applications in the fall of her senior year:

> While attending Harvard Summer School, I had, for the first time, the opportunity to choose from a vast number of courses. I wanted to explore subjects I knew little about, ones that differed from the basic academic subjects offered in high school. I chose Biomedical Ethics because I was interested in the ambiguity and complications a study in ethics would afford. I was not disappointed. The class consisted of undergraduate and graduate students. Some students in the class were currently working in the medical field. The diversity of the class provided an environment for heated debates. Small group discussions were held often, and gave me the chance to share my thoughts. We applied many different ethical theories to controversial questions.
>
> The debate concerning euthanasia was the topic that interested me the most. The question of euthanasia has become increasingly important as medical technology has advanced. Even if

euthanasia were to be practiced, a differentiation would still have to be made between active euthanasia which involves killing a patient or passive euthanasia which allows a patient to die. At some point in our lives, many of us may have to face the choice of euthanasia either for ourselves or for our loved ones. As the class related each ethical theory to euthanasia, I felt persuaded by parts of each theory. I struggled with every argument, trying to form my own opinion. I discussed this question not only with classmates; I also felt compelled to talk with my friends and roommates about it.

Depending on their personal background, everyone I talked to felt strongly in favor of or against euthanasia. I was finally able to form my own eclectic view of the topic, using parts of various points of view and arguments. In fact, I wrote my final paper on my view of euthanasia. In addition to learning much about the difficulties ethics addresses, I realized that the course was also a journey of self-discovery. It forced me to search within myself for answers, allowing me to formulate a personal ethical perspective. It was, indeed, a memorable summer of learning and discovery.

What university would not be interested in Martha after reading this statement? Her experience led to the outcomes all colleges hope their students will gain. She was an active participant, she was mentally and emotionally engaged in the topic, and she learned much about her own value system as a result. The reader learns a good deal about Martha from this brief, but clear and honest, description of her thinking and level of participation in an advanced classroom environment. Martha's summer at Harvard was a positive complement to her excellent school record, high test scores, and community service commitments. By the conclusion of the admissions process she was offered places at Columbia, Duke, Chicago, Johns Hopkins, Stanford, and Harvard (the latter two from the wait list). Martha chose to enroll in Columbia after second visits to her top three choices.

We hasten to tell you that a meaningful summer experience does not have to be of a strictly academic nature. David, for instance, attended the American Academy of Dramatic Arts summer acting program to sharpen his skills and to decide if he would apply to performing arts university programs or to a professional drama school. He also wanted the opportunity to live in a city, since he had spent his entire life in a small Southern town.

Some students gain confidence by participating in rigorous outdoor programs, while others participate in study-abroad programs that include living with a host family. It is now common for very competitive athletes, both men and women, to attend sports camps where they can improve their skills through intensive coaching and practice, and possibly catch the attention of college coaches who visit these camps for recruitment purposes.

Here is a short list of some summer programs you may want to consider. It is intended to give you an idea of the wide range of opportunities. Research through various directories and conversations with your counselor, coach, parents, and friends can help you identify the right program for you.

A Sampling of Summer Opportunities

Pre-College Programs (offering a wide variety of fields of study)

Boston University
Brown University
University of California, Berkeley
Cambridge University, England
University of Chicago
Columbia/Barnard College
Cornell University
Duke University
Georgetown University
Harvard University
Johns Hopkins Center for Talented Youth
Northwestern University
Oxford Advanced Studies Program
University of Pennsylvania
Pennsylvania State University
Stanford University

Tufts University
University of Virginia
Yale University

Specialized Programs

American Academy of Dramatic Arts (Acting)
American Farm School, Greek Summer
Aspen Music School
Boston University (Film Studies, Communications, Journalism, TV, Writing)
Bryn Mawr College (Writing for College)
Carnegie Mellon University (Art, Architecture, Engineering)
Cornell University (Architecture, Engineering)
Duke University (Writers' Workshop)
Harvard University (Career Discovery in Art and Architecture)
Interlocken Center for Experiential Learning
MIT (Science, Engineering, Computer Science)
Mount Holyoke College (Math for Women)
National Science Foundation Research Projects
New York Film Academy
New York University (Tisch School of the Arts Programs)
North Carolina State University (Nuclear Science and Technology)
Oxford Media School, England (Film, TV, Creative Writing)
Putney Student Travel and EXCEL Programs (Travel, Service, Pre-College)
Rassias Language Programs at Dartmouth College and Abroad
Rhode Island School of Design (Art, Design, Architecture)
Sea Education Association (Woods Hole SEA Summer Session)
Skidmore College (Creative and Performing Arts)
Syracuse University (Architecture, Engineering, Communications)
Walnut Hill School (Dance, Theater Arts)
Washington University (Architecture, Art and Design, Engineering)
Where There Be Dragons (Asian Travel and Cultural Studies)

Worcester Polytechnic Institute (Science and Mathematics
for Minority Students)
Yale University (Junior Statesman Summer Session)

Boarding Schools Offering Enrichment Programs

Choate Rosemary Hall School
Hotchkiss School
Loomis Chaffee School
Northfield–Mt. Hermon School
Phillips Andover Academy
Phillips Exeter Academy
Portsmouth Abbey School
Saint George's School
Suffield Academy
The Taft School

Who Should Take Enrichment Courses?

Ideally, every applicant to a selective college would benefit from some
kind of academic enrichment beyond the walls of his or her high school.
We recognize that this is not universally possible for a variety of practical
reasons, yet large numbers of candidates present themselves to the admissions committees with a breadth of new experiences that strengthens
their chances for admission. If you are one who has not had these opportunities, how do you meet the competition and shine in your profile? The
answer is by stretching yourself within your high school and the local
community to enrich your intellectual or talent foundation. There are
likely to be those additional honors or Advanced Placement courses that
would expand the quality of your program and expose you to a subject of
interest in greater depth. There are area colleges that offer summer programs of study during the day or evenings, so that you can still work or
volunteer while building a stronger profile. Arts and performing arts programs abound during the summer months in virtually all communities.
Search for such opportunities through your local newspapers or on the
Internet. What impresses admissions committees is the effort to learn as
much as you can and test yourself in areas you have selected. It does not
matter if the setting is near home or in an exotic location.

Take Mathias as an example. A student in the upper 5% of his competitive private day school in Connecticut, Mathias had taken four honors courses in his junior year and planned to take two honors, two Advanced Placement courses, and an introductory architecture class in his senior year. He and one of his classmates decided to spend six weeks before their senior year at Harvard's Career Discovery in Architecture program to test out their potential interest in the subject. This experience not only gave Mathias an appreciation for the field of design and architecture, allowing him to determine if this would be his future area of study, it also showed an added range of academic diversity when he applied for Early Decision to Dartmouth. In the early fall he sent to the admissions office six drawings of an urban development project he had worked on with a Harvard professor. The willingness to give up six weeks of summer vacation to work at an intensive pace paid off, and Mathias was admitted to Dartmouth in December. He was to major in political science and history eventually, as he found these disciplines more to his liking. His classmate, Peter, confirmed his passion and talent for architecture through the exposure at Harvard. He decided to apply early to Yale because of its combination of liberal arts and architecture concentration. Peter, too, presented a portfolio of his designs and a three-dimensional project that had received raves from his Harvard professor. In December Peter received a letter congratulating him on his acceptance to Yale.

Katerina was a student at a New England boarding school for her last three years of high school. Her talent as a pianist and her love of music became evident in her early schooling. She studied piano with the same instructor throughout lower and middle school. Katerina spent two summers at an advanced music camp in upstate New York, where she studied with a teacher whom she admired greatly and who encouraged her to continue with her training. When she decided she would like to have the experience of a boarding school, she looked carefully for one that had a strong music department and that would prepare her for a top college. Katerina took advantage of every advanced music course and performing group her school offered her. She also worked with an excellent piano instructor outside of the school community as time allowed.

A good but not outstanding academic performer, Katerina knew two things about herself: She wanted to continue with her piano in college, and to enjoy a well-balanced academic and social life since she was not 100% certain she would eventually become a performing artist. Through her research and visits to a number of campuses, Katerina discovered that Vanderbilt University would meet all her criteria. She applied to the School of Music within the university, which required her to perform before the music faculty. Her personal statement told the story of her teacher in the summer music program and the ways in which this woman had influenced her. Katerina was admitted into the School of Music at Vanderbilt after receiving several letters from the professors who had heard her audition. They commented on the way her understanding and feeling for the pieces she performed were so evident, special qualities that came from her exposure to advanced courses in music throughout her school years and her summer enrichment experiences.

Improving Your Grades

Grades reflect effort, motivation, focus, and interest as much as they do anything else. Consistently high grades in the most demanding curriculum, of course, also are a characteristic of students of exceptional talent. But as we hope you have discovered, you do not have to be a genius to achieve an A grade. Think of the higher grades you have received already. Were they not the result of more work and more enthusiasm in the subject matter?

Good study habits and organization will also bring good grades. You can waste time studying if you have not learned how to organize your work and absorb what you have read. Cramming for exams is one of the most notoriously bad study habits, often concealed by success in an exam, which pulls up lower grades you have received as the result of not studying effectively. Many bright students discover the truth of this when they are faced with a heavy load of honors and Advanced Placement courses in their junior or senior year.

Your effort to improve your grades will be taken into account by admissions officers. "We don't expect perfection," said one dean. "Most people stumble once in a while." So if you should stumble in a particular course or over a term for personal reasons, there are ways to pick yourself up, start again, and improve your grades.

There are four important factors to think about in becoming a successful student:

Motivation

You have to feel that higher grades are important to you, in order to make the effort to change your study habits and your classroom habits, too. One motive you may already have is the desire to be admitted to a college that your review of your record to date indicates would now turn you down. A realistic self-appraisal tells you that your performance falls short of the standards the top colleges expect of a successful candidate.

Time

All of us are fully capable of wasting time. We can only suggest that you tighten your schedule, reduce the amount of time spent on less important matters, and increase the time you spend studying assignments. Doing these things will not automatically lead to higher grades if your mind wanders when you read or if you fail to take notes. But combine added time to improved study habits and you are bound to raise your grades. You will also indicate to your teachers your commitment to learning the subject matter.

Rereading

You do not have to read everything twice, not if you comprehend the material the first time. But much academic work requires a second reading. Professors do it, lawyers do it, your teachers do it, and you will do it someday when you are engaged in your chosen career. Figures have to be checked, novels have to be reread if you are to appreciate the subtle themes and well-written passages that make for a great work of literature, history has to be digested again so that you can comprehend the important issues and elements that influence the events that have shaped our world. In college you will be expected to read and understand greater amounts of information in all your courses, so now is the time to develop the habit of reading and rereading what counts.

Reviewing

Successful students constantly review their course work so that they do not have to cram for tests and exams, thereby forgetting all the information immediately after the test. If you do not have this essential habit already, make a promise to yourself to spend at least fifteen minutes each day reviewing your homework for the next day. You will find that by final exam time you need only go over material you are unsure about. The benefits of "the reviewing instinct" will not only lead to grades that help you get into the selective college you desire, they will help you to handle college work once you are there.

Your Academic Record and Your Test Scores

The conclusion of this step prepares you for Step Four, on how to take advantage of admissions tests. The thought we leave you with is this:

YOUR ACADEMIC RECORD IS MUCH MORE IMPORTANT THAN YOUR STANDARDIZED TEST SCORES IN THE SELECTIVE COLLEGE ADMISSIONS PROCESS

Not a single one of the dozens of top colleges we have surveyed put the SAT or ACT scores ahead of a strong, challenging curriculum in the admissions process. All stated that high school students bent on gaining admission to a selective college should be less concerned about test scores than about the quality of their academic work. The dean of admissions at Washington and Lee echoed the sentiments of all the top college admissions officers: "Worry more about program, personal productivity, and performance, and less about standardized scores." Wake Forest University even joined the ranks of test optional colleges recently, making the argument that test scores were not an essential part of its admission process.

What about the student with a mediocre academic record and exceptional test scores? A senior admissions officer at Princeton University had this to say: "This situation means that a bright student must develop the self-discipline to do course work in order to qualify for selective college admission. Test scores in and of themselves will not lead to acceptance to a demanding university."

Step Three Checklist

✓Make sure your curriculum for four years includes the best courses in English, science, mathematics, language, and history, as well as some courses in the arts and computer science.

✓Take as many honors courses as you can handle successfully.

✓Take Advanced Placement courses if at all possible.

✓Use your notebook to compare your academic record with the academic requirements you wrote down in Step One.

✓Take enrichment courses outside of school if you can, either during the summer or at night.

✓Work for good grades. You will never regret it. Weak marks are not invariably insurmountable, but try to bring them up through more effort and improved study habits.

STEP FOUR:
Make Standardized Tests Work for You

Approach Tests as Opportunities

What do we do about that test!? Among all aspects of the college admissions process, perhaps none strikes such dread into the minds and hearts of college applicants (and their parents) as the SAT. The power of this standardized "assessment" (formerly "aptitude") test to torpedo or gild a student's application to selective colleges and universities remains central to college admissions mythology. Media focus on "The Numbers Game" associated with the SAT and ACT test prep industry, and college admissions has raised the hype, and the ante, to new levels. What should parents and students really know and do about the standardized testing?

The unfortunate truth is that testing still matters, in fact, more than it used to. Compelled by rankings guides, an abundance of available public information, and better educated and more demanding consumers, colleges are frantic about showing good numbers. Humans love easily quantifiable statistics, hard facts that we can hold on to, and the SAT and ACT provide just that. We are seeing the highest number of students going to college in history, but the more selective colleges and universities are still competing for the "best students," the biggest endowments, and the most favorable press. Those little score range sidebars in the guidebooks can mean the difference between "better school" and "safety" in the minds of many parents, students, alums, and trustees.

Thus, like it or not, the SAT plays an increasingly important role in college admissions. Yet it is still second fiddle to consistent good grades through a strong curriculum. And an increasing number of colleges, such as Bowdoin, which has made the SAT optional for a long time, are searching for ways to de-emphasize the role of this No. 2 pencil test. The research and practice in learning disabilities, attention disorders, and multiple intelligences continue to suggest that the SAT is not an accurate measure of many students' potential to succeed in college.

Several trends in standardized testing deserve mention here. We have already discussed the Advanced Placement (AP) exams and their role in displaying your mastery of course material. There are three other tests that you may build into your repertoire: the SAT and SAT Subject Tests (both administered by the Educational Testing Service, or ETS, for the College Board) and the ACT (formerly called the American College Testing program). The trends to be aware of: (1) Standardized tests have become *more* rather than *less* important in recent years in evaluating applicants to most of the selective colleges, even though they are still less important than curriculum and grades; (2) students have more opportunities to take tests, and more selection among tests, in putting together a strong testing profile; and (3) test preparation options have become more prevalent, more diverse, more and less expensive, and more important. We focus much of our discussion on the SATs, which are for the majority of applicants to selective colleges the most common and important tests to consider even though almost as many students take the ACT (some 1.5 million) and every college now accepts the ACT in place of the SAT, and sometimes Subject Tests (e.g., Yale and Brown). We will cover the ACT and multiple test-taking strategies, however.

Your adviser and the media have probably alerted you to changes in the SAT over the past few years. The name has changed from the Scholastic Aptitude Test to the Scholastic Assessment Test and now simply to the SAT, but the College Board long ago disabused the educational world of the notion that it was testing native aptitude, that is, intelligence. The SAT tests reading, math, and writing capabilities; the SAT Subject Tests test knowledge of specific subjects. The biggest recent change to the SAT was the addition of the writing (with essay) section, emulating the PSAT and replacing the SAT II writing test. Many colleges continue not to use the writing section to evaluate students, though this is slowly changing as evidence seems to suggest that the writing section is as or even more predictive of freshman-year performance than the critical reading (formerly verbal) and math sections. You will see us sometimes note, and many colleges continue to report, a combined two-section Reading + Math score as opposed to a three-section score total.

Other changes to the SAT include the elimination of the analogies in the critical reading section and the addition of more short and long reading-comprehension paragraphs. In the math section, Algebra II–level math was added to the content.

Subject Tests can weigh more heavily in your folder than the SAT. They are opportunities to show your competence in specific areas. Yet psychologically the SAT remains so important as a way of demonstrating institutional success that we will devote much of this step to helping you achieve the best SAT scores within your ability. You will be able to use your College Board scores to display your academic strengths.

In this step you will get to know more about test taking, and you will approach the SAT, ACT, and the Subject Tests with the same confidence you have in your work in school. How will you achieve such confidence? In the same way you are dealing with other admissions requirements, by:

1. Learning test procedures: familiarizing yourself with these tests, the nature of the questions, and the time limits for answering them.

2. Emphasizing your strengths in scheduling tests to your advantage, in the same way that you are playing to your strengths in school.

3. Understanding the relative importance of tests in admissions decisions.

We will waste no time discussing the validity or fairness of the SATs, and we suggest that you postpone any critique of college testing until you have completed the tests. The changes that have been instituted in the SAT have been in response to criticism. Whether these tests will ever satisfy the critics is beside the point. Our experience is that despite all the worrying, students' SAT performance tends to correspond to their level of high school performance. Colleges are fully aware of why some students' SAT scores are lower than their grades, and they make allowances accordingly in admissions decisions. A student with a certified learning disability or attention disorder may seek permission to take extended-time tests, and international students may present the Test of English as a Foreign Language (TOEFL), for example, to supplement their SAT scores and to show their level of language proficiency. Students from disadvantaged backgrounds, and without access to the best one-on-one test prep services, which can indeed make a great difference in eventual scores, do have access to many low-cost and free materials to help them prepare themselves for the tests, and colleges will look at their test scores in the context of their socioeconomic and school background.

Those who score well on the SAT sections concentrate on the questions, not on the issues that have arisen in public about testing. Talk to high-scoring students to verify our experience in the importance of having a positive attitude at test time.

Here's what we have been told by some students:

Aggie, who went on to the University of Pennsylvania: "I told my counselor that the SAT had me scared stiff because my PSAT scores were mediocre. He asked me what I had done to improve my testing ability. That's all he had to say. Instead of listening to the kids around me moaning about winding up in a community college, I got hold of practice tests and went through them. By the time I went into the test center, I was relaxed. My scores were 100 points higher than the PSAT taken six months earlier."

Wilson, after scoring 1000 on his first SAT in his junior year at a New York private day school: "I kept grousing at home about how awful the SAT was going to be, in order to prepare my family for a shock. My father said, 'Do you know what a self-fulfilling prophecy is?' He told me I was psyching myself into a poor performance. Was I really that stupid? So how do you psych yourself into a good performance? I got my father to give me a vocabulary test every week. I wasn't worried about the math SAT. Well, I got a 570 in the verbal and 620 in the math."

Danielle, who scored 1250 on her second SAT after attending tutoring classes: "I couldn't believe the 1100 I got, spring of junior year." She attended a rural Virginia high school, but arranged to go to prep classes on weekends in Washington, D.C. "By the time I had finished the course, I had answered so many practice questions, I just knew I couldn't help but improve. I said before walking into that test center, 'Danielle, you'll get a 1200.' Somebody was listening. Me!"

Hugh: "I made a point to talk to some top seniors in my prep school about the SAT. 'Piece of cake,' they said. 'With your grade point average, you've got to do well.' I mentioned someone with good grades who got clobbered. 'LSE,' they said. 'Low self-esteem.' I decided to watch out for signs of LSE in others and stay clear of them. I guess I never caught the disease. That's how I interpret my 1350 scores."

FOREIGN LANGUAGE TESTS

Foreign language tests are given both with and without a listening option. The November SAT language Subject Tests are administered with both a reading and a listening component, while tests on other dates contain only reading sections. Consider your personal foreign language strengths, and have a discussion with your teacher. Are you better at listening and understanding a language, or do you do better when you only have to read, or vice versa? If you want a chance to listen and respond to questions, as well as to read and react, then you should consider taking your language test at least one time in November, probably during your senior year.

The SAT tests are administered by schools, not at national administration centers. It is important to ask your language teacher if your school has been registered with ETS to give either or both of these types of tests. It is possible that your school may not be, in which case you should ask that they contact ETS to arrange for appropriate test administration procedures, or you may need to check with ETS yourself to identify other test sites in your area which offer the test you are interested in taking.

Andy, a strong student at a suburban New York public school, scored 67 critical reading, 70 writing, and 80 math on his PSAT. He was clearly a good tester, but he was unsure whether he could bring his verbal scores in line with his math. "I have been taking SAT Subject Tests for a long time, so I really don't get too worked up about these tests. I worked with a tutor after the PSAT who helped me to focus on particular areas on the verbal sections. I knew that I could do better, and I had scored in the 70s on my writing section, but math is my usual strength. When I took the test in January, I felt really relaxed, and I was confident when I came out of the test. But I was totally surprised when I got my scores back, and I had flip-flopped. I had a 720 on the math, and an 800 on the reading."

Acquaint Your Parents with Tests

Your parents can help you in this step by going over practice tests with you, checking on extra work you do to build vocabulary, and reviewing your math. It is important that they spend some time reading through the College Board guide booklets and Web site that you will be using extensively. They will be impressed by what today's college-bound student is expected to know, and they will encourage you. Your parents will also be essential in helping you to plan your testing schedule, to evaluate your past performance, and to connect you with outside support if you feel that you need it. Paying for, taking, and reporting tests to colleges is an expensive and complicated business, and your parents can be your allies in this process.

Learning About Tests

There is no mystery about the tests. Two free booklets on the SAT and Subjects are available at all schools, as is one on the ACT, and you should study them as you would a textbook. Even more is available on the College Board and ACT Web sites. These should serve as your guides for the specifics of each test you will encounter. Your knowledge of what is being tested, how questions are presented, how they are scored, whether to guess or not with answers you do not know, how much you can accomplish in a given test period—will build your confidence and help you to avoid unnecessary mistakes.

See these materials as a starting point in your exploration of the SATs. The College Board makes a great deal of information available, including practice tests and answers to frequently asked questions

(FAQs), on its Web site and in a book series called *Real SATs*. A potentially overwhelming amount of information is now available on the Internet and from private test preparation services, some of which are nationally known organizations, others high-cost local businesses, and still others smaller personal services. On the Web are a multitude of startup businesses designed to prepare you for tests. Evaluate with care any potential local, national, or Internet-based services before signing on, and find out more about their materials and practices. References from friends, teachers, and other students in your school can help you to make a right choice of materials, services, and tutors, should you go that route. Our resource list on pages 102–105 includes a number of good Web sites to help you learn more about the SATs and other tests.

Myths About the SAT and ACT

The College Board has explicitly attempted to dispel two myths about the SAT and ACT. One is that the SAT measures intelligence, and the other, implied by the first, is that coaching or tutoring cannot help you improve your SAT scores. Rather, the SAT measures developed verbal and mathematical reasoning abilities; these abilities are helpful in succeeding in college-level academic work, and thus the SAT is one tool that admissions officers use in comparing students from schools with differing academic and grading standards.

The assumption of admissions committees is that when a student with high grades gets mediocre SAT or ACT scores, he or she was not as well prepared as the student with high grades and high test scores. This says nothing about a student's intelligence, and the colleges know this, because they are willing to admit a certain number of students with lower test scores than most of their first-year students. Such students seem to overcome their weaker college preparation in one or two years, and often wind up on an academic level with those who entered with higher scores.

This fact should encourage anyone who consistently scores below 600 on the reading, writing, and math portions of the SAT. We cannot say too strongly that if you score low on the SAT, there is nothing wrong with your intelligence.

Coaching or Tutoring May Help

Students should take advantage of every opportunity they have to prepare for the SAT or ACT beginning at least in the junior year in order to give themselves the best chance they have to make these tests a nonissue. But how?

Here is the crux of the issue: We have found that those students who make the most improvement on the SAT do so by gradual, diligent work over a long period of time. On the verbal sections, reading and writing matter most. Word lists, vocabulary building, attention to grammar and language structure—these activities over several years can dramatically change a student's verbal and writing ability. So Level One is practicing with some of the many good word, grammar, and practice test books on the market. A new development is the availability of Internet-based interactive tutoring programs. Many students find twenty minutes a day, or an hour every few days, to be very helpful in approaching test prep.

Level Two is taking a class, which can present students with strategies and drills, but can often be a waste of time if not taken seriously. Level Three is hiring an individual tutor for one or more test sections. Often, individual tutoring can address learning and study skills and knowledge gaps, in addition to practical work on the SAT or ACT. Of course, this comes at a price, and again students must be dedicated and take the tutoring seriously to achieve progress.

In evaluating these three levels of preparation, families should use PSAT score reports or the ACT PLAN as templates—areas that need work are often first identified on these. Additionally, for a solid student who has serious trouble on the PSAT, SAT, or ACT families should consider a more extensive learning evaluation that may help students to understand why they are having difficulty on this particular kind of standardized test.

So, the bad news? Testing matters more than ever at many of the most desirable institutions, and if you score poorly, you may lose your chance of admission in the face of increasing competition. The good news? There are many inexpensive strategies for preparing for tests which can work well over a longer period of time, and if you score well, you can bolster your chances of admission, placement into higher-level college courses, and qualification for merit-based scholarships at some non-Ivy institutions.

Since the SAT measures "developed" reasoning abilities, development can be aided by teachers, coaches, tutors, and through dedicated self-improvement: that is, practicing basic mathematical operations and reading. While the College Board and private test preparation services differ in their assessment of the average score increases to be gained through test prep programs, it is clear that improvement can range from 50 to 250 or more points on the combined math and verbal score. If you get a combined score of 1000 the first time, you might get 1140 the second, raising you, for example, from 500 in the verbal and 500 in the math to 570 in the verbal test and 570 in the math. If you score in the high 1200s or 1300s on your first SAT or on your PSAT, then you probably have a good chance of raising your scores into the 1400s over time.

While test prep services do claim to show high average score improvement for their students, they tend not to make individual score improvement guarantees (although some services allow a student to retake a class for free if his or her score fails to increase by a certain amount). They make clear that you must be an active participant in classes or tutoring sessions in order to get the most out of the material. You must work to develop the reasoning abilities tested by the SAT. No tutor can develop them for you.

Many students we have worked with have improved their SAT scores with the help of tutoring programs. The decision to attend one should not be casual. The course may cost more than $700. It will require self-discipline—class attendance and homework. There is no guarantee that your scores will improve after you have been tutored. If your counselor and teachers feel that this approach will be useful, and if you and your parents agree and can afford the tuition, we would say, "Get some help, from a personal coach or a group class." But before you sign up for a course, remember the limitations: You cannot expect ten sessions of a tutoring class to change your scores from mediocre to brilliant. Ask yourself, "How best could *I* spend that time preparing for the SAT?"

Williams College Class of 2012 Profile

	SAT Critical Reading	SAT Math
750–800	36%	32%
700–740	25%	28%
650–690	16%	18%
600–640	12%	13%
550–590	5%	7%
Below 550	1%	2%

Class Rank in High School Class (of those reporting rank)

Top Decile	88%
Second Decile	8%
Third Decile	3%
Below Third Decile	1%

Total Applications

Total men applied	3,479
Total women applied	4,069
Total men admitted	600 (17%)
Total women admitted	676 (17%)
Total men enrolled	251
Total women enrolled	284

Early Decision Applications

Men applied	284
Men admitted	108
Women applied	316
Women admitted	115
ED applicants admitted	37%
Class admitted ED	42%

What Are Good SAT Scores?

One subject not covered by the College Board's introductory booklets is the significance of your scores. The perfect score for writing, math, or reading is 800; the lowest is 200. All selective colleges publish freshman class profiles that provide an idea of these students' average SAT scores. Detailed profiles can show you specifics on what percentages of students scored in what particular ranges on the SAT. Typically, reporting the *middle 50%* range has become the standard means of reporting SATs. That is, colleges report the range of scores that the middle 50% of enrolling students (a different group from applicants, or, sometimes, admitted students) scored. That means 25% of students had scores above this range, and 25% scored lower. If you are in the middle of the middle 50% range, you can assume that *by the one variable of SAT scores,* you represent an average first-year student on campus. If your scores are well above the middle 50% range, you are likely to be at the top of this college's applicant pool, and if you are well below the middle 50%, this school may be a real stretch for you. Again, this does not take into account your courses, grades, and the other factors important in making an admission decision for you.

A student with low grades and high SAT scores runs the risk of being thought lazy. A student with high grades in easy classes but low SAT scores may have his grades and course work devalued.

So what are good SAT scores? If both low scorers and high scorers, according to the middle 50% concept, qualify for admission under certain circumstances, where is the standard? It lies in what the majority of any entering freshman class achieves. You can tell from a school's profile and your own self-assessment, and realistic goals for test performance, whether you will be at the top or bottom or in the middle of a college's SAT range. The upper and lower 25% bands at the top colleges are often the exceptions. You only need worry if you are in the lower group. Most applicants in that range will have a special talent or circumstance that makes them attractive in other ways.

Colleges try to help students to determine if they are potential candidates by listing the class standing, GPA, and other information of recently accepted candidates as well as their SAT scores. In the accompanying list, you can quickly tell whether your test scores match up with the sample. Feel free to ask the admissions staff at any college for such information if you have trouble finding it in guidebooks or on the college's Web site.

Sampling of Combined SAT and ACT Scores, 2007 Freshmen
(middle 50%)

	SAT CR+MA+WR	ACT Composite
Amherst	2000–2290	29–34
Bates	1270–1410 (CR+MA)	N/A
Bowdoin	1950–2200	29–33
U California Berkeley	1800–2170	N/A
Carleton	1960–2220	29–33
Colorado College	1830–2090	27–31
Cornell	1290–1500 (CR+MA)	28–32
Dartmouth	1990–2320	29–34
Emory	1940–2210	29–33
Georgetown	1300–1490 (CR+MA)	29–33
Harvard	2090–2380	31–35
Kenyon	1870–2130	28–32
Lehigh	1240–1390 (CR+MA)	N/A
Middlebury	1950–2220	29–33
MIT	2040–2310	31–34
U North Carolina	1800–2090	26–31
Northwestern	2010–2270	30–34
U Pennsylvania	1990–2270	29–33
Pomona	2060–2280	29–34
Princeton	2080–2360	30–34
Rice	1950–2260	29–34
Smith	1740–2080	25–30
Swarthmore	2040–2300	27–33
U Virginia	1800–2130	N/A

Washington University	1370–1530 (CR+MA)	30–33
Wellesley	1960–2210	29–32
Wesleyan	1950–2230	27–32

HIGH SATS AT SELECTIVE COLLEGES AND UNIVERSITIES

Here is some evidence for the rise in high SAT scores at elite schools during the past twenty years. One must note that the SAT was "recentered" in 1996, resulting in a spike in average verbal and math scores and significant increases on the high-end verbal scores. This data is not adjusted for recentering. What is presented is the percentage of enrolling freshmen in 1989 scoring 700 or above on the old math and verbal sections, and of those enrolling in 2007 on the new math and critical reading sections (first administered in March 2005).

	Math		Verbal	
	1989	2007	1989	2007
Brown	37%	66%	17%	64%
U California Berkeley	33%	50%	7%	33%
Cornell	40%	60%	10%	41%
Emory	15%	45%	4%	32%
Georgetown	61%	51%	5%	53%
Northwestern	20%	63%	4%	53%
U Pennsylvania	41%	69%	9%	54%
Stanford	55%	74%	24%	67%
U Virginia	27%	39%	8%	32%
Yale	54%	78%	33%	78%

Source: Chronicle of Higher Education 5/11/08, from "Realizing Bakke's Legacy: Affirmative Action, Equal Opportunity, and Access to Higher Education" (Stylus Publishing, 2008).

The SAT Reasoning Test

The SAT has three parts, critical reading, writing, and mathematical. The collective name for them is the SAT Reasoning Test, or SAT. The old College Board Achievement Tests are now known as the SAT Subject Tests. Let's look at the SAT reading part first.

SAT Critical Reading

There are three critical reading sections: two 25-minute and one 20-minute section. These sections consist of passage-based reading and sentence completion questions.

Passage-Based Reading

Passage-based reading accounts for over 70% (forty-eight questions) of the verbal test, and consists of a variety of passages from the humanities, social sciences, natural sciences, and narrative fiction and nonfiction. Passages may stand independently, or there may be a pair of passages consisting of related and opposing views. Three types of questions are asked about the short and long reading passages: Vocabulary in Context, which test your understanding of the meaning of words as used in the reading sample; Literal Comprehension, which examine your understanding of the facts discussed; and Extended Reasoning, which comprise the largest proportion of questions and which ask you to analyze information and arguments and read for deeper meaning and inferences.

Reading questions test your understanding of the passages and vocabulary. Since you will be reading thousands of words in college, answers to these questions show your probable ability to understand class assignments. You cannot spend too much time evaluating and reevaluating every word. You will need to read the available answers, and then quickly and carefully go through the passages to determine which answers are correct. You will need to read for meaning, looking for key words and phrases. Questions require students to look for the meaning of words in the context of the passage, to demonstrate understanding of the content, and to reflect on the ideas and arguments presented.

THE IMPORTANCE OF BUILDING YOUR VOCABULARY

Your vocabulary increases over the years without effort, but to give you the edge required by selective colleges, you must make an effort to build it up further by keeping a pocket notebook or computer file in which you jot down new words and their definitions. On the SAT, you will not be asked to write down the definitions of words. Rather, your knowledge of vocabulary will allow you to correctly respond to verbal questions, whether in the form of reading paragraphs for meaning or completing sentences' missing words.

You may use any number of the vocabulary-building books from the test prep companies, including, of course, a good dictionary. Building vocabulary can be a steady, ongoing process for you from now on, one that will help you not only on the SAT verbal sections, but also on your class assignments and in your own reading. Read with a dictionary by your side. Whenever you encounter an unfamiliar or uncertain word, look it up, and write the definition in your notebook. Also, read outside your normal class or casual reading books. Read the front page or cover story of a major newspaper or magazine. You'll gain not only vocabulary but also knowledge of current affairs.

Sentence Completion

The nineteen questions that give you a choice of words with which to complete a sentence correctly are testing your ability to see relations between parts of a sentence. Sentence Completion tests your understanding of the logical structure of language, as well as the meanings of words.

In sentence completion questions, you will be provided with a choice of five words to complete a sentence with a blank in it, or with a choice of five pairs of words to complete a sentence with two blanks. You will have to test the word or word pair choices to see which make the most sense in the sentence at hand. You will need to look for meaning, consistency, and appropriate fit.

Read to Develop Verbal Skills

Invariably those who score high on the verbal part of the SAT are skilled readers; they read a great deal and read widely. Between the time when you take the PSAT in the fall of your junior year and the SAT the next spring, you can do much reading. But if you have not been a reader before your junior year, how do you suddenly turn into a reader? And what should you read?

We suggest that you consult your English teacher and come up with a reasonable variety of extra reading to do. Periodically you should then report to the teacher what you have read. A good teacher will observe how well you read. Unless you concentrate on and absorb reading matter, you are wasting your time. To read well, do not try to read too fast. Take notes or, if you own the book, underline and make notes in the margins—magazine articles should be underlined and reread.

Francis Bacon said, "Reading maketh a full man," and we today would add, "and woman." The more you read, the more enjoyable and useful reading becomes. Your practice tests will reveal the extent to which you must expand your reading. If you were to read a passage a day in a book like the *Norton Reader* or any other collection of prose passages, you would soon find yourself with a larger vocabulary and an ability to grasp new ideas and new information more quickly.

Such a program is an enrichment of your mind as well. Preparing for the SAT in this way allows you to sample the kinds of reading you will do in a liberal arts college. You need not think of this extra reading as a means to passing a test, and if you are enrolled in a strong English program, you may have enough assigned reading from class to develop your verbal skills. This reading is the kind of practicing that musicians do; it is how athletes perfect their running, skating, or serving. It is an exercise, in this case, to develop your mind, to make you interesting to yourself and to others.

Seen in this light, the SAT reading comprehension questions become a service to you. Read passages that puzzle you, read passages you disagree with, open your mind to the treasures of the written word. Read sophisticated magazines like the *New Yorker,* the *Atlantic Monthly, Scientific American,* and the *Economist* once in a while.

Above all, read with a dictionary at hand, take down new words, and build your own vocabulary list. A good vocabulary will help you get a good verbal SAT score. You can keep your list of words and their definitions in the back of your admissions notebook as a reminder that this will help you in your efforts to get into your favorite college. Boxes of vocabulary cards are turning up on coffee tables in the homes of college candidates. They provide amusement, even stimulation, but you do not build a vocabulary only by trying to learn words in isolation. In learning a foreign language you build vocabulary as you read, as you study grammar, and as you try to understand pronunciation. Learn to deepen appreciation of your own language in the same way.

When you consciously carry on a reading program that builds vocabulary, you will find that reading assignments for your courses will become part of the program, and you will improve your course work accordingly.

You can improve your speed in the analogies if you put questions to yourself about the meaning of words. G. K. Chesterton made this witticism: "Art is limitation; the essence of every picture is the frame." Do you see the analogy he was making? Limitation is to art as a frame is to a picture; knowing where to stop, whether it be in a drip painting or a portrait, is all.

Discuss with friends and family what you are reading. When someone tells you that you are wrong, that you misread a passage, take the comment to heart. Merely to be literate is not to be a good reader. If you dislike reading, have trouble concentrating when you are reading, or have difficulty with spelling words, you may have a learning disability or attention deficit disorder (see next page). This is no disgrace, and it is correctable. You can be tested for a learning disability in school or by an outside professional. Students who have documented learning disabilities may qualify for extended or untimed tests in school and on standardized tests like the SATs. An SAT accommodation for extra time must come either from your school or through a direct request to ETS. Such a request must be accompanied by certification from a recognized educational specialist.

ADVICE FOR LEARNING-DISABLED STUDENTS

In the last two decades, most colleges have recognized that some students have learning disabilities or attention disorders that impact not only their academic performance but, often more noticeably, their success on timed multiple choice tests like the SAT. One such disability is dyslexia, a learning disability that does not necessarily prevent the student from doing college work and even earning high honors. Famous dyslexics include Thomas Edison, Albert Einstein, and Woodrow Wilson. Many students with learning disabilities such as dyslexia and attention deficit disorder (ADD) qualify for extended-time testing on their SATs, and they can use this to their advantage. Colleges will not know that you have had any accommodations. We cannot say to students and parents forcefully enough: Take advantage of this accommodation if you qualify for it, at least once. It could make a major difference in your scores. And if you have a learning disability or attention disorder, *share* this information with colleges to which you are applying. Not only will colleges be able to use this knowledge to help them evaluate your academic record and SATs, they will be able to make a decision about admission based in part on whether they feel you will be successful in their academic program. If they decide not to admit you, then, as we have said earlier, you probably would not have wanted to go there anyway!

One of the best ways to present information about your learning style to colleges is to address the matter directly in a covering letter or supplemental essay in your application that describes the nature of your learning disability or ADD, the ways in which this has affected your academic and test performance, and what you see as your strengths and weaknesses.

SAT Mathematics

The math portion of the SAT includes two 25-minute and one 20-minute section. Forty-four questions are multiple choice questions on regular math. Ten are student-produced "grid-in" response problems. It is recommended that students use a calculator for the test. The "grid-in" questions require that you produce your own answers rather than select one from a set of multiple choice alternatives. The quantitative questions will require study. The math SAT section includes math through Algebra II: Numbers and Operations; Algebra and Functions; Geometry and Measurement; and Data Analysis, Statistics, and Probability.

Work on Mathematical Skills with a Teacher

Math is not magic. You can improve your math skills with practice, but you probably need the help of a teacher or a tutor. It will not take up much of a teacher's time to show you arithmetic, algebra, and geometry books you can use to review your skills. Remember that the SAT is primarily based on algebra I and II, geometry, and grade-school arithmetic, so you will be reviewing subjects you should already know. Some students need more directed help because of a lack of skills. Think positively: You can be helped to overcome math weaknesses or anxiety.

Some students are gifted in math and easily score in the 700s on the SAT math test. Most selective college applicants are well enough trained to score at least in the 600s. A PSAT score lower than 50, therefore, calls for remedial work. This will help you in your math courses, and may enable you to take an honors math course in your senior year. You may be able to get help in this work from a math whiz in your school.

A prep course drills you in the kinds of operations you will need to understand for the math SAT. It forces you to take practice tests, revealing weaknesses that you then learn to overcome in class sessions.

SAT Writing

The newest section of the SAT is the writing, which was adapted from the old SAT II writing test. Although many colleges remain skeptical of the writing section, tracking students' scores but not using them for evaluatory purposes, we are already seeing signs of changes in colleges' attitudes toward this part of the SAT. Data is beginning to suggest that the writing section is as or even more predictive of first-year college academic performance. More colleges are reporting a three-section score summary in their profiles for entering students, as well. We expect that this trend will continue.

The Essay

The writing section consists of one 25-minute and one 10-minute section made up of multiple choice questions, and one 25-minute section consisting of a student-written essay. The entire SAT begins with this essay, during which you'll be asked to respond clearly and comprehensively to a prompt. You will need to develop a reasoned argument with a point of view supported by personal and/or other evidence gained from your academic studies. The essay is scored by two readers on a 1 to 6 scale so that 12 is the highest score. This score is worth one-third of the total writing section score.

To do well on the writing section, not only do you need to write enough to make your argument, but you also need to write clear, concise sentences in well-organized paragraphs. This is basic expository writing 101, and practice in your school assignments and in SAT prep work will help you improve your style, content, and form so that you can master this part of the writing section. Another aspect of the writing section to be aware of is that colleges can go online to view your timed, monitored SAT essay. Yes, it is considered to be "first-draft" quality, but also a reasonable representation of your writing capabilities. Thus, when the college compares this known quantity to the application essays you have submitted, they are hoping to see a consistent relationship.

Identifying Sentence Errors

There are three types of multiple choice writing questions: identifying sentence errors, improving sentences, and improving paragraphs. The first type of question asks you to recognize mistakes in language usage and conventions in standard written English. You are given a sentence that might have one error or no error at all. Four words or phrases are underlined, and you must choose one that appears to be a mistake, or the fifth choice of no error in the sentence. You are not asked to supply the correction to the sentence.

Improving Sentences

For these questions, you do need to recognize and correct mistakes, as well as identify proper English usage. You are given a sentence with all or part of it underlined. Your first of five answer choices indicates no change to the sentence. The others offer alternative ways of phrasing part or all of the sentence. The key here is to identify the clearest, least ambiguous, most effective option. This tests your vocabulary, as well as your knowledge of basic grammar, punctuation, and sentence construction.

Improving Paragraphs

Here you are given a draft paragraph and asked to identify improvements to it. After reading the paragraph quickly, you proceed to questions based on it. You may need to fix words, phrases, or sentences to improve the overall passage or clarify its meaning. You must pay attention to organization of the paragraph, sentence transitions, and logical ordering of the sentences.

Selective Colleges and Universities with SAT/ACT Optional or Flexible Policies (Selected List)

An increasing number of selective colleges and universities, typically smaller institutions, are making standardized tests optional. Sometimes they will require an interview, an extra writing sample, or a portfolio instead. Many specialized colleges of music and the arts also do not require tests.

Bard College	Annandale-on-Hudson, NY
Bard College at Simon's Rock	Great Barrington, MA
Bates College	Lewiston, ME
Bennington College	Bennington, VT
Bowdoin College	Brunswick, ME
College of the Atlantic	Bar Harbor, ME
College of the Holy Cross	Worcester, MA
Connecticut College*	New London, CT
Denison University	Granville, OH
Dickinson College	Carlisle, PA
Dowling College	Oakdale, NY

Drew University	Madison, NJ
Franklin and Marshall College	Lancaster, PA
George Mason University*	Fairfax, VA
Gettysburg College	Gettysburg, PA
Goddard College	Plainfield, VT
Guilford College	Greensboro, NC
Gustavus Adolphus College	St. Peter, MN
Hamilton College*	Clinton, NY
Hampshire College	Amherst, MA
Hartwick College	Oneonta, NY
Hobart and William Smith Colleges	Geneva, NY
Johnson and Wales University	(multiple campuses)
Knox College	Galesburg, IL
Lake Forest College	Lake Forest, IL
Lawrence University	Appleton, WI
Lewis and Clark College	Portland, OR
McDaniel College*	Westminster, MD
Middlebury College*	Middlebury, VT
Mount Holyoke College	South Hadley, MA
Muhlenberg College	Allentown, PA
New England College	Henniker, NH
Pitzer College	Claremont, CA
Prescott College	Prescott, AZ
Providence College	Providence, RI
Rollins College	Winter Park, FL

Saint John's College	Annapolis, MD
Saint John's College	Santa Fe, NM
Saint Lawrence University	Canton, NY
Salisbury University*	Salisbury, MD
Sarah Lawrence College	Bronxville, NY
Smith College	Northampton, MA
Susquehanna University	Selinsgrove, PA
Union College	Schenectady, NY
Ursinus College*	Collegeville, PA
Wake Forest University	Winston-Salem, NC
Washington College*	Chestertown, MD
Wheaton College	Norton, MA
Wittenberg University	Springfield, OH
Worcester Polytechnic Institute*	Worcester, MA

* Indicates that the college has a "flexible" policy: See school Web site for more information.

Tips on Taking the SAT

The following tips have been used for a number of years by our students. You should start following them when you do your practice tests. They will be habitual by the time of an actual SAT.

1. Plan your time carefully. Spending too much time on a question can be as detrimental as giving a wrong answer.

2. Answer first the questions to which you know the answers. Then, if you have time left, return to the unanswered questions.

3. There is only one right answer. If you identify it, do not waste time working through the other possibilities. Go on to the next question.

4. Guess shrewdly on answers that you do not know. Wrong answers carry a larger penalty than unanswered ones, but your chances for a higher score will be improved if you guess—provided you can first eliminate at least one or two choices.

5. In reading comprehension passages, underline important information as you read through the test. There is no penalty for marking the worksheets, and doing it will help you recall important information. Likewise, in mathematical sections use the white space as a worksheet.

6. Pay particular attention to words like *but, not, however,* and *therefore.* They are key words that often signal the major thoughts of a passage.

7. Wherever possible, use mathematical shortcuts, cancellation of fractions, estimation, removal of decimal points, and so forth.

8. Memorize math formulas. Formulas such as $a = l \times w$ for the area of a rectangle are often given at the beginning of the test section, but it is quicker to have them in your head.

9. Don't be sidetracked by secondary answers or answers that are true but not directly related to the central questions.

10. Be so familiar with each test and section that you do not need to spend time reading the instructions to know what is required of you.

Inasmuch as the SAT is given in the morning, after you have presumably had a good night's sleep, do not take practice tests at midnight or when you are tired. Take them during the day.

The College Board's Advice

The College Board has its own set of "test-taking tips," which appear in its materials. You should reread them until you know their gist by heart. Here is how you might fix them in your mind with key reminder sentences.

1. Questions increase in difficulty from beginning to end of each section. Exception to the above: Reading passages get harder, but the questions have no order of difficulty.

2. Omit questions you don't know at all; go to the next section.

3. Answer easy questions first before spending time on harder ones. Correct answers on easy questions count just as much as correct answers on difficult ones.

4. You don't have to answer every question. Answering 50% to 60% of the questions correctly can produce average or slightly above average scores.

5. Omitting some questions may not affect your score adversely.

6. Guess at the answer if you know at least one choice is wrong.

7. For a wrong answer you lose a fraction of a credit. For a correct answer you get one credit. Omitting an answer will result in neither gain nor loss of credit.

8. If you do not answer any questions in a section, you will receive the minimum score for that part.

9. You can use the test book for scratchwork or reminders if you have time to go back to omitted questions.

10. Make no extra marks on the answer sheet! (Be sure to score the question you are answering; you can get mixed up when you omit questions.) Check your answers sheet.

11. Mark the answer sheet correctly! Give only one answer for each question by filling in the oval completely. Use a No. 2 pencil.

12. Keep track of your overall time, as well as time spent on each question.

SAT Procedures

We wish to distinguish the SAT from the Subject Tests, which will be discussed later in this step. Let's review the SAT procedures.

1. Check with your counselor in the fall of your junior year about taking the PSAT/NMSQT (National Merit Scholarship Qualifying Test; it is sometimes taken by sophomores). This warm-up for the SAT does not go into your admissions application, but you can qualify for a National Merit Scholarship if you score high enough. We recommend that you take it for practice and use your PSAT score as a diagnostic tool for planning your review for the SAT.

2. The SAT is taken for the first time in the winter or spring of your junior year. Although some schools, particularly competitive private schools, are pushing their students to take an SAT in January of junior year, we find that this is not a wise strategy for many students. If you are not ready, if you have not had time to review for the SAT, or if your PSATs were significantly lower than you expected, do not take the SAT in January. Plan to prepare for it gradually and take it for the first time in March or May. You will still have at least two additional opportunities to retake the test down the line. Even though you can use the Score Choice program now to control which tests you will eventually send to colleges, there is little point in taking the SAT if you do not have a reasonable chance of getting a good score on at least one section. And remember, you must report the entire SAT from a given test date, not just one selected section. Some colleges may also continue to ask you to submit all your test scores to them in any event.

3. To register, create an account online at the College Board's Web site.

4. In registering, you are allowed to select answers to the Student Questionnaire, a survey that you need complete only once. This reports to colleges and scholarship organizations such information as your GPA and intended major and career.

5. The SAT is held at many test centers in each state. You are free to take the test at any center that you choose. If you want to make sure

you can take the test at a particular center, such as your own school, make sure to register well before the deadline.

6. Tests are held on Saturdays (or alternate days for those with religious exemptions) starting at 8:30 A.M. Arrange to be early and bring identification, your registration ticket, two No. 2 pencils, erasers, snacks, and a calculator.

7. Standby testing may be available if you have missed the registration deadlines.

Your counselor will go over all this with you. These bureaucratic procedures should give you no trouble, but we are constantly amazed at how casually some students handle details. Do not be casual about the SAT, no matter how confident you become as a result of careful preparation for the tests.

COMPUTER-AIDED TEST PREPARATION

If you like to work on the computer, and a few bells and whistles entice you to stay focused, and interactive work on particular problem sets under your own tutelage and self-discipline works as a strategy for you, then you are in luck. There are numerous programs and Web sites available at low cost to help you prepare for the PSAT, SAT, and ACT to let you set the pace in your test prep. Check out a few of the sites listed on our Internet Resources list as part of your strategy of making standardized tests work for you.

Preparing for Your First SAT

Take the PSAT/NMSQT

The PSAT taken in October of your junior year (or sophomore year for practice) is your warm-up. It is shorter and is not submitted to the colleges. However, since it is also the National Merit Scholarship Qualifying

Test, a high score qualifies you for this valuable award (see Step Nine). If you are among the 16,000 semifinalists, you will want to include this fact in your applications for admission, because colleges are mightily impressed by this group of applicants. You will also receive letters from many colleges soliciting your application, some of them selective colleges that seek as many strong students as possible. To this end, more and more students are taking the PSAT for additional practice in the tenth grade. Ask your school if the PSAT is offered to sophomores, and if you are unable to take the test there, ask if you can take it elsewhere. If you feel that you have a decent chance of making it into the National Merit competition by attaining scores above their selection index, then you should begin to review for the PSAT test during the summer and fall before your junior year. The selection index varies in each state, but is typically above 205. The index score consists of your scores on the three sections of the PSAT added together. If you score 70 on each section, for example, your index score will be 210, generally high enough to get you into the National Merit competition.

Your PSAT scores are predictive of how well you will score on the SAT you take the following spring. The PSAT is scored between 20 and 80, so you add a zero to see what your score is likely to be on the SAT. If you have unimpressive PSAT scores by the standards you hold, you have from December (when the scores are announced) to May or longer to develop your verbal and math reasoning ability. Your scores will very likely come up to at least the higher end of the score range reported on your PSAT report if you put in some work and review. It is more likely that following the strategies outlined in this step, you will bring your scores up even higher, especially by fall of senior year.

Take SAT Practice Tests

Three to four months before the SAT, start taking practice tests. These last several hours. Set aside enough time so that you will not be interrupted. You can find practice tests on the College Board's Web site and in its *Real SATs* books as well as books by the Princeton Review, Kaplan, McGraw-Hill, and Peterson's, to name just a few. Taking as many practice tests as you can will acquaint you with the nature of the tests and give you confidence when the time comes to take the actual SAT.

Score the Sample Test and Study the Results

You need not score a sample test at once. Psychologically, you would do better to put it aside and score it later, when your mind is no longer preoccupied with getting the right answers. When you score it, take your time and be accurate. You gain nothing by giving yourself a mark better than the one you actually earned.

The board has good suggestions to follow about analyzing your performance. If you feel comfortable going over this and any other sample test with a teacher, doing so can be helpful. After taking several sample tests, you will know your weaknesses and can work to overcome them. For example, if you score in the 500s on the reading test and in the 600s on the math one, work on those parts of the reading test that gave you the most difficulty.

Taking the SAT Itself

After so much work on preparation, the SAT itself need not be the traumatic experience for you that it is for some students. For one thing, you already know what to expect. If you have scored 1900 in practice, you are likely to score close to this in actuality. Hoping to do better than you did in practice is not realistic, and neither is fearing that you will do worse.

Taking the SAT Again

Most students take the SAT during the winter or spring of their junior year and the fall of their senior year. Some take a third SAT in an effort to improve their score. Three is enough. The likelihood of further improvement, if there has been any, is slight. There is usually some improvement between junior and senior year, especially if you do more work, review, and get coaching during the summer. Taking a postgraduate high school year will sometimes help a student make a considerably higher score, but is not a reason in itself to pursue a PG year. If you plan a fifth year of high school, wait until the fall of that year to take your third SAT.

We urge you to take no more than three SAT tests for the following reasons: For strong students overall, most colleges will look at a set of two or three SAT scores and take the highest section scores from among the tests. Additionally, for new scores to be higher in a statistically significant way, they need to be 30 or 40 points above the previous scores. That is, they need to be above the *range* of reported scores you have already earned. A 650 on the math test, for example, may be reported as a 650 score with a range of 620–680. This means that on any given day, with any given test, you would have scored as low as 620 and as high as 680. For you to post a statistically significant higher score than 650, you will have to score above 680.

Finally, the SAT is important, but not as much as your grades. Concentrate first on your grades, and, particularly if your SATs are not improving after a third test, realize that your grades will matter even more if you are to get a good reading by the colleges. Devote your efforts to your regular schoolwork and activities. If you can show tangible results in your course work or in some activity, it will count more in your admissions folder than a fourth or fifth SAT score or a sight improvement in one section. Accept the fact that your scores tell you a certain truth about your preparation for college at this point. You need not think that your capacities for verbal and mathematical reasoning will remain forever at your present level. Remember that you are continually developing these powers, and that it is quite possible for you someday to surpass not only your own present scores, but those of others who currently score higher than you do.

SAT SUBJECT TESTS

Many selective colleges require candidates to submit two or three Subject Test scores. Like the SAT, you can take many SAT Subject Tests and then, using the *score choice* option, *withhold* your accumulating scores until you decide which tests to release to their score report that goes to the colleges. You may retake an SAT Subject Test, and choose to report an individual test result from a test date on which you took two or three (the maximum you can take on a test date). The SAT Subjects are given in these subjects:

English
Literature

History
U.S. History
World History

Foreign Language (Reading Only)
French
German
Modern Hebrew
Italian
Latin
Spanish

Foreign Language (Reading and Listening)
Chinese
French
German
Japanese
Korean
Spanish

Mathematics
Mathematics Level 1
Mathematics Level 2

Science
Biology E/M
Chemistry
Physics

The SAT Reasoning Test is offered seven times per year. Most SAT Subject Tests except foreign language and world history are offered six times per year. The world history test is offered twice, in December and June, as is Latin. The foreign language tests requiring reading and listening are offered only in November. French and Spanish are offered five times per year, and German, Hebrew, and Italian only once.

To an admissions committee, the Subject Tests provide more tangible evidence of your capacity to do the advanced academic work of college courses than does the SAT. They test you in subjects you know, and you can prepare for them with a sense of mastery of the material on which you will be questioned.

Because Subject Tests can be taken as early as the freshman year, they offer the selective college applicant an opportunity to construct an impressive testing record. By taking a number of tests over four years, you will be in a position to choose the three best scores for the admissions committees' consideration. But you can also submit all of your Subject Test scores, and students who begin taking them during their freshman year usually have scores that are satisfactory and often more than satisfactory.

To drive this point home, put yourself in the position of an admissions committee looking at two transcripts. One shows six Subject Test scores averaging 700. The other shows three Subject Test scores that average 700. The committee has to think that the student who took the extra three Subject Tests is more academically aggressive, more daring. Students who successfully exercise this option put themselves in a very strong competitive position for admission to the most selective colleges.

In contrast to the SAT, which is one three-plus-hour test, there are twenty-one different one-hour Subject Tests. You may choose what tests to take and when to take them, and you may take as many as three tests on one date. First-round Early Decision applicants should submit their scores in the fall with their applications. Their last opportunity to take the tests and have them count in the first-round review is in October or November. Such applicants would be advised to take their SAT Subjects by spring of junior year. Taking an extra Subject Test in November of your senior year will help you if your score is good, but you will have to rush your score to the college, without time for you to assess it and its place in your application folder. Early Decision Round II allows students more time to take SAT Subjects and SATs, into December, and possibly even January.

The Ideal Subject Test Program

The ideal is to take as many SAT Subjects as you can, starting in your freshman year, in those subjects expressly required by colleges to which you plan to apply, and in those that are particular personal strengths. By your senior year, you may already have compiled a record of impressive Subject Test scores. Then, as a senior, you take SAT Subjects at the most advanced level. See our testing schedule on the next page for a generalized testing schedule.

Concise Academic and Testing Schedule
Grades 9–12

Grade	Course Selection	Possible Tests
9	English Biology (Laboratory) History (Ancient or World) Math (Algebra I or Plane Geometry) Language (first or second year)	*June:* SAT Subject Tests in Biology, World History

10	English
	Chemistry (Laboratory)
	Math (Plane Geometry or
	    Algebra II)
	Language (second or third year)
	History (World or U.S.) or
	Computer Science or Fine or
	Performing Arts
		October: PSAT
		June:
		SAT Subject
		Tests in Chemistry,
		    Math Level 1, U.S. History

11	English Physics (Laboratory) Math (Algebra II or Precalculus) Language (third or fourth year) History (U.S. or European) Electives	*October:* PSAT *January/March/May:* SAT I *May/June:* SAT Subject Tests in Physics, Math Level 1 or 2, Language, U.S. History

12	Advanced English	*Oct/Dec:* SAT
	Advanced Science	*Nov/Dec/Jan:* ·
	Math (Precalculus or	SAT Subject Tests in Literature,
	Calculus or Statistics)	Math Level 2, Science, Foreign
	Language (fourth or fifth year)	Language
	Advanced History	
	Electives (Computer Science or	
	Economics or Political Science	
	or Music or Art History)	

Rules of Thumb for Subject Tests

1. Most colleges do not require specific Subject Tests, though some programs, such as engineering and international relations, might.

2. If a college requires two or three Subject Tests, they should be in areas reflecting your strengths and college intentions: e.g., science for engineering or premedical students; history or foreign language for prelaw, political science, or foreign-language majors; literature for English majors. Of course, if you can produce multiple strong tests in areas inside and outside your major areas of interest, you will be an even more attractive and balanced applicant.

3. If you are not certain of your future field of study, take a Subject Test in a terminal course, such as United States History or Physics, a subject not continued in the senior year.

4. If you plan to take advanced-level courses in your senior year, you can leave the Subject Test until then.

5. For twelfth grade courses: If you have followed the suggested program the first three years, you should be able to emphasize your particular areas of talent and interest beyond English, mathematics, and language. Take Advanced Placement courses, if available in your school, in those subjects in which you have excelled. Take SAT Subject Tests during the fall in those subjects that you have continued into your last year of high school. Be prepared to take not only Advanced Placement

exams, but also SAT Subject Tests in May and June of senior year, in order to gain college course placement and credit.

Your teachers and your counselor can help you decide how many of these tests you ought to take. But you must assume the responsibility for asking about and registering for the tests. This schedule is often followed by students who enroll in the Exceedingly Demanding colleges.

Tests are given on six scheduled Saturdays throughout the year, as specified in the College Board's registration information. Refer to their brochures and Web site to plan your schedule. The tests should always be taken as soon as possible after completing a course. You will see that the best time to take Subject Tests is June, after you have studied a subject for a full year. In your senior year you can take tests in November or December, or even January, if you need to complete your requirements.

Your Subject Test scores will usually correspond to your grades in those subjects. Should there be a discrepancy, a lower score than your grades would seem to warrant, you can repeat any Subject Test in an attempt to bring up your score. By the time you submit the three Subject Test scores that selective colleges require, you should have had good or excellent scores, in line with your SAT results, on three out of a possible eight or nine tests. Furthermore, if you have discovered an area of concentration in which you are strong, your Subject Test scores will reflect this academic commitment, an important consideration in being admitted to the Exceedingly or Very Demanding colleges. If such a program is not possible for you—if you are taking Subject Tests for the first time in your senior year, for example—you still can make them count heavily in your favor by taking them in your strongest subjects.

Preparing for a Subject Test is a matter of going over material in the course you have recently completed, bearing in mind the kinds of questions you will expect from taking practice tests, just as you did for the SAT. In fact, if you are able to take Subject Tests in your freshman and sophomore years, you will feel more comfortable about preparing for and taking the SAT; you will be a veteran. With this in mind, and given the *score choice* option, some students get on the bandwagon early, taking the science and Math Level 1 tests in their sophomore or even freshman years, just for practice.

Use the College Board's guides to taking the SAT Subject Tests, its *Real SAT* Subjects book, and other guides published by test prep groups to get ready for individual SAT Subjects. Take practice exams, go over practice questions, and examine the content of the material that the test is covering. Talk with your teacher if you think you need more focus in a particular area that was not emphasized in class. You should practice for any test early in the process, in order to allow time to work on any weaknesses the sample tests reveal. Plan your test schedules far enough ahead to allow you to prepare for each Subject Test. The best preparation is strong course work, of course, but you will want to take a practice test, review the course, and concentrate on any areas of uncertainty.

Tips on Taking Subject Tests

Like the SAT questions, Subject Test questions get harder toward the end of a section, with the exception of questions on reading passages and diagrams. This means that as the questions increase in difficulty, you will be slowed down. So read all the questions once, answer those you know, and do not get rattled if you cannot finish a section. Many students who have respectable Subject Test scores leave questions unanswered. The unanswered questions do not count against your score. As with the SAT, guessing is advisable if you can identify one wrong answer.

It's the reading passages and diagrams themselves that increase in difficulty, rather than the questions. The questions themselves are not presented in order of difficulty, so you may find the first question harder to answer than the last. All you can do is go through the questions and waste no time on those that completely baffle you; leave them unanswered.

Testing: Major Points to Remember

You will have to add SAT and SAT Subject Test preparation to your homework schedule. The challenge is to exercise self-discipline, for it is one thing to write an assigned paper for English class and quite another to assign yourself a book or magazine article to build vocabulary for your reading and writing SAT. One solution is to write brief periodic reports to teachers on the test preparation you undertake. Doing this has the effect of obliging you to do needed preparation and allowing a teacher to help you make the best use of your time.

The success of test prep courses or individual tutors lies in part in the discipline they impose on students by giving them workbooks and making them come regularly to tutoring sessions. You can prepare for tests by studying an extra half hour a day for a month prior to a test. Be sure to allow added time to take practice tests. This kind of schedule will make it unnecessary even to think of cramming, a practice you no doubt have been told is seldom fruitful.

Average SAT and ACT Scores

ACT (2008)

	Composite Score	English	Math	Reading	Science
Men	21.2	20.1	21.6	21.2	21.3
Women	21.0	21.0	20.4	21.5	20.4
All	21.1	20.6	21.0	21.4	20.8

SAT (2007)

	Critical Reading	Math	Writing
Men	504	533	489
Women	502	499	500
All	502	515	494

The ACT

The ACT assessment is an alternative to the SAT program. We will not debate the merits of each test here. Suffice it to say that each program has its strengths and weaknesses, as does standardized multiple choice testing in general. Every college in the U.S. accepts the ACT in lieu of the SAT, and sometimes as a substitute for both the SAT *and* SAT Subject Tests. That is, one can apply to an Exceedingly Demanding, Very Demanding, or Demanding College with *either* the SAT and two or three SAT Subjects, *or* the ACT, or, in some cases, a combination of the ACT and SAT Subjects.

The ACT consists of four distinct tests in English, mathematics, reading, and science as well as an optional writing test. The English test is a forty-five-minute, seventy-five-question multiple choice test covering written English punctuation, grammar, usage, and sentence structure, as well as "rhetorical skills"—strategy, organization, and style. It employs five prose passages followed by multiple choice questions. The questions cover content in six areas, under two main divisions. The usage/mechanics questions cover punctuation (13%), basic grammar and usage (16%), and sentence structure (24%). The rhetorical skills questions cover strategy (16%), organization (15%), and style (16%). Students receive three scores on the English test: a total score covering all seventy-five questions, a usage/mechanics subscore covering forty questions, and a rhetorical skills subscore covering thirty-five questions.

The mathematics test includes sixty multiple choice questions to be answered in sixty minutes. Students should bring calculators to answer questions in six content areas, under three subsections. The twenty-four pre-algebra/elementary algebra questions cover pre-algebra (23%) and elementary algebra (17%). The intermediate algebra/coordinate geometry subsection includes eighteen questions on intermediate algebra (15%) and coordinate geometry (15%). The eighteen plane geometry/trigonometry questions cover plane geometry (23%) and trigonometry (7%). Again, students receive a total test score based on all sixty mathematics questions, in addition to subscores on the three subsections.

THE RISE OF EARLY STANDARDIZED TESTING OPPORTUNITIES

We have already discussed the availability and desirability of taking the PSAT in tenth, or even ninth, grade, in advance of its "official" administration in eleventh grade. The ACT has long offered its PLAN program to help tenth graders assess their academic readiness and begin long-range planning for college and career. If the

PLAN is available to you, we encourage you to take it in the fall of sophomore year. If these tests aren't enough, and early enough for you, there are others you can consider. The ACT's EXPLORE program is offered to eighth and ninth graders to help them plan for high school courses and long-term college success. The College Board announced its ReadiStep program for eighth graders in fall 2008, designed to gauge student achievement in reading, writing, and math. For a long time, students have also taken the actual ACT or SAT for such talent-search programs as the Johns Hopkins Center for Talented Youth (CTY). We have our concerns about the overemphasis, stress, and overreliance on standardized testing in this country, to be sure. Nevertheless, we encourage students to take advantage of these various testing programs as ways to open up academic and other enrichment opportunities, to gauge skill levels related to high school and college success, and to identify gaps to work on during their high school years. Put into perspective, such tests can be useful tools.

The reading test consists of forty multiple choice questions on four prose passages that are allotted thirty-five minutes in total. The test questions are evenly divided among one passage each in social studies, natural sciences, prose fiction, and humanities. This test concentrates on students' reading comprehension and analytical skills. Students receive a total test score on the forty questions, and two subscores, one in social sciences/sciences reading skills covering the twenty social studies and natural sciences questions, and one in arts/literature reading skills covering the twenty prose fiction and humanities questions.

Finally, the science test has forty multiple choice questions to be answered in thirty-five minutes. This test, according to ACT, "measures the interpretation, analysis, evaluation, reasoning, and problem-solving skills required in the natural sciences." Biology, chemistry, earth and space sciences, and physics are covered. This science test is the major difference between the ACT and the SAT, which has no such science section. The ACT science test offers seven sets of scientific information, each in one of three formats: data representation, such as graphs and tables (38%); research summaries (45%); and conflicting viewpoints (17%). Students receive only a total test score based on all of the science questions.

For us, the optional ACT writing test is optional in name only. If you are planning to submit the ACT to a selective college, you should take the writing test just in case. This test is quite similar to the SAT writing section, and if you have prepared for that, you should be in good shape. The ACT writing test lasts thirty minutes and consists of one essay response to a prompt. It is scored on a 12-point scale.

When you see ACT scores reported, they are on a scale from a low of 1 to a high of 36. The composite score is arrived at by converting the raw score for each of the four tests to the 36-point scale, and then averaging the four scaled scores. A composite score of 30, for example, is at the ninety-sixth percentile of all test-takers.

If you attend a high school where most students take the ACT as a matter of course, then by all means you should begin your testing program with the ACT. Just as with the SATs, you can conduct a self-assessment and comparison with the published scores of selective colleges to determine whether your ACT scores are within average ranges of different schools. You may decide that you would like to try the SAT at least once, and that you may be able to put together a more impressive testing portfolio by taking SAT Subject Tests in those areas of personal strength. The good news is that the ACT is universally accepted, so that if you are in an area where the ACT is the more familiar testing program, you will not be at a disadvantage in applying to selective colleges. As always, review the requirements and recommendations of each individual college to determine which tests are preferable for you.

SHOULD YOU TAKE THE ACT INSTEAD OF THE SAT? DOES IT MATTER?

Yes, the ACT test is an alternative to both types of SAT tests, and the ACT is accepted by competitive colleges. While students on the East and West coasts generally take the SAT on a regular basis, many students in the Midwest and South more often encounter the ACT. Colleges that accept the ACT assert that they view it identically to the SATs, and they are able to compare scores on each test, even though they are on different scales. Testing experts continue to debate the merits and fairness both of standardized testing in general, and of differences between the SAT and ACT in particular.

Some students find the ACT easier than the SAT, noting the ACT is a more substance-oriented test. This changed to some degree when the SAT dropped analogies and added writing and higher-level math to the test. We generally recommend staying with either the SAT or ACT program, although there is little harm in taking both as a trial, as long as this is not too much of a diversion from classes or from continuing to build up a strong SAT profile. A student may take both the SATs and the ACT, and then not submit the weaker set of scores. We do find some students just do better on one or the other of the ACT or SAT.

We should note that competitive schools may wonder why a student in a particularly strong Eastern public or private school has chosen to take the ACT when the SAT combination is the more common path. Additionally, the SAT Subject Tests offer a student the opportunity to show mastery of content in a variety of subject areas. Some elite colleges continue to require Subject Tests in addition to the SAT or ACT (e.g., Dartmouth), while others do not (e.g., Yale). In evaluating the ACT and SAT, students should examine the different test books and take evaluatory practice tests to see whether they are producing significantly different scores with either program. Look to the college guidebooks and individual schools' literature to compare average SAT and ACT scores. Most of all, consider which test or combination of tests will allow you to present your strongest profile to colleges.

Step Four Checklist

✓Think of standardized tests like the SAT as opportunities in the admissions process.

✓Consider a program of self-teaching, coaching, or tutoring to improve your scores.

✓Read the College Board's and ACT's own test guides, and review them in preparing to take the tests.

✓Take the practice tests the College Board and ACT provide.

✓Find other test preparation information and materials on the Web, at the library, and at bookstores.

✓If possible, begin taking SAT Subject Tests in your freshman year.

✓Take a Subject Test as soon as possible after finishing a course in the subject of the test.

✓Consider the ACT as an alternative to the SAT, particularly if you are having trouble with the SAT or if students in your school tend to take the ACT.

STEP FIVE:

Excel Outside Class]

Excellence as an Admissions Factor

Most applicants to any selective college are "average in their excellence"—that is, they excel above most of their classmates academically, but when considered in a group none necessarily excels over another. How, then, will *you* stand out from other qualified applicants within the selective college pool?

Admissions committees look to candidates' nonacademic qualifications to distinguish the students who will add high-caliber diversity to their first-year classes.

Denise, for example, was a junior at a large suburban New York high school, where she was achieving A and B grades in a solid Regents curriculum. She was not in the most advanced courses possible, and felt that she did not have one great talent that colleges would be looking for. She was going to be captain of her varsity tennis team, but would not be a competitive athletic recruit. She was not class president, but saw herself as "an extremely outgoing, social, humorous person." We saw Denise as a "people person" whose friends were extremely important to her, and who was very socially aware and perceptive. "I love to write, especially creative writing," Denise told us. And we noted that she was a reporter for the newspaper, a peer counselor, and had her own columns published already. "What do you mean you don't have a special talent?" we asked her. Denise's mother agreed. "She is a gifted writer and shows real creative promise," she had told us. "Denise's greatest achievement has been her ability to connect with people from different backgrounds and abilities."

We encouraged Denise to see her perceptiveness and her writing as real and identifiable skills, and to do more in these areas, which she clearly enjoyed and excelled in. We suggested an advanced course load for senior year, stretching in those areas that fit with these strengths, including AP English, AP Studio Art, and AP Government or Psychology. We then talked about possible outside activities, internships, and programs that would allow Denise to shine. She pursued more involvement with the school newspaper, began writing more creatively on her own and with the guidance of her English teacher, and sought outside involvements. During the summer, she attended a writing program at Barnard College. She started winning awards, including a New England Young Writers Conference Award and a Scholastic Press Award. Her confidence increased dramatically, and Denise was writing like never before. For the fall, she secured an internship with the *New York Times,* which began publishing a bimonthly high school magazine as venture with Scholastic Press. Denise brought up her SAT reading and writing scores into the high 600s and pursued every writing and publishing opportunity she could find.

As Denise continued to look at specific colleges, she now had a real focus to her search. Strong writing and communications programs were key for her, and we encouraged her to expand her list geographically to include some of the excellent middle-sized universities around the country, such as Washington University in St. Louis, Vanderbilt, Emory, Northwestern, and Tulane. Denise visited these colleges early in her search process, which required advance planning and commitment of time during her junior summer. Through a good self-assessment and through feedback from us, Denise decided that Northwestern and Emory were her first two choices, but that Northwestern might be too much of a stretch, given her SATs. Denise carefully evaluated Emory, wrote essays discussing her passion for writing, included samples of her written work and a list of her awards and involvements, applied for Early Decision, and was accepted.

Without her pursuit and discussion of writing, Denise would have been a good but not likely admissions prospect for Emory. Her presentation of her sincere interest and participation in this area distinguished her from hundreds of applicants with similar academic profiles.

In the long run, most students will finish academic work in college or graduate school and spend the rest of their lives in some kind of useful service in the professions, business, government, the arts, the media, education, or information technology. Every selective college, with its strong body of alumni, takes enormous pride in training the men and women whose responsible leadership makes the world work. Admissions committees look for applicants whose excellence reflects an inner need to use their personal strengths, energies, and talents for a socially useful purpose.

The Spiritual Qualities of Excellence

The ways in which you excel embody your personal sense of who you are. You excel in ways no one else can. Your interests guide your choice of activities, and your personal convictions and qualities inspire and enrich your performance. No book can tell you how or in what to excel—but we *can* help you identify and emphasize your particular areas of excellence. And we urge you, above all, to listen to your own inner voice that inspires your unique capabilities, be they athletic, artistic, intellectual, political, social, or charitable. We have heard again and again from admissions committees that they look for students with a passionate commitment to one or several interests, not for candidates who have many minor activities without a deeply held conviction about any of them. Pursue your passions.

In working with thousands of students, we have observed (and admissions officers confirm this) that those who excel at any activity exhibit four qualities. If you recognize these traits in yourself, you can be sure that selective colleges will spot them, too:

A willingness to compete with yourself as well as with others. You ask more of yourself, striving to better your performance. You wrestle with the devil in you that would persuade you to take it easy. After Charles Lindbergh flew the Atlantic in 1927, he wrote a book called simply *We*, referring to himself and his plane, the *Spirit of St. Louis*. But there was another person that he recognized as part of himself. One person was the determined pilot who wanted to be the first to make a solo flight from New York to Paris. The other was the demanding physical self that urged him to sleep—and probably crash into the ocean. Quite consciously he fought off this threatening demon to keep flying for thirty-seven hours, and to become a world hero symbolic of the adventurous spirit. Of course, you need to sleep, but you also need to push yourself and test your perceived limits.

A positive outlook on life, with less tendency than others have to use drugs and alcohol. A jovial, extroverted manner does not necessarily reflect a positive outlook. You may be the strong, silent type like Lindbergh. Your positive outlook embodies a healthy optimism and a confidence that reassures those around you. Your competitive spirit inspires even your opponents, who trust your honest striving. You rely for stimulus on your innate optimism rather than on substances.

Good organization in use of time and study habits. You have learned that there is time for everything as long as you are aware of what must be done. You do the important thing first, and the trivial things take care of themselves instead of eating into the study hour. You get enough sleep, you have added energy as a result, and you get things done more efficiently.

A concern for others, which often earns you the role of leader. You have been praised for your personal qualities at home and in school, and so you respond warmly and genuinely to others. Your self-confidence and capability inspire people to have confidence in you and to seek you out to fill leadership roles.

Nonacademic Excellence as an Admissions Factor

Selective colleges seek real students, of course, not paragons. What will admissions committees look for as indicators of excellence in your nonacademic record?

Naturally, it helps if you are captain of an athletic team, president of your class, valedictorian, editor of the school paper, or head of the dramatic or debate club. Colleges often proudly list statistics about the numbers of these individuals in every first-year class.

DIVERSE EXAMPLES OF INDIVIDUAL EXCELLENCE
FROM GRINNELL'S FIRST-YEAR CLASS PROFILE

Selective colleges love to brag about the amazing individual students they have enrolled, and their statistics can give you some idea about the interests of your potential classmates. You can also see the many different ways in which you can stand out. Here is an example from a top small liberal arts college:

According to Grinnell College in Iowa, one 390-member first-year class included:

- 206 National Honor Society members
- 129 musicians (24 different instruments)
- 102 involved in drama/theater (4 club presidents)
- 83 community service tutors
- 69 members of wildlife/environmental clubs (3 presidents)
- 67 athletic captains
- 66 members of debate, forensics, or mock trial teams (6 captains)
- 50 peer helpers
- 49 workers in homeless shelters
- 33 National Merit Scholars
- 31 valedictorians
- 29 hospital volunteers
- 23 Scouts (7 Eagle, 2 Gold, 1 Life)
- 20 student council/government presidents
- 15 high school newspaper editors
- 15 literary magazine editors
- 11 All-State vocalists
- 11 state academic team/decathlon champions (2 world competitors)
- 8 yearbook editors
- 4 All-State athletes
- 2 licensed pilots
- 1 belly dancer

However, while it helps to be number one in some activity, this is not essential for admission. Selective colleges also regularly list the number of valedictorians whom they reject. Yet selective colleges would not be able to fill their freshman classes if they restricted admission to football captains, class presidents, and presidents of the National Honor Society. You, too, will be an attractive candidate if, like Denise, you have shown commitment in some activity and have been recognized for excellence in and out of school. Even if you happen to be a star, you will be competing against others like yourself—athletes, editors, dancers, community leaders. *Your* excellence must stand out.

Admissions officials look for three essential characteristics in your nonacademic performance: commitment, development, and recognition.

Commitment

You know the student who gets involved in so many activities that you cannot keep track of what he or she is doing. But a whirl of activities does not impress selective admissions directors. They are looking for maturity, which takes the form of sticking to a few things to show positive results.

Gene, for example, swam a lot. He was always in the water. He swam on the varsity team in his small, rural New York high school. He competed in the American Athletic Union's national swimming program. He was named All-State. Gene was not an Olympic-class swimmer, and he wanted to be a novelist. Duke accepted him on Early Decision in part because he would fit into their swimming program, but also because they appreciated his single-mindedness that they thought might someday bring America a new literary voice.

Alice, in a suburban Saint Paul high school, was on the cross-country ski team, but she also had to earn money for college. Instead of taking the first minimum-wage job she could find at a supermarket or fast-food outlet, she canvassed her community for some opportunity to use her decorating talents. She approached a handsome store that sold inexpensive home furnishings, including wooden racks, occasional tables, folding chairs, and simple plastic containers in tasteful colors, and offered to join the sales staff as a decorating consultant, helping people pick items that would work well with their existing furniture, wall colors, rugs, and curtains. She made more than the minimum wage and on occasion was asked to visit homes and develop decorating plans. Her skill and experience made her a semiprofessional decorator at the age of seventeen.

Walter played football for his rural Vermont high school, but had no winter sport except recreational skiing. Knowing the basketball players, he heard them complain about lack of team support. For the last two years of high school, he became the team mascot, wearing a bird costume to represent an eagle. A rather shy person, Walter found that concealed as a bird, he lost all inhibitions, and he became such a hilarious figure on the sidelines that crowds came to watch him. His pep rallies in town brought new fans to the school, and for the last two seasons, the basketball team won more games than it lost. Walter was considered a factor in this success.

You have been urged to take risks academically by stretching, going for the more demanding courses, doing the extra paper, and generally going beyond the minimum asked of you. Nonacademic commitment calls for the same kind of stretching, risk taking, and sacrifice of time and energy.

Noelle was on her school ski team in Colorado. But she also joined a group of super-skiers who were being rigorously trained in a program for national competition. Every day she found herself skiing with far superior skiers, some of them boastful and quick to put her down. Because she was among the weaker skiers, her time for the slalom run was among the slowest, and she was forced to ski with the last skiers. Her runs were made after the course was worn and icy, a catch-22 situation—weak skier, forced to accept the worst conditions; good skier, great conditions, improved technique. But Noelle got points for trying and gradually moved up to the middle of the group. She knew she was not of Olympic caliber, but she was determined to ski as well as her limitations permitted. Admissions committees love this kind of commitment.

One word of caution: We do urge students not to commit themselves to any activity only for the purpose of getting into college. If you feel you have not involved yourself sufficiently in one or two activities, make the commitment to do something you like to do, something you know will be useful to others as well as to yourself. It may be that taking a part in the senior play will give you a better chance of getting into Oberlin, but what will this mean to the drama coach and the rest of the cast?

They want you to be part of their joint effort of putting on a good play. That's the commitment they expect. And so do the colleges.

Development

Nonacademic activities should change your capacities or outlook. Even a menial job requiring no skill can develop in you good habits such as punctuality, careful work, and a cheerful manner with your associates and your supervisor.

Development usually occurs more quickly when you set goals. Agnes wanted to give up her piano lessons after six months. They bored her. But her teacher said, "It's because you don't think you're improving, and that's true. I'll make a deal with you. If you'll practice this Haydn minuet for one hour every day for a week and you don't play it any better, I'll give you up as a pupil."

Stung, Agnes grudgingly said, "Oh, all right." But inside she was saying, "I'll show her." After a week she played the little dance without a mistake, and the teacher said, "I'm sorry, Agnes, I can't give you up yet. You seem to be improving. Now do the same thing with this Mozart sonata." Agnes continued her lessons and eventually played in school recitals. We are mentioning less conventional activities outside class, because you know already what it takes to develop yourself in sports, journalism, theater arts, or class government. Colleges do not ask that you do anything in particular with your nonacademic time, but they expect you to do something that pays off in ways that you can measure and describe, such as:

- Specializing as a camp counselor in safety and lifesaving, then working as a safety volunteer in your community, or getting involved with the EMT or paramedic squad.
- Assisting the local tennis or golf pro in summer to qualify to give lessons while in college to help pay your tuition.
- Working for the local paper or radio or TV station as an intern or apprentice in order to become a campus reporter for a metropolitan paper or radio or TV news service.
- Starting a part-time catering service with a plan to offer the same service for faculty receptions.

- Volunteering in political campaigns to learn how to organize voters on a college campus.
- Building Web sites for local families, companies, or schools, in order to improve your computer science, information technology, and consulting skills for later use in your college major and career.
- Tutoring kids in your local middle and elementary schools, and becoming a camp counselor, to gain more experience for your college major in education and eventual career as a teacher.

All such activities show development, and this attribute will catch an admissions committee's attention. Again, your goal should be development of a skill or some personal quality, not just college admission!

Recognition

When they evaluate your achievements, admissions committees rely on the recognition you have received. Keep all tangible evidence of your accomplishments, from certificates for perfect attendance to the paddle you won at camp. Save newspaper clippings describing your participation in community events, and consider these as possible items to be mentioned in your college applications or to be sent to the colleges as exhibits.

Seek recognition for your contribution if none seems forthcoming. Isabel worked in the paraplegic ward of a veterans' hospital in Indiana all summer between her junior and senior years of high school. She was warmly thanked, the men gave her flowers, and all signed a card. When she filed her college applications, she requested a letter from the doctor in charge of the ward, describing how much her work had meant to the veterans. This letter accompanied her applications and substantiated her one-line description of this valuable public service work.

When you complete an internship, employment, or volunteer experience, it is more than appropriate to ask your supervisor for a letter of reference describing your involvement and contributions. Almost always, you will be furnished with a supportive recommendation thanking you for your work. Keep these letters in your admissions file, and continue to update your list of honors, awards, recognitions, activities, and work experiences.

Areas of Nonacademic Excellence

In contrast to the detailed academic requisites for admission, selective colleges' standards for nonacademic achievement are expressed vaguely. As exemplified by many of the comments of admissions officers in *The Hidden Ivies,* selective colleges are indeed looking for that extra something that defines a student's commitment, development, and recognition: their passion.

What is clear is that selective college admissions offices are looking for something more than just strong academic preparation. From Pomona's catalogue: "Pomona College admits a freshman class representing a broad range of interests, viewpoints, talents, and backgrounds. . . . Special talents or experiences in science, music, drama, art, journalism, athletics, community service, and other fields, as well as evidence of originality, energy, motivation, and leadership potential, are also considered in the admissions process."

And from Princeton's: "The Admissions Office staff seeks to identify those candidates who seem best qualified to take advantage of Princeton's academic programs and to select from among them those who will form an undergraduate body with a wide representation of interests, backgrounds, and special abilities. The Admissions Office staff considers each applicant individually. Those candidates who apply for admission to Princeton should have demonstrated significant academic potential, as well as strength of character and maturity, and show promise of making some contribution to the life of the University."

By intention, selective colleges leave enormous latitude for accepting a variety of meaningful activities as measures of a candidate's initiative and commitment.

Varsity Sports

A good athlete, as you know, will be considered for admission separately in the admissions committee's athletic round. You can discover whether you qualify for the athletic round of a selective college simply by asking your coach, the admissions office, and the coaches of the colleges. In many cases athletes know from letters of solicitation before they are seniors that their talents are valued by a number of colleges. The more selective colleges do not "recruit" athletes as do colleges whose teams act as farm clubs for professional leagues, although there is certainly variance in this respect among such selective colleges as Duke, the University of North Carolina, Williams, and Brown.

"We don't do recruiting in the Ivy League," former Dartmouth basketball coach Gary Walters once told us in an interview. "Student enrollment work is the euphemism we use."

Athletes give the place a tone, a Harvard dean used to say. A tone of vigor, grace, and physical control. Remember that Harvard, so often first in events, built America's first football stadium back in 1900. No longer national football powers, the Ivies have abandoned what has been called their "mucker pose," which put athletes above scholars. Today many faculty members are former athletes. Before he became president of Harvard, Derek Bok had played varsity basketball for Stanford; William Bowen, Princeton's former president, was a state tennis champion in Ohio.

If you are among the athletes destined to play varsity sports in college, you must also have a respectable academic record for admissions. In a selective college you will be a so-called scholar-athlete, even though you may never have thought of yourself as a scholar. You will be carrying a heavy academic schedule. Should you be the object of desire of two or more Exceedingly Demanding or Very Demanding colleges, you will need the help of your coach and counselor in making decisions about the applications you will file. You should apply to several colleges and anticipate the possibility of not being admitted to one that has urged you to apply. Coaches cannot admit anyone. They can only plead for some applicants, and they never get all they ask for from admissions committees. So play it safe, look after your own interests, and remember that you can get burned. Take every promise from a college coach with a big grain of salt, and have a broad list of colleges to which you can apply. Coaches may try to convince you to commit to an Early Decision round-one or -two application, and you should evaluate this option for yourself carefully before making such a commitment.

As you go through the admissions process, you, the athlete, will have a few more responsibilities than the non-athlete. You will need to register with the NCAA (www.ncaa.org) and review their requirements for academic standards and recruiting procedures. You will need to contact coaches at colleges in which you are interested, presenting them with a cover letter, résumé, and perhaps films (see Step Eight).

You will need to gain an understanding of the differences between Division I athletic teams, which are more competitive, and Division III teams, which are less competitive, offer fewer scholarships, and do not recruit as heavily. You will need to decide which level is realistic for you to aim for, and which you prefer in terms of your athletic commitment. You will need to decide if athletic scholarships are important to you (see Step Nine), and you may need to make a choice if you are a multi-sport athlete about which sport you would like to continue in college.

Many a high school star, however, is destined to try out for varsity sports in college, only to be cut from the squad: a cruel blow, but not fatal. Selective colleges have wonderful intramural sports, and you may take up a new sport in college—squash, rowing, boxing, the marathon, cycling, or rugby. Your excellence and drive will find a new outlet. One undergraduate organized a horse-jumping team at Princeton. You may start you own water polo, surfing, or ultimate Frisbee club, for all we know. The admissions office will not be surprised.

We like to recommend that athletes take the "freshman stairs test" when they are considering their college choices. Think about being accepted to a college you are considering, perhaps as an Early Decision choice. Imagine your arrival on campus the first week of school. You are unpacking, emptying your bags on your bed. Down the stairs you go, carrying an empty box for the Dumpster. But your new roommate has left a pile of books on the landing, which you don't notice until it is too late. You trip, you slide, you break your leg. It looks as though you won't be on the team this year. Do you still want to be where you are?

UNDERSTANDING THE ATHLETIC ROUND

The athletic round is simply a session in which the admissions committee considers the applications of good athletes separately from other applications. This, of course, means that very good athletes with reasonably good academic records are strong candidates. But they are competing among themselves and so in the athletic round there are both admissions and rejections.

Frank Leana, author of *Getting into College*, warns parents and applicants to beware of the promise of admission by a coach. "A college coach does not make the final decision to admit or deny. Only an admissions committee makes that decision," he says.

No coaches are present in the athletic round, ever, though they may have talked to admissions personnel urging acceptance of certain athletic applicants. Athletes should talk to coaches at schools they are thinking of applying to, to find out what might happen if they're admitted. Most coaches will tell you what they're looking for. "We need no more goalies. Sorry." Or, "Yes, we could use a good point guard. I hope you'll apply. I'll put in a good word for you." If you're rejected, don't blame the coach. He had nothing to do with it.

WOMEN ATHLETES

The picture of padded women playing ice hockey, or sports bra– clad women soccer players celebrating after a goal, is no longer out of the ordinary, especially after the successes of the U.S. women's ice hockey and soccer teams at the Olympics and World Cup. These teams were both driven by female athletes with selective college connections.

Selective colleges have extended most athletic activities to include sports for women. Women athletes are included in the athletic round of admissions, and an outstanding woman athlete has greatly enhanced chances of admission.

Sports participation outside school, such as equestrianism, golf, or sailing, should be included in admissions applications. Comments by instructors and news reports of honors won will reinforce an impression of an active candidate.

Due in large part to the increasing enforcement of Title IX, a federal law demanding equity in athletic opportunities for female athletes at all levels (see Step Nine for more on Title IX and scholarships), women's sports programs at the college level (and in high school) have been growing at a fantastic rate. More women are playing competitive sports from grade school through high school, and more are going on to play varsity sports in college.

Because of the parity rules, colleges must provide comparable funds and sports for female athletes. Now, women do not play big-time football, and men do. Imagine the resources in terms of money and numbers of athletes required to keep a men's football program running. To achieve parity, colleges must fund and fill spots for large numbers of women on many different teams. Some of the sports that women are being recruited for and excelling at include both traditionally male sports, such as ice hockey, soccer, and lacrosse, and the more traditional women's or co-ed sports (at least in the U.S.) of field hockey, horseback riding, sailing, golf, squash, tennis, basketball, cross-country running, track and field, crew, fencing, skiing, softball, swimming, and volleyball.

Non-Varsity Sports

The high school athlete who will not play on a varsity team will not be considered in the athletic round. Nonetheless, your athletic accomplishments will be a strong consideration in your factor as a representation of nonacademic excellence. Most admissions officers are athletes, though not necessarily of varsity caliber, either. "When admissions officers get together, they seem to wind up talking about sports," a Middlebury admissions officer told us. They love athletes, because from experience they know that athletes have the drive and optimism that will carry them to the top in many other things they do. The selective colleges have strong athletic programs and amazing facilities, which they want to see put to good use.

Extracurricular Activities

There are no special rounds in admissions for editors, class presidents, band leaders, debate captains, Amnesty International organizers, or even concert pianists. In the search for diversity, admissions committees consider each applicant on his or her merits. The more intense your commitment, the more outstanding your achievement, the more it will help you. But just as the athlete must apply to several colleges, so must the future editor of the *New York Times* (though if it were possible to identify this student, there would be competition among the top colleges to enroll him or her).

However you have excelled, you can anticipate competition from other applicants. But some college will prove to be the one that particularly appreciates you. Your excellence will be recognized and welcomed as an addition to a diverse first-year class. It is the right approach to excel at the one or more activities you truly enjoy, and then to apply to colleges that seem to fit your academic and extracurricular interests. It is the wrong approach to try to fit your activities to your perception of what one or more colleges are looking for. You should identify colleges that offer you good opportunities to pursue your interests, colleges that seek applicants who will take advantage of their programs.

Savor your extracurricular passions, whatever they are, and take them to the next level. In your presentation to the colleges (Step Eight), you will showcase your strengths and celebrate your individuality.

Community Service and Employment

Almost every student is involved in some kind of volunteer service or work. Take a look at any college application, including the Common Application as an example, and you will see sections designed to allow you, the applicant, to detail how you have spent your time: academic honors, awards and recognition; extracurricular, personal, and volunteer activities; summer activities; work experience. You are asked to *prioritize* your lists, and to note how many hours per week and how many weeks per year you are engaged in these activities. You may attach an additional résumé to provide more information on special talents. There is also a short essay topic that asks you to talk about the most meaningful of the involvements you have listed.

It is important to remember that you do not need to fill in every space in this part of the application. There are only so many hours in a week, and you cannot successfully balance a part-time job, fifteen hours of community service, club leadership, and being a varsity captain (and get some sleep, and do well in your courses, and not get sick within a few months . . .). Just because there are multiple sections and spaces in an application does not mean you will be an unsuccessful applicant if you leave something blank. If you have not worked a lot, what have you done with your time? If you have had a job, and that has prevented you from being a star athlete or an active school club member, what have you learned from your work experience? If you have been on a traveling state soccer team, or a competitive YMCA swim team in addition to your varsity participation in school, and you have attended summer athletic camps, and have actively trained in the off-season, what has this meant in your life? Colleges will understand that you could not also have done several other activities well, without compromising your academic work, your personal and family life, and your success in your key area of interest.

VOLUNTEER SERVICE AT WASHINGTON UNIVERSITY IN ST. LOUIS

Both urban and rural schools actively encourage community service, and urban schools have become particularly interested in fostering student engagement in their city surroundings. Washington University is thrilled that over two-thirds of its undergraduate student body participates in volunteer activities and community service. The university boasts the largest university branch of the YMCA/YWCA in the country. The Campus Y, located right next to the Student Center, hosts some twenty-five different programs in which students can participate, including working with children, improving the environment, and helping the disabled. According to the university 57% of WU students participate in community service at some time during college, and 24% do so all four years.

Examples of service and employment activities that are less directly related to school and that applicants present to colleges include 4-H Club membership, religious organization involvement such as Emmaus, Bible study, or Temple Youth; nursing home work, carpenter's apprenticing, secondhand car salesmanship, scouting, bank teller jobs, camp counseling, volunteer firefighting or EMT duty, auxiliary police duty, Web site maintenance, sailing instructing, fund-raising, political campaign management, school representation at town meeting, being an extra in the opera or theater, breeding dogs or horses. Anything you do with enthusiasm on a sustained basis is worth bringing to the attention of an admissions committee.

Routine jobs such as pumping gas, waiting on tables, washing cars, or delivering pizza may show a willingness to work, but such activities by themselves do not demonstrate excellence. Rising in a job, even a notch, shows competence. Otherwise, it would be wise to explain why you chose to spend many hours earning a minimum wage—because you needed the money, because you were earning it for college, because your family owned a restaurant and needed your help in the kitchen, because you like fixing cars and want to be an engineer, or because you are handy with computers and working for a tech company seemed a perfect match. You will note that in some college applications, you are even asked to discuss what you did with your earnings.

Evaluating Your Areas of Excellence

Recognizing your particular excellence carries Step Two—Determine Your Strengths—to another level of exactitude. You are positioning yourself to make more rational choices of colleges you would like to visit, colleges where you think you have some chances of admission.

For college admissions you will be presenting a "snapshot" of your particular areas of excellence. As we have said, admissions committees want well-rounded classes more than they want well-rounded students. Some call the desirable students of today "angular" to emphasize this distinction. Ask yourself these questions and answer them in your notebook:

- What is my most outstanding achievement outside class?
- How can I best call attention to this in my applications?
- How would I rate this achievement: excellent, good, fair?
- How does my excellence match with campus activities at particular colleges [to help identify institutions that will be especially appreciative of what you do]?

In athletics your rating is often determined for you by the competition. If you are your track team's second-fastest runner of the mile, you know where you stand, and you are able to quickly determine how your times compare to those of runners at different colleges. Other sports, such as soccer and lacrosse, are more difficult to comparatively evaluate than those with fixed times or distances, such as swimming, cross-country, and the javelin toss, because of the different school and league competition levels. Your coach and college coaches will have to help you to determine your ability relative to that of athletes from other regions.

Other activities may have to be rated on the basis of what your teachers, counselors, and/or peers say of your performance. Likewise, your rating of an activity outside school may require a statement from a supervisor or someone you work with, such as the head of a camp or the Red Cross director. Again, colleges want students who will participate in their programs and use their wonderful facilities.

You need not show these evaluations to anyone immediately. Think about them, revise them, then test them with your counselor or your parents. It may be that you underestimate yourself. Your counselor may ask, "Why not mention your chess?" It never occurred to you. Or your counselor may say, "I don't think sewing is going to carry much weight," if you have mentioned routine mending. But knitting sweaters with your own original patterns is worth mentioning on an application. One admissions officer opened a package from an applicant to find a quilt, all the more remarkable since the applicant was male.

GROWTH IN COMMUNITY SERVICE

Community service, or public service, or volunteering has become increasingly prevalent, popular, and important today. Many high schools have requirements for community service that specify a minimum level of student involvement during the high school career. Many colleges have begun to institute such requirements, and to tout the benefits of their service learning, volunteer action, and internship programs.

We encourage students to engage in community service, because it is good for them and for others. Colleges admire service involvement, but not if it is hollow, forced, or to the detriment of academic success. Colleges look for service leaders, students who truly are passionate about giving back to others, and whose record shows a committed pattern of service-related activities over time. Some of the service/adventure programs are wonderful growing and exploring experiences, but students should not see these as things to do because they look good for college. If you have the opportunity to go to Costa Rica, speak Spanish, explore the rain forests, and help a local community there, then go for it! However, do so because you are excited about this experience, and do not feel that this is a substitute for, or better than, getting involved at home.

As we have told many students and families, you do not need to go to Central America or India to help people. There are many volunteer opportunities and needs right in your own backyard, wherever you live. Some organizations with lots of connections and possibilities: the American Red Cross, Americares, Greenpeace, Habitat for Humanity, the Salvation Army, the Sierra Club, and Teach for America. Two research sources you may wish to consult are *Peterson's Guides to Summer Opportunities for Kids and Teenagers,* and *Peterson's Internships.*

In Step One—Know the Selective Colleges and Their Admissions Requirements and Procedures—and Step Six—Make the Most of Campus Visits and Interviews—you will discover how your own areas of excellence correspond to campus opportunities and to the character of different institutions. Continue to reflect on your activities outside of class and to refine the evaluation of your performance. You are learning to know where you stand in relation to others, and if you do not stand as tall in your own esteem as you would like to, then STRETCH.

Step Five Checklist

✓Remember that being number one academically is not essential to excellence. Concentrate on excelling in your own fashion.

✓Identify the nonacademic areas in which you demonstrate the three characteristics of excellence: commitment, development, and recognition from others.

✓Stretch yourself to excel in a few nonacademic activities. Even routine jobs are opportunities to commit yourself, show development, and receive recognition.

✓Pursue your extracurricular passion as far as you can take it.

✓Get references from employers, supervisors, and those for whom you have volunteered. Keep track of recognition you have received for your work, service, or activities.

STEP SIX:
Make the Most of Campus Visits and Interviews

Looking Under the Hood

Although "virtual tours" online, guide services, and a decreased emphasis on formal interviews have changed the ways in which students learn about colleges, visiting campuses remains an important tradition among applicants for admission. And in spite of the changes just mentioned, it still is a pleasant ritual. Both colleges and secondary schools look on a campus visit as an opportunity for enlarging a candidate's understanding of what four years of university training can be like. A few hours spent touring the campus and gathering random impressions is mere tire kicking. The potential candidate should also look under the hood. For an understanding of the unique character of each college visited, a day ought to be devoted to each of those that deeply interest you. If possible, you ought to spend one night in a dorm.

Philip Smith, a former dean of admissions at Williams, once suggested that students should subject each college to the 10:30 test. You stay overnight and observe what happens after 10:30 P.M. on a weeknight, when students drift out of the library or begin closing their textbooks in their dorms. Is there obsessive studying until 2:00 A.M.? Are students playing beer-can hockey or discussing politics? Is there much drinking? How does the atmosphere suit your own tastes, and could you get your work done and survive socially?

Campus visits can have a powerful influence on your motivation. When you are told that your academic performance does not stand out enough to make you a strong candidate, you may determine in your senior year to make an all-out effort to exceed your past performance in class. You may become so enamored of a college and its campus that you say to yourself, "This is the place. Now, what do I have to do to get there?"

Your Turn to Choose

All through the admissions process you are concerned about being admitted to a good college, which has the power to choose you from among a number of good applicants. Now the situation is reversed. You are the one who chooses to apply to one college and not to another. Yes, even as the numbers of applicants rise, the most selective colleges want more good applicants. The colleges lose to other colleges over half the applicants they admit, so they are anxious to impress you on your campus visit. They are the sellers; you are the buyer.

Again and again we have been impressed by the stories of students who, upon visiting a particular college, were able to see themselves there as a student, or were able to determine that they did not feel comfortable in that place. The initial and succeeding visits to a top-choice college serve to establish and confirm reactions, and first impressions are, right or not, often indelible.

When asked why they chose their college, current students often think back to their first hours on campus as a high school junior or senior. "I immediately felt at home there," they say. Or, "Everyone was so incredibly friendly." "The library was amazing," say others. "Everyone was clearly academically serious, but at the same time I felt very welcomed."

Take advantage of your being in the driver's seat at this time in your life to discover as much as you can on your campus visit. Test the claims made in brochures. See for yourself how good the library will be for your particular interest. Will you be able to talk to the great professors, or are they available only to seniors and graduate students? What sports programs will be open to you? Is the social atmosphere congenial to your personality?

All selective colleges are good for most of their students, but not all selective colleges will be good for you. You can likely survive, and even gain a good education, in almost any place. The question is, where will you be happiest, and most successful? A campus visit will provide the essential basis for your judgment when the time comes to fill out applications—and later when you must decide where to enroll. Take notes on each visit, using the College Visit Summary Sheet on page 233. Copies also appear in the Appendix.

Preparing for Campus Visits

Experience proves that campus visits are most productive if you will take the trouble to follow a few tested routines:

Before each visit, quickly review any notes you have made about the college in your notebook, so that you arrive on campus "briefed," as it were, and prepared to enlarge your knowledge and alter preconceptions about the place. Review the college's viewbook and browse its Web site.

Note any questions you have after your review and research. You may want to ask these of a tour guide, interviewer, or leader of a group information session.

From your long list of colleges you have considered, pick a reasonable number, eight to ten, that you can feasibly visit. Try to see some contrasting models or types of colleges, some larger, some smaller, some closer to a city, some more rural, and so on, to give yourself perspective.

You may want to see schools on your list which are farther from home first if you will not be able to get to them later in the year, or you may start close to home, and, if you are on the right track, see a select group of schools farther away during senior fall.

Work out a timetable so as to be prompt for tours or appointments. Study road maps and plane schedules; get directions from the college (these are often in the back of viewbooks or on the Web site).

Know where you will stay overnight. If you do not plan to stay in a dormitory, line up your lodging in advance to avoid anxiety en route. Colleges will usually have suggestions for local places to stay.

Dress appropriately. Show that you take the interview seriously. This means, for one thing, no sneakers and no T-shirts. You should look clean and well groomed. Males ought to wear jackets. Neckties are optional. On a hot day, if the interviewer is in shirt-sleeves, a male ap-plicant can take off his jacket. Females should avoid flamboyance—no glamorous makeup or attention-getting hairdos. In short, look natural and seek no "special effects" that will distract the interviewer. Admis-sions officers interview many students and, like most people, retain first impressions long after an interview. The impression you should leave is that of a self-confident young person who cares about appear-ance but does not strive to make a unique statement with a garment, hairstyle, makeup, or an accessory. You can have style, but be sensitive to the fact that this is a professional meeting. You should not wear a baseball cap or sunglasses, and if your style is more "alternative" (nose ring, mohawk, black eye shadow, purple nails, combat boots . . .), that's fine. Just consider toning it down for a day. You will still be able to tell if this is the right college for you.

Have a game plan for each campus, listing what you want to see and do, but leave spare time to accept invitations to an athletic event, a student play, a class, a party, or some other activity. Try to talk to one or more faculty members, a coach, a student editor or radio station manager, a theater-arts director, or someone involved with the activities that interest you.

College Visit Summary Sheet

Before visiting a college, be sure to review carefully the information in the school brochure or Web site. Upon completion of your visit, write in your responses to the issues contained here. Do this for each college visited and then compare your summaries for each.

COLLEGE OR UNIVERSITY: _____ LOCATION: _____

Date of visit: _____ Interviewer: _____

STUDENT BODY

(Impression of student body in terms of appearance, style, friendliness, degree of interest and enthusiasm, diversity of social, religious, ethnic background.)

ACADEMIC FACTORS

(How serious about academics is the college and its students; how good are the facilities for academic pursuits; how varied is the curriculum; how strict or flexible are the requirements; how appropriate is the college for your interests?)

CAMPUS FACILITIES AND SOCIAL LIFE

(How complete and modern are the facilities, such as dorms, library, Internet system, student center, athletic complex; how active is the social life, how diverse is it; is it a suitcase or commuter campus?)

OVERALL IMPRESSIONS

(What you liked least and most; what seemed different or special. What type of student do you feel would be happiest there? Are you the type?)

RATING

(On a scale of 1 to 5, with 1 being the top grade, rate the college on the basis of your interest in it.)

When Your Parents Visit Campuses with You

You may visit some campuses on your own, perhaps with a friend, or perhaps to stay with an older friend who is a current student. However, you will most likely see the majority of your college campuses with a parent. Parents are wonderful allies in the admissions process, but like you, they need to understand how admissions decisions are made. Anxiety can spoil a campus visit and prevent you from absorbing the experience. To allay their tension—and your own—discuss your concerns frankly, and be sure to tell your parents how much you appreciate their help and caring. Pass on some of the facts and information from your research, and anticipate some of the concerns your parents will have. For instance, parents should not feel offended because they are not invited to sit in on the interview—the interview is with the candidate. Warn your parents that you may prefer not to discuss the interview immediately after it is over.

Explain how spending a night in a dormitory will be useful, so that on some campuses you may accept an invitation to stay in a dorm instead of a motel. Make plans to meet your parents in the morning in such cases.

Incidentally, the way to arrange for a dormitory stay is first to try to contact an undergraduate you know and ask to be put up for the night. If you know no one, the admissions office will usually have a list of undergraduates willing to let you stay overnight. We have found that some colleges are discouraging overnight visits like this until senior fall, or after an application has been submitted, or even after a candidate has been accepted. Too many non-students staying on campus and sitting in on classes can disrupt a college's functioning. Check with each college about their policies in these areas.

Following a visit, do not elicit too many opinions from your parents. Tell them your reactions first, so that they will be cautious about dampening your enthusiasm or overselling a place you did not like. Let their criticism of the dormitories or the economics lecture come, if it does, after you have had your say. Then weigh their observations, even noting them in your College Visit Summary Sheet as something to consider later. This approach will prevent you from taking views contrary to theirs just to assert your independence.

The College Peer Group Impact

In deciding where to enroll, you should consider among other characteristics the kind of students you will be thrown together with. According to Professor Alexander W. Astin's study of over 200 institutions, the impact of the peer group is the most pervasive of 190 environmental characteristics that affect the individual student's development. Astin studied more than 20,000 students and 25,000 faculty members for his 1997 book, *What Matters in College*, a sequel to his acclaimed *Four Critical Years*.

The peer group's values will have the strongest influence. If you see telltale signs of a "party school" atmosphere at a college, unless your resistance is strong, you can be drawn into time-wasting, debilitating carousal. At the other extreme, you might feel alienated and become withdrawn on a campus where intense interstudent competition and overworking are the norm.

Another surprising finding of the Astin study was that college faculties oriented to research rather than to teaching turn off students, whose cognitive development consequently suffers. This is not to say that if you personally are oriented to research, you will not benefit in a research atmosphere. But the average student will do well to recognize the possible influences the students and the faculty of such an institution may exert. Appropriate questions during campus visits can flush out the negative impacts Astin has observed.

We found similar evidence in our survey research for *Inside the Top Colleges*. Students clearly stated that two of the most important aspects of their experience at highly selective colleges were whom they were studying and socializing with, and who was doing the teaching. Access to involved faculty teaching courses in their area of interest, and building lasting friendships with bright peers with similar interests, made all the difference to these students.

The Best Time to Visit

The best time for visiting campuses is when they are in session, in fall, winter, or spring of your junior year or fall of the senior year, but not on a big football game or house-party weekend, nor when exams are being held. You want to be on campus when there is neither unusual excitement nor intense seclusion, to see what normal daily college life is like.

More and more students visit campuses during the summer, because this is the only time they can get an admissions office appointment, or get away from school, sports, or other responsibilities. We have found, for example, that by September, if not earlier, almost all the most selective colleges that still interview on campus have no appointment openings in the admissions office until the following spring—for applicants to the next freshman class. If you visit in the summer, you ought to return during the fall to see the campus when students are there.

Some timing and strategy hints:

• Begin visiting during the fall, winter, and spring of junior year. No interviews at this time, just campus tours and information sessions. The two high school vacation periods of Presidents' Day weekend and spring vacation may be times when you are out of school, but colleges are in session.

• Save some time in late May or early June to visit colleges, which may still be in session when you have just finished school.

• Make appointments *before the summer* for interviews at selective colleges during the fall.

• Save some time in late August and early September for visits when colleges are back in session but you have not yet started school. You may interview at this time.

• Columbus Day weekend is another good long weekend to visit colleges in the fall when they are in session.

What to Look for on Campus

Having worked with many students after fruitful campus visits, we find that they usually return with new impressions and different thoughts about places they knew only from written material, pictures, and what people had told them. These changed ideas are more valuable when the student organizes them into a coherent pattern that can be used in later decision making. To return and say "I had no idea Oberlin College was such a neat place" is all very well, but it is not particularly helpful when you are asked to compare it with another "neat place." Why is it neat?

The College Visit Summary Sheet should be photocopied so that you will have enough copies for all your campus visits, and you should fill it out immediately after the end of the visit. Students who have used this sheet tell us that they take notes during the visit and then consult them when filling out the sheet.

To gather the kind of information you will need, you should put questions to the admissions staff, students, faculty, coaches, alumni, and employees like campus security personnel. The following questions have been used by applicants who have worked with us on admission strategies. There are too many to ask of any one person, such as an admissions officer, and you may not be able to ask all of them at every institution. After a couple of visits, you will develop your own investigative routine, and will discern which questions are most important to you.

The Social Concerns

• What are the living arrangements in dormitories or fraternity or sorority houses? What options are there for choosing roommates? Is off-campus housing available at reasonable rents? Are there residency requirements or guaranteed housing? For which years?

• Are there coeducational dormitories by floor? By building? None? Are there quiet study hours? If so, are the hours enforced? Are there upper-class student RAs (resident advisers) or faculty in the dorms?

• Is student housing adequate and pleasant? Are students happy or unhappy with accommodations? How are roommates assigned? How flexible is the school about changing or reassigning roommates?

• If there are fraternities and sororities, what percentage of the students belong to them and what percentage live in them? Is there first-year rushing? What is the college's official attitude toward them? Is there a stated policy on possible fraternity or sorority discrimination?

• What are the social opportunities if you choose not to join a Greek organization or club, or if they do not exist on campus? What facilities are available for parties, dances, and other activities? Is there another formal residential life system, based on clusters or social houses, for example?

• What activities, such as concerts, speakers, informal athletics, and tours, does the college sponsor? Do most students remain on campus on weekends, or is it a "suitcase" college?

• What is the makeup of the student body in terms of geographical origin, and what are students' academic interests? What are the most popular majors? How many students go on to graduate school?

• Are there advantages to the school's size? Disadvantages?

• How good is campus security? Is crime a concern? Is there alcohol or drug abuse?

• Is there much political activism? Is there pressure to conform, or can you "do your own thing"?

• What control do students have over campus social and academic life?

• Is there a diverse student body to allow for exposure to a variety of backgrounds and experience? What percentage of the student body is African American, Hispanic, Asian, Native American, or international? What percentage is Catholic, Protestant, Jewish, or other significant religious faiths?

• Are the facilities for various religious groups adequate? If the college is church-affiliated, how do students of differing faiths fit in?

• How are ethnic and racial minorities accommodated? Are there special programs and facilities for minority members who want them? Is there affinity housing? A multicultural resource center?

- Are jobs available to those not on financial aid? What services are there for job placement in summer or after graduating?

- What is the ratio of men to women? Is there any evidence of sexism?

- For single-sex colleges: What arrangements are there for dating? What are the social activities?

- What are the most common student complaints? What procedures exist for students to convey their complaints to someone in authority? What do students say they like most about the college?

Before leaving any campus, make sure that you have been provided with all relevant statistical data you may not have found on the college's Web site or in their viewbook. Often, colleges will make their longer course bulletin or catalogue available in their admissions office, along with many smaller pamphlets and brochures describing particular clubs and programs.

The Academic Concerns

- What departments are considered outstanding, average, or weak? (Admissions officers and faculty members can be surprisingly candid about this.) Is there more academic opportunity than is listed in the catalogue (special research projects, field trips, and so on)? Perhaps a new program has been recently created?

- Can you create your own interdepartmental major?

- Do you have to do independent work? Are there off-campus reading periods? What would be your chances of getting into an honors program?

- Are there college-sponsored foreign study programs? Internship opportunities? How easy does the college make it for students to participate in these activities, and how many students take advantage of them?

- Are classes large or small? How many lecture courses will you take? In courses with large enrollments, are there small sections?

- Is the faculty available to students after class? (Ask students this one.) Is there diversity in faculty background? That is, do most of the members come from different regions or from one region? Have most of them been educated at one kind of university or at many different kinds of universities? Is there ethnic, racial, international, and gender diversity among the faculty?

- Are most course requirements cut-and-dried, with two-hour exams, one paper, and a final examination? Or is there individuality in the way different professors grade and structure their classes?

- Are introductory courses taught by professors or by graduate assistants? Are freshmen taught by top members of the faculty?

- What recognition is there for advanced courses taken in high school?

- How good is faculty advising? Are there remedial or tutorial services? Is there a learning support program, and if so, how well developed is it?

- How good is the career counseling and placement office in helping students plan for jobs or graduate schools?

- What are the most important factors influencing admissions decisions?

- In the interviewer's (or tour guide's or alum's or professor's) view, what makes this college distinctive, compared to other colleges of its size and type?

The Facilities

- What health care arrangements are there?

- Does the library have most of the research materials you will need in your field?

• Are freshmen given space and carrels in the library for study? If not, is other space assigned for study? Where?

• How good is the bookstore?

• Are there enough parking spaces? Will you need or be allowed to have a car?

• Are laboratories kept up to date? Are art studios available? How good is the theater? Are there music practice facilities?

• Are athletic facilities taken up mostly by varsity sports, or will you be able to use the gymnasium, pool, or tennis courts on a regular basis? What kind of intramural athletic programs are there?

• Is the campus well wired or wireless for the Internet? Are dorm rooms, commons areas, and the library connected to the Internet? Is there a campus intra-net, including e-mail services and a common laser printing facility? Are students furnished with or expected to have their own laptop or desktop computer? How up-to-date are the public computing facilities?

• What kinds of accommodations and facilities are available for students with disabilities?

• What commercial outlets are nearby? How are town–gown relations? Are there restaurants and motels nearby for visiting relatives and friends?

• What meal plans are available? What dining facilities are available? Are students happy with the facilities and choices? Can students get food deliveries?

CAMPUS COMPARISONS

Students who keep track of their campus visits help themselves by keeping their reactions to schools fresh in their minds after they have seen multiple campuses. They also help their counselors by giving them a good pattern of contrasts to react to. This is a good basis for continuing to develop a student's final list of colleges. We recall one student who visited six campuses in the Northeast, and made careful notes on each. She sent her reactions to us in advance of our second meeting with her. She was so perceptive and complete in her analysis that we were quickly able to help her both narrow and expand her eventual college list from this initial foundation.

Here is an example of two campuses compared by a student.

COUNTRY CAMPUS

Student Body

Informally dressed, friendly, kind of suburban, laid back, very athletic, rah-rah, frat parties big deal, few minorities. Weekly paper, good literary magazine. Strong theater.

Academic Factors

Small classes, library cubicles for seniors, big computer center, new micro bio lab, few government courses, profs accessible, writing course obligatory.

Campus Facilities and Social Life

Dorms have suites, common room, social programs, lectures. Dining hall self-serve, fair food. Social life determined by fraternities. Sororities very quiet, have housemothers! Six squash courts.

Overall Impressions

Very comfortable feeling here. Many students are like me. The two profs I met urged me to apply. Said their premed program is tops. Is there enough challenge here?

Rating

2—Might apply to this college.

URBAN CAMPUS

Student Body

Much high fashion, rush-rush, involved in politics, downtown stores, rock concerts. Much beer, no drugs. Many minorities, foreign students. Daily paper, top radio station.

Academic Factors

Exciting lecture on Truman Doctrine—500 in hall. Computer required for accounting. Library jammed. Grad students teach many courses.

Campus Facilities and Social Life

Skyscraper dorms, huge cafeterias, beer/wine with fancy meals. Mass protest on Chechnya followed by torchlight parade. No squash courts. Frisbee big.

Overall Impressions

I felt I was in another world, a very exciting but unsettling place. Not sure some students aren't loafing. More like the real world. Not gentle.

Rating

4—Not for me. Too unstructured.

THE USES OF COLLEGE GUIDEBOOKS

As you visit campuses you will probably be looking at one or two campus "inside" guidebooks or Web sites based on the observations of undergraduates or recent graduates. Some are obviously amusing and deliberately vulgar. Others pronounce on institutions summary judgments that may be the opinion of one person, or perhaps a few self-appointed critics. So long as you do not take their assertions as gospel, such books or sites can help you to look more closely at an institution, to question students and others about assertions such as the impersonality of the professors or the *Animal House* character of fraternity life. They can give you a broad overview and comparison of multiple institutions, and a quick factual reference guide.

It is always useful to check any opinion about a college with other sources, and to examine the foundation of each reference's material. Who is doing the writing? From what sources? With what experience? If rankings are involved, how are they developed? Individual guidebooks can be more or less instructive for you, but your own campus visits and ongoing research will provide you with your best measure of different colleges.

The Optional Interview

You will know from catalogues and other sources that some colleges do not offer an on-campus interview, but the policy of most selective colleges is to make both the on-campus interview and an additional or substitute alumni one optional. You should be aware that there is disagreement about the importance of the interview. When a college tells you that the admissions office interview, or an interview with a member of an alumni schools committee working as a volunteer for the college, will not affect your admissions chances one way or the other, can you believe this? We believe you can.

In recent years, a number of selective colleges have done away with on-campus interviews altogether. Princeton, for example, offers only group information sessions on campus. Others offer interviews, but declare them "informational," as opposed to "evaluative." Some admissions offices, such as Middlebury's and Yale's, train current students to handle most interviews.

We have been told, "We can't make definitive judgments on the basis of twenty minutes or half an hour with the student." Wellesley has claimed that no student has ever been turned down on the basis of an interview. "A good student can have a bad day. We look at the overall record," an admissions staff member said.

As a rule of thumb, those colleges where the interview plays relatively more of a role tend to be the smaller liberal arts colleges.

If the interview is crucial, how can it be optional? One explanation is that with so many applicants from all over the country, it is impossible to interview all of them. Another is that colleges have decided that interviews are unfair because they are too subjective: They may reward the smooth-talking average student while penalizing the quiet scholar, or lead to bias against individuals from different cultural backgrounds than that of the interviewer. To which we say, this is precisely why the interview does not weigh heavily in the folder. As an admissions officer in the 1960s, Howard Greene interviewed hundreds of students for Princeton, and he always enjoyed the candidates who challenged him with sharp questions about the college. Yet never was an interview a deciding factor in accepting or rejecting a candidate. Since then, interviews have become ever less important. In the admissions process a report on an interview is largely useful to confirm and support other evidence about a candidate.

HOW TO READ A COLLEGE CATALOGUE OR WEB SITE

College catalogues, sometimes called "bulletins," can have a deadly quality. The prose is antiseptic and impersonal, but for a reason: A catalogue is a contract. The student can hold the college to what the catalogue says. So a catalogue should be read for what it is, a description. Most of the contents can be taken at face value. It is important to read selectively about those areas most relevant to you.

From the catalogue may be gleaned most of the information that will help you evaluate the college according to your preferences and priorities. Due to rising costs, colleges often are not sending full catalogues to interested students. They are often available only at the admissions office, and/or for a small fee. It is often easier to access a college's Web site (where some catalogues are available online), and read its glossy brochure. A catalogue offers detailed and specific information on courses, requirements, and characteristics of the college. Every catalogue puts the college's best foot forward and avoids negative comment, so the catalogue makes every college sound good. The question is—is it good for you?

Begin with the academic qualities. You are going to college first of all for academic training, not for the social life, athletics, glee club, or mountain air. Unless you find the right academic atmosphere, the rest will be superficial and meaningless to you.

What are the degree requirements? Is there a thesis? How about interdisciplinary majors? Are there pass/fail options? The bulk of a college catalogue is taken up with course descriptions. Look for what is not offered to see if you might be short-changed. If you are interested in becoming a geologist and there are only a few courses in this field, then this college, which may be otherwise excellent, is not for you.

Special programs of study offer clues to a college's strong points. Are you interested in creative writing? The catalogue will tell you just how much academic training you can expect.

The catalogue should give an indication of the percentage of faculty with doctoral degrees and what the ratio of faculty to students is. Top colleges have few faculty who lack a Ph.D. and the faculty-to-student ratio is one teacher for every ten students or so. The catalogue will not tell you how many teaching assistants (graduate students) you will be taught by. Nor does it always say what percentage of the college's graduates go to graduate school, nor what distinction the alumni have achieved.

Description of facilities should be scrutinized. Is there a swimming pool, hockey rink, tennis courts, student center? How many books does the library have? Small colleges tend to have in the range of 150,000 volumes, while universities have one to three million. Is there a science center? A theater? Is there a computer facility for students' use? Is the college's technology up to today's standards and demands? Whatever a college does not list, it usually does not have. A catalogue is an inventory of assets.

The catalogue describes living arrangements and costs. Must the student take meals in common? Can he or she live off-campus? Are dormitories large or small? High-rise or low? If there are fraternities and/or sororities, there will be extra costs and perhaps concerns.

The makeup of the student body will tell you whether you will feel comfortable there. The number of out-of-state students may be low. How many international students are there? How diverse is the student body ethnically and racially?

The size of the endowment may be listed. Some small colleges have as much as $700,000 per student in endowment, while other top colleges have between $150,000 and $300,000 per student. Obviously they have more to offer than a college where the endowment is only $30,000 per student. But some colleges with low endowments receive large donations for current operations.

The athletic programs listed will tell you whether you can engage in your particular sport. Not every college has rowing, sailing, fencing, hiking, and so on. In a city college, where do you exercise? Is the pool open daily, and at what time?

A catalogue is no substitute for a visit to the campus, but rather, an aid to the visit. Read it before and during the visit. It will stimulate questions as well as provide answers.

In addition to catalogues, colleges offer brochures, online videos, Web pages, and DVDs. On its Web site, Middlebury offers its answers to the Common Data Set program, which many selective colleges participate in to provide standardized and more reliable data, as well as Middlebury's submissions to various guidebooks. Some college materials are simply promotional and must be read with care, while others are highly informative. They are not contractual in nature like the catalogue, and may be issued by a department without central administration control. Since many private colleges are struggling to maintain or increase enrollment, reliance on sales promotion is increasing. The intelligent student will do well to "look under the hood."

It should be remembered that admissions decisions are arrived at by a committee. You will recall from Step One that decisions about the weakest and best candidates are arrived at quickly, so the interview can have little bearing on these decisions. The remaining candidates compete for places on the basis of their accomplishments. If an interviewer in a committee makes a case for a candidate who has made a very favorable impression in the interview, others can challenge the interviewer by pointing to candidates they think are stronger— candidates who may never have been interviewed.

Our own research and other polls of college admissions officers consistently have placed the interview at the bottom of those factors considered important in the admissions process. And since colleges have made interviews optional, it would be unfair or even discriminatory for them to penalize students who did not interview.

You should see interviews as a two-way street: a chance for you to learn more about the college from an admissions representative, alumnus, or senior student; and a chance for them to learn more about you and what is important to you. You should be prepared to ask meaningful questions in an interview, related to your interests and your perception of the college. You should be familiar with the college's programs and ready to talk about yourself. Your questions should be genuinely probing and should never concern information easily obtained in the catalogue, viewbook, or other publications. Nothing irritates an admissions officer more than a candidate who wastes interview time with such questions as "How many students do you have?" Or, "Do you give credits for AP tests?"

In short, we urge that you keep the interview in perspective and use it constructively to ask serious questions that will help you decide (1) whether you would be happy at the college and (2) whether your candidacy will be strong or weak. Our general advice is to take advantage of as many opportunities for on-campus and alumni interviews as is feasible within your campus visit schedule, especially at those schools that are likely top choices for you. However, see these interviews as informational learning opportunities and chances for you to represent your level of interest in the college, rather than make-or-break interrogations.

The Myth About Blowing the Interview

A successful businesswoman graduate of a Pennsylvania liberal arts college told us that she was turned down by Bowdoin because she was so rattled during the interview that she made a poor impression. No college will tell any candidate why he or she was turned down. If a candidate chooses to believe that the interview was the reason, what can we say? By now you should be convinced that admissions decisions ride on no one single factor.

In plain English, YOU CANNOT BLOW YOUR ADMISSIONS CHANCES IN AN INTERVIEW. The worst that can happen is that an interview will confirm what the admissions folder already is telling a college: This candidate is not for us. Conversely, a very successful interview will not convert an unlikely candidate into one likely to be accepted.

For the candidate in the middle, a strong interview may become a minor plus in the evaluation, but such factors as teacher recommendations, end-of-semester grades, and, importantly, essays will matter much more.

The person interviewing you will want to know why you are interested in the college, and what you think the college has to offer you in particular. It is never the intention of an interviewer to grill you or intimidate you, though you may feel this was the case. If you are very nervous about interviewing, you may choose not to do so. If you go forward with an interview and find you are very nervous, feel free to take a deep breath, look your interviewer in the eye, and say, "I'm just a bit nervous. I'm very interested in your college, and this interview is important to me." The likely reaction? You will be reassured, comforted, and asked to say more about why you are so interested in the school. You cannot blow an interview.

One-on-One Interviews at Some Selective Colleges

COLLEGE	CAMPUS INTERVIEW
Amherst	Not offered
Bard	Strongly recommended
Barnard	Recommended
Bates	Strongly recommended
Boston College	Not offered
Bowdoin	Strongly recommended
Brown	Not offered
Bryn Mawr	Strongly recommended
University of California—Berkeley	Not offered
California Institute of Technology	Not offered
Carleton	Strongly recommended
Carnegie Mellon	Strongly recommended
Case Western	Strongly recommended
University of Chicago	Strongly recommended
Claremont McKenna	Recommended
Colby	Strongly recommended
Colgate	Recommended
University of Colorado—Boulder	Not offered
Colorado College	Recommended
Columbia	Not offered
Cornell University	Not offered
Dartmouth	Not offered
Duke	Not offered
Emory	Not offered
Georgetown	Not offered
Hamilton	Strongly recommended
Harvard	Recommended
Haverford	Strongly recommended
Johns Hopkins	Strongly recommended
Massachusetts Institute of Technology	Not offered
Middlebury	Recommended
New York University	Not offered

University of North Carolina—Chapel Hill	Not offered
University of Notre Dame	Not offered
Oberlin	Strongly recommended
University of Pennsylvania	Not offered
Pomona	Strongly recommended
Princeton	Not offered
Reed	Strongly recommended
Rice	Strongly recommended
Smith	Strongly recommended
Stanford	Not offered
Swarthmore	Strongly recommended
Tufts	Not offered
Vanderbilt	Not offered
Vassar	Not offered
Wake Forest	Strongly recommended
Washington and Lee	Strongly recommended
Wellesley	Strongly recommended
Wesleyan	Strongly recommended
Yale	Recommended

This information is subject to change, and students should check with each college to ask about on-campus interviewing and its importance. Some colleges may strongly recommend alumni interviews in addition to or instead of on-campus interviews. Unless stated otherwise, all these on-campus interviews should be considered OPTIONAL, and not highly important in admissions. Where interviews are "strongly recommended," colleges prefer to talk with applicants, but do not penalize students for not interviewing on campus. In some cases, these colleges may offer or even require interviews for applicants to special programs or for special groups of applicants, such as legacies or underrepresented minorities.

What If You Do Not Have an Interview?

Since at almost all colleges interviews are optional, the lack of an interview will have no bearing on your admission. It would be a pity for you to decide not to apply to a college because you were not interviewed. Information you lack can be obtained by a telephone call to someone at the college.

The primary benefit of an interview is the information you gather from it, and the impression you take away about the college.

The Golden Rules for Interviews

A typical *good* interview was Tim's at Middlebury. He told us he arrived on a cool July day wearing a seersucker jacket, button-down shirt without a tie, khaki pants, and loafers. The admissions officer began by asking him about his trip, what his impressions of Vermont were, what other colleges he was visiting, and then asked why he was considering an application to Middlebury.

Tim said, "I've heard about your language program from my French teacher, who got his master's here." The admissions officer immediately pointed out that the summer graduate program in languages was independent of the undergraduate program, and that majoring in French at Middlebury would be no different from such a major at any good small selective college. This candor Tim found refreshing.

The next topic was skiing. As a Rochester boy Tim skied either in New York state or Canada; he was on his school ski team, and hoped he might be good enough to ski for Middlebury. He was told that from his record this looked like a reasonable ambition. The interviewer then asked Tim if he was considering applying for Early Decision. Tim said no. The interviewer said that he should ask his college adviser's opinion, but from what Tim said about his academic record, he looked like a very promising candidate.

Tim came away from Middlebury with a strong feeling about the college, but did not apply for Early Decision because he preferred Colgate. In his notebook he wrote: "Apply here if Colgate does not accept me ED."

Not every interviewer will be so direct or forthcoming about your chances for admission or your athletic participation, and don't feel that you have to press your interviewer for some such statement. But do look for hints as to whether you fit the profile of the average admitted applicant.

Theodora's interview at Wellesley was not satisfying. She found herself drawn into a discussion of her rural Massachusetts high school and her somewhat uneven grades. It was a mediocre school sending fewer than half the students to college, and so there was no incentive to do well, she explained. Politely, the interviewer asked if Theodora was a self-starter. Did she need others to inspire her? Would she be able to keep up in a very competitive environment? Her response was overly defensive, she realized later. She explained she was a very competitive person. Her basketball coach, she said, considered her one of the most aggressive players she had ever coached. Was this a compliment? the interviewer asked with a laugh. Theodora slumped in her seat, and mumbled something about the coach playing favorites.

The interviewer said nothing for a moment. Then she said kindly that this did not seem to be Theodora's day, and invited her to return when she felt more sure of herself. Back at school, when she complained to her college adviser about the "cold" interview, her adviser asked her to put herself in the admissions officer's place and give an impression of Theodora. It took a while for her to see that her negative attitude was holding her back. Her adviser taught her little interview tricks, like putting one foot in front as she sat, so that she would be thrust forward and prevented from slouching. In time Theodora learned not to overestimate herself (she was not qualified for Wellesley), and subsequent interviews at other colleges were more satisfactory.

Tips for College Interviewing

QUESTIONS YOU MAY BE ASKED:

- Tell me about yourself.

- What do you hope to get out of college? What academic and extracurricular activities will you pursue? What are your goals?

- What do you know about our college and why are you interested in us?

- Tell me about your current high school. How are you doing academically?

- What are your academic interests? Do you have an idea about what you might major in?

- Where do you see yourself in ten years?

- Tell me about your favorite teacher. What do you like about him or her?

- What are your strongest and weakest subjects? Why?

- What do you like to do with your free time? What are your favorite sports, hobbies, interests? Tell me about your involvement with them.

- What are some of your favorite books and authors? Why do you like them?

- Tell me about your friends and family.

- How would your friends describe you? How would you describe yourself?

- If you could relive one moment in your life, what would it be and why?

- What other colleges are you looking at? Why?

- What have you done during your summers?

- What are your personal strengths and weaknesses?

- Is there anything in particular you would like to discuss?

- Do you have any questions? [Feel free to ask questions throughout the interview. Possible subjects might include social or weekend activities at school, or courses, sports, clubs, fraternities or sororities, art, music, theater, computer availability, gymnasium or workout facilities, and so forth. You might also have questions about ethnic and religious diversity.]

GENERAL TIPS:

- Learn as much about the school as you can prior to your interview. Read available brochures, college magazines, or other campus publications. If possible, talk with students who have attended the college. Browse the Web site.

- Review in advance the above list of questions you may be asked. Think of questions you might ask if you were interviewing a prospective student. You might want to discuss the above list with your parents or friends.

- In order to keep the questions and your proposed replies fresh in your mind, use the night before your interview to jot down some notes about what you want to be sure to cover.

- Develop your answers fully, but avoid running on and on. Keep the point in mind. Open up and talk freely about yourself. Be honest, and avoid plain yes or no one-word answers.

- Dress neatly, relax but don't slouch in your chair, and remember to look your interviewer in the eye as you speak. Listen attentively to what he or she has to say. Remember to be yourself. Don't pretend either through your replies or demeanor to be what you are not.

- Have a firm handshake when you arrive and when you leave.

- Arrive early, and well rested. Remember to have breakfast or lunch prior to your meeting. Relax and prepare to enjoy your college visit and interview!

- Thank your interviewer for his or her time, get his or her card, and send a brief thank-you note or e-mail when you get home.

Every interview, and every student, is different. But here is some general advice for you to take to heart:

Be yourself. Do not try to be what you think the interviewer wants or expects of all applicants. Be natural. The interviewer knows that students are often nervous, and he or she will help to put you at ease. As the interview progresses and you reveal your true self, the interviewer can help you decide if this college is appropriate for you.

Be confident. Be self-assured, but not cocky. Know that you are interested in this college, and that it is reasonable for you to be applying.

Be expressive. Be discursive, conversational, and offer up information easily. Don't make your interviewer work too hard to learn things about you.

Be prepared. If you have done your homework and are generally familiar with the college, with your own interests and priorities, and with why you are there, you will be more comfortable and secure.

Ask questions. Coming prepared with one or two questions is the easiest way to overcome your own nervousness. Here are three examples of questions asked by applicants with different interests:

- I am very interested in theater productions. In school I enjoy designing sets. Can I get involved in drama here without majoring in your Theater Arts Department? I am thinking of majoring in history.

- In school I am taking four years of French and three social studies courses. Is it possible to combine a major in French and political science, and realistically spend a semester or a year abroad?

- I have a mild language disability, which I am proud to say I have not let stand in my way. I have worked hard in all my courses, and have taken several honors courses.

The only subject to give me problems is Spanish. Is it possible to have a language requirement waived or fulfilled in some other academic way?

Be thoughtful. You can take time to offer sincere and well-considered responses to questions. This is not a timed game show, and there are no wrong answers. This is about getting to know you.

Be clear about your goals. Leave the interviewer with a sense that there is a logical fit between you and the college. If you know who you are, where you want to go, and how you want to get there, how does this particular college fit into your future? What are you looking for out of college that this school can provide?

Find out where you stand. Before leaving an interview, you should have an idea of what your admissions chances look like on the basis of information you give the interviewer about yourself. No selective college can promise that you will be admitted, and many times interviewers will try to refrain from being overly definitive, but you generally will be given a frank answer to your question. Here is the range of answers you can expect:

"You will be a strong candidate. We hope you will apply."

"On the basis of what we know about you, you will face stiff competition. Please apply here, but be sure to apply to a good list of other colleges as well."

"Frankly, you would not be a strong candidate. You, of course, may apply. Conditions do change. But as of now you probably would not be admitted."

The third answer leaves an opening for the college to react to a sudden surge in your grades, or a brilliant achievement in athletics, the arts, or some other field. But unless such a change occurs, you would be advised not to apply to this college.

If You Cannot Visit Some Campuses

Usually students are interviewed at the college, when such interviews are available, by someone in the admissions office. But when this is not possible, students may be interviewed by an alumnus or alumna who is a member of the committee of volunteers helping the admissions office. Some local alumni clubs interview hundreds of candidates each year. Some students will interview both on campus and, later in the admissions process, with an alum. These interviews usually take place once you have submitted your application to the college, from November through February.

Alumni interviews do not put you at any disadvantage. In fact, these give you the opportunity to ask the interviewer why he or she is glad to have attended the institution. Looking back, what made it special; would he or she go there again in its present form? If the interviewer cannot answer a particular question, they can obtain the information for you by a phone call. Remember that these alums are volunteers. They are performing this service for their college because they feel connected to and proud of their alma mater. They will enjoy talking about their experiences, and their hopes for the college in the future. Their main goal, apart from imparting their enthusiasm to you, is to help you (and the admissions office) decide if you "fit" the college.

You can certainly get into a selective college without visiting the campus. You may find it impossible to visit far-off places, and you may have to rely on what you know about a college from catalogues, friends, and alumni enthusiasts. A New Jersey girl decided that the University of Michigan was her first choice. After enrolling there, sight unseen, she observed wryly, "It's like Paris. You don't have to see it to know you want to go there."

Another way to see colleges these days is via the Internet. Many colleges offer "virtual tours" online. While it is no perfect substitute for a real campus tour and visit, such Web browsing can help you to determine whether you are interested in making a campus visit happen, or whether a college is not appropriate for you at all.

So while we highly recommend a number of campus visits, we know that there are reasons why you may never get to the campuses of some colleges of great interest to you. If you apply somewhere you have never visited, you will have other campus visits as a basis of comparison.

However, before you actually enroll in such a college, we would highly recommend visiting during April open house or orientation sessions (see Step Ten) if at all possible, to ensure that your expectations for the college are met.

After Campus Visits

A thank-you letter to the admissions office or an interviewer (alumnus or on-campus) for having seen you is a nice gesture. A letter will go in your folder and will be a sign of your interest in the college. Such letters should be relatively noncommittal unless you have already made a decision to apply. Your saying to an admissions office that a college is your first choice is taken with a grain of salt. The experience of admissions committees is that there are so many variables between the time you visit and the time you might enroll that the sincerest statements of intention can become meaningless. Your letter, then, is a courtesy, not a persuader, but you should say nothing you do not mean. The essays and personal statements that go with applications are powerful persuaders. Save your efforts to make a strong impact for these important creative statements. Your thank-you note can be in the form of a handwritten card, or even an e-mail. Ask your interviewer for his or her business card, which will have the full name, title, address, and e-mail on it.

Trying to butter up admissions officers is counterproductive. Admissions directors and their staffs are amused by such obvious attempts to win their favor as, "I love your tie!" The applicant who appeared for his interview at Columbia in tails got nothing but scorn for his flamboyance. A wordy letter after an interview is worse than no letter. Polishing the apple does not go over well in admissions.

Use Your Summary Sheet

When all your campus visits have been completed, you will have your College Visit Summary Sheet to consult for each college. Some you will file and forget, having decided that you will not apply to colleges that do not suit you. You wondered what a college would be like. It looked beautiful in the literature, but you have found it too remote, or too dedicated to the arts and without enough science emphasis. You are surprised to learn about a college that you had not considered, and now you feel very strongly that it is your first choice. Another college has reacted so favorably to you that you feel almost certain that it will admit you. It may become your second choice. A state college you considered somewhat less selective turned out to be one of the most exciting places you visited. You will apply there.

The rating you give each college will not necessarily correspond to the order of your choices. You may have visited Stanford just to see what it is like, and you may rate it higher than the colleges you will apply to. Or you can be surprised by a phone call from the alumnus of a college you have not visited, asking you to consider his college. A brilliant mathematician had made Rensselaer her first choice after visiting the campus, but when a Princeton alumnus in her New England town asked her to consider applying to Princeton, she made that her first choice and was admitted.

As you go over your College Visit Summary Sheets you will begin to arrive at important decisions about where to apply, so you want to be careful to avoid snap judgments and impulsiveness. Now is the time for discussion with counselors, teachers, friends, and family. Get their reactions to your reactions. Your self-assessment shows that you will be an above-average candidate at most of the Exceedingly Demanding colleges, and your visits to both urban and rural, large and small schools have led you to confirm your preference for larger, urban campuses. You say you want to apply for Early Decision at the Wharton School of Finance at the University of Pennsylvania. Your counselor thinks you will be almost certainly deferred, but not rejected. And the university has not discouraged you. So you decide to apply in the hope that being deferred will result in your being admitted to the University of Pennsylvania in April as a liberal arts rather than a business school candidate. Your counselor will remind you that you should file perhaps six other applications.

Knowing What Is Important to You

They say that every choice is a sacrifice, that there are trade-offs required in decision making. In winter you long for summer, but then come the mosquitoes. So it is with colleges. You look at Columbia's rich curriculum and you look at the urban campus. You can't have one without the other, and you may not want the excitement New York offers. In visiting campuses it is useful to set up characteristics that clash, and to ask yourself what means more to you.

Here are some dichotomies we use in helping students reach decisions about specific colleges:

Quality of reputation and programs vs. location

Quality of reputation and programs vs. size

Quality of reputation and programs vs. single-sex environment

Quality of reputation and programs vs. distance from home

Quality of reputation and programs vs. personality or tone of campus and students

Academic prestige vs. appropriate curricular interests

Academic pressure vs. participating in extracurricular activities and sports

Bear these conflicting characteristics and others in mind as you talk to people on campus; ask how others have resolved them. You may find that a high school football star at an Exceedingly Demanding college has decided to drop his sport because he is not going to be a professional football player, but an accountant, so he has chosen to put academics first. You may say, I have a chance to be on the tennis circuit, so I would rather attend a college that allows me time to play lots of tennis. Or, teaching is most important to me, so I would rather attend a smaller college, even though it is farther away from the city and is not as diverse as I would like.

Considering a Major Subject

During a campus visit the question of majoring in a subject may come up. Some high school students know already that they will major in chemical engineering or history or fine arts. Most freshmen enter college with no clearly defined academic program in mind. In your discussions with students and faculty members, you should realize that college is an exploratory process for most students.

Liberal arts colleges do not pressure first-year students to make up their minds about a field of concentration. Their curriculum is like a pyramid, with the base laid in the freshman year in survey courses in the arts, humanities, sciences, mathematics, and the social sciences. In sophomore year the choice of electives narrows somewhat as you take courses with possible majors in mind. Then in your junior year you concentrate on one major subject, or on a combination of subjects like French language and French history or biology and chemistry. By senior year the narrowing of interest requires more concentration in your major field, plus a thesis, project, field work, or some special research. Of course, this pattern and structure vary across liberal arts colleges, and those students choosing to enter an engineering school, music conservatory, college of art, or school of business, for example, will have less flexibility and will be required to specialize much earlier. The good news is, most students are not only encouraged to explore new and different academic disciplines in the liberal arts, they are required to do so.

Jeffrey enrolled at Lewis and Clark with no idea of what his major might be. At his private day school in Seattle he had earned an A in an honors biology course, and at Lewis and Clark he had been assigned a biology professor as his adviser. The adviser steered him to several biology courses during his first four terms. Jeffrey found it impossible to get an A in any of them for all the work he did, while he got A's in economics, geography, and social ethics. By the end of his sophomore year he had decided to major in business administration and minor in social ethics. His ambition was to work for a corporation with a large program of community service. It was pointed out to him that his biology courses were not wasted and that they might help him if he should work for a drug company or go into agribusiness. Thus the pyramid's base supported the subsequent structuring of his college program.

Test this pyramid concept as you meet faculty members or graduates of a college, to see how their undergraduate programs worked out. Ask about their advising programs, flexibility in structuring majors, course requirements, interdisciplinary study, and opportunities for dual majors or minors. You will find much similarity in undergraduate programs, yet each college will have particular academic strengths that may appeal to you. This kind of investigation may have the effect of changing your senior high school course choices to allow you to take a college-level course in economics, for example, instead of studying a language.

When you visit campuses, and perhaps are asked about your possible major, you may be very clear if you know exactly what you plan to pursue. However, if you are like the majority of students, who have developed interests but are not ready to commit in one area, you may talk about your academic and extracurricular (music or fine art) strengths and focus, your interest in one or more programs at the college, and your desire to explore subjects across the liberal arts to obtain a broad-based education. Remember that expressing interest in one or another major, even later in your applications, does not commit you absolutely to following that path once you are at college. It is only an initial sense of your preferences and abilities.

Considering Your Options

Your campus visits will sharpen the focus of your selective college admissions process. When the visits are over, you will have a much clearer understanding of which colleges are right for you. The number to which you might apply can be reduced to a reasonable group. Which of these might admit you? Some have more or less assured you that you would be a strong candidate, although there are never any guarantees. Others you thought might be a possibility for you now look doubtful, and you wonder whether to apply to them. You begin to draw up a list of your preferred colleges and you discuss them with your counselor. "What chance do I have for Vanderbilt? What about Washington and Lee?" you ask. "What do you see as the major differences between these two places, and which do you think might suit me better?" At this point you know you are ready to calculate your chances for admission to those colleges where you feel you would love to spend a happy four years. This you will learn to do in Step Seven—Find Your Place in the Class Pie Charts.

Step Six Checklist

✓Plan your visits to college campuses. Phone or e-mail for information on campus tours, group information sessions, or interviews well in advance. In the case of on-campus interviews at the selective colleges, which you should take advantage of during the late summer and fall, you should call in the spring to make appointments.

✓Prepare for the visit by reviewing the material you've collected in your notebook about each school you will visit. Formulate questions you want to ask.

✓Prepare your parents for the visit, to allay their (and your) anxieties and enlist their support.

✓Try to stay overnight in a dormitory for the "10:30 test."

✓Remember that interviews are useful primarily as opportunities to learn more about a college. They are not important in admissions decisions, and are not offered everywhere.

✓Review the Golden Rules for Interviews and practice some interview questions with a parent, friend, or counselor to make the most of each interview you have.

✓Ask many questions—of students, faculty members, admissions officers, staff members—and note your impressions for the College Visit Summary Sheet.

✓Refer to the questions in this chapter in considering the character of the student body, the nature of academic work you may do, and the quality of the facilities. Give each college an overall rating, from 1 down to 5.

✓Revisit campuses (1) if you have visited in the summer when no students were there; (2) to talk to faculty, coaches, and others who may have a direct interest in your admission; (3) if you visited for a tour and an information session in the spring, and would now like to interview at a serious college choice; and (4) if you had a shorter visit in the spring or summer, and would now like to spend the night at a serious college choice. Do not call the admissions office a second time if you have already interviewed.

✓Use your campus visit notes to help you decide where to apply and possibly to inspire you to improve academically and intensify your extracurricular commitments. Your visits may lead you to add schools to your list that are similar to those you liked, or to drop colleges similar to those you did not.

STEP SEVEN:

Find Your Place in the Class Pie Charts

We think you will find this step both stimulating and enlightening. Visualizing the admissions decision process can help you understand where you might fit into the goal of the top colleges to create a well-rounded class of talented and unique individuals. As we have indicated throughout the steps, selective colleges are in the enviable position of choosing students who have achieved excellence in their academic work and one or more nonacademic roles. You will learn, through our presentation of the classic pie chart representing a typical admitted class at a top college, what your chances for admissions are by identifying your appropriate slice of the pie. If you comprehend the philosophy that underlies the selective universities' admissions policies, you then can determine how you should present yourself to appropriate colleges.

Yale states in its admissions information, "Diversity within the student population is important, and the Admissions Committee selects a class of able and contributing individuals from a variety of backgrounds and with a broad range of interests and skills. . . . Qualifications include not only the reasonably well defined areas of academic achievement and special skills in nonacademic areas, but also the less tangible qualities of capacity for involvement, commitment, and personal growth."

Stanford University has noted that with an increasingly large and competitive applicant pool, "We continue to look for diversity of background, interests, and experience; accomplishment in all fields of endeavor—the arts, sports, and community service; integrity and a passion for learning and doing."

How does an admissions committee screen such a large body of talented men and women to offer admission to only 7% to 15% of the applicants? In addition to the key factors of high school curriculum, test scores, and recommendations, the committee gives a great deal of attention to the other factors listed in the pie chart below. Many candidates make it through such a fine screening because they fit into one or several of the special categories that help top colleges to build the diverse and dynamic classes they seek. For example, one-quarter of the class might represent minority backgrounds, 6% are from international backgrounds, 15% athletes of exceptional talent, and 12% sons and daughters of alumni.

You can see from this chart how a selection committee can begin to sort out from the large number of candidates those they will pick in order to create the diverse class they want to enroll.

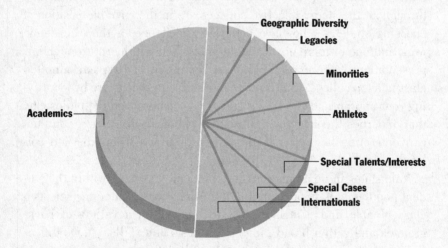

Finding the Competitive Edge

You know all about admissions requirements and procedures; you know your academic and nonacademic strengths; you have visited most or all of the colleges of interest to you. But you also know how much competition there is for the places in the top colleges, and you want to apply where you have the best chance of acceptance. You have worked hard through your high school years and thus dislike the idea of ending up in a much less selective college than you believe you can cope with successfully. You have to ask yourself, therefore, "Where do I have a competitive edge? What are the conditions that narrow the competition and provide me with a better chance of acceptance? Are there any significant differences among the selective colleges on my list that could help me find my special place in the entering class?"

With your understanding of the diversified class that selective colleges construct, you can gauge your chances of acceptance at any college by dividing the present first-year class's composition into a number of categories, and matching them against your own profile. Every top college shares this information in a statistical format with guidance counselors, who are willing to share this information with you. The same information is available to you when you check individual colleges' Web sites. In Step One you learned about the admissions process known as "rounds," in which students classified in general categories are considered together. Let us take a closer look at the eight categories within which successful candidates fall, and see how they can influence your chances for admission at the colleges you hope will admit you.

THE MISSION OF THE IVY COLLEGES TODAY

Dartmouth must be a place of opportunity for students of all backgrounds. It is hard to imagine education taking place in an environment that is fully like-minded. . . . And so Dartmouth seeks to attract a student body that reflects the richness of the world in which we live, and to offer an education that enables and empowers. Learning at Dartmouth has always been a multifaceted phenomenon. It occurs within such diverse settings as classrooms, laboratories, libraries, residence halls, athletic and recreational venues, and campus meeting and activity rooms. Our purpose is to encourage a residential and social community that is inclusive, to foster a sense of belonging and acceptance, that brings together its diverse student body as equal members in the Dartmouth community.

—James Wright, president of Dartmouth College

Eight Admissions Categories

Academics

As you review the selective college pie chart, you see that one-half is dedicated to academics. We want to make sure that you understand two critical facts: (1) Any of the other special slices of the class pie will give you an edge in the selection process only if you have the strong academic profile we have described; (2) the greatest number of successful applicants are those with the most outstanding academic credentials, i.e., top grades in the most demanding curriculum available, very high class standing in their school, commensurate test scores, and indications of serious intellectual interests. Keep in mind that the mission of the major colleges and universities is to bring together exceptional students with the exceptional resources of faculty and learning facilities they provide.

Legacies

Each college has its own policy and rules about admitting alumni-related applicants, and the admissions and alumni affairs offices are the only reliable sources of this information. Applicants and their families ought to ask either of these groups what exactly the policy is at the college under consideration. Here are the possibilities a selective college can consider in the separate round referred to as "legacies":

1. Only the children whose parent(s) graduated from the college

2. Both children and grandchildren of alumni

3. Applicants related to, but not children of, alumni

4. Applicants who have a sibling enrolled

5. Applicants whose parents are graduates of the undergraduate
   college versus those who hold graduate or professional degrees
   from the university

Contrary to the rumors that often circulate within communities, no
selective college will automatically admit the son or daughter of an
alumnus who has made substantial financial gifts to the institution but
has played no active role in the college's well-being or advancement.
The alumni who win the respect and attention of the admissions committees are those who volunteer to interview applicants in their home
community, raise money for the college, serve on special visiting committees to the university or the board of trustees, or head their local
alumni club. In other words, the college will not allow a family to buy
a place in the class for a certain price regardless of their offspring's
qualifications for admission. Many an alum's son or daughter has been
turned down by an admissions committee, despite their parent's promise of a large gift to the institution. The rare exception that is made
occasionally by one of the top colleges seems to catch the attention of
the community and gets enlarged into a given policy for all wealthy
legacy candidates. This is simply not true.

Most colleges state that alumni-related applicants have about a two-
or three-to-one better chance of admission than students in the applicant pool as a whole. Nonetheless, each year as many as 50% of those
candidates in the legacy category are turned down. If they do not meet
the standards of their competitors, they will not be invited into the
class. On the other hand, a 35% to 50% frequency of admission is significantly greater than the odds the other applicants face. All of the
Ivies, for example, now admit under 15% of the total applicant pool.
The reasoning behind the favored status of legacies is the belief that
long-standing traditions that are a trademark of the top colleges are
carried forward by succeeding generations of students who have grown
up with the stories of these customs and traditions. You may consider
yourself a probable candidate for admission to Georgetown, for example, because your father or mother graduated twenty-five years ago and
has recounted his or her experiences to you. But you cannot count on
this because of the many other competitive candidates applying, and so
you must consider your other options as well.

In all our years of counseling, we have seen many high school students rebel at the notion of applying to the college their mother or father attended. While we understand the psychological desire to separate their personality and goals from their parents', they often miss out on the opportunity to apply to a very appropriate college for themselves, one where their legacy status can help them be accepted. We urge you to search out those colleges that are right for you on all counts, and if one of them happens to be one your parent attended, do not eliminate it only so that you can make a statement of your independence. It will be hard to justify ignoring a selective college where you have such a connection, since it may be one of your best chances for admission. If you are admitted but then decide to go elsewhere, nothing is lost as long as your family does not make the final decision for you. As you begin your college search, ask your parents directly: "If I am admitted to your alma mater, will you try to make me enroll?" They should answer no to this question and let you get on with your search for the right college for you.

One of the positive fallouts today of the legacy policy selective colleges adhere to is the fact that every year thousands of exceptional young men and women graduate from supposedly elite colleges. They, in turn, create legacy status for the children they will raise in the next generation. The continuity is a positive force that enables great institutions to maintain their independence and educational leadership as time and events change the world around them.

We view faculty connections as a subset of the legacy category. An applicant who has a parent on the faculty or administration of a selective college has two things going for him or her: probable admission to the institution and partial or free tuition. It is generally understood that the children of full-time employees merit special consideration if they apply, since they tend to know the college well and their family gives a great deal to enhance the life and the academics on campus. Some colleges pay for the tuition in full at their own school or at any other the student attends. It is important to check with the admissions office regarding their policy on both the admissions and financial assistance fronts. But a selective college will not admit a borderline faculty child who is likely to falter or even fail. He or she must meet the high standards set by the committee for all applicants.

Minorities

Members of minority groups who apply to selective colleges are considered one of the special categories to ensure that the goal of achieving significant diversity within the class is accomplished. Like applicants in all of the other special categories, minority candidates must compete on the basis of their academic capabilities and strengths, since there are more applicants in this group than can be admitted. Given the present public debate on the merits of affirmative action and the emotions this policy has engendered on both sides of the issue, we want to make two vital points clear: First, the top private colleges and universities view a well-educated young man or woman as one who has exposure to all kinds of ideas and people with religious, cultural, ethnic, and racial backgrounds that differ from their own. Reaching out to students of color is one of the missions, therefore, of the admissions committees. Second, minority applicants are not accorded a special privilege or right to admission. They must earn a place, like all other candidates, on the strength of their abilities and performance and with the confidence that they can take advantage of the richness of the colleges' offerings. This is the ultimate criterion for minority admissions.

Minorities are now defined for the purposes of the admissions process as including economically and educationally disadvantaged Asians and Caucasians, African Americans, Hispanics, and Native Americans. They do not usually include most Americans of Japanese, Chinese, Korean, or Southeast Asian extraction.

Minority group and economically disadvantaged applicants are considered in a special round because many, if not a majority, have the burden of weaker schooling and poor test preparation. Admissions committees take into account in weighing the credentials of disadvantaged candidates the lack of opportunity to prepare themselves as readily as suburban high school or independent school students. They also consider the motivation and determination of such students to push themselves beyond the boundaries of their environment to seek further education. First-generation college students, not all of whom are minorities, are highly sought after by selective colleges, which see the enrollment of such students as part of their mission. As we noted, in many cases, first-generation students comprise a significant proportion of each class, as high as that of alumni legacies.

If you are an applicant from one of the groups listed above, you may be contacted by an admissions officer who belongs to a minority group or an alumnus who lives in your area and has gotten your name from your registration for the PSAT or SAT or has read about your exploits in the local newspaper. You should ask to speak with members of your group who are presently attending the colleges you have initial interest in. You should also draw up a list of these colleges and see if there are other categories into which you fit. Are you an athlete; have you a musical or writing talent? At what college will you most likely have an added edge? Minority group applicants wind up like all other applicants, winning some, losing some, with admissions offers from two or three of five to seven colleges where they applied. We encourage you to apply to more rather than fewer colleges so that you also increase the odds of winning the financial award you may need to attend a top college. Remember that each college determines its financial aid packages on the basis of its interest in a candidate and the amount of scholarship resources it has in hand.

Athletes

Selective colleges love good athletes for their talent, perseverance, courage, discipline, and confidence. Star athletes are often positive role models for non-athletes. They frequently take on leadership roles in the campus community and are not hesitant to stress school spirit and participation. But the top colleges insist that their athletes be serious students, prepared to meet all of the rigorous academic requirements, graduate in good standing, and move on to careers that benefit the community as well as themselves.

Graduates of the top colleges who were recruited on the basis of their athletic talent often continue their sports interests by supporting amateur athletics or raising money for their colleges' sports programs or national and international athletic competitions such as the Olympics. Some former athletes are so appreciative of the impact athletic competition had on their personal opportunities that they have endowed a chair for the coach in their sport: a Yale alumnus endowed the

varsity football coach's position, and a group of former Princeton basketball players endowed the coach's position for the same reason. At
Dartmouth, a large number of alumni of all ages who played rugby
during their time on campus have raised the money to build an endowment to support a coach and their own clubhouse. These are the binding traditions that give certain campuses their unique tone.

Selective colleges differ on their policy of awarding athletic scholarships. The Ivy League institutions, for example, joined together as a
league to establish common athletic policies on recruitment of athletes
and scholarships. A majority of the Eastern top colleges do not give athletic scholarships, using their resources to award aid solely on the basis
of need, which, of course, includes many athletes. Many of the larger
selective universities in the other regions of the country do have substantial budgets for athletic scholarships.

A student-athlete who will need substantial amounts of aid to pay
for four years of college should consider the advantages and potential
disadvantages of applying to both categories of selective schools. For
the nonscholarship group of colleges, you will have to rely on the aid
package offered you, which typically is a combination of grant, loan,
and work-study funds based on your need. An outright athletic scholarship signifies two important factors: First, the level of play and the odds
of making a varsity team are significantly more competitive; second,
there is the risk of losing your scholarship if you sustain an injury or do
not make the team. We encourage those students who are competitive
athletes to consider colleges more on the basis of the right choice educationally if their ultimate goal is to attain a diploma. It may be wiser
to use the athletic edge for admissions purposes, knowing that whether
or not you continue to play a sport in college will be entirely your
choice.

Why do good athletes have an edge in admissions to the top colleges? Because colleges like to have winning teams for the spirit this
engenders on campus and among their alumni. Former President Na-
than Pusey of Harvard is said to have told an assistant after watching
Yale beat Harvard 54–0: "Don't let this happen again!" Since that
time Harvard has had one of the most successful athletic programs of
all the non-scholarship-granting universities. To attract strong scholar-
athletes, selective colleges must recruit them. This means that in the

athletic round, when only the folders of the athletes recommended by the respective coaches are considered, admissions committees are under pressure to take applicants who might not make it through the competition without their star quality. It is not uncommon for a coach or alumnus to bring to the attention of the admissions committee a top athlete who is in the middle of his or her high school class and might not consider applying to a highly selective college. Another benefit of the recruitment of student-athletes is the identification each year of a number of disadvantaged students of athletic and academic distinction who otherwise would not know that they were of interest to a selective college.

The "buyer beware" theme applies to athletic recruitment, however. Athletes have to reckon with the competition for precious places in the selective colleges. Coaches do not have the power to admit candidates on their own, and their reassurance that "I want you" and will "help you get in" should not be taken as an offer of admission. Coaches lose many battles on behalf of a prospect with the admissions committees. They can let the committee know what they believe are the chances of an applicant making the varsity team in their sport, but they cannot demand the admission of anyone. We have seen many student-athletes who relied on the word of a coach get turned down. In the meantime, they had not followed through on all of their applications and they ended up without any good choices.

Special Talents and Interests

Talent is a broad category that goes beyond creativity and encompasses many fields of endeavor. You may have a talent for languages that is attractive to selective colleges in this era when language concentrators are increasingly scarce. We encouraged Linda, who attended a competitive New England boarding school, to apply to selective colleges like Yale, Vanderbilt, Georgetown, and Emory on the basis of her impressive background of study in Russian history and language. She had spent the summer prior to her senior year on an immersion program in Russia to learn more about the culture and to improve her speaking ability. These universities had good to strong departments in this discipline and were eager to enroll students who would take advantage of their resources. Linda was admitted to three of these universities ahead of a number of competitive classmates on the strength of her special talent and now attends Georgetown.

What do you consider your talents? Professional assessment of talent is what impresses admissions committees. When they read about a student who has performed vocally in competitive settings and her voice teacher writes that she has the talent and drive to become a professional performer, the committee will take notice.

But to what colleges should talented students apply? We encourage students who have both high academic standing in their high school and a special talent to include selective colleges among those they are considering. Professional schools of music, art, or drama, as examples, are highly specialized and will not provide you with the balanced education that will prove valuable and enriching in your future. Unless you are very sure about pursuing your special talent or interest to the exclusion of most others at this time, you should explore selective colleges where you can gain a liberal arts education while continuing simultaneously to develop your talent at a high level. You can always attend a professional program later on when you have had enough exposure to be certain this is your chosen career.

We have, from time to time, discouraged uniquely talented students from considering top colleges because they were focused exclusively on their interest and might not have had the patience and discipline required in an academically demanding college. These students may, in fact, be better served by following their interest to the highest level possible. If they succeed in making a career out of their talent, that is fine; if not, they can always enroll in a well-rounded college or university later on. Howard Greene had just this experience when he was an admissions officer at Princeton. Eric, a professional violinist who had distinguished himself as a young virtuoso performer, decided at age twenty-five to take a sabbatical from his music to get the liberal arts education he felt was a missing part of his life. He was encouraged to apply to Princeton and was admitted, although this was rare for an older student. Eric contributed greatly to the community by sharing his exceptional talent through performing and instructing beginning students interested in the violin. He, in turn, received wonderful exposure to the literature, history, and philosophy that he had always wanted to study.

Individual talents may be best developed further in a selective college where the necessary faculty and facilities are available. This is true of such areas as writing and leadership of others, for example. Contacting teachers in your special field of talent to discuss their programs and how they can assist you is the right way to go about sorting out the best place for you to enroll. The admissions committees, in turn, are likely to be more interested in you, since they want to continue the reputation of their outstanding programs. They also know that what can lead any outstanding student to apply to their college is the excitement and energy certain programs or activities engender on campus.

International Students

Nationals of other countries are of interest to selective colleges because of the diversity foreign students add to the community. We distinguish non-American citizens from American students living abroad with their families. Internationals are considered in the selection process as a group for several reasons: It is the usual practice to have one member of the admissions committee responsible for all applicants from abroad so that he can train himself in the different academic and grading systems of foreign countries. These officers also visit each year secondary schools around the world from which numbers of students regularly apply to their college. You will notice in the literature of all selective colleges a brag sheet regarding the number of foreign countries represented in the student body. The purpose of this is to underscore the cosmopolitan mix of students and the global reputation the college enjoys. Having a good group of international students is the result of maintaining a special piece of the admissions pie which can vary from 5% to 20% of the total admitted group in a given year. Every year almost half a million international students enroll in American colleges and universities, many of them in top colleges throughout the United States.

We need to warn international candidates that a majority of colleges do not have designated scholarship funds for non-American citizens. If you will need financial aid to attend college here, you must do the research we recommend in Step Nine to determine which institutions do provide scholarships for internationals.

Americans who live abroad and attend national or international schools are also appealing to selective colleges, because of their broader perspective on the world and other cultures. This student frequently has learned a new language, sometimes an exotic one, and has traveled more widely than the typical American student. We encourage such candidates to write extensively in their applications about the nature of their experiences abroad and what they can add to the college's environment. As the global economy continues to define the nature of the world of commerce, increasing numbers of businesspeople live abroad with their families. Admissions officers pay close attention to the students who have taken advantage of the opportunities this provides them to grow intellectually and culturally.

Geographic Diversity

All selective colleges seek geographic diversity in their entering class. This involves reaching out to students from faraway or non-traditional locations.

A selective admissions officer may not tell you that where you come from is a plus in your profile, but you can tell that it may well be by examining the college's published list of students and their home states. If your locality turns up infrequently, you can consider your chances of acceptance a good reason to apply to selective colleges outside your home region. We have had very good results bringing to selective college admissions officers' attention strong applicants from high schools that rarely have qualified applicants.

It is not unusual for too many students from the same public high school or private school to apply to the same small band of selective colleges. The admissions officers have to ask themselves, "What will these candidates add to the life at our college, since they appear to have similar socioeconomic backgrounds, common interests, and goals. Will they relate to students different from themselves?" The staff at the Consulting Centers counsels applicants to avoid the "bunching effect" and to diversify their targeted list of colleges geographically.

We will refer in Step Eight to a talented young woman who applied to a host of Ivy League universities from a small town in central Ohio. She was fortunate to have traveled extensively in her young life, but she grew up in this small town and attended its high school and thus had an interesting perspective on the advantages and disadvantages of a small community. She was helped in her candidacy by fitting into a slice of the admissions pie that, together with her excellent academic profile, proved of great interest to the admissions committees.

Special Cases

This is a tricky category, to say the least. Every college is faced in each year's admissions cycle with a small group of applications that call for special consideration. They can include the son or daughter of an influential supporter or a well-known public figure. Usually the president or a trustee of the institution is involved in making a recommendation to the admissions committee regarding such candidates. Even the most prestigious universities enjoy the publicity and added glow that comes from the enrollment of a member of a highly recognizable family. Contrary to the rumors that a large number of such special cases are admitted to the selective colleges, senior administrators tend to leave the decision making to the professional admissions staff. College presidents have told us how rarely they have interceded on behalf of an applicant. We urge families not to rely on seemingly important contacts to help get their child admitted to a college that is beyond their grasp, since the odds of its helping them are slim and it is probably the wrong college for their son or daughter.

CHURNING THE APPLICANT POOL

In the interest of diversifying their student bodies, the top colleges in the East are deliberately cutting back on the numbers of applicants they will admit from high-density areas, particularly the New York metropolitan area. Selective colleges that have very large pools of applicants from this area every year are sensitive to the tilt in the nature of their community that accepting a disproportionate number from any one area creates. There is no question about the greater competition, therefore, in winning a place in one of the top Eastern colleges from New York suburban high schools and Manhattan day schools. The same dynamic applies to areas like Boston and Washington for certain highly desirable colleges. As one dean of admissions reported to us, "We worry about a critical mass of one type of student." Another said that their students from other parts of the country felt they were not well received by the cliques sometimes formed by the students from large urban communities.

To take these places, the Eastern colleges will be looking for good students from other sections of the country, including both rural and urban areas. Colleges in the South, Southwest, and West, in their turn, are conscious of the regional dominance of their student bodies and are eager to have applications from outstanding Eastern students.

In all cases the goal is also to achieve national recognition, which leads to an ever greater variety of talented candidates. This means that many qualified applicants in the metropolitan areas may not be admitted to their preferred Eastern colleges. While you can never be certain of an acceptance anywhere, your chances, if you are an East Coast student, are likely to be better at one of the outstanding colleges in the other regions of the country. Smart applicants will include at least several top colleges outside of their area on their list of applications.

The Different Approach to State Universities

In developing a strategy for selective state universities like the University of Virginia, North Carolina, Michigan, and Wisconsin, and the College of William and Mary, you should pay special attention to the issue of quotas on out-of-state applicants. Most public universities must limit the number of places available to "non-state-taxpayers," thus creating greater competition for admissions. Because of the large number of applicants to be processed, the admissions committees normally set cutoff scores on the SAT or ACT and class rank. Depending on the university, this could mean a combined SAT score above 1900 or 2000 and class standing in the top quintile or decile of your high school class. You need also to find a special category in the class pie to give you a real chance for acceptance. For some students, identified talent as a future varsity athlete will work; for others, applying to one of the universities' specialized schools such as engineering, music, architecture, or education with a documented commitment to the field, which can be measured by a portfolio or performance or special course work, can make the difference. For minority students there is still a serious interest in your applying to the state universities, but a number of judicial decisions and legislative changes have eliminated or restricted affirmative action policies. Nevertheless, if you are a strong student who meets the academic requirements set by the selective state schools, you will be given close consideration.

INDEPENDENT SCHOOLS AND COLLEGE ADMISSIONS

A generation ago the quality and size of suburban high schools around the country began to put the traditional "prep schools" in their shadow. These famous old places were deemed too elitist by the rising tide of baby boomers putting their children in public schools. Over time the private schools have regained their eminence, but in new and exciting roles. They began by abandoning the term *private* in favor of *independent,* which better describes their mission. Through huge financial aid programs they have broadened dramatically the composition of their student bodies racially, ethnically, geographically, and socioeconomically. Today many families seek out the independent schools not only for the quality of their education but also for the diversity of their communities, which sometimes can be greater than that of the exclusive suburban high schools, which reflect only their local communities.

Admissions committees perceive applicants from the top independent schools as being well prepared for rigorous college work and socially mature because of their residential experience in broad-based environments. In a real sense, the selective secondary schools have done some of the identification and recruitment work for the top colleges. The Choate Rosemary Hall School in Connecticut, as a good example, enrolls students from over forty countries and almost all fifty states, and provides financial aid for over 20% of its students.

The Eastern independent schools no longer enjoy virtually automatic admissions to the top colleges, as they did prior to the 1960s, but they continue to send their top students in disproportionate numbers to the top fifty or so colleges each year. Choate, for example, sends the largest number of its graduating classes to such top colleges as Pennsylvania, Brown, Georgetown, Yale, Cornell, Tufts, Columbia, Johns Hopkins, Emory, New York University, and Bowdoin. Today's independent school student must compete with the best of the public high school applicants for a place in the selective colleges.

Your Pie Chart Analysis

The eight applicant categories can be approximately quantified in percentages that vary from one institution to another. One college may enroll 20% alumni children, and another only 15%. An Eastern college may enroll 75% of its students from east of the Mississippi; a Southern college may enroll 50% of its students from below the Mason-Dixon Line.

These percentages provide you with a means for estimating the intensity of your competition for admission at different selective colleges, all of them, as you know now, determined to construct a diverse student body. You can use the classic pie chart at the beginning of this step as a graphic aid to add in the percentages of each category for the colleges you are considering. You can convert data from the first-year profiles issued by the colleges into individual pie charts. You can then locate your own place in those charts to understand how you compare with the competition. You will be able to see from the data or size of the slices where the competition is great and where it is moderate.

WHAT HIGHLY SELECTIVE (EXCEEDINGLY DEMANDING) MEANS
A Georgetown Class

Georgetown had 16,171 students apply for the class of 2010. Only 3,305 were offered admission. A total of about 1,580 men and women chose to enroll. What are the credentials of the class? Thirteen percent internationals, 29% students of color and ethnic backgrounds. Ninety percent of accepted students, ranked in the top 10% to 15% of their high school class. Middle 50% SAT scores were 680–760 critical reading, 670–760 math.

You would find the Georgetown pie chart enlightening in terms of the breakout of the regional, international, minority, talent, athletic, legacy, and academic categories we have drawn. A close study of the pie chart would help you to determine if you have any chance of admission to Georgetown. You can find this information on the Office of Admissions Web site.

Developing Your Own Pie Chart

The statistical profile for the class of 2012 admitted to Princeton, one of the most selective universities in the nation, reveals the significance of some of the categories given special consideration in the decision process. While only 9.9% of the total applicant group was accepted, legacies and minority students were admitted at much higher rates. If you study carefully the demographic information that all selective colleges make public, you can learn if geography will be an asset or a detriment. For example, Princeton tells you which states have the highest representation in the undergraduate college. You can readily see that there is no competitive edge if you are from New Jersey, New York, Pennsylvania, or other populous states like California or Texas. A strong applicant from an underrepresented state may well be helped in the competition. We can tell you from personal experience in the admissions office that well-qualified applicants to Princeton from such states as Montana, Utah, and Oklahoma were given special consideration within the geography category and thus accepted. In the class of 2012, there were no enrollees from New Mexico, Idaho, Wyoming, or Montana, and very few from a number of New England, Midwestern, and Southern states.

Children of alumni have an advantage in applying to Princeton. You can see that almost 14% of the class were legacies. This figure is not a statistical aberration for the class of 2012. Princeton has long honored the ties its graduates maintain to the university, which is reflected in their generous gifts for endowment and buildings, and in volunteer activities to enhance the university's reputation and quality. Though it varies, we estimate that qualified legacies have double the odds of admission at universities like Princeton and Dartmouth. Now, double 10% are still tough odds. . . .

It is also clear that minority candidates are given a decided edge in the selection process. This reflects the university's ongoing commitment to diversify its student population. Princeton's trustees and administrators adhere to a vision of a meritocratic community rather than one based on aristocratic elitism. As we have indicated, those institutions with large endowments can afford to act on their principles and make it possible for any qualified candidate to enroll. Fifty-five percent of the class was offered need-based aid. One hundred and forty-one members of the class were internationals.

The category for special interests is also reflected in the data that compare engineering majors to liberal arts majors at Princeton. A student with a serious interest in studying engineering at the undergraduate level may have a statistically better chance for admission. Although one-quarter of each class is dedicated to engineering majors, the number of qualified applicants to fill this portion of the class is less than for bachelor of arts students.

It is more difficult to quantify the numbers and percentages of students admitted because of athletic or special talents. You can be sure these pieces of the Princeton pie are represented with approximately 10% each of scholar-athletes, outstanding artists and performers, debaters, writers, and school and community leaders.

All of the top colleges and universities will share with you the data you need to design your personal pie chart and to determine if you have good reason to apply.

Princeton University Profile, Class of 2012

Applicants: 21,370
Admitted: 2,122 (9.9%)
Enrolled: 1,243

Percentage of Applicants Admitted, by GPA Range

16.4%	4.00
11.0%	3.90–3.99
9.6%	3.80–3.89
6.2%	3.70–3.79
5.1%	3.60–3.69
4.9%	3.50–3.59
4.1%	Below 3.50

Percentage of Applicants Admitted, by SAT Range

28.1%	2300–2400
10.6%	2100–2290
6.2%	1900–2090
2.3%	1700–1890
0.6%	1500–1690
0.0%	Below 1500
4.4%	No CEEB Scores

Composition of Enrolled Class

96.8% ranked in the top decile of their class (of those whose schools rank)

50/50 Male/Female Ratio

13.7% Legacies

Middle 50% SAT: CR 690–790, MA 700–790, WR 690–780

School Type Graduated From: Public 56.2%, Independent Day 20.8%, Independent Boarding 9.4%, Religious 12.9%, Home Schooled 0.5%, Military 0.2%

Ethnic/Racial Diversity: African American 7.6%, Asian American 16.7%, Hispanic 7.6%, Native American 0.4%, Multiracial 5.6%, International 11.3% (from 45 countries)

You can quantify a pie chart by putting numbers into the slices. Take the total number of admitted applicants and divide each of the eight categories to see if your profile matches positively with any of them. If Princeton, for example, admits a high percentage of minority students and alumni children and you fit one or both of these categories, you will have a definite advantage over the thousands of other qualified candidates. If you have an excellent academic record and you see that among your target colleges one is very underrepresented by your home state while another has a large number of students enrolled, you can figure which one is likely to be more interested in you.

You should follow this analysis for each of the eight categories of the pie to arrive at a final list of colleges that will give you your best chance of admission. Your aim is to identify the colleges where you fit into the most slices of the pie. Therefore, when you have finished charting your prospects at one college on your list, turn to the next, and so on, until you have a series of charts that represent your admission chances.

Pie charts are for our own use and can be drawn freehand. We can tell you from our many years of counseling students that pie-charting has made the difference for many strong applicants. Students who were anxious and depressed that they were focused only on colleges where their odds of being admitted were poor were convinced by using the pie chart system to broaden their list of colleges logically. We think of many students who discovered how their athletic ability or musical talent or interest in anthropology or classics led to acceptance by targeted colleges that had not been on their original list.

Analyzing the fields of concentration that undergraduates at Stanford University select, as an example, reveals a large percentage of engineering, biological/life sciences, computer science, social science, and history majors. By contrast, a small percentage of students major in foreign languages, literature, or philosophy, religion, and theology. If any of these are of genuine interest to you as demonstrated in your present studies, you should consider applying to Stanford with a strong statement of your commitment to participating in one of these programs.

Two Case Studies

Here are pie charts copied from those of two students we counseled, Audrey and Jim. Audrey, in the upper 15% of her high school in Illinois, was vice president of the senior class and captain of the varsity field hockey team. Her mother was a Smith College graduate. After her research into some twenty colleges of possible interest, Audrey was particularly keen on applying to Smith, Colorado College, Pomona, and Northwestern. She drew these four pie charts:

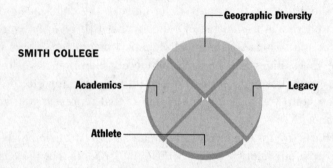

Audrey drew her Smith pie chart first in a schematic way, cutting the pie into four equal slices and finding herself in four of them, as opposed to only three of them at Colorado, two at Pomona, and one at Northwestern.

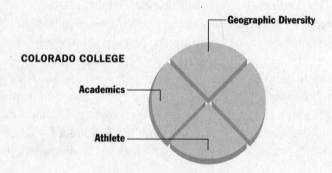

At Colorado Audrey felt that she would be considered in the athletic round since the coach expressed great interest in her, and that coming from Illinois gave her some geographic diversity. She checked the college's statistics and noted that her academic credentials matched up very nicely.

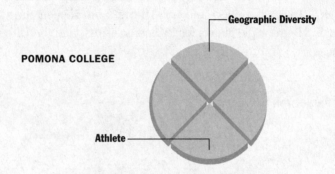

POMONA COLLEGE

A careful study of Pomona's statistics indicated to Audrey that she had two potential advantages working for her: her athletic ability and her regional background. She recognized that her academic credentials placed her in the middle of the last two classes admitted to the college.

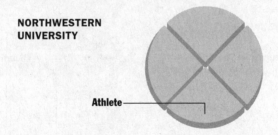

NORTHWESTERN
UNIVERSITY

Audrey felt, after looking at her Northwestern pie chart, that her chances were not as good as at the other three colleges. As with Pomona, her academic profile placed her in the middle of the Northwestern pool. Her high school class had at least twenty students planning to apply to Northwestern. She was not even certain her athletic ability would call attention to her application, since she had not heard from the field hockey coach.

With this picture of her chances laid out before her, Audrey decided to apply to Smith, Colorado, and Pomona. She would not submit an application to Northwestern. In early April, Audrey received acceptance letters from Smith and Colorado and was placed on Pomona's wait list.

Jim, a minority student in a Newark, New Jersey, high school, was in the upper 10% of his class and an All-State hurdler on the varsity track team. He drew pie charts for Princeton, Tufts, and the University of Chicago.

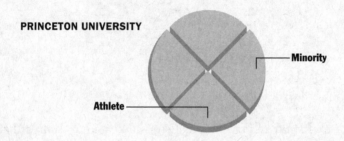

PRINCETON UNIVERSITY

Minority

Athlete

At Princeton, his pie chart showed he would be considered in both the athletic and the minority rounds. His academic record positioned him in the upper middle range for the previous year's admitted class.

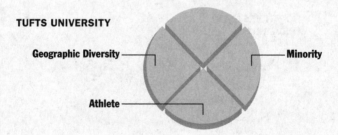

TUFTS UNIVERSITY

Geographic Diversity

Minority

Athlete

Jim's Tufts pie chart showed that in addition to his status as an athlete and minority candidate, he would be attractive as a candidate from an urban New Jersey high school. His academic performance and test scores placed him in the upper quintile of Tufts's profile.

Drawing his chart for the University of Chicago, Jim made the regional diversity slice much larger than for Tufts, since Midwestern universities have fewer Eastern applicants, and a recent visit from an admissions officer had confirmed the school's interest in qualified candidates from his high school. Jim also drew a larger athletic slice after receiving two letters from the varsity track coach, who stated that Jim's times would make him a starter on his team as a freshman.

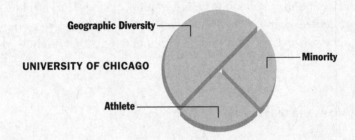

Jim rated his chances at Chicago as excellent, very good at Tufts, and least good at Princeton. He decided to apply to all three and to cover himself with an application to his home state university, Rutgers. The outcomes for Jim were quite exhilarating. He was offered places at all four colleges and after visits to Chicago and Princeton, he chose Chicago for its urban location and generous financial aid award.

Emphasize Your Uniqueness

Doing pie-charting is tailoring admissions to your size. Within each category there are literally thousands of variations, and these can provide opportunities for you to emphasize your strengths and to identify your distinctive characteristics. Now consider the categories where these very features will place you within small slices of the pie.

Every student has a unique profile, and every selective college its unique diversity and mix. Bringing the two together will reveal the institutions most likely to respond favorably to your application. Are you a creative writer or a poet? Colleges like Vanderbilt and Kenyon have a long and cherished tradition of outstanding faculty who teach writing to serious undergraduates. If your academic credentials are in line with the requirements of these colleges, your special talent can give you an advantage in admissions.

Are you a rower? Highly selective universities like Harvard, Cornell, and Pennsylvania have a major commitment to their crew programs. The coaches seek experienced high school rowers every year to ensure their winning tradition. If you are a committed athlete in this field, you will have a distinct slice in the pie chart that could make the difference between acceptance and rejection. Here is a Harvard chart that helped twin brothers realize their dream to attend the university. At first Roger and Raymond were hesitant to consider Harvard because of the intense competition. But once they each drew a personal pie chart, they saw that they had several unique talents that might work for them.

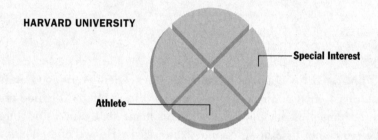

HARVARD UNIVERSITY

Special Interest

Athlete

Their competitive experience on their high school team and their year-round training brought Roger and Raymond to the attention of the Harvard rowing coach in their junior year. He followed their development through their senior year to be certain they were at a level of ability and commitment that would help his program. Once he knew that both boys had excellent grades and test scores, he encouraged them to apply early to Harvard, from which they received "likely letters" in September informing them of their almost certain admission.

The other pie slice that helped them through the decision process was their strong background in the study of Greek and Latin. Both Roger and Raymond wrote enthusiastically in their applications about their passion for classical language studies. Their courses in high school and in a summer program reinforced their interest. Harvard accepted both.

Pie-charting opens your eyes to admission possibilities. It is up to you to decide where you really want to go. In studying pie charts you have two general situations: Either you fit into a number of categories and therefore have extra competitive chances, or you are unique and are competing against few applicants. For example, an admissions committee, noting that you are both an alumnus's child and a talented athlete or musician, will be more inclined to admit you than another applicant with your profile minus the athletic or musical gift.

On the other hand, a particular college seeking students for certain programs within their college will look closely at applicants for those programs. While pie-charting is not an exact science, we can tell you from experience that it has proved to be one of the most reassuring tools an applicant can use to sort out admissions chances. Further, it can help you highlight those colleges that match up the best for you in terms of your interests and talents.

Consider the case of Arnold, an outstanding student who attended a competitive high school on Long Island. He had excellent grades in the most demanding courses the school offered and he was a school leader. His SATs were all in the 700 range. In the summer prior to his senior year he interned in Washington with his local congressman. Should he consider Harvard, he asked his counselor? In terms of his capabilities, the answer was yes. But twenty other strong students in his class were applying to Harvard. Yale, Princeton, and Brown were other top choices. But he knew he faced similar competition within his class for these schools as well.

In thinking through his strategic plan by designing a personal pie chart, Arnold discovered that Dartmouth had precisely the academic program and resources he wanted, and it gave him a better chance for admission for two reasons: geography and the Nelson Rockefeller Center for Political Studies. Arnold read the description of the center as a premier program for training undergraduates about public policy and civic leadership. Dartmouth receives thousands of applications from highly competitive Connecticut and Massachusetts students but not as many from Long Islanders because of its northern New England location. Arnold's work as president of his school's Model United Nations program, his campaigning for local congressional candidates, and his internship in Washington made him an appealing candidate for the Rockefeller Center program. After a visit to the Dartmouth campus and an interview with a Rockefeller Center professor, Arnold applied Early Decision and was accepted. His awareness of the right program for him and his better chance for acceptance were triggered by his use of the pie chart exercise.

Travis was an intellectually mature young man who attended a Westchester County, New York, high school that sends almost 100% of its graduates on to college. He knew by his senior year that he was going to study philosophy and religion as an undergraduate, and then go on for a Ph.D. He should have been a natural candidate for one of the top research-oriented universities, including the Ivies, where the faculty in the philosophy departments was outstanding. But Travis did not test well on the SAT, despite several attempts to improve his scores. He made the mistake of lingering too long on questions that intrigued him, turning them over in his mind like the good philosopher that he was. This is a fatal test procedure, and it put him in the 1100 range when he probably could have made a significant jump if he had agreed to intense preparation to break him of his habit, admirable though it might be, of mulling over answers in such depth.

After meeting with a counselor at the Educational Consulting Centers, Travis focused his search on the small selective colleges noted for sending a high percentage of their graduates on to doctoral degree programs. He confirmed the advice he had received that top-ranked small liberal arts colleges like Carleton, Grinnell, and Oberlin had excellent philosophy departments and that the number of candidates who applied for this major was small. We described the advantages of these colleges to Travis just as we have in *The Hidden Ivies*. So his special interest matched up favorably on his pie charts. Another advantage would be his regional diversity, since all three colleges are located well outside the metropolitan New York region. His pie slices for Grinnell and Oberlin were large ones, since these Midwestern colleges were eager to enroll excellent students from the Northeast corridor to diversify their community, especially with students from his high school, which enjoyed a national reputation.

A third factor for Travis in applying to these colleges was financial; they are somewhat less expensive than the Ivies, and they have substantial financial aid programs. All three colleges accepted Travis and offered him generous scholarship packages that made it possible for him to attend. After an April visit to all three campuses, he chose Carleton on the basis of the warm welcome the philosophy faculty gave him and their promise of encouraging him to undertake research projects with them early in his undergraduate career.

Will it help your admissions chances if you know as an applicant what you want to major in? Yes, but only to the extent that you realize what the competition is in your field. For example, only the very strongest candidates have a chance for admission to MIT's computer science and electrical engineering programs. RPI, Cal Tech, and Carnegie Mellon University are overwhelmed with applicants wishing to major in these fields as well as in chemistry, physics, and mathematics. At the same time, other great universities, including some of the Ivies, are working hard to attract excellent students in these disciplines in order to build their departments. The competition for premedical places is heavy at all the Ivies as well as at Johns Hopkins, Emory, Rochester, Washington in St. Louis, Berkeley, Stanford, Duke, and Vanderbilt, among others. Using different examples, the same dynamic will hold true for students planning on becoming lawyers.

So, to draw a pie chart relating to a specific academic discipline, you will have to contact the colleges themselves or check their Web sites to find out how many students major in your field and how many go on to graduate school in the particular discipline. You must realize that even admission to a selective college is no guarantee that you can get into specialized upper-class programs such as the Woodrow Wilson School of Public and International Affairs at Princeton or the McIntyre School of Commerce at the University of Virginia. Be careful how you choose your college based on your field of interest.

The fact is that the majority of freshmen arrive on campus without a clear idea of what their major will be, so not knowing what you want to study is the norm and is not a major hindrance to admission. The appeal of the liberal arts colleges is that they offer you an opportunity to explore their many offerings in order to discover where your interests lie. Thus we urge you not to try to fit into a piece of the pie by arbitrarily deciding that you will opt for a specific academic program. Some students have applied and been admitted as engineering concentrators only because selective colleges with engineering departments had fewer candidates. The result has been that those students who had no right to be engineers would enroll and, after a year of torturous studies, transfer to the liberal arts division of the college. There has to be legitimate interest and aptitude for the indicated field of study to make sense for you to apply for any particular specialty. You can be sure that selective colleges look carefully at an applicant's background for evidence of a sincere commitment to the field of study expressed in the application.

Review the notes you took on your campus visits, using the College Visit Summary Sheets included in the Appendix, to discover how your uniqueness can be fitted into a slice of the freshman pie chart where the competition may not be overwhelming. If you need further information, go after it. Phone the college admissions office and ask to be connected with academic or extracurricular departments to get your questions answered. You can probably get all or most of your answers from a search on the college's Web site. We encourage students to e-mail department heads, coaches, and any relevant person to make personal contact.

Drawing Pie Charts in Your Junior Year

Usually applicants need not calculate their chances for admission until they are ready to decide where they will apply. There are cases, however, when a student will benefit by drawing some pie charts in junior year. Lincoln, for example, was under the impression that his grades were good enough for him to apply to an Ivy college—until he began making a few pie charts with our encouragement. What he discovered was that many of his competitive classmates in his suburban Washington, D.C., high school had already taken a number of advanced courses. How could he catch up if he were to be a viable candidate for the colleges he had in mind? He decided to enroll in Cornell's Advanced Placement Summer Pre-College Program and to take courses in advanced history and French. Not only did he perform well and receive two A's, he was able to get credit from his high school and thus take other advanced subjects in his senior year. Lincoln now had a rich academic profile to match his extracurricular strengths as captain of the varsity tennis team and president of the debate team. Now able to apply from a position of strength, Lincoln was admitted to two of his three top choices. As it turned out, he enrolled in Cornell because his summer exposure informed him of the many advantages Cornell had to offer. This positive outcome would not have happened had he not charted his course, so to speak, in his junior year.

Andrea visited Howard Greene's office in the winter of her junior year to discuss her interests and ambitions. She attended a magnet school in Philadelphia where she was an outstanding student with a particular passion: Chinese culture and language study. She needed direction on which universities were strong in this discipline and what she had to accomplish to have a serious chance for acceptance. We recommended she visit five selective colleges that offered Chinese studies, including Brown, which was in the process of adding faculty and resources to this program. A visit to the campus that included meeting with several members of the department stimulated Andrea to enroll in a summer language program in China, which we recommended to her. In the early fall of senior year she plotted her personal pie chart, which indicated that her optimum chance for admission to an Ivy university was at Brown because of their encouragement and interest in building a larger department in Asian studies.

Andrea's pie chart looked like this for Brown. She was admitted on the Early Decision plan, having secured impressive letters of recommendation from her high school instructor and the director of the summer program she attended. Further, she had remained in contact with the two Brown professors she had met the previous year, and they subsequently endorsed her candidacy.

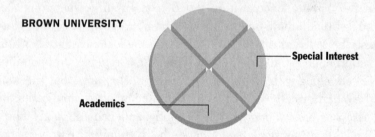

BROWN UNIVERSITY

Special Interest

Academics

More unusual is the case of Janice, a student in the top 5% of her class in a rural high school north of Boston. Janice decided as a sophomore that she wanted to go to Harvard. Her father, a successful businessman, wanted her to attend a prominent day school noted for its success in sending graduates on to very selective colleges. It was a known fact that this school enrolled an unusually large number of students with Harvard-educated parents, making the competition still greater for a non-legacy candidate. But Janice's counselor told her that no one from her small public high school had applied to Harvard in years, and he calculated that if she finished near the top of her class, she would have a better chance of being admitted. Warning her against competing with twenty-five applicants from the private school under consideration and not standing at the top of her class, he convinced her of her unique status in a rural public school that could give her a number of advanced courses to demonstrate her ability and motivation.

This is the pie chart that applied to Janice's situation for Harvard:

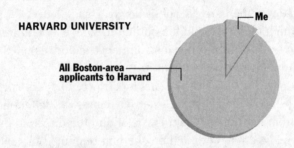

Janice drew her pie chart this way to show how slight her competition was based on location and school competition. Had she applied from the private school within the Boston suburbs, she would have found it difficult to distinguish herself from hundreds of similar candidates. She realized that in one sense, she was competing only against herself from her small high school. True, she had to be a fully qualified candidate along with all the others in the Boston area, but she would not be pitted directly against a number of comparable applicants. Janice also was able to demonstrate her independence and motivation by taking all that was available for her on her own initiative in her school. She was admitted to Harvard as well as to Vassar (where her mother had gone), Middlebury, and Wesleyan.

Independent School Pie-Charting

Premier boarding schools like Exeter, Andover, Choate, Hotchkiss, Deerfield, Lawrenceville, Milton, St. Paul's, and Groton are no longer the automatic feeder schools to the Ivies they once were. The competition within their own highly selective classes makes acceptance to the very top colleges more challenging than ever. Therefore, how did a girl like Melissa with a solid B average and 1300 SAT scores estimate her chances for admission to Dartmouth, Williams, Amherst, and Harvard after four years at Choate? In the academic slices of the pie charts of these extremely competitive colleges, her chances did not look favorable. In what slices of their upcoming freshman classes could Melissa encounter fewer opponents for a place?

Melissa was one of the major campus leaders at Choate. She served on the Judiciary Committee and the Student Council. What proved to be more significant was her talent as a competitive squash player. Melissa captained the varsity women's team and in her senior year was ranked nationally as the number two women's player in the country. College coaches were recruiting her heavily as she entered her senior year. She knew that her four top choices had serious squash programs. Her pie-charting showed that she was virtually alone in this slice of the pie charts at each of the colleges. Would this fact be sufficient to gain admission to at least one of them? Academically she was below the average of their usual admitted class.

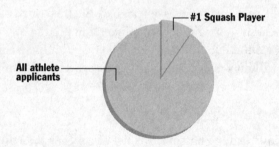

Melissa drew one pie chart for Williams, then realized that the same three charts could be drawn for Amherst, Dartmouth, and Harvard. There was no applicant like her in any of the three athletic rounds. But in satisfying the special talent category, the admissions committees at all four colleges accepted Melissa.

List Your Competitive Advantages

With your charts spread out in front of you, you are ready to list the colleges and the pie slice or slices that give you an advantage at each. For instance, you could list them in this way:

COLLEGES	MY SLICE OF THE PIE
1. _____	Computer Science Talent
2. _____	Legacy
3. _____	Athlete
4. _____	Geography
5. _____	Minority
6. _____	Foreign Languages
7. _____	Community Service Leader

You may have several slices at some schools, or none at all that matter for one or two of the colleges. Next, you can qualify the admissions situations at each as Most Likely, Likely, and Possible. Impossible situations you simply erase from your list!

You will get a genuine psychological lift from such strategic planning. Instead of worrying if you can get admitted to any good college, you will face the daunting task of applying with increasing assurance and thus will do a good job of writing essays and presenting yourself.

Decide Where You Want to Apply

You are now ready to narrow your list of colleges to between eight and ten where you will apply. Your choices will reflect the range of your possibilities, based on everything you have learned thus far in the Ten-Step Plan.

Consult with your counselor, and select one school where you have rated your chances "Most Likely." Next, choose a college where you judge your chances to be "Possible," say, 50–50 or even less, but there are rational reasons for you to apply. Between these extremes, you will also choose three or more colleges where your chances are reasonably good. We urge you to avoid the tendency to overload your list on the least likely side. Find a balanced bell curve from most to least likely, with most of your choices falling somewhere in the middle, and you are ready to contact the colleges for application forms or download them from their Web sites.

Step Seven Checklist

✓Consider the general categories of diversity, and identify those that apply to you.

✓Create pie charts to represent your standing within each category for each college you are considering. Use published class profiles, your notes on the colleges, and other sources of data available to you.

✓Review your strengths and unique characteristics, and identify the variations on the general categories where your uniqueness will be emphasized. Explore college programs where this will give you a competitive edge. Use unusual academic interests and talents, defined career goals, and non-traditional backgrounds to find your possible niches.

✓List the colleges you are considering and the slices of the pie that give you an advantage at each. Rate the colleges as "Most Likely," "Likely," and "Possible."

✓In consultation with your counselor, select between five and nine colleges where you will apply. Make sure your choices span your admissions possibilities.

✓Now begin the work of completing thoughtful applications.

✓Determine who will be the most appropriate recommenders to support your talents and uniqueness. Ask them as early as possible if they will write on your behalf to your college choices.

STEP EIGHT:

Present Yourself in the Best Light: Marketing Your Strengths and Writing Top Essays

We consider self-marketing one of the most confusing issues in the selective college admissions process today. The extraordinary rise in the number of qualified applicants can veil the individual, who is liable to fall into a classification by quantifiable merit and achievement and to become faceless in the process. What does an overburdened admissions committee do when forced to make choices among candidates whose folders would be virtually indistinguishable if the names were blanked out? We will begin this step by focusing on presenting yourself to the admissions committee. We will then help you understand the role the personal application and essays play in the decision process.

Given anywhere between 5,000 and 35,000 folders to review, with each one representing an individual's dossier, a committee is bound to make decisions that may sometimes appear arbitrary. Jack is accepted and Jill is not, despite the fact that each is perfectly capable of doing the academic work and contributing to the vitality of campus life. Marketing yourself therefore becomes essential. Why shouldn't you be offered that precious place rather than someone else with similar qualifications? Your objective is to force a committee to choose you because its members really are aware of your individuality and what a difference it can make to the incoming class. Otherwise, the committee is just as liable to choose someone else who appears to be like you. There should be no way of misreading or second-guessing your qualifications.

When to Market Your Strengths

Your marketing efforts begin when you have a sure sense of your strengths and know the colleges that are most likely to appreciate them. This usually occurs near the end of the admissions process, when you file your applications, and it continues right up to the time when admissions committees begin their final decision sessions— December for Early Decision or Action applicants, January through March for second-round Early Decision or regular applicants.

Many applicants do not take advantage of selective colleges' open folder policies: that is, admissions personnel are willing to continue to examine the folders of strong candidates right up to the time when final decisions are made. It is, of course, possible to be rejected early in the process without knowing it as the committees make internal decisions on those candidates they deem unqualified or not exciting enough to consider in comparison to the many excellent choices before them. Marketing cannot reverse such decisions. But because you are applying to a group of colleges of varying selectivity, you must expect to win some and lose some. What we know from our years of advising thousands of well-qualified students is that marketing your strengths in the appropriate manner will improve your chances of winning a place in a top college.

SUGGESTIONS FROM TOP COLLEGE DEANS

*Be yourself through the admissions process. Don't put
on a persona that is not your own.*
—Dean of Admissions and Financial Aid, Cornell University

*Do not make your application look like it was
filled out on top of the mailbox!*
—Director of Admissions, Connecticut College

*Tell about all your personal credentials. Just being
number one in the class is not going to make
your application successful.*
—Director of Admissions, University of North Carolina

*Students should do their best to let the admissions office
know what is important to and about them, and not be shy about
their accomplishments. It is hard to capture yourself on pieces
of paper, but it is important to try because that is all
the admissions office has to look at.*
—Senior Admissions Officer, Swarthmore College

*It is important to remember that admissions decisions are
not made by gatekeeping computers but by humans who exercise a
considerable amount of human judgment. Tell us, therefore,
all that you can about yourself.*
—Senior Admissions Officer, Williams College

*Recommendations can help a student when they shed light
on a special quality, experience, or talent, and when they provide
strong evidence of a student's enthusiasm for learning or
distinguished extracurricular involvement.*
—Director of Admissions, Kenyon College

What Does Marketing Involve?

We use this commercial word, *marketing*, because selective colleges have become in a real sense a marketplace dominated by the forces of supply and demand. They are no longer inhibited by tradition. Admissions officers spend considerable time on strategic planning to attract the best students each year. They use the language and strategies of the public marketplace to make certain their message will be heard across the landscape of education. As a consequence, they expect students to make the best case for themselves for why they should be admitted. Of course it is a given that good taste and using appropriate means of marketing oneself are the gold standard in the admissions process. This will make an overworked admissions committee wide open to your efforts to have your folder be one that must be flagged and labeled "Admit."

Marketing in college admissions comes down to three factors:

- Assessing your strengths
- Assessing the colleges that want students with your strengths

- Communicating clearly and passionately these strengths to the colleges

Marketing yourself will take thought and study, and it will not result in acceptance letters from every college. We think of Mary Lou, captain of her high school tennis team, winner of several interscholastic tournaments, and ranked among the top regional players in New York state. She convinced herself that she could get into the University of North Carolina and the University of Virginia on the strength of her tennis, despite a mediocre academic record and 1100 combined SAT scores. Although she had received a letter in her junior year from the varsity tennis coaches at both universities, she hadn't heard from either one in her senior year. She did not accept these facts as a reality check on her limited chances for acceptance, and, as was anticipated by her counselor, both universities rejected her.

Marketing herself with the tennis coaches was a waste of time. Mary Lou was not aware that out-of-state applicants must score over 1250 on their SAT and rank in the top quarter of their high school class to be considered for acceptance. The exception to these admissions bars would be for a fabulous athlete, musician, writer, and so forth. Mary Lou was a good tennis player within her Northeastern region, but she did not understand the level of competitive tennis in other regions of the country and the high quality of the sport at both of these nationally ranked university programs. She did not take the counsel of her own coach, who understood the level of play that would make her a successful college athlete.

Mary Lou's efforts should have been focused on private colleges with Division III athletic programs where the coaches would have been interested in her as a competitive player for their team. Here is where her self-marketing would have resulted in a number of acceptances. It is not enough to put time into promoting one's talents; it is vitally important to know which colleges will respond positively.

Make a Marketing Plan

The three marketing steps—assessing your strengths, identifying the colleges that will appreciate your strengths, and communicating your strengths—take time and thoughtfulness. Early Decision candidates should have their marketing plans ready by September of senior year. So let's review what is involved.

To help you organize your plan for marketing yourself, we have drawn up a Strengths Assessment Form for you to fill in.

Assessing Your Strengths

Our form suggests how you might go about reassessing your strengths in the light of all you now know about yourself from earlier introspection begun in Step Two. You have come to a critical moment when doubts must be put aside and weaknesses ignored. Whatever about you is strong must become stronger during your senior year because you are about to put your best foot forward for all the college world to see.

In using the form, keep your observations to yourself until you have clearly identified your strengths. Dare to be proud of your achievements; personality, and abilities that can make any college community a better place for having you as a member. Then discuss them with others who know you well, be it your parents, a counselor, teacher, coach, or best friend, to confirm your own judgment. Nine out of ten times, we have found, you will uncover appealing strengths or qualities that you have taken for granted. No one's judgment is perfect, as we saw in the case of Mary Lou, the tennis player. Her sins, so to speak, were overrating herself and not listening to the counsel of people who knew more than she did.

We are all guided by our wishes, and sometimes they are fanciful because we want something so badly. It is wise to be skeptical of praise, because your elders, particularly your parents, and your friends have their wishes, too; they wish for your success and fulfillment of your dreams, and so they encourage you, sometimes too enthusiastically. On the other hand, we believe that parents know their children far better than you and others may give them credit for. In the greater number of instances, they know where your strengths lie, and where you have fewer competencies. Listen to them rather than discounting their advice out of hand.

Ultimately, you must be the person who decides how you are going to help admissions committees bring a blurred picture into focus. You want these committees to see you clearly for who you really are and what you have to offer their institution.

MY ADMISSIONS STRENGTHS ASSESSMENT

(This form is not exhaustive. Use it creatively to sketch a logical college plan, substituting your own ideas wherever appropriate.)

STRENGTHS	ACTIVITIES	OTHER ADVANTAGES
ACADEMIC	**SCHOOL ACTIVITIES**	**STRENGTHS OF CHARACTER**
Grades _____	School Government _____	Independence _____
Class Rank _____	Class Officer _____	Reliability _____
Test Scores _____	Publications _____	Courage _____
Honors _____	Music _____	Persistence _____
Special Projects _____	Drama _____	Patience _____
Extra Credits _____	Clubs _____	Tolerance _____
Advanced Placements _____	Other _____	Concern for Others _____
Outside Courses _____	**OTHER ACTIVITIES**	**SKILLS/TALENTS**
Related Work or Internships _____	Community Service _____	1._____
NONACADEMIC	Work _____	2._____
Sport _____	Internship _____	3._____
Sport _____	Religious _____	4._____
Letters _____	Political _____	
Captaincy _____	Unique Travel _____	

COLLEGES LOOKING FOR MY STRENGTHS

College: Strengths: College: Strengths:

College: Strengths: College: Strengths:

MARKETING STRATEGY

Communicate my strengths to:

       Admissions Committee___

       Faculty Members___

       Administrators___

       Coaches___

       Minority Affairs Officer___

       Alumni___

By means of:

       Direct communications by telephone, letter, or e-mail_____

       Additional essays___

       Exhibits: Tapes___

             Portfolio___

             Newspaper Clippings___

             Audition___

       Added recommendations: employer, minister, coach_____

Review your self-assessment checklist and ask yourself if you have left anything out.

Identifying the Colleges

While getting to know the colleges, you will have picked up many hints about their programs, their departments, and their facilities, and you may in your pie-charting exercise have spotted a need you might fill at one place or another. You know by now that Hamilton is interested in your international experience and Japanese fluency from living abroad with your family, or Duke in your dedication to public affairs, or Davidson and Washington and Lee in the combination of academic talent and racial diversity that you will add to their community. We can go on with thousands of examples to make our point.

We have an important guideline to share with you to help in this process: In any of the means of communication you have with a college—from their viewbook to a tour of their Web site to an interview—note down the academic programs they boast about, the new facilities they have committed great amounts of money to build, and the emphasis they give to any other of the eight categories of the pie chart you now know by heart. A new performing arts facility on campus, for example, will impel the admissions committee to recruit truly talented students. So will a new hockey rink or computer science center. An announcement of a new or expanded academic department also serves as a clue to the merits of steering your application in this direction when appropriate to your interests and training.

You should query your counselor, teachers, coach, and others who know your strengths for ideas about college programs suited to your capabilities. Admissions officers or the heads of special areas keep these people informed through mailings and calls about special-interest activities and programs. It is possible that late in the admissions process, you may discover a college you have not researched or visited. The thing to do is to telephone the department or the coach you think might appreciate your strengths. You will save yourself a good deal of trouble by getting the information directly from those who know what they are looking for. If you are encouraged to apply after this conversation, contact the admissions office to request an application and to tell them a bit about yourself. The wonders of the electronic age make it exceedingly easy to communicate with college people in all departments by e-mail, so there is no excuse not to act on your own behalf if a college that interests you comes into the picture.

MANY WAYS TO APPLY TO COLLEGE

Despite the increasing complexity of the admissions process, colleges are making it easier to submit an application. The days of handwriting one's life story in tiny spaces, or plunking away on a clunky, if full-of-character, typewriter, are past, and the era of electronic filing and Common Applications are here. Here are just some of the ways to apply:

PAPER COPIES of the application can be filled out by hand (or typed) and mailed to the admissions office. Paper copies can be downloaded from a college's Web site, or ordered by phone, mail, e-mail, or in person. This method shows perhaps the most individuality, and, when combined with delivery-notification mail, can provide the most sense of "it got there in hard copy" reassurance. Beware of sloppy handwriting, off-kilter typing, your dog eating it, or "It got lost in the mail." Most selective colleges do *not* prefer hard copies, which require data entry into their database systems. This makes them costlier and more subject to human error.

THE COMMON APPLICATION can be obtained from your school guidance office or downloaded from www.commonapp.org, printed and filled out, and mailed in. The best way to use the Common App is to fill it out and file it online. The Common Application can be used for multiple colleges, some of which require a supplement. Multiple ways to fill this out make this a good option. Many top colleges, including Harvard, Williams, Yale, and Dartmouth, have made the Common App their primary application. We recommend using the online Common App whenever and wherever possible, paying careful attention to required supplements.

THE UNIVERSAL COLLEGE APPLICATION: A newer alternative to the Common App, this can be filled out online, as well. It is accepted by a broader group of colleges, since it does not call for member institutions to require an essay or teacher reference from applicants. See our Internet Resources list (pages 102–105) for additional standardized application services.

Word to the wise: Always print out and make copies of everything. Once you have submitted an application, wait at least a week, and then feel free to call an admissions office and ask, "Is my application complete?" Lost recommendations, SAT or ACT scores not sent directly from the testing service, and lack of a transcript are common reasons for a delay in reviewing your application. When you apply online, you will receive an e-mail confirmation of receipt. You can usually also log on to the college's Web site to check your application status.

Communicating Your Strengths by Documentation

Documentation is the key to communicating your strengths to the admissions committees. It may seem paradoxical that you want to bring all that paper in your folder to life, but you have to realize that an admissions committee has to work with pieces of paper, photos, tapes, drawings, or other palpable evidence of who you are and what are your accomplishments. When push comes to shove—and it does in committees as members compete among themselves to admit one candidate over another—whoever is in your corner will glance at documentation in your folder. It may simply be a penciled memo that you have brought up your grades during the fall semester of senior year, or it may be a copy of a speech you have made for a local community program you volunteer for. It could be a reminder that the head of the music department called to say you would be a significant addition to his department's program.

If more candidates realized the importance of appropriate documentation, there would be less effort spent on ineffective efforts to capture admissions officers' attention. We know of no way to gain admission to a top college by creating a sensation—such as an oversized Christmas card to the dean of admissions saying you hope to be admitted as your Christmas present, or sending a DVD or YouTube link showing off your card tricks or tap dancing. Yes, desperate students without real substantive skills do these things.

By marketing we do not mean adopting the creative tactics of advertising or publicity firms. Admissions officers are far from stuffy—in fact, they are unlikely to survive the pressures of their job for very long without a sense of humor—but they universally believe flamboyance or shallowness belongs more on stage than in the academic world. Show-off applicants usually do not make it past the first round of folder reading.

Documentation will be supplemental evidence supporting your claims to be a more deserving candidate than others like yourself. For example, Bernard's résumé of his soccer talent in the accompanying box provides all the relevant information a college soccer coach could ask for. Bernard sent this to the coaches at the six selective colleges he wanted to attend, along with a packet of newspaper clippings reporting on the quality of his play and leadership on the field. These write-ups provide an objective appraisal of his own description and that of his high school coach.

Now, we ask you, would not this small but vital bit of documentation be more persuasive than a brief summary standing alone on the application form? You will note that Bernard did not confine his report to soccer; he also mentioned his academic strengths and other interests. He understood that an Ivy League athletic coach needed to know if he could meet the stringent academic admissions standards. Bernard sent an unofficial copy of his school transcript to the coaches as confirmation of his intellectual abilities and motivation. The sum and substance of his profile convinced the Dartmouth coach that Bernard would be designated a scholar-athlete and that he could successfully manage his studies and participate in the soccer program. After meeting Bernard and reviewing some game tapes, he made known to the admissions committee that Bernard was one of his top three prospects in the applicant pool. For his part, Bernard let the coach know how his August training camp went and the results of his first three games in the early fall of senior year. Bernard also informed the coach as soon as he made up his mind to apply for Early Decision consideration at Dartmouth. The admissions officers were impressed by all the information now in his folder. They reviewed his academic and athletic credentials as a whole and read him as a scholar-athlete candidate. He received his letter of acceptance in time for holiday celebrations.

SUBMITTING SUPPLEMENTARY MATERIALS

Here is what Harvard has to say on its supplement to the Common Application about supplementary materials. Like many elite colleges, Harvard has high standards for these types of materials and will want to see only those that are of the top level of quality.

The required components of the application to Harvard provide an ample basis on which to make our admissions decisions. However, students with very exceptional talents or achievements may send music recordings, slides of artwork, or selected samples of academic work (e.g., creative writing) for us to consider as part of their application files. At the discretion of the Admissions Committee, submissions may be evaluated by faculty. Supplementary materials are neither required nor expected—and should be sent only if the applicant's work is unusually advanced.

Yale sets a similarly high bar in its application, and even has clear advice about which types of YouTube videos are appropriate!

BERNARD'S SOCCER RÉSUMÉ

Midfielder
Lincoln Soccer Association
Lincoln, CT

SCHOOL TEAM	Lincoln High School, Lincoln, Connecticut
	2-Year Varsity Starter—34 consecutive games
	Assists—Leader (12) Junior Year (2006)
	All-County 1st Team (2004)
	All-State—Honorable Mention (2006)
	Elected Captain for 2007 season
	Varsity Coach: Steve Walzer
CLUB TEAM	LSA Select Team 6 years
	Teams made it to State Finals 5 times
	2005—Selected to participate in exchange program with West German team
	2005–2007—Assistant Coach for Select Team
	2004—Scholarship Award for Service to Soccer Community (Coach, Referee, Player)
SELECT TEAMS	2006—CT 16 1/1—Under Select Region I Tournament
	Captain, Starting Center Midfielder
	2005—CT 16 1/2—Under Select Region Tournament
	Attended Region I Tourney where started all 7 games

SELF-ASSESSMENT	Strengths: Intensity, Vision
	Weaknesses: Dribbling
ACADEMICS	1990 SAT Combined Score
	1st Decile
	Many Honors Classes
OTHER INTERESTS	All-State and Captain of Lincoln High School
	Ski Team
	Writer for school newspaper
COACH'S COMMENTS	"Certainly he has one of the highest work rates of anyone in the county. He was consistently solid, both offensively and defensively all year long." (Steve Walzer, Lincoln High)
PERSONAL DATA	Height: 5'7"
	Weight: 135 lbs.

Why Be Bashful?

In telling Bernard's success story to other applicants, we often hear back, "I'm just not that pushy. I find it hard to brag about myself." Neither do we believe in bragging. Marketing your strengths is not bragging; it is communicating. Colleges want to know who you are. They give you an opportunity to reveal yourself on your application through answers to questions and in the personal essays. Most ambitious students who have worked hard for their accomplishments take advantage of this opportunity, which they do not look on as bragging. But they stop there, despite the fact that colleges urge them to tell them anything about themselves they ought to know in considering these students' candidacies. We tell almost every student who comes into our offices that they will be more upset if they allow the admissions officers to second-guess them in regard to who they are and what they stand for. This is a bigger risk than is speaking for yourself in an honest and direct manner.

Another kind of résumé that we encourage is the one that Karen prepared. It helped her get into Williams from a competitive suburban Maryland high school. A B+ student with strong courses and a combined SAT score of 1300, she was also a varsity swimmer and team leader. It was certainly helpful to be the daughter of an alumnus, but Karen was concerned about the fierce competition for a place at Williams and her above-average but not brilliant academic profile. She constructed a résumé because on her Williams application there was only room to list piano, voice, and chorus, plus her participation in church choir. The résumé presents a much fuller picture of Karen's accomplishments. We found it impressive and forthright, but not overstated.

KAREN'S MUSIC-RELATED EXPERIENCE

TRAINING

VOICE LESSONS (alto) (2006–07)

PIANO LESSONS

    Popular/Jazz/Classical (2002–06)

    Classical (1998–2002)

DANCE

    Jazz—Langton Dance Company (2004–05)

    General—Turner Dance Class (2000–03)

SCHOOL SINGING GROUPS

    CHAMBER CHORUS (High School) (2005–07)

        Group of 16; perform mostly choral works,
        primarily a cappella

    FESTIVAL CHORUS (2004–07)

        Group of 60; perform sacred and secular choral music

    SPECIAL CHORUS (Junior High) (2003–04)

        Group of 25; perform sacred/contemporary music at
        school and at state events

        First prize in regional competition

MUSICAL STAGE PRODUCTIONS

    Trial by Jury (High School) (2006)

    You're a Good Man, Charlie Brown (High School) (2005)

    Best of Broadway (Langton Dance Company) (2004)

MUSIC IN THE COMMUNITY

    ST. LUKE'S CHURCH (Summers, 2006–07)

        Musical accompanist for Sunday School (2005–06)

        Church Choir (Soloist) (1999–2005)

    WILLOW WOOD NURSING HOME (2005–06)

        Entertain groups, piano and singing, accompanist
        to singing groups

OBJECTIVES AND GOALS

I plan to pursue the study of music in college, possibly as a major. I want to be active in extracurricular activities that are music related. In addition to participating in the college's chapel program I will join one or more of the community service organizations that perform musically for the benefit of others. I expect that music will always be part of my life, but at this juncture of my education I want the benefits of a liberal arts education.

Report New Developments

After you send in your applications, keep the colleges informed about new successes: high marks, a research paper that is praised by your teacher, chairmanship of a committee, an award, an athletic accomplishment. Make sure that you do not repeat what is already in your folder, and document it—photocopy your report card if it is exceptional, photocopy an award, a newspaper clipping. You can e-mail brief updates and attach pdf files for colleges at key points in the process, and when there is something significant to report.

Whatever the committees do not know about you constitutes a new development and should be shared. Do not hesitate to ask a teacher or coach or musical director to send a new or updated recommendation if you are excelling under their tutelage since you formally applied. Most important, keep up your grades throughout the winter and spring terms of senior year. An improvement demonstrates your true motivation to excel in your studies, while a decline shows just the opposite. Many a candidate has learned the importance of this by failing to get admitted in the spring because their grades dropped after they sent in their application. Others made their acceptance happen by working to improve their record right up to the end of the academic year, when they were considered for admission from the wait list.

Get That Extra Recommendation

Your teachers' recommendations will probably be strong if you have chosen the right teachers and have been a strong academic performer. Thousands of applicants get wonderful recommendations from one or two teachers. When you secure that extra one or two letters of support from teachers in major subjects, however, you distance yourself from the pack. Read Beth Ann's supplementary recommendation from her college adviser. You will see that it is not boilerplate or cliché-ridden, but thoughtful and convincing. A B student in a strong private day school near Philadelphia, Beth Ann was rejected by several Ivies despite her college varsity potential in three sports and leadership in two of them. She was, however, put on the wait lists by Duke, Middlebury, Haverford, and Carleton. She held out until admitted to Middlebury for their winter term. The extra recommendation, which was supported by her senior year teachers, got her that extra consideration from four selective colleges. It helped to explain how serious she was about her studies and told about her efforts to make up for earlier missed work.

BETH ANN'S EXTRA RECOMMENDATION

Bright, motivated, cultured, and well traveled, Beth Ann is an attractive girl—charming and coltish. She is involved in studies, three varsity sports, chorus, yearbook, friends, and succeeding in all endeavors. Additionally, she is conversationally fluent in French and German, having lived abroad in 8th grade where she attended a French-speaking Swiss gymnasium.

Academically, Beth Ann's achievement record and demanding curriculum place her in the top quarter of a competitive class of 80 students, all of whom will attend selective colleges or universities. She is taking an academic overload this year (four courses are required), including English, American History, and French V, which are considered "advanced courses"—the equivalent of first-year courses at most colleges. Because of her year away, she missed some of our sequential material. On her return, by dint of summer tutoring, she skipped Algebra I entirely and went directly into Geometry in 9th grade. She also omitted Latin III (having tutored herself during the summer) in order to catch up to her classmates; her B grade in Latin IV is thus a real tribute to her effort, energy, and interest. Occasionally Beth Ann feels some academic pressure, but then, who doesn't around here? By and large, she copes well.

Beth Ann's teachers say of her: "The quality of Beth Ann's writing improved during the course. Her final essay was moving and well written. Her other English essays and comments in class reflected her enthusiasm and the accuracy of her reading." "Beth Ann is a pleasure to have in math class because she is always so involved and focused on what is going on. She should be proud of her work this year." "Beth Ann has performed impressively this year in history. Her essays have been well informed, well organized, and well written. She puts diverse information together well and differentiates well between the relevant and the trivial."

An excellent athlete, Beth Ann is a starter on our hockey team and a varsity squash and lacrosse player also.

Beth Ann has the brains, the training, and the determination to be successful at Middlebury. She has been a high achiever here and a contributing member of the school community; she's socially adept and appealing, and she comes from a sophisticated and intellectual family. Thus this recommendation gets our very warm support.

Talking to Alumni

Most parents who went through the admissions process a generation ago are surprised to learn that very few colleges today grant personal interviews in their admissions offices. The combination of the huge number of applications and the potential for overly subjective reactions has made this a non-factor in the decision process today. This should not be interpreted as a lack of interest by the colleges. What has replaced the on-campus interview is the application, with the opportunity to write in depth about yourself, and the alumni interview in your home area.

After the deadlines for applying have passed, the alumni committees that are now a part of the admissions process for all selective colleges will interview candidates at the request of the admissions offices. If you are contacted by a college alumnus, by all means take advantage of the opportunity to meet with this college representative. An interview will never have the effect of reversing a positive decision of an admissions officer; as we have said already, you cannot blow an interview. But having an enthusiastic graduate in your corner is helpful.

Usually, alumni reports confirm the judgments of the professional staff in the admissions office. A highly enthusiastic review may turn a skeptical reader of your folder into a believer. One major role of the local interviewer is to be aware of high school students in his or her home area who have received publicity for success in the arts, school or community leadership, or athletics. The alum can substantiate for the admissions committee the applicant's level of achievements. One of the vital roles local alumni play often is to encourage students who have accomplished a good deal to consider applying to their alma mater. Admissions staff are frequently tipped off to a deserving prospect by an alumni representative. If there is a substantial time gap between submitting your application and not hearing from the local alumni representative, you should e-mail or call the admissions office and ask for the name of the person. You can take the initiative in making contact, which will only help your cause.

If You Know a Trustee

Not infrequently a parent will say, "George So-and-So has been a trustee of my son's favorite college for years, and he is a very good friend." The parent proposes to get in touch with George right away. George may well be amenable to such an approach and will actually write a glowing letter about a candidate he has known since birth. But, perusing it, the admissions committee finds no additional information that can help them decide on the candidate's qualifications. Warmth and friendship are insufficient documentation, no matter who makes the recommendation. The question "Is this candidate better than dozens of others?" remains unanswered. It also runs the risk of alienating the admissions officers, who wonder why the applicant had to use "a heavy connection" to help his or her candidacy. Irritating overworked admissions evaluators reading thousands of folders in the dead of winter is not an especially good idea.

When George's letter does not make the difference and the candidate is rejected, a close friendship may cool. Our advice is the following: Never ask anyone of importance in the particular college—trustee, donor, diligent fund-raiser, or administrator—to write a recommendation for you without doing two essential things: giving the person a copy of your application and arranging for you to meet with that person for a meaningful period of time.

Busy people who may have known you for years do not know the details of your school career and accomplishments. They will, however, usually take the time to look over your application. If they do not feel that they can honestly recommend you, they will say so in most instances, and the friendship remains intact in the long run. If they do recommend you, after your meeting and a review of your dossier, their recommendation may well be persuasive. No admissions committee wants to receive a letter from someone in the university community asking why a recommended applicant was rejected, while another deemed less attractive was admitted.

One further word of warning is called for. As a parent, you do not want to put your son or daughter and yourself in a compromising situation. How can you ask a friend or acquaintance to support your child's candidacy in earnest when their college may not be of major interest? Ask yourself, "Why should this person I have contacted support my son to his college when there is no certainty that he will attend if admitted?" You all need to be comfortable that this college is, in fact, his first choice.

After Marketing, What?

In the box below are further examples of creative marketing. They are put here to stimulate your thinking, or to be imitated if you so choose. You and your college adviser are the best marketers of your strengths. Of course, you must keep your college adviser informed about any new initiatives you take, so that he or she can respond knowledgeably if a query comes from the colleges about some documentation you have submitted. You may well be informing your adviser of exciting information that he or she was unaware of. This could impel him or her to follow up on your behalf during that critical period in the evaluation process.

CREATIVE MARKETING

The only limit to marketing your strengths is your imagination and energy. Here are a number of marketing strategies that have worked for applicants to top colleges.

SEND TO ADMISSIONS:
- A copy of an award or citation received in your senior year
- A newspaper clipping about your achievement
- A particularly striking word of praise written by a teacher about a paper or project
- The school paper carrying results of your selection to the National Honor Society or Headmaster's List or to be speaker at graduation
- A prize story that has appeared since you submitted your application—or a drawing, photo, or art exhibit, etc.

SEND TO THE APPROPRIATE FACULTY MEMBER:
- A paper or project of exceptional merit
- A model you have constructed of a building for architecture or design class
- A software program or Web site you have developed
- A report on a business you have started
- Music you have composed or a film you have produced
- A translation prepared by you from a foreign language into English, or vice versa, for a faculty member who teaches that language
- News of a conference or seminar in Washington on politics and government that you have attended recently

Write an Exciting Essay

Applications today involve writing—responding to thoughtful questions lucidly and imaginatively. The goal is to write an essay or personal statement that will touch the mind and possibly the soul of the admissions committee and thus inspire its members to admit you. Because the nature and quality of your writing about yourself have become so crucial to your presentation, you should begin working on your essay, trying out different ideas and practicing your writing, at least six to eight weeks before you actually file your applications. For those applying for Early Decision or Action or through the rolling admissions process of the state universities, this means starting your writing in late August and continuing through September and October. For regular admissions, it means starting your work in mid-October at the latest, and we recommend that all students begin the writing process, completing the Common Application, for example, during the summer.

Why Colleges Want Essays

It is clear that to enliven, personalize, and strengthen your application, you need to describe some of your intangible qualities that move beyond your obvious record of grades, activities, and test scores. Committees can learn far more about you through your self-disclosure in your essay writing than from a twenty-minute personal interview. How does the application assist the committee in its deliberations? Here is what Dartmouth says about its admissions review process, noting both the importance of the essays and learning more about the applicant as an individual. The former dean of admissions at Dartmouth also once pointed out that the essay is the first part of the application an admissions officer at Dartmouth looks at:

> Dartmouth incorporates an individual, holistic approach to the reading of applications. In reading files from an applicant, we thoughtfully consider the achievements of an applicant with respect to the opportunities available in his or her environment.
>
> Each application to Dartmouth is:
>
> Independently reviewed by at least two and usually three members of the Admissions staff.
>
> Evaluated for the tangible academic accomplishments which are represented by grades and test scores and supplemented by essays, recommendations, and interviews.

Carefully considered for qualities such as passion for ideas, dedication to learning, leadership, compassion, integrity, motivation, and sense of humor.

Evaluated for significant extracurricular involvements and interests beyond the classroom—ranging from community service and debate to athletics and drama.

A senior admissions officer at Amherst addressed the essential role essay writing and content play in the evaluation of applicants:

The essay questions enable an admissions dean to look beyond test results, grades, and class rank to better understand the applicant and to personalize the process. Although writing ability is important, it is not the only thing that a dean will see. An essay can be well written but uninformative, meaning that I have no better perception of who you are as a student or as an individual after reading the essay than I did before reading the essay, nor do I see how your strengths are different than those of many other talented applicants. Essays are a way to express yourself, share thoughts, and display creativity. Write from your viewpoint. Stay away from the same topics that others choose to write about. By being an individual, you distinguish yourself from the group and give us the opportunity to see your strengths.

Stanford University further emphasizes how essays fit into the context of a lengthy and deliberate review of applicants. Again, the personal presentation in the application provides a vital supplement to a student's record of academic and extracurricular achievement. There is a good deal of information for the serious applicant in these remarks by a dean of admissions at Stanford:

The thorough and elaborate evaluation process in which almost the entire admissions staff is involved each winter and spring cannot be reduced to a quantifiable formula. We attempt to blend the information contained in references with the data from academic credentials. We spend many hours (including nights, weekends, and holidays) reading and rereading files. Each application is carefully reviewed, sometimes by as many as five admissions officers. Each admissions officer reads hundreds of folders from a wide variety of applicants, thereby acquiring a strong sense of the strength of the pool. . . . Also of importance to us are applicants' essays and references from teachers and others who know them well. We take into consideration personal qualities—how well an individual applicant has taken advantage of available resources, whether he or she has faced and withstood unusual adversity, and whether the applicant shows promise as a contributing community member.

You can be assured that there is more involved in this complicated process than merely grades and test scores. Your essay writing provides you with an opportunity to influence an admissions committee directly, in your own words. You can help them to connect the dots that complete the full portrait of you, the applicant. A thoughtful, well-crafted, and personal statement sets you apart in the crowded field of other qualified candidates. So let us help you by sharing our thoughts on how to approach your writing, how to determine what are worthwhile topics, and how to jump-start this daunting process.

A Few Examples of Sparkling Essays

Adelaide wrote the following essay, and was admitted to Harvard, Dartmouth, and Princeton on the basis of the quality of her essays and the personal qualities reflected in them. Other candidates had equal or better academic records of excellence, but the committees saw the special qualities of this young woman that put her in a different category for consideration.

Standing in my front yard one day this summer, I watched a car creep up and down the road past my house four times before it finally turned into my driveway. Roads in my New England town are thin and winding, and all the trees look the same, so my parents and I are used to giving directions to travelers who have taken wrong turns. However, this driver was not lost or looking for help, but rather returning at a slow speed deliberately, to a territory whose every bump and twist he knew perfectly. When the man stepped out of his car, he introduced himself to me as the boy who had grown up in the house that I live in now. And though I did not recognize the stranger standing in front of me, I felt I already knew the boy of whom he spoke.

For seventeen years I have collected old glass marbles and Matchbox cars as they have surfaced from an abandoned sandpile in my backyard. I connected quickly that the man in my driveway was the child responsible for their burial, and I told him of my collection. He laughed as he remembered his pile of toys in the sand, and when I asked him why he had left them there when he moved, he answered, "I used to play with them every day, and when I was finished playing at the end of each afternoon, I would just leave everything there until the next morning."

His explanation sounded simple. When he was young, he would play with his toys when he wanted to, go inside when he wanted to, and return to his sandpile the next day. However, the fact that the marbles and Matchbox cars are still buried today suggests that there was one morning when the boy woke up and decided not to play. There was one exact moment in time when something changed, when he did not return to his sandpile, and he has not been there since.

The idea that there are singular, unpredictable moments in time that divide one stage of life from another has greatly affected my life. I am conscious that something that I am active in today may become part of a past stage without my realizing it, and so I commit myself to each project with the belief that I will never do that particular activity in just the same way again.

For example, if I want to publish a short story today, I am not going to worry that I would have a better vocabulary to write it with in ten years. And when I volunteer to teach illiterate adults, I do not question whether I would be more effective after a few more years of my own education. For today I can pursue both of these activities with the capabilities of a seventeen-year-old, and although the story I write and the class I assist may not be as

successful as they would be if I tried them again in ten years,
they will invariably be a reflection of my best effort at this point
in my life. For as long as I believe that my life comes in stages
whose beginnings and endings are invisible, *this* moment is
always the right time to write and to work, and I am never too
young to try anything.

Doesn't this story that appears so simple on the surface but that considers deeply moving thoughts about life and its evolution move you? Adelaide is obviously a gifted writer, but instead of showing off her skill she focuses on a simple event that arouses a host of feelings and reflections. You can understand why admissions committee members would want to have a girl with her soul and talent in their community. It should also be obvious that there is no need to have experienced a tragedy in your life or a world-shaking event to be able to convey who you are and what matters to you.

A former director of admissions at Middlebury observed for us, "When in doubt about an applicant, the admissions committee always takes a second look at the personal statement and the essay. It can tell things that no teacher or counselor can express so convincingly about the character and inner light that shines in a person." How true this is.

Adelaide switched on her inner light to reveal her character, and she did it artfully and without false modesty. This caliber of thought and writing did not come easily, and certainly not automatically. She practiced writing her thoughts on this small event until she understood for herself why it had such significance. She then wrote and wrote again the story that she finally presented to the several colleges. Rarely can even the best students dash off a convincing essay that conveys something about their character. All writers have to work hard to establish in their own minds what they are trying to convey to the reader and then actually get the story down in a way that will instruct their audience as to who they really are.

Here is the personal story by Katerina, a young woman now studying music at Vanderbilt, that let her inner light shine through. Her goal was to have the admissions committee understand her personality and her commitment to her music. Reflecting her own values off of the experience of her music teacher allowed her inner spirit to show forth.

The feeling of inadequacy is present in each of our lives at one point or another. I felt it when I forgot the last two measures of Chopin's Nocturne in C Minor during my annual piano recital. It engulfed me every time I heard Jennifer Boxwood, my competition, play Claude Debussy. I experienced it when I listened to a thirteen-year-old prodigy play a twenty-two-minute variation of Bach's first three-part invention. Yet, the time I felt most inept in relation to another person and her ability happened while I was attending an intensive training course in all areas of music at The New York State Music Festival and Institute at Hartwick College during the summer of 2005. Although these events continually made me question my "unique talent," which I relied on in order to maintain my self-confidence, I never considered actually quitting the thing I loved most until I met Jungeon Kim at the New York State Music Camp.

I recall the evening very clearly, in which I met the greatest influence in my life. I knocked on her door feeling confident that my preparation, talent, and natural aptitude would present me positively to the renowned piano teacher. A tiny Korean woman, nearly half my size, opened the door and whisked me inside her living room to the seven-foot Steinway, a sight all its own. Mrs. Kim watched as I performed my most difficult piece: Rachmaninoff's Prelude in D. Flushed and out of breath as I finished playing, I moved away from the monster piano experiencing a certain vulnerability only felt when awaiting a reaction. Mrs. Kim, who did not utter a word, took over the piano bench, and only slightly glancing at the music played my piece. I interpreted this as her way of showing me how the music should have been played. The retards were perfect, crescendos sweltering, chords crisp and in sync, staccatos resembling raindrops, and the tempo as precise as that of a metronome. Not only did this minuscule woman fail to miss a single note, she remained completely placid throughout the entire prelude. Fifteen minutes and eight pages later, I was shocked, disillusioned, and heartbroken due to the fact that my best effort had been surpassed in so short a time.

I immediately came to the conclusion that my skills, in comparison to Mrs. Kim's, were nonexistent. The woman must have sensed my dismay, because she became incredibly sympathetic, telling me, in her strong Korean accent, that "everything takes time and practice." I truly believed that in a world of achievement-oriented people, there was little room for those who relied on effort. I thought it was all natural talent that led to such excellence. Upset by my new realization, I did not even think that Mrs. Kim had worked in order to gain her musical success until she comforted me by sharing her background.

Mrs. Kim had practiced the piano for nine hours a day for twenty-eight years. Beginning at the age of four, she had always wanted to become a classical concert pianist. Entirely self-motivated, Mrs. Kim lived for the piano, but when she failed to win first place in a state Bach competition, her domineering parents forbade her to continue playing the piano. Determined to succeed, she continued practicing in an attempt to study at Juilliard eventually. Forbidden to study music, Mrs. Kim's parents pushed her in the direction of medicine, but she kept practicing the piano. Working at a local restaurant, Mrs. Kim earned enough money to purchase a round-trip plane ticket from her home in California to New York City. Telling her parents she was working late that night, Mrs. Kim skipped school that day, flew 3,000 miles to New York, and begged the prominent Head of Admissions from Juilliard to listen to her play. A week later, Mrs. Kim received a letter of acceptance from the conservatory with a full scholarship. Impressed with their daughter's determination, her parents agreed to send her to New York. All of Mrs. Kim's persistence had paid off.

Reflecting on Mrs. Kim's experience, I now realize that intensive effort is critical in order to succeed, and the initial feeling of inadequacy is necessary as a motivational force. Most important, I realize that with continual effort and persistence, I can achieve whatever I desire. This is the way I plan to approach the next stage in my life.

You Are the Topic

The word *essay* suggests a paper written for a course, formal prose on a subject you have studied or researched. This is not what admissions committees ask you to write. They are providing you with the opportunity you should eagerly welcome, to write about yourself, for two or three double-spaced pages. We believe the term *personal statement* better conveys the purpose of the exercise. The capability to word-process your writing for the applications means that you have no excuse for presenting a disorganized, sloppy, or thoughtless personal statement.

Here is a list of guidelines for writing about yourself which students have found useful:

- Know thyself better than anyone else, before you begin to write. Make a list of your personal qualities that make you special. Review your list of strengths that reveal the asset you will be on campus.

- Be honest. Do not embroider or shade the truth.

- Be relaxed. It is your story you are relating. Therefore, you are in charge of your presentation.

- You set the theme, the style and tone, the setting, and the spirit of your story.

- Trust your own instincts. The message you have decided to send to the admissions committees is important and right, because it matters to you and should be shared if a group of strangers is to know you.

- Take risks. Try a topic that may be considered slightly offbeat or unusual, even controversial in nature, if it has relevance for the selection process. Dare to talk about yourself, but don't try to shock the reader for shock's sake. Do feel you can write on a sensitive issue that brings insight to the committee.

- Be humorous and demonstrate your ability to laugh at yourself or at least not take yourself too seriously.

- Don't be overly modest. It is not that appealing and often comes across as false modesty or coyness that is insincere.

- *Show* who you are through an incident, a major event, a crisis, or a tragedy rather than *tell* a committee who you are and what you stand for.

- Develop a strong introduction to catch the reader's attention. It makes all the difference. You cannot ask an overworked admissions officer to wade through half of your statement before he comprehends what you have in mind to tell him.

- Keep your story simple, keep it brief, keep it focused on one theme or point.

- Keep it yours. You own it; it is about you. Do not let others tell you what you must write about and how to write it.

- Do accept offers by your parents, counselor, or a friend who knows you well to review and react honestly to your writing. They may be able to tell you how it appears to an outside reader, and whether your language comes across as readable and well organized.

- Know that there is more than one kind of appropriate essay writing. The nature of your theme should determine the style and tone of your expression. You can create a serious, lighthearted, dramatic, reflective, or straightforward story. The choice is yours.

- Focus on one or two major points that you want to come through about yourself. Do not attempt to relate everything that you have experienced and are interested in. Focus on the primary idea that expresses the essence of who you are.

- Choose a personal topic to write on. While you may have a concern for issues like world hunger, overpopulation, or gun control, you will find it more difficult to describe yourself as opposed to an issue.

- Avoid sounding pompous, arrogant, bombastic, all-knowing, or like a smart aleck. The committee will immediately wonder why they would want you in their community.

- Avoid self-promotion and hucksterism. Let your accomplishments and record speak for you. Overselling will make the committee suspicious of your genuine worth.

- Make your voice be heard in your writing. Use your natural style and language to communicate your thoughts, but be certain not to fall into too casual or colloquial a style.

- Proofread your final draft several times to be sure you have not made any errors.

The Final Test of a Good Personal Statement

You are finished when you put down your pen or turn off your computer and say to yourself, "That's it; I have given the essay my best effort. I have shared a major piece of myself with a group of strangers so that they will know me better. I believe in myself and what I have accomplished. I know that I have some special features I can bring to the college campus, and I feel I have conveyed them clearly and honestly to the admissions committee."

We believe it will help you to get started in designing your personal statement by reading a sampling of what other applicants have created. Again we reassure you that each of these writers struggled at first with their choice of topic, and the final product you read here went through three to four drafts before it read well. Each of these pieces displays the qualities, in one fashion or another, that admissions committees look for.

Isabella began her statement with this opening: "I am purely and simply the shortest person I know!" She is able to laugh at what she considers a handicap, her height. Continuing in this light vein, she manages in an opening punch line to let the reader know she is a very serious person: "I figure I will be the first child therapist who can see eye-to-eye . . . with her patients." Isabella shows early signs of becoming a child therapist with a wonderful sense of humor, which is her goal. Her essay helped her get accepted to Harvard.

> I am purely and simply the shortest person I know! So much of my life has been colored by this fact that in matters of direct personal importance it ranks very close to the top of my list. When I was three years old, the pediatrician thought perhaps I was a dwarf—but no such luck. (Dwarfism, I figured, would definitely qualify me for minority-group status and make me a shoo-in at Harvard.) Today I can reach the 4'11" mark, thanks to years and years of ballet lessons, where I learned to stretch my neck and hyperextend my legs through the hip sockets. But that's it—unless I am "en Pointe"—and walking around in toe

shoes all day is positively hazardous to one's health (not to mention one's toes).

And so I have learned to cope with, take advantage of, and compensate for my shortcomings (pun intended). I grin and bear it when the middle-aged crowd coos and gurgles and says, "How cute—how old is this little one?" I also know to answer with a single-digit number lest they go into cardiac arrest on learning I am practically old enough to vote. I try to have my social life revolve around activities other than large parties and dances because other people's belt buckles do not make interesting conversation. I have talked my mother out of sending me on errands to butcher shops, bakeries, and delicatessens, because no way can I reach the little machine that gives out the numbers that allot you your turn.

The advantages: I consider myself an honest and law-abiding citizen, but when the chips are down and allowance runs short and baby-sitting prospects are dim, I am not above letting ticket-takers at museums, theaters, and ski lifts assume that I am in the "eleven-and-under" category. I have more clothes than anyone else I know; I get "hand-me-ups" from my younger sisters as well as "hand-me-downs" from the older one. Traveling is easy because one can pack many more small-sized clothes in a suitcase than average ones.

Finally, the compensating. I have wanted to be an actress ever since I played a Munchkin in my fourth-grade production of *The Wizard of Oz*. But my dreams were dashed when I subsequently read an article in the *New York Times* which quoted a famous director as saying that being a commanding presence has a great deal to do with having a large and imposing physique. So I substituted a career in psychology. Aside from a very real interest in the subject, I figure I will be the first child therapist who can see eye-to-eye, literally as well as figuratively, with her patients.

Other compensations: my very loud voice, my larger-than-life enthusiasms, and determination to be the smartest and the best—because I am never going to be the biggest!

Lewis Carroll's Alice (of Wonderland fame), when drinking her potion and shrinking to subnormal size, said, "Why, there's hardly enough of me to make *one* respectable person!" Nonsense, Alice, take it from someone who's lived it that size has nothing to do with respectability—or brains or talent or determination. And, besides, there are ways to add inches emotionally and mentally, if not physically. I know that becoming one of the 10,000 of Harvard (and the only Munchkin), for example, would do that for me.

Alice wanted the admissions committee to understand her experiences as an émigré to the United States and the influence her experiences in her home country had on her values and future goals. She wrote from the heart and shared her inner light with a committee of strangers. Alice succeeded in making a national medical issue in her home country her own issue in this compelling story. Columbia accepted her on the basis of her special qualities as exemplified in this statement:

I had never seen so many people at the mercy of such uncontrollable circumstances. They were stripped of their personal dignity, dealing with their pain in their own ways. I cannot, hard as I might try, banish that scene from my mind. As I stood amidst the shouting doctors and nurses, the moaning patients, and the sickly heat of the room, a part of me reached out not only to the patients in the room but to those who might potentially be subjected to this inhumane treatment.

My grandmother, the victim of two paralyzing strokes, lay uncomfortably on an old rolling stretcher with a high fever for two hours before a doctor came to see her. As we waited, a doctor and a nurse examined an old man on a stretcher next to my grandmother's. The man was lying on his side, his face contorted in silent agony. Another nurse walked haphazardly through the emergency room that day, trying to sweep the gritty, dusty floor with a broom and a dustpan made of half of a large tin box. I could still read the writing on the box. It must have been a large container of vegetable oil. I wondered at her attempt to clean such a crowded room. Sanitation could only have been regarded as a technicality.

Many elderly people were in the emergency room that day, their faces aged and lined by pain and suffering, their expressions devoid of hope. Doctors and nurses were short-tempered and in short supply. We had to beg a doctor to come to my grandmother. The longer we waited, the more desperate the situation seemed to become. The sight of my grandmother's helpless state wrung my heart and triggered waves of frustration and despair.

The situation I have described happened in Chunghun, Taiwan, a town near my maternal grandparents' home. This scene symbolizes for me much of the motivation for what I want to do with my life. I was born in Taiwan in 1990. When our family business expanded in the 1990s, my father transported his family to Ohio to head the North American branch of the business. I arrived in Ohio in 1996 and began my education here.

I came speaking no English, but I learned the language within two months. As quickly as I learned English, I also learned the American ways. Although I love America and this town in which I have lived the last eleven years of my life, a part of me has always remained faithful to my native country. Taiwan has become my cause and my motivation to further my education.

My family, both maternal and paternal, has been in Taiwan for over twenty generations. Although we can trace our ancestors to the Chinese mainland, we consider ourselves truly Taiwanese. We no longer share a culture with those Chinese people of our ancestral homes. Instead, we have adopted a distinctively Taiwanese culture. For hundreds of years, the Taiwanese people have been oppressed. Most recently, the Japanese held Taiwan for many years until the end of World War II, when it was given to China. When the Chinese Nationalist leader, Chiang-Kai Shek, suffered defeat at the hands of the Chinese Communists, he retreated with his troops and countless numbers of fleeing refugees to Taiwan. The Chiang family and those who followed them from the mainland ruled Taiwan with an iron fist up to thirty years ago when the Taiwanese people finally began to regain control of their country. To this day, friction and struggle persist between the native Taiwanese and the followers of Chiang from mainland China.

In the last twenty years, Taiwan's economic miracle has raised the standard of living significantly. However, many social problems have developed as a result of the rapid growth of the country. I visit Taiwan twice a year since all my relatives still live there. I know that the cities are crowded, alive, friendly, fresh. Many places are even glamorous. Yet behind all of this show of wealth, certain aspects of the nation need time to catch up with the country's rapid development.

The effects of democratization and economic expansion have had serious influences on the people. From the large increase in violent crimes and teenage delinquency, to the unsuccessful attempts to find a solution to the dire problem of health care, the social problems that plague the country are varied and numerous. These problems are inevitably a part of any society, but a country like Taiwan has been deprived of the time needed for orderly social development and a workable infrastructure to sustain its economy. The populace is still in a transition stage. The obstacles that must be overcome in order for the country to be complete in all aspects cannot be solved by wealth only. Meanwhile, the masses suffer daily. People like my grandmother need help now. They cannot wait. To this cause I have dedicated myself.

My move to America was by chance, dictated by my father's professional career. Yet I feel it has given me an extraordinary opportunity. Having spent the greater part of my life in this country, I have come to love and respect my adopted land in many ways more than my native Taiwan. Looking back at the last eleven years I have spent here, I have learned to appreciate the environment in which I grew. The entirety of my education has taken place in the U.S. It has taught me the worth of democracy and the democratic system. I have had the opportunity to experience the values and mores that epitomize American society. I have fully embraced the laws, the benefits, and the freedoms given to every individual in this country.

Using what I have learned here, I hope to further the reorganization and democratization of my native land. During the next few years, I want to devote myself to studying sociology and psychology in order to understand social behavior and community development. With a background in the social and behavioral sciences, I will then work to accelerate the social development of the Taiwanese healthcare systems. The people of this stubborn and proud country who have survived so much tragedy and hardship over time, deserve the basic amenities and securities that most Americans are blessed to have.

As I look into the future, I hold within my heart the picture of that emergency room. It serves as my inspiration. It represents for me the innocent, suffering masses waiting for help. God willing, I will be able to help improve the life of the common Taiwanese citizen. Then I look further into the future where I hope to participate in the establishment of a bridge of cooperation between the East and the West, particularly one between the two countries I love most, my native land and my adopted one.

One of our central themes as we counsel students is to encourage them to take the lead in establishing their identity for the committees. We say, don't let a group of strangers who are judging you decide who you are, what matters to you, why you have achieved what you have, or why you have stumbled at times. Here are a few common situations that you should explain in your writing:

- Poor grades in a particular term due to serious illness
- Low test scores due to a specific learning disability
- Missing advanced courses due to limited offerings of your high school
- Community service as your most significant commitment rather than school clubs or athletic teams
- Few extracurricular activities because you work after school and weekends to put away money for college
- Little time for outside activities because you live with a single parent and have to help with your brother or sister
- Multiple school changes, and thus a confusing transcript, because of family moves or other circumstances

Feel Comfortable in Writing About Yourself

Although applicants understand that the point of responding to the questions on an application is to move beyond the statistics of their profile, they are often hesitant to share with the committee the most important issues or events in their lives. We are asked all too often by a student, "Can I really tell them about my innermost thoughts or the tragedy that has affected my life? Won't they be turned off by learning about my family's circumstances or my dreams?" Our emphatic response is *no*. If you figure that the members of the admissions committees have to read thousands of essays over a two- to three-month period, you can appreciate the impact a genuine story can have.

The brilliant short story writer Edgar Allan Poe believed that the critical consideration in any composition is the effect the piece will have on the reader. His recommendation was to start with the effect desired, then to create the story, being certain to include enough facts to give weight to the composition. Additional good advice is to consider the denouement, the point of your writing, "before anything be attempted with the pen," sage words for the amateur writer. Think of what you want the conclusion and purpose of your essay or story to be.

One of the most gifted essayists in American letters was James Thurber. His style of writing can serve as a model for anyone who wants to write in a personalized manner with a tone of simplicity that conveys deep feelings. Student writers can learn much from reading any of his essays. Here are the opening lines to Thurber's affectionate memory of his father in his essay "Gentleman from Indiana." Thurber was a master at creating an opening that hooked the reader into wanting to read on.

> One day in the summer of 1900, my father was riding a lemon-yellow bicycle that went into pieces in a gleaming and tangled moment, its crossbar falling, the seat sagging, the handle bars buckling, the front wheel hitting a curb and twisting the tire from the rim. He had to carry the wreck home amidst laughter and cries of "Get a horse!" He was a good rider, but he was always mightily plagued by the mechanical.

> — James Thurber, *The Thurber Album* (Simon & Schuster, New York, 1952, p. 110)

Jonathan had the courage to share a sad event in his childhood that led him to the positive attitude that guides his life today. He responded to one of the standard questions on the Common Application, "Indicate a person who has had a significant influence on you, and describe that influence." Dartmouth, Colgate, Davidson, and Duke had no doubts about this young man's strengths and future contributions.

December 30, 1992: My parents, my uncle, and I were flying home from visiting family during the Christmas holidays when I was one year old. We were in my father's small plane and planned on landing at an airport near our home in Vermont. There was zero visibility but a light on the instrument panel indicated that we were approaching the airstrip. Everything went dark suddenly, and the plane started shaking as if it were being enveloped by a tornado. My father had miscalculated our altitude, and we had dropped below the tree line. We crashed into a thick forest. Both wings were ripped off by the large pine trees, the woods clawed at us until we smashed into a tree, killing my father.

Although the death of my father was almost impossible to come to terms with for my family, everyone who knew him felt he had lived each day to its fullest and that he would not have regretted a minute of his life. He tinkered with electronics in high school, building a robot in his free time. He took a year off from college to devote himself to campaigning for a politician in whom he believed strongly. He created a computer program, which was revolutionary at the time, that could help analyze the demographics of voting districts. My father installed a wood stove and built a solar hot-water system on our house, so that we only had to pay $2.00 for fuel during the oil crisis. All of these accomplishments are what many people dream about and never have the drive or confidence to try. If my father had put these things off, he never would have felt fulfilled.

My father was not a technological recluse, a man who buried himself in the garage with his gadgets. I have heard story after story as I grew up about the many sides to this man. The warmth of his character deeply affected the people close to him. His cheerful attitude, instinctive kindness, and forgiving nature put a spark and energy into the lives of those whom he touched. His example pushes me to give to others and to take as much as possible from my daily life.

At the same time, I have also grown up with a screaming hole in my life; a chasm that is so deep it forces me to take notice. It reinforces how easy it is for someone's life to be so fulfilled one day and suddenly over the next.

By understanding the fragile nature of life, I realize how important it is to appreciate all that is around me while I have it. This is to my advantage because since I have grown up with this understanding, I have taken a positive, happy outlook. I can be fascinated by street sewers and where they lead to at the age of three, to the concepts that underlie calculus and advanced physics. When my peers ask me how I can be cheerful in the physics class at 8:00 in the morning or when it is 3:00 A.M. and I am not yet finished with my history term paper, I never know how to respond rationally. Should I tell them it is because my father died when I was one year old? I think they would not understand.

Although I cannot recall my father on a personal level, he has inspired me for the seventeen years of my life. I know I am on a mission to live my life to the fullest, to inspire others with my enthusiasm for all things bright and beautiful, and to appreciate every moment just as he had.

Thurber's recollection of a favorite college teacher is another marvelous model of the adage that simple is more. Many students choose to write about a teacher who has influenced their thinking or left a memorable impression. Consider here the small details about Thurber's teacher that create a feeling of recognition.

I will always remember my first view of Joseph Russell Taylor, in one of his English classes at Ohio State, more than thirty-five years ago. He was round of face and body, with yellow hair, pink cheeks, and fine blue eyes. He usually wore a brown suit, and he always brought to class the enchanted artistic world he lived in, of whose wonders he once said, "It is possible that all things are beautiful." His friends thought of him as one of the permanent things of life, and when we heard that he was dead, the light of the day diminished.

A hopeful Ivy League applicant displayed a combination of his serious and humorous sides with this Thurberish style of writing:

> Mr. Nugent plodded down the ramp to the classroom on the first day of school, clad in his scary jet-black cloak and a graduation cap. Anxiously waiting, we had no idea what to make of his garb. He explained that he wanted us in the "college frame of mind" so as to immediately place us on track for the year's AP Calculus curriculum. He was as intimidating a figure as I had been warned.
>
> The feared Mr. Nugent passed out the syllabus and started to read it aloud. When he got to his grading and homework scale, he intoned, "And we all are starting off the year with the summer assignments completed and ready to hand in now." Everyone scurried to scrounge up the chicken scratch pieces they had completed in the wee hours of that very morning. I kept my cool and casually opened my backpack to take out my picture-perfect notebook containing the solutions to every odd-numbered question in the textbook's first six sections.
>
> The line for the class stapler had dissipated by the time I realized that I had left my Calculus books at home. I had a vivid picture of them shimmering in the light, squared perfectly in the center of my desk. I stared into my bag in disbelief. I have always believed there is a reason for everything, that anything that should happen will happen when and where it is supposed to. At that moment, however, I could not see why God would reward my newly found, impeccable study habits with an "unprepared," a zero on six homeworks, and the worst initial impression possible. I could not believe that God had let me down, after all the trust I had invested in him.
>
> Mr. Nugent weaved down the first row and back up the second, looking over shoulders and solemnly staring at the papers through his reading glasses. I was the only one with nothing to show for myself. How could this be happening to me? I had done everything right. *What had I done wrong!?*
>
> When Mr. Nugent hovered ominously over my desk, I apologized and explained, as calmly and nonchalantly as my rapidly beating heart would allow, that my books were "on their way," as

if notebooks take buses and arrive at school by themselves. He just gave a cold blank stare as I struggled to tell him that I would go home and get them somehow. But the reality of the situation was, "What was I to do?" Officer Meyer, the campus security guard, was patrolling to ensure that no student would attempt to leave unexcused during the school day. Was he guarding the gate? Would he sympathize or suspend me? I imagined strolling out of the school's front entrance, muttering prayers in the hope of making the one-eighth-mile trek to the car undetected. I could not risk it.

I asked Mr. Nugent where I could find him immediately after school. He said he had a meeting but I could put my notebook on his desk.

I went to my last-period government class and stared at the clock as seconds slowly ticked away. The teacher was rambling on about mock trials when in my stupor, I heard the magical words, "That's enough for today." It was now 1:57. I could make it home in minutes. There would be at least ten minutes of the first day of school left by the time Mr. Nugent got the papers.

At home, the books were sitting in the center of my desk as I had pictured them. I grabbed them into my arms like an infant I needed to protect, zipped back up the road, and was back on campus in record time. Who was thinking about the local police stopping me when I had Mr. Nugent to deal with?

I waited outside the classroom as Mr. Nugent wrapped up the final minutes of Algebra 2. As the last pupil left, I made my entrance. I walked toward the desk at which he was sorting papers and said, "Here it is, Mr. Nugent," as if he were the one anxiously awaiting "the arrival." "Okay," he muttered without deigning to look up at me.

"So, was it a good summer?" I asked, attempting to break the ice floe between us with this exquisitely original question. Getting a little personal couldn't hurt, I thought, as I crossed my fingers, hoping there had been death in his family or some other unforeseen catastrophe.

"Good." He looked up for a second before returning to grading papers. "My wife and I traveled. It seems that . . ." I suddenly noticed the ring on his finger. The silver band with a cross cut out was a ring which I was familiar with from a Christian jewelry catalogue. As he finished his story, I debated mentioning the ring. I have learned through my own religious experience that some people are not comfortable discussing their faith. I am a committed Christian, though, so I figured he would not take the small comment to be anything other than what it really was. "Say something, say something!" echoed in my head until I finally found the courage to blurt out, "It's a James Avery."

Mr. Nugent put down his pen and looked up at me for a frozen moment. Dead silence.

"I have been trying to think of the name of the designer for about twenty years," he exclaimed, with animation no less. He continued to stare at me dumbfounded. "Nobody has ever been able to identify it. I thought it was James something, but I bought it years ago in Texas and have no records on hand to tell me."

The Hallelujah Chorus was blasting in my head. The monster that everyone had described had a core—and not only did I hit it, but I also shared it.

"What is it called again?" he asked. I said he probably purchased the ring in Waco, at the James Avery headquarters. I was correct. He asked my affiliation and where I worshipped. By the conclusion of our conversation, he was telling me that it was going to be such a pleasure having me in his class. I could not believe my eyes and my ears. My feet did not touch the ground as I waltzed back to my car and drove home, slowly this time, reflecting on the best first day of school I had ever experienced.

How would I have felt if my notebook had been where it was supposed to be, when it was supposed to be there? Another day would have passed in which I did not thank God for all he does for me, all the time. As I glanced down at my James Avery ring with the word FAITH inscribed, I could not help but smile. My ring had never made so much sense to me.

Rewrite, Rewrite, Rewrite

When Winston Churchill had finished a manuscript, he went to work on galley proofs. Maddeningly, he would return to the publisher thousands of words of corrections, costing thousands of dollars to be reset, for which Churchill, naturally, had no intention of paying. The publisher eventually recovered this expense in the sale of the great Englishman's bestsellers on the history of England and the two World Wars. Churchill believed in what he preached. He offered his countrymen during the darkest days of World War II his "blood, toil, tears, and sweat," and he asked it of himself at his own writing.

Looking at a text over and over again, you will find ways to improve it; by adding or cutting, by rewording, reparagraphing, changing punctuation, or adding a small vignette or fact, your opening may be spiced up or changed. You may spot bad taste, exaggeration, clumsy phrasing, the wrong word, and too flowery a word. You will eliminate all clichés such as *well, you know, it was like exciting, he is awesome, you know what I mean*, and *on and on and on*.

We recommend two books on proper writing and English usage. Buy them and keep them at your elbow as you work over your drafts. The first is the smallest and the most used of all primers on writing: *The Elements of Style*, by William Strunk Jr. and E. B. White. It is only seventy-one pages long, but packs a ton of useful information that will bail you out of many a writing dilemma. The second reference is *Modern English Usage*, by Wilson Follett. This is a masterpiece of sensible advice for finding the grammatically correct phrase, the word that really means what you intend to say. The combination of these two sources will carry you through your college years after you have used it to help you get admitted.

We think of a meeting in the early fall of Meghan's senior year. She had a germ of an idea that she wanted to develop into her personal presentation. She felt that writing about the uniqueness of her cultural roots would tell the admissions committees the source of her values and beliefs. It was not an easy topic to do justice to without sounding self-important or unfocused. Three rewrites led to a tightly organized statement that pleased Georgetown University, where she is now studying.

> "My mother is from the Middle East and my father is from the Middle West."
>
> For most of my life, I have used the above phrase with relative ease to describe myself. A few years ago, however, I began to feel that such a simple phrase did not even come close

to describing my identity as an individual. How on earth can a girl with an Episcopalian father from Kansas City, Missouri, and a Jewish mother born and raised in Tel Aviv, Israel, adequately define her background in one word? The situation only deteriorated when I began to take standardized tests and was faced with a forced response to "Who am I?" and none of the categories listed applied to me.

Gradually, I have begun to overcome the initial unease caused by my unique situation, and have learned to cherish my family's diversity. I have learned that saying "My mother is from the Middle East and my father from the Middle West" means more than just a simple geographic play on words; rather, it sums up the unusual and special qualities that make me who I am.

While my background could be construed by an outsider as anything but "normal" or "usual," I can honestly say that I would not have it any other way. Rather than attending only one type of religious school, I instead went to Hebrew School and Synagogue on Saturdays to study the traditions of Judaism, followed by Church School and Services to study the foundations of Christianity. My parents explained to me that they sent me to learn both religions so that I could make an informed decision later in life, while accepting both family traditions.

I recall with warm memories how Thanksgiving in Kansas City with my American family consisted of football games, pumpkin pie, apple cider, and playing in the snow. Passover celebration in Tel Aviv with my Israeli family embodied the rituals of Hebrew prayers, roast lamb, falafel, matzoh bread, and circle dancing. I always looked forward to both holidays with an open mind (and stomach!) because I was special enough to enjoy and affiliate myself with two different kinds of cultures.

Perhaps the most influential aspect of the two families I have grown up with is the way in which they have inspired me for the future. My American father and his family have encouraged me to remain true to the traditional values which make the United States a privileged country in which to live. Freedom, democracy, capitalism, opportunity, freedom to worship—these are all the virtues a Mid-western family is raised in. The pride for the country in which I live, and my desire to protect that feeling which they have instilled upon me, has encouraged me to develop my interests in government, law, social services, and politics. Likewise, my mother and her Israeli family, having been strongly affected by the Arab/Israeli conflict in the Middle East, have always encouraged me to remain a strong woman, and help solve problems. The trauma suffered by my family in Israel in the last few years has compelled me to devote much of my life to helping end racial/religious struggles and working toward ending world conflict around the globe. In addition to sparking these interests, both sides of my family have helped inspire my dedication to studying history as a way to better understand the forces which have shaped their lives and mine.

My background, although at times frustrating to describe succinctly, has ultimately prepared me to approach all new ideas with a fair and open mind. I treat the attitudes, culture, customs, and religions of both my American family and my Israeli family as equally compelling. By exposing myself fearlessly to the most important aspects of life on both sides of my family, I feel that I can understand better the ways in which my unusual background has molded and affected me. I feel my willingness to accept widely diverse ideas within my immediate family has prepared me for larger world challenges.

My interest in interacting with people from different cultural and national backgrounds drew me to enroll in a large, internationally known boarding school. My goals have been realized in my three years in this school; I have thrived in this richly diverse and culturally, intellectually sensitive environment.

I have discovered that the underlying values, hopes, dreams, concerns of the majority of individuals are similar, whatever their spoken language, their religion, their customs. It is possible that the next time I am asked, "Who are you and where do you come from?" I will respond that while my mother is from the Middle East, and father from the Middle West, I am right on the bridge in the middle.

Other Kinds of Essays

Because the personal application in its entirety has replaced the interview as a guide for admissions committees, there are a number of different kinds of questions included. Two of the most important after the lengthier personal statement concern how you spent your last summer, and what subject interests you the most and why.

Remember one of our cardinal rules: There are no trick questions on college applications. Admissions officers want to know as much about you as they can, and these kinds of questions allow you to relate other aspects of your life that are important to you. We have already encouraged you to use your summers in a productive and meaningful enterprise. This is good for your personal growth, and therefore informs the colleges that you are prepared to take on the challenges of their heady environment. Signs of intellectual curiosity and excitement for learning will naturally influence their opinion of you.

SUPPLEMENTAL ESSAY QUESTION EXAMPLES

In our book *Presenting Yourself Successfully to Colleges,* we discuss at length a number of different essay types, such as the "Why Us?" supplemental essay, which asks you to talk about the logical fit between you and the particular college at hand. Here are some current supplemental essay topics required by selective colleges and universities for you to consider:

Johns Hopkins University

1. Respond to the following, using whatever space and medium you like: Communities define our lives. Those you are born into, those you make yourselves, and those you fall into by accident—communities of all types influence us and help shape us. Describe a defining community in your life and what it means to you.
2. Write a brief essay in which you respond to the following question: Johns Hopkins offers forty-nine majors across the

schools of Arts and Sciences and Engineering. On this supplement, we ask you to identify one or two that you might like to pursue here. Why did you choose the way you did? If you are undecided, why didn't you choose? (If any past courses or academic experiences influenced your decision, you may include them in your essay.)

Tufts University

We invite you to think beyond boundaries when you answer the questions below. Take a risk and go somewhere unexpected. Be serious if the moment calls for it, but feel comfortable being playful if that suits you, too.

I. REQUIRED SHORT ANSWER (50 words). Which aspects of Tufts' curriculum or undergraduate experience prompt your application? In short: "Why Tufts?"

II. REQUIRED SHORT ESSAYS (200 words)

1. There is a Quaker saying: "Let your life speak." Describe the environment in which you were raised—your family, your family home, neighborhood or community—and how it influenced the person you are today.
2. Self-identity and personal expression take many forms. Use the richness of your life to give us insight: Who are *you*?

III. OPTIONAL ESSAY. Tufts develops leaders who will address the intellectual and social challenges of the new century. Since critical thinking, creativity, practicality, and wisdom are four elements of successful leadership, the following topics offer you an opportunity to illustrate these various characteristics. We invite you to choose one and prepare an essay of 250–400 words. (And it really is optional!)

Williams College

Imagine looking through a window at any environment that is particularly significant to you. Reflect on the scene, paying close attention to the relation between what you are seeing and why it is meaningful to you. Please limit your statement to 300 words.

Gettysburg College

1. How did you become interested in Gettysburg College? (750 characters)
2. Gettysburg College students are engaged learners and "make a difference" both on and off campus through their academic and extracurricular activities. Describe a situation in which you have made a difference in your school or community and what you learned from that experience.

Lafayette College

Describe an intellectual or creative interest or accomplishment. (2,000 characters)

University of Richmond

Tell about an experience where you had to leave your comfort zone. How did it change you?

University of California

The Personal Statement

In reading your application, we want to get to know you as well as we can. There's a limit to what grades and test scores can tell us, so we ask you to write a personal statement.

Your personal statement is your chance to tell us who you are and what's important to you. Think of it as your opportunity to intro-duce yourself to the admissions and scholarship officers reading your application. Be open, be honest, be real. What you tell us in your personal statement gives readers the context to better understand the rest of the information you've provided in your application.

A couple of tips: Read each prompt carefully and be sure to respond to all parts. Use specific, concrete examples to support the points you want to make. Finally, relax. This is one of many pieces of information we consider in reviewing your application; an admission decision will not be based on your personal statement alone.

1. Describe the world you come from—for example, your family, community, or school—and tell us how your world has shaped your dreams and aspirations.
2. Tell us about a personal quality, talent, accomplishment, contribution, or experience that is important to you. What about this quality or accomplishment makes you proud and how does it relate to the person you are?

PRINCETON UNIVERSITY

1. Please tell us how you have spent the last two summers (or vacations between school years), including any jobs you have held, if not already detailed on the Common Application. (2,500 characters)

2. Using a favorite quotation from an essay or book you have read in the last three years as a jumping-off point, tell us about an event or experience that helped you define one of your values or changed how you approach the world. Please write the quotation at the beginning of your essay. (500 words)

Make a note to yourself that these questions call for shorter, even more focused responses. It is frequently harder to write a brief, informative description than a longer, rambling one. We offer you two final writing samples for your study. Once again, we reassure you that the first tightly written statement did not come easily to the writer, who took three rewritings to get it right. It is a serious, but also witty, explanation of a Yale candidate's favorite subject.

Mathematics is not beautiful. It is practical, precise, and it smells like chalk dust and damp blackboards. A sadistic old man invented it many years ago to torture young, fun-loving high school students. Schools still teach it to everyone so they learn to appreciate the outdoors. Or at least that is what I thought until I met Ms. Gold.

One thing anyone who has ever had Ms. Gold will tell you is that she does not teach; she flies. Once she gets started, all the words just begin soaring out of her mouth in gusts and blasts, and she is halfway through the first paragraph before you know what hit you. As you turn to pull out your notebook, her hands whirl across the blackboard splashing formulas and examples in every direction.

The first week of class is a blur, but when you catch up, you start wondering how you ever went any slower and how many notebooks you will exhaust before the term is over. It took me three notebooks, using both sides of every page, and by the end of the course I was still talking notes on the back covers.

This was the hardest course I have taken at my high school, but the rewards have made the torture seem trifling. I am not talking about learning good study habits or test-taking skills—these are lessons I learned at other times from other teachers, as well as on my own. I am talking about the sort of things I could only learn writing at 3,000 words per minute, trying to keep up with a woman with short, gray hair who still wears white stockings, who manages to have more energy than you had when you were a five year old. At this speed, amazing discoveries occur.

The numbers appear on the blackboard mysteriously before one can even think of writing them down. The theorems roll into each other with a rhythm and progression I never expected from mathematics. Concepts start to make sense and through this understanding there emerges a world of new intellectual opportunities. There are practical applications, for one thing. I can now calculate bacterial growth rates and the volumes of irregular three-dimensional packages. Did you know that any equation could be expressed as an infinite series?

Ms. Gold taught me how to look at math in a different light.

She showed the meaning of all those trite little phrases that math teachers tell their students over the years, like "Mathematics is the international language" and "There is truth in numbers." Ms. Gold taught me how to speak calculus, how to breathe it, and most of all, how to enjoy it. The magnificence in math comes not from getting the right answer, but from understanding where it came from. I now look at a formula or theorem and understand not just what it means, but how it originated. In a real sense, I have learned how math was born. I see how each letter has come together to form the sentences and clauses of this universal language. This is a breathtaking experience for me.

I was so moved by my math "happening" with Ms. Gold that I decided to take more of it; voluntarily no less. I spent last summer at Harvard Summer School taking Multivariable Calculus. My professor could not fly like Ms. Gold, but amazing discoveries in mathematical concepts still occurred. I learned that learning is not about speed but the road one chooses to take that matters.

The pace has slowed down considerably within the high school's math department because Ms. Gold decided to retire last June. She will not teach another BC Calculus class, but I am certain our class made her proud because 20 out of 21 students in her class received a grade of Five on the Advanced Placement exam. I know she has more time now to tend to her beloved garden, but I cannot help thinking that she misses teaching advanced math at 2,000 RPMs. After all, flowers are beautiful and alluring, but then so is calculus.

China

I left my home in New York without realizing the magnitude of the trip I was to undertake. For some odd reason, the thought of spending several weeks in the People's Republic of China seemed no different to me than vacationing at Orlando's Disney World. Although alone, I was at ease during the flight to Hong Kong and ferry ride to Shekou. As I disembarked, the first thing that caught my attention was a pair of armed soldiers wearing traditional red armbands. As I recalled my lessons about Mao's Red Guard and the Cultural Revolution, I finally understood that I had entered mainland China.

The period that followed was challenging and rewarding. As a summer intern for the Standard Chartered Bank in Shenzhen, I worked with Wang Rui Ping, a senior bank officer. Wang taught me about banking in China—the history of its changing economy, and the emergence of private enterprise. After work and on weekends, I lived with him, his pregnant wife, and his parents. Wang helped assimilate me into his family and culture. His father woke me at six-thirty every morning to teach me tai chi, a discipline of martial arts that exercises the mind and body. After work, Wang and I relaxed by reading, listening to Chinese music, viewing old photographs, and discussing everything from international politics to American films.

The most challenging part of my stay was overcoming the language barrier that I faced with Wang's parents, who did not speak a word of English. As I expected, early communication with them was held through Wang. However, by the end of my stay, I was amazed at how well we communicated using gestures, facial expressions, and intonations. I knew my assimilation into Chinese culture was complete when I understood his parents, who had been imprisoned during the Cultural Revolution, held political and social views that were profoundly different from the entrepreneurial outlook of their son.

This trip was the highlight of my international experiences. Although I enjoyed touring the Middle East with my family and visiting Europe as a Student Ambassador, Western culture, American style, now dominates these regions. China, on the other hand, has a unique and ancient culture that differs substantially from mine. Nevertheless, my summer experiences made me aware of the parallels between cultures. Irrespective of an individual's looks, language, or geographical location, there are certain values shared by middle-class families around the world. We all wake in the morning, study or work during the day, enjoy leisure time, believe in some faith, and love our family and friends. While the political systems under which we pursue these activities may vary, the common goal of enjoyment through success does not. Living and working in Shenzhen this past summer will significantly impact my thinking and outlook as I continue to grow in the years ahead.

Step Eight Checklist

✓Begin marketing your strengths when you file your applications, and continue right up to the closing of your folder—December 1 if you are a candidate for Early Decision or Action, otherwise late March.

✓Create a marketing plan to make use of all your self-scrutiny, as well as to raise fresh awareness of what distinguishes you from other applicants. Assess your strengths, identify the colleges that need or want them, then communicate to the colleges the nature of your strengths by means of documentation.

✓Document evidence of your strengths with outstanding essays you have written, creative writing, art, newspaper clippings, recent report cards, commendations, awards, résumés of athletic experience, speeches, or tapes.

✓Get an outside opinion of creative work before sending it to admissions offices, which will ask faculty members about its quality in most cases.

✓Avoid flamboyance or gimmickry, but do not be bashful. Admissions officers admire candidates who speak from a position of strength and accomplishment.

✓If you add recommendations to your folder, give a copy of your application to the person who is writing the college on your behalf. This is especially important if the person is a trustee or an administrator of the college.

✓Alumni admissions volunteers can help you receive close attention from the admissions committees. Get an interview with an alumnus once your application has been sent in.

✓Keep in touch with faculty members and coaches by telephone or e-mail. Let them know about your latest achievements.

✓Your college adviser should be informed of your marketing efforts. Give him or her copies of your letters and exhibits sent to the admissions office. An adviser can be more helpful in backing up your candidacy when armed with new information.

✓Take an inventory of your attitudes, expectations, and achievements as you search for essay topics that will allow you to reveal your personality.

✓Be sincere, be clear, be spirited, and be personal in your writing.

✓Practice, write drafts, then polish your writing.

✓Proofread your writing. Get an A in applications—no mistakes, please.

✓Keep copies of all your drafts, organized by college, so you can refer to them as you rewrite.

✓Share your nearly final draft with someone who knows you well to get feedback on whether you are perceived accurately through your writing.

STEP NINE:
Plan Your Selective College Finances

Financial Aid Problems Have Their Solutions

With the current cost of a selective private college education at over $50,000 per year at some of the most competitive institutions, financial aid becomes an almost universal consideration for candidates. Even the selective public universities charge a premium for out-of-state students. Scholarship resources are increasing, and selective universities have begun attempts to restructure the ways in which they calculate a family's ability to pay for college and to keep tuition increases under control. Nevertheless, more and more students are and will be borrowing and working their way through college, sometimes postponing their enrollment to build savings, and graduating with record levels of debt. During this decade, about 60% of bachelor's degree recipients have borrowed to pay for their college education. Average student debt per borrower increased 18%, from $19,300 in 2000–01 to $22,700 in 2006–07 in 2007 dollars. Average debt per B.A./B.S. recipient rose from $10,600 to $12,400 in the same period. And remember, this is before students have added the financing of a graduate degree into the mix. Between 1980 and 1990—one decade—college costs rose in real dollars by over 100%. Average published tuition and fees at four-year public and private institutions doubled between 1977 and 2007. The Federal Pell Grant, initiated in 1972, which had been a key cornerstone for a financial aid package for the very needy student, dropped in purchasing power dramatically. The 1999–2000 maximum award was

100% lower in its value for meeting college tuition costs than it was twenty years before. In 2007–08, the maximum and average Pell Grant rose for the first time since 2002–03. Yet the maximum Pell covered just 32% of the total costs at a public four-year college and 13% of private college total costs, compared to 50% for public and 20% for private colleges twenty years before.

This, however, is not the first time in American history that lack of sufficient means has been an obstacle to a college education. During the depression of the 1930s the selective colleges still managed to attract students whose families were suddenly almost penniless. We know that if you want to attend a selective college badly enough, you can find the money to pay for it, if not now, then in the future, after graduation. Estimates are that over $142 billion of aid was provided to college and graduate students from all sources (grants, federal loans, work-study, and tax credits and deductions) in 2007–08. Students borrowed $19 billion more from state and private sources. Undergraduates received an average aid package of $8,896 ($4,656 in grants and $3,650 in federal loans). Total aid increased by some 84% between 1997–98 and 2007–08 after adjusting for inflation.

HIGH RETURNS FOR COLLEGE DEGREES

Why is it worth getting a college degree? The "wage premium" paid to workers with a college degree relative to those with just a high school diploma has soared over the past three decades. This investment in our "human capital" is likely to remain valuable in the years ahead.

Since about 1980, the wage premium has risen fairly steadily and dramatically, from about 25% to over 45%, according to one study (Economic Policy Institute, 2/8/07).

It is therefore crucial that you resist the temptation to lower your expectations and decide not to attend a selective college for purely financial reasons. Certainly there are low-cost options, but you get what you pay for. In the long run the benefits of a selective college education far outweigh the difficulties encountered in paying for one. Some of these benefits, such as the intellectual quality and diversity of one's peer group, access to top faculty, strong and wide curricular offerings, and entry into a well-connected alumni network, are difficult to quantify, but they are tangible. Strategies for meeting the costs will require sacrifice and self-discipline. But also remember that some of the most expensive private colleges have the largest endowments and greatest resources for financial aid, often supporting, in full or in part, half of all students on campus, so that talented but needy students have every opportunity to make the most of their abilities. Polls have shown that financial aid offers and low relative tuition have become increasingly important in students' selection of colleges over the last few decades.

Just as there is academic and nonacademic competition, however, so too is there competition for financial aid. In this Ninth Step we want to acquaint you in a general and introductory way with financial aid and scholarship issues, how to overcome them as others have done and will continue to do, and how to conduct further research into obtaining aid for yourself. Our book *Paying for College: The Greenes' Guide to Financing Higher Education* provides further information on this topic.

NEW FINANCIAL AID POLICIES HELP LOWER- AND MIDDLE-INCOME STUDENTS

In the face of rising tuition costs and critiques from policy makers and the public that they were not doing enough to help lower- and even middle-income families to afford college, many selective private and public colleges and universities added more to their financial aid budgets during the 2000s. A number of institutions eliminated loans for all, most, or many students; capped the maximum amount of loans a student would need to borrow; reduced or eliminated the overall parent and/or student contribution toward the cost of a college education for all or, more typically, the lowest-income portion of enrollees; and instituted a number of policies to make their education more affordable. Despite the economic difficulties that began in 2008, including the loan crisis and decline of the stock market, which led to the erosion of many college endowments, we expect that this financial aid trend will continue among at least the wealthier colleges in the decade to come. Here is a list of many of the institutions that have made significant changes to help families afford their costs of attendance. We encourage you to examine their financial aid policies carefully and not to let their sticker prices deter you from applying. If you are admitted, they will do all they can to help you.

Amherst College
Bowdoin College
Brown University
California Institute of Technology
University of Chicago
Claremont McKenna College
Colby College
Columbia University
Cornell University
Dartmouth College
Davidson College
Duke University
Emory University
University of Florida
Harvard University
Haverford College
Indiana University, Bloomington
Lafayette College
Lehigh University
Massachusetts Institute of Technology
University of North Carolina, Chapel Hill
Northwestern University
Oberlin College
University of Pennsylvania
Pennsylvania State University
Pomona College
Princeton University
Rice University
Stanford University
Swarthmore College
Tufts University

Vanderbilt University

Vassar College

University of Virginia

Washington University in St. Louis

Wellesley College

College of William and Mary

Williams College

Yale University

The New Trends

The new trends, as we noted in our introduction, are (1) the disappearance of need-blind admissions policies at all but the most heavily endowed colleges, both public and private; (2) an increasing number of financial aid packages in which academic achievement is rewarded; (3) a larger dependence on borrowing to pay for undergraduate as well as graduate education; and (4) new state and federal scholarship, loan, and investment programs.

Selective colleges, with their large endowments, are in a better position to help undergraduates financially than institutions dependent on tuition for much of their income.

Financial aid can influence your choice of college, of course. Many applicants and their families will shop around for the best bargains among selective colleges. There are colleges—including some of the most expensive in the country—that offer large scholarships to the very best applicants, and there are selective state institutions where tuition is roughly half that of private selective colleges. The military academies are selective and they cost a family nothing. ROTC scholarships provide a four-year all-expenses-paid college education. There are postgraduate military commitments with both of these routes, of course, and there are other options, too, which we will discuss.

> Of the several thousand colleges and universities in the U.S., fewer than 400 have endowments in excess of $100 million. These endowments typically mean endowment-per-student ratios of $100,000 or more. These funds not only help support financial aid for needy students, but also cover the gap between the actual cost of providing a college education and the tuition paid by a full-pay student.

Despite the higher cost of selective colleges, there has been no drop in the number of applicants for admission. On the contrary, applications continue to rise at record rates and in record numbers.

How Financial Aid Works

Financial aid comes in a "package" consisting of three elements: grants and scholarships, loans, and work-study. Scholarships and grants do not need to be repaid, while loans do. Loans have become an increasingly larger portion of financial aid. Aid packages vary because of college policies and available funds. It is possible for a candidate to receive an admit-deny notice, meaning that the candidate is admitted but is denied scholarship aid, on the grounds of not needing it. Such a candidate can still borrow at low interest and work on campus, and parents can still participate in tuition plans that save money, or borrow at favorable interest rates.

If you qualify for financial aid, based on a calculation of your and your family's *expected contribution* and *ability to pay*, you will be expected to meet your share of costs from your savings and jobs, and you will pay back any loans in installments, usually after graduation. Your parents and you will be responsible for paying the difference between the financial aid package (which includes sums you contribute from savings and job earnings) and the total annual cost of your education.

Your parents are not strangers to meeting their financial obligations. Yet the college years may impose the most strains yet encountered on the family budget. An appreciation of your parents' willingness and ability to help you at this time will strengthen family bonds.

Example of Costs and Financial Aid Calculations: Stanford University

Stanford's 2008–2009 student budget:

Tuition	$36,030
Room & Board	$11,182
Books & Supplies	$1,455
Personal	$2,325
Orientation Fee	$438

Transportation	varies
Total	$51,430

Stanford uses a version of the Institutional Methodology (IM) of the College Scholarship Service to determine parent and student expected levels of contribution. Students are required to file the FAFSA, and Stanford utilizes the Federal Methodology (FM) to determine contribution levels for Pell Grant, Cal Grant, Stafford Loan, and work-study programs.

Stanford generally expects students to work during the summer, contributing $1,700 in their first year toward their education, and during the school year, earning at least $2,500. Students are also expected to contribute 5% of their savings each year toward their college costs. Yet Stanford has eliminated all student loans, as well as the entire parent contribution for families earning below $60,000 per year. Parents earning below $100,000 per year pay no tuition.

Example of Aid Packages for Different Recipients: Yale University

As with some of the other most selective institutions, Yale moved to make its costs less prohibitive for lower- and middle-income families, and to keep its tuition increases low. Families earning less than $60,000 per year are not expected to pay anything at Yale. Those earning between $60,000 and $120,000 will pay between 1% and 10% of family income, and those earning $120,000 and above will pay an average of 10% of their income. Yale has replaced all loans with grants. Yale's Web site provides some case studies of different financial aid packages under its old and new policies.

CASE STUDY 1:

COST OF ATTENDANCE 2008–09 (without travel, which varies)

Tuition	$35,300
Room and Board	$10,700
Books and Personal	$3,000
Total Cost	$49,000

FAMILY RESOURCES

Parents' Income	$60,000
Parents' Assets	$100,000

EXPECTED CONTRIBUTION	Old Policy	New Policy
Parental Contribution	$4,450	0
Student Contribution	$2,500	$4,400

CASE STUDY 2:

FAMILY RESOURCES

Parents' Income	$90,000
Parents' Assets	$150,000

EXPECTED CONTRIBUTION	Old Policy	New Policy
Parental Contribution	$12,550	$2,950
Student Contribution	$4,400	$2,500

CASE STUDY 3:

FAMILY RESOURCES

Parents' Income	$180,000
Parents' Assets	$200,000

EXPECTED CONTRIBUTION	Old Policy	New Policy
Parental Contribution	$38,150	$23,050
Student Contribution	$4,400	$2,500

One can see the differences in Yale's new policy, which benefit lower- and middle-income families. The lesson here again is that families should not rule themselves out of either the admissions or the financial aid pools. Yale notes that for 2007–08, 43% of Yale College students received need-based aid from Yale and that over $62 million of need-based aid controlled by the university was offered.

Paying for College: The Ten Key Principles

1. **College is worth the cost.** College is well worth the cost and sacrifices you might have to make. It is a valuable investment in your future. You will earn more during your lifetime and have

greater career flexibility, opportunities, and security. Form a family partnership to work together to make a college education a reality.

2. **Saving is important.** Begin saving for college as early as possible, but it's never too late to start. Savings are the key to all other financial assistance opportunities. Consider tax-advantaged savings plans like your and other states' 529 Plans. Save regularly and show colleges you're serious about completing your degree. More savings means less loan debt.

3. **Good students have good choices.** Good students will have good choices. Good grades in strong academic courses will create many opportunities for admission and for need-based and merit-based aid. Students, your number one job is doing well in school.

4. **Don't let costs limit options.** Do not let the costs of individual colleges limit your options. A majority of students do not pay the full tuition costs, and many of the most expensive colleges have the most generous financial aid programs. Suspend disbelief and believe you can afford college.

5. **Apply for aid.** Apply for financial aid, if you will need it, at the same time you apply for admission. Financial need will not affect your odds for acceptance in the greatest number of cases. Work with college financial aid officers as a helpful source of information and guidance. They are there to help you manage the costs of college and navigate the complexities of securing aid. Estimate your Expected Family Contribution (EFC), prepare your tax and financial aid information, and file the FAFSA, PROFILE, and institutional aid forms as close to January 1 of senior year as possible.

6. **Use available resources.** Make strategic use of the many information sources on need-based and merit-based scholarships available to you on the Internet, in bookstores and the public library, and from colleges. Be certain to meet with your high

school guidance counselor and use the resources in your school's college counseling center. Contact college financial aid counselors directly and see them as friendly, helpful guides to assist you in paying for college.

7. **Create a diverse application pattern.** Applying to a broad-based group of colleges will create more opportunities to attend a college that suits you and one that you can afford. Consider colleges that offer different types of financial aid programs, including need-blind and merit-based awards.

8. **Consider public universities.** Consider your state's public university system. Look for tuition bargains, special honors programs, and transfer possibilities within the public system. Apply early through rolling admissions programs.

9. **Consider two-year colleges.** Consider beginning a two-step college education by enrolling in an inexpensive two-year program that leads to transfer to a four-year college. In addition to considerable savings for the first two years, many opportunities for admission and financial aid may be available for the next two years of your education.

10. **Evaluate your aid packages.** Understand and carefully evaluate your aid package from each college. Comparisons of the different awards can be significant in terms of outright grant money versus loans. Consider the long-term implications of taking on loans. Compare other possible conditions of each aid package: Is the scholarship renewable for four years? Is there a work component? Do you need to maintain a certain grade point average? What will be the total cost of attending different colleges. Consider appealing your aid packages in an appropriate manner.

SOURCE: *Paying for College: The Greenes' Guide to Financing Higher Education* (New York: St. Martin's Press, 2004).

Apply If You Need Aid!

Every financial aid official of the colleges we are in contact with has urged us to get this message across: APPLY FOR AID IF YOU NEED IT! Let the *college* determine whether you are eligible for aid.

The College Scholarship Search Service has said: "The only way to know for sure if you're eligible for financial aid is to apply for financial aid." One way to get an initial sense of aid eligibility is to use some of the calculators and aid estimators available at fafsa.ed.gov and collegeboard.com.

What happens when a family decides it is ineligible for aid, and therefore does not apply for it? The cost of college becomes the chief consideration in deciding what college you want to attend. This is reversing the sound procedure of deciding what colleges you really like, and then taking the necessary, and sometimes difficult, steps to meet the bills.

So the rule is: If your parents say that an expensive selective college is beyond their means, persuade them to apply for aid. The worst that can happen is that you will be turned down for a scholarship. Aid, remember, includes tuition payment plans, low-interest loans, and possible job opportunities for you. Just because you are not considered eligible for aid does not mean that the college will not help you at all.

A director of financial aid at Princeton has said, "Don't fail to apply for financial reasons. Don't opt yourself out of the applicant pool."

Scholarships Based on Merit

Most selective college applicants will be familiar with National Merit Scholarships, which are awarded to several thousand students a year now on the basis of performance on the PSAT/NMSQT. The criterion for the awards is scholastic excellence among competitors. Financial need is not a consideration. These awards are a testimony to the students' capacities and studiousness.

The National Merit Scholarship, the most widely distributed merit award, is modest by comparison with merit scholarships offered by a number of selective universities. The University of Virginia, for example, offers up to thirty-five Jefferson Scholarships to top-achieving students. These awards cover the full cost of a student's education.

The old-fashioned tradition of helping deserving students by giving them scholarships has largely yielded to government provision of grants based solely on financial need. To be deserving no longer means to be among the top students, but simply to be a student who cannot meet all the costs of college. There is resistance by some donors to private colleges, who insist that scholarships be a reward for academic performance. Corporations have also stepped in to fill gaps in aid by offering competitive merit-based awards.

Meanwhile, the Ivies and that small group of other top colleges that have determined to award *only* "need-based" aid are finding themselves in a difficult position today. They are losing great students to public and private institutions that offer a lower price tag, merit-based financial awards, or both. And, competing among themselves, they are starting to blur the definitions of "need" and "merit," and to adjust the loan/grant/scholarship/work proportions of their need-based awards to entice highly desirable students to enroll. Since the group of twenty-three private top institutions (including all the Ivies) were accused of price fixing and forced by the U.S. Justice Department to abandon their collaborative discussions on individual students' aid packages in 1991, competition, guesswork, and mistrust between institutions have increased. Students may now indeed secure substantially different aid awards among these schools, if not in overall value, than in the proportion of the aid that must be repaid. Many top colleges, even some of those on our list of wealthy schools offering more attractive financial aid packages, are somewhat "need-conscious," meaning that near the end of the admissions process, for perhaps 5% to 10% of applicants, they consider only those who can afford to pay most or all of their way.

Many other colleges admit students without considering their need for aid, but then do not offer them enough support to make it possible for them to attend. Admissions offices at top colleges, including Williams, Carnegie Mellon, Swarthmore, and Harvard, have actually begun encouraging students to fax them their best offers of financial aid from other institutions. If the student is seen as a strong member of the admitted pool of candidates, he or she may receive a better offer, in terms of either additional money, a reduction in his or her loans, or both. Colleges are even practicing various forms of "enrollment management," calculating not only a student's ability to pay, but also his or her willingness to pay, paradoxically punishing those who express the most interest in a college because they are likely to need the least amount of aid to entice them to enroll. We have noted the moves of some of the wealthiest colleges to make their aid packages more attractive and workable for middle-income families, and the College Scholarship Service has been revising its expected contribution formula as well. Colleges have utilized a combination of the CSS formula and the sometimes more generous Federal Methodology to craft individual aid offers attractive to particular students.

What conclusions should students and parents draw from these trends? (1) They should become good, informed, flexible negotiators, willing and able to constructively, actively, and honestly approach colleges in which they are interested for better aid offers; (2) they should expand their college list to include schools that offer both need-based and merit-based awards; (3) they should again realize that merit is everywhere the best strategy. Apart from and in addition to showing significant financial need, merit will in every case help students to get the best offers from different colleges. And it is the students who are at the top of a *particular* college's admitted applicant pool who often get the most attractive awards from *that* college.

Ultimately, we should continue to wonder whether we are witnessing the demise of need-based financial aid overall, as top colleges compete to get the top small percentage of students to enroll.

In what may have become a financial aid arms race to the bottom, some top colleges may spend themselves into an inability to support all of their students in the fairest way possible in order to enroll a small group of the most talented students. Writing in 1996 in the *New York Times Magazine,* Andrew Delbanco, a professor at Columbia University, discussed "sending the limo," the phrase Ivy League admissions officers use to describe what happens when a non-Ivy school uses an attractive financial offer to lure away a strong student. He noted that "competition for exceptional students has gotten so intense that the Ivy League financial-aid structure is starting to crack." This trend has continued, with merit-based financial aid representing one of the fastest-growing sectors of the aid pie. The clear implication is that the future of need-blind and need-based aid is threatened by too many limo trips originating from selective college campuses.

Let us illustrate one approach to merit- and need-based aid with an example. Cindy, among the top three Merit Scholarship finalists in her large urban New England high school, applied to several Ivy League colleges and was admitted to all of them, as well as to Vanderbilt. Her family could be described as middle-income, and they felt that considerable scholarship money would be necessary to carry Cindy through four years of a selective college.

The Ivy colleges offered Cindy similar aid packages, for it is still their custom not to compete for students by outbidding each other with larger, merit-based scholarships overall. While they are no longer able to confer in the spring to compare aid packages of students admitted to two or more of these colleges and adjust packages that are out of line, the Ivies and a few other top colleges still use roughly similar financial aid formulas that result in generally comparable total aid packages for the same student admitted to multiple-schools. Cindy's Ivy need-based awards were all about $5,000.

ENROLLMENT OF 2007 FRESHMAN MERIT SCHOLARS

In the fall of 2007, 8,262 freshman Merit Scholars were enrolled, 4,845 at 226 private colleges and universities, and 3,317 at 136 public universities. The list below shows the colleges and universities enrolling the largest numbers of Merit Scholarship winners (50 or more), and the number whose scholarships were funded by the college or university, rather than the National Merit Scholarship Corporation or other corporate sponsors. Readers will likely be surprised by some of the names in this group, showing the active pursuit by a diverse set of institutions of top students as identified by the Merit Scholars program, the attractiveness of public universities across the country, and the lack of merit-based awards at some schools. Note that, proportionally, some very small colleges enroll quite a few scholars, and some very large universities don't enroll many at all.

(Data Source: National Merit Scholarship Corporation)

Number of Freshman Merit Scholars Enrolled

285 Harvard College

283* University of Texas, Austin (232)

249* Northwestern University (186)

231* University of Southern California (195)

204* Washington University in St. Louis (154)

196* University of Chicago (156)

183 Yale University

179 Princeton University

175* University of Oklahoma (137)

173* Texas A&M University, College Station (134)

172* Vanderbilt University (116)

168* University of Florida (132)

166* University of North Carolina, Chapel Hill (127)

164 Stanford University

159* New York University (137)

159* Rice University (95)

150* Arizona State University (127)

138 Massachusetts Institute of Technology

118* Ohio State University, Columbus (93)

115 University of Pennsylvania

100* Georgia Institute of Technology (73)

96* University of Minnesota, Twin Cities (73)

95* Brigham Young University (70)

90 Duke University

87* Purdue University (66)

84* Baylor University (70)

84* University of Illinois, Urbana-Champaign (56)

83* Carleton College (64)

80 Brown University

73* University of Alabama, Tuscaloosa (60)

70* University of Arizona (58)

68* University of Tulsa (55)

68* Harvey Mudd College (52)

66* University of Nebraska, Lincoln (54)

62 Columbia University

62 University of Michigan, Ann Arbor

60* Emory University (40)

60 University of California, Berkeley

59* Tufts University (43)

57* Indiana University, Bloomington (42)

51* University of Maryland, College Park (38)

51 Dartmouth College

50* Clemson University (37)

*Signifies that Merit Scholarships sponsored by the college are included; the number sponsored by the college is in parentheses.

Vanderbilt, however, offered her a $9,000 scholarship. In fact, this situation had been anticipated when Cindy first discussed admissions with us and mentioned the family concern about paying for college. She was told that the Ivies are generous, but that there are colleges and universities anxious to attract top applicants away from them. Among such well-endowed institutions, Vanderbilt is building a reputation for strong academic programs preparing half the student body for graduate school, which might have been difficult at an Ivy college where Cindy would have had to work at a job to pay her bills.

Cindy's case is not unique. The box above shows the forty-three institutions enrolling fifty or more National Merit Scholars as freshmen in 2007, each with scholarships of up to several thousand dollars.

Most get further scholarship offers from outstanding institutions or corporations. Some Merit Scholars require no aid, yet their education is largely paid for by the colleges and the government. We should also mention the significant National Achievement Scholarship Program for African American students which awards additional funds and recognition.

The Ivies are not complacent about losing students like Cindy, and they do not lose all the National Merit Scholars. They continue to be proud of the fact that they reserve their largest scholarships for those with the greatest need. Other selective colleges that give scholarships to the very brightest students regardless of need include North Carolina, Virginia, Lehigh, Johns Hopkins, Michigan, Duke, Emory, Washington University in St. Louis, Northwestern, and the University of Rochester. It is good fiscal strategy to apply to one or two of these colleges when money is a concern. We should note that every year, individual colleges revise their financial aid approach, and it is important for applicants to check each college's information carefully to determine its current financial aid policies when they are applying.

Scholarships by the Hundreds

It used to be said that there were so many scholarships that some went begging for lack of applications for them. This is less often the case today, thanks to the computerization of scholarship data. Even so, a great deal of scholarship money often remains on the table for students with particular interests, backgrounds, locations, or talents, because these students are unaware that they are eligible for such non-need-based awards. We have provided a list of mainly Internet-based sources that will lead you to scholarships for which you may be eligible.

Corporations and organizations that sponsor scholarships include the American Legion, the Coca-Cola Scholars Foundation, DuPont, Duracell, the Bill and Melinda Gates Foundation, Intel, the Jaycees, the Masons, the National Honor Society, the Rotary Club, Toyota, Wal-Mart, and the YMCA/YWCA. National fraternities and sororities, as well as labor unions and employers, are other potential sources of scholarships. When beginning your search for scholarships, you should make a list of your affiliations. These can include:

- Activities
- Volunteer and work experience
- Your hometown, county, and state
- Your potential college choices
- Your possible college majors and career plans
- Your athletic involvement
- Your demographic information (gender, race, ethnicity, age, disability, military backround)
- Your parents' involvement in unions, companies, fraternal organizations, their colleges, and the military

Some of the awards available from private sources are lucrative. The Intel Science Talent Search Scholarships, formerly known as Westinghouse (www.sciserv.org), award a $100,000 first-place four-year scholarship, as well as additional significant amounts to the next few dozen winners. The awards are for use in scientific fields of study. This is a tough one to win: Candidates must complete a significant science-related research project and be lightly qualified academically.

The Toyota Community Scholars Program has 100 awards of between $10,000 and $20,000 available for students with a focus on leadership and community service. Winners are selected based on merit, and the awards are open to students in all academic fields.

Be sure to ask your counselor for the latest news about scholarships you may be eligible for in your region, and to actively pursue your research in the library, the school resource room, and on the Internet. In your search, you may find or be approached by organizations claiming to guarantee you awards and access to privileged information. Be aware of potential scams, and skeptical of services that seem too good to be true. You can find most information on your own with care and persistence, and scholarships advertise in many places in order to find suitable applicants. Some of the best, and free, computerized scholarship search services are on the Internet, including Peterson's, the College Board, FastWeb, and others listed in our Internet Resources list (pages 102–105). Start with www.finaid.org, the U.S. Department of Education at www.studentaid.ed.gov, and some of these services before ever considering a fee-based search service. And, if you do decide you want more help and are willing to pay for it, look for references from services you are considering, and think about contacting the Federal Trade Commission or the Better Business Bureau if you think you are being taken advantage of.

Financial Aid for Multicultural Students

The good news? There may be *money* available for you if you are a member of a minority group, a group that is underrepresented in higher education. Colleges are seeking to expand their diversity in many different ways, as we have discussed, not the least of which is ethnic and racial heritage. If you are a talented student who is African American, Hispanic, or Native American, for example, you will have access to college-based scholarship aid, particular corporate awards, and funds from organizations dedicated to improving minority representation in academia, in addition to the other forms of federal and state financial aid discussed in this chapter. Washington University in St. Louis offers the Ervin Scholars Program, granting up to ten African American freshmen renewable scholarships covering full or partial tuition and an annual stipend of $2,500. These scholarships are awarded on the basis of academic merit, service, and leadership in one's school or community, three qualifying factors that are consistent across many scholarship awards.

Some examples of minority-specific scholarship funding organizations include:

- AMOCO Foundation Undergraduate Scholarship Program for Hispanic students who intend to study engineering and other sciences

- Armstrong Foundation–National Achievement Scholarships for African Americans who have National Merit Achievement Status

- Hallie Q. Brown Scholarship Fund, National Association of Colored Women's Clubs (nacwc.org)

- The Jackie Robinson Foundation (jackierobinson.org)

- Jesse Arias Scholarship Fund for Hispanic students interested in careers in law or public policy

- McDonald's Hispanic American Commitment to Education Resources (HACER) Program (rmhc.org)

- NAACP Scholarships

- The National Hispanic Scholarship Fund (www.nhsf.org)

- Organization of Chinese Americans Scholarships (ocanational .org)

- Presbyterian Church (U.S.A.) Native American Grant (www .pcusa.org)

- United Negro College Fund Scholarships

- U.S. Department of the Interior, Bureau of Indian Affairs, Higher Education Grant Program (www.doi.giv/bia)

- Xerox Technical Minority Scholarship (xerox.com)

A major resource and opportunity center for students of color is A Better Chance, a nationally prominent organization with a history of supporting talented minority youth in high school and college. For more information on ABC, go to their Web site at www.abetterchance .org. There they also have links to and information on colleges that are affiliated with ABC's programs and that are particularly interested in attracting and supporting students of color. ABC's record of recruiting, selecting, and supporting motivated and intelligent students of color is unparalleled, and ABC Scholars, who have graduated from top private and public schools across the country, have gone on to many top colleges with significant financial help. A recent ABC graduate, currently attending Columbia University, was asked by ABC about his college search process and his advice for other minority students. "The thing that I found most helpful," he noted, "was talking to the students" at different colleges. "I cannot emphasize that enough. Black students, white students, undergrads, grad students, everyone!!!!! The most important questions were ones regarding financial aid." His advice for students of color? "DO NOT SELL YOURSELF SHORT!!!!! When everyone heard my college list, they advised me to choose more safety schools. You have to reach for the stars. Be realistic, but also take a chance. It is better to have some kind of chance and apply than not apply—a 100% no. Also, talk to African Americans at each college and ask them about social life, academic workload, their personal experience, the black community, etc." This student also advised prospective applicants not to take their initial aid offer as final. "I am glad that I negotiated the financial aid package. My responsibility lessened by $2,500—it may not be much to some, but that was a huge burden off my shoulders."

See our list of additional Internet resources on pages 102–105 and pursue the other routes of aid we discuss here. Just remember that when you conduct *your* search for aid, see your racial or ethnic identity as an asset, and include it as one of your personal characteristics when filling out search or aid forms.

Financial Aid for International Students

One of the key criteria for qualifying for aid from the U.S. and American state governments, which supply the vast majority of aid in the United States, is American citizenship or "permanent resident alien" status (a green card). That means that if you do not meet either of these qualifications, then you are unlikely to gain grants or loans through most of the financial aid systems discussed here. However, do not despair, because many of the private colleges with strong financial resources are actively seeking talented international students to bring to their campuses. You need to help them by finding out which colleges offer some aid (covering full or partial need) to international students, and by contacting their admissions and financial aid offices. Often, these colleges make one or a few aid awards specifically directed at international students, and the competition is stiff. You must have strong grades and test scores and a good application to the college. The important point to note is that colleges that offer aid, whether based on need or merit, to international students do so from their own pockets, and without the help of the federal government. Thus, such aid is more precious, harder to come by, and difficult to find. International students with need should make sure when evaluating an aid offer or merit award to ask about tuition, room and board, fees and living expenses, and, importantly, travel allowances to and from home. Awards may cover only partial and not full need. Thus, international students should seek supplemental sources of aid, from U.S.-based scholarship providers or, in some cases, their own home country governments or organizations.

Anna came to us from Romania after spending an exchange semester at a high school in Colorado. An extremely talented student, she had scored over 1300 on the SATs, without practice, during this junior year experience in the United States. She was determined to return to America for college, but her family, although comfortable in Romania, would not be able to pay for any of her college tuition in the U.S. market. Our task: matching Anna's interests academically and socially with a college that would not only admit this strong student, but also provide her with scholarships to cover the total cost of her education, from tuition to fees to books. Anna spoke several languages and had major interests in international relations, international business, and comparative languages. She was an A student in a difficult curriculum in Romania, but, due to the structure of the system there, had few extracurricular activities. Nevertheless, her international travel and study experiences, as well as the story of her upbringing in Romania, made for interesting and compelling essays.

We knew that Anna's list would have to be expansive, because many colleges, when made aware of an international student's full need, will decide not to admit the student if the college does not have the aid available, even if the student is academically qualified, because the college knows the student will be unable to attend. Anna was initially interested in urban East Coast universities, which seemed more familiar and diverse to her. She centered in on Columbia as having the right programs and environment for her. We encouraged her to expand her list to include a number of those colleges listed below, which would not only have international aid available, but also find Anna's unique background and interests a wonderful contribution to their campuses. Anna applied to some of the most competitive schools, which, as we have discussed, have deep resources, and to a broad mix of other colleges. Her list included Columbia (Early Decision), Amherst, Yale, Dartmouth, Princeton, Harvard, Penn, Brown, Gettysburg, Connecticut College, Mount Holyoke, Colorado College, Bates, and the University of Bridgeport (CT). Her list was top-heavy, but she wanted to give herself a chance at a number of Exceedingly Demanding colleges.

Anna was rejected from Columbia early, and from all the others except Bridgeport and Colorado College, where she was accepted, and Mount Holyoke and Connecticut, where she was wait-listed. It turned out she had overreached with many schools, but by balancing her list, she had found some good options. We felt that Connecticut and Mount Holyoke might have taken Anna if she had given one of them a sense that they were her first choice, but she had a full aid package from Colorado College, an excellent school only an hour from where she had lived with an American family during her junior year, and she enrolled there.

A SAMPLING OF U.S. COLLEGES AND UNIVERSITIES OFFERING MORE AID TO INTERNATIONAL STUDENTS

Amherst College

Bates College

Bowdoin College

University of Chicago

Colorado College

Connecticut College

Dartmouth College

Dickinson College

George Washington University

Gettysburg College

Hampshire College

Macalester College

Massachusetts Institute of Technology

Mount Holyoke College

University of Pennsylvania

Trinity College (CT)

Washington University in St. Louis

Wesleyan University

The State University Option

Our list of selective colleges includes more than fifty state universities and colleges. You may decide to apply to one or more of them for other than financial reasons, but certainly their lower costs make them attractive, too. For the very brightest students, some like North Carolina, California, Georgia, Texas, and Connecticut have financial aid packages that lure students from the private selectives. Chapel Hill's Morehead Scholars receive a four-year "free ride," the academic equivalent of athletic scholarships. Georgia's HOPE scholarships (now adopted in some form by at least fourteen states) pay full tuition at any state university in Georgia for those with a GPA of 3.0 and above. Public institutions, especially for in-state students, can even without need-based or merit-based aid prove to be great deals for students when compared to the selective private colleges. At about $14,000 per year on average for in-state students, public universities are significantly less expensive than the selective private colleges.

Many applicants to the public universities believe that they will get a fine education at a great university for far less than it would cost at a private college, even if they do not receive aid. The public universities are trying to attract more top students through special programs in addition to larger amounts of merit-based financial aid. With many top students considering both public and private options, admission to the top public campuses, and to selective honors college programs at the state universities in particular, has become increasingly more competitive. The University of Maryland, for example, has reported that average SAT of first-year students enrolled in its honors college in 2008 was 1400 (CISTMA), and weighted GPA was 4.28, statistics comparable to those for students at many Exceedingly Demanding private colleges and universities.

The University of Virginia's Echols Scholars Program invites "avid learners" to take advantage of special opportunities on campus, including freedom from course requirements, course selection priority, a shared first-year living experience, special faculty advisers, and an Echols learning network. Echols Scholars make up about 10% of UVA's students in each class, and are among the best and the brightest at the university. Said one Echols Scholar on UVA's Web site, "I was accepted into many private universities of similar standing to UVA, and many had incredible departments that I wished to study at. However, the cost to attend these universities was inordinately high, beyond affording. What the Echols program does is turn UVA into one of those schools for me. Of course, UVA is great alone, but the Echols privileges certainly make the university a better learning environment." Top public honors programs are competing effectively with top private colleges, and their students compare favorably to their private college counterparts.

If you are admitted to a selective state university, though, before you enroll at what you and your family consider an excellent "bargain," visit the campus if you have not already done so, and make sure that you really like the college, and not just the money. Some students and their families ignore the state university option until the last minute, then apply "just in case." Then, almost on a whim, they get out the pocket calculator and on the basis of comparative figures decide that, after all, the state university is best. The first time the student sees the campus is registration day. The educational experience may be great, or the student may find the institution unsuitable after a year and transfer elsewhere. A campus visit is worth the travel expense. As we mentioned, the large public universities have made great efforts to institute residential college, honors, and critical thinking programs to emulate the smaller universities and liberal arts colleges and to provide a more supportive and stimulating environment for students. Nevertheless, there are great differences between the excellent state universities and the private small and middle-sized colleges and universities, which bear thorough examination on the part of students and parents.

NONRESIDENT VERSUS RESIDENT TUITIONS IN STATE COLLEGES

State residents gain significant tuition, and admissions, advantages over their out-of-state counterparts. That is one reason that out-of-state students are so interested in gaining residency in the state where they are attending college. It is also a reason that students in every state should consider their public university as *an* option which they can rule in or out, or keep on their college list alongside of selective private colleges. To give one example, at the University of Virginia, of the most selective public universities in the country, Virginians could expect to pay $9,940 in tuition and fees ($20,173 total costs) for 2008–09, as compared to $29,790 ($40,473 total costs) for non-Virginians!

Military Options

All the military academies are selective. Appointments, arranged through your congressperson or senator, are given only to good students. Once you are accepted, though, your expenses for four years are covered. You, of course, agree to join one of the six military services—Army, Navy, Marines, Air Force, Coast Guard, or merchant marine.

Selective colleges with ROTC programs admit applicants who then apply for admission into the Reserve Officer Training Corps on the various scholarship programs. Acceptance can mean an all-expense-paid college education in a civilian setting, and an agreement to serve a term as an officer in the armed services after graduation.

Other military-related issues: If you or your parents are veterans, you will have access to a number of specific government and scholarship programs dedicated to members or veterans of the armed forces. Additionally, many states grant military waivers to those in the military, giving you immediate residency status, and thus reduced tuition, even if you just arrived in the state.

AmeriCorps represents a non-military option that allows you to trade service for loan reductions or education support. The Corporation for National and Community Service (www.cns.gov) provides more information about this program, which allows you to teach, work in shelters, or clean up the environment, for example, in exchange for financial assistance for future or past college tuition.

Athletic Scholarships

If you are a strong athlete, consider the possibility of competing for athletic scholarships, which are most often and most significantly awarded by National Collegiate Athletic Association (NCAA) Division I (the most competitive) colleges and universities. These include such athletic powerhouses as the University of Michigan and the University of Texas. Some 125,000 scholarships are offered each year by about 1,000 NCAA-affiliated institutions, totaling about $1 billion. Over 300 scholarships are offered by the smaller colleges of the National Association of Intercollegiate Athletics (NAIA), and some of the over 500 schools in the National Junior College Athletic Association also give athletic awards.

Female athletes should know that due to the increasing enforcement of Title IX, a law that requires equal opportunity for men and women athletes, more money and scholarships are being made available to women. See Step Seven for help on evaluating yourself as a potential athletic recruit, and Step Eight on presentation for more information on communicating with college athletic departments and coaches. It may be very worth your while to evaluate your prospects as a college athlete, to pursue the recruiting game, and to seek out some colleges where your athletic strengths could not only help with admissions, but also provide you with a significant sports scholarship.

Saving Time and Money

If you can complete your undergraduate education in three years instead of four, you save one year's college costs. This may be possible by taking several Advanced Placement courses in high school that allow you to enter as a sophomore. If you can get credit for college courses taken elsewhere, doing this can shorten your time in college. The three-year plan is not popular because part of the selective college experience is the four years you spend with your professors and classmates. Nevertheless, earning college credits in high school can save you time and tuition, and room and board money.

Work Versus Scholarships and Loans

Today, almost all students earn money in college and on vacation, whatever the family income. Students who earn money as part of their aid packages usually are assigned jobs by the college's financial aid officer, although students may have some discretion in finding jobs particular to their interest or skills, including research assistant work with faculty. For those students who are not eligible for aid, there may be employment opportunities on campus. If not, a student employment agency lists jobs off campus with reliable employers. Job markets, of course, vary. A student not receiving aid who nonetheless is expected by the family to earn money while in college will do well to determine how much work will be available. Another point to remember is that colleges today recommend no more than fifteen hours' work on a job in a week. Longer hours result in weaker academic performance, and that is counterproductive.

Research has shown that there is a connection between student employment and a higher GPA—to a point. That is, students who do not work tend to perform less well than those who work under about fifteen hours per week. Students may wish to work to supplement their spending money, to take care of bills, and to fulfill the requirements of financial aid packages. However, too much work can be detrimental to a student's undergraduate studies. And a poor GPA can negatively affect graduate admission and career opportunities. According to some estimates, 66% of college students plan to work during school, and only 56% plan to take out student loans. Again, students are encouraged to pursue financial aid, including loans and scholarship possibilities, in order to keep their working hours below fifteen per week.

The colleges use the Preliminary Estimated Contribution as a *guideline* in working out their aid packages, hence the description as preliminary. In the end the colleges themselves administer student aid, so they are the final arbiters of what a student and family must pay. Colleges are therefore free to provide more aid or less than the Preliminary Estimated Contribution.

IMPACT OF COLLEGE COSTS

In 2007, freshmen surveyed by UCLA's Higher Education Research Institute indicated significant concern about college costs. More than half had some concern about financing college, while almost 10% indicated this was a major concern. In terms of why they selected their college, 39.4% noted that it was very important that the college had offered financial assistance, and 36.8% noted the cost of attendance was very important.

Splitting Your Colleges

Some students attend public institutions for a year or two, then transfer to a private selective college, or to a selective state university that originally turned them down. This certainly saves tuition money, but we must warn you that the most selective colleges take very few transfer students. Additionally, transferring into a college, especially a small college, may put you at a social disadvantage, because friendships have developed and it is not easy to break into circles that are frequently rather closed. But if financing your education is a primary consideration, or if your academic record necessitates it, this is a strategy to consider seriously.

Federal Student Aid Programs

There are a number of federal student financial aid programs, which presently amount to almost $100 billion a year. New aid programs and additional funding of current programs are under discussion even as we write. Remember, grants you do not need to repay, loans you do, and work-study requires your employment. A good starting resource on federal student aid programs is available at www.studentaid.ed.gov.

Federal Pell Grants. Named after their sponsor, Senator Claiborne Pell, the grants, in varying amounts, are distributed essentially on the basis of need to students from lower-income families. Based on the Expected Family Contribution (EFC) calculation, Pell grants help more than 5 million students annually, with a maximum award of $4,731 in 2008–09.

Federal Supplemental Educational Opportunity Grants (FSEOG). Federal funds distributed by the colleges to a few need-based students in relatively small amounts. The maximum award is $4,000 per year.

Federal Stafford Loans. Low-interest (6.0% in 2008–09, down to 3.4% by 2011–12) loans made through a bank, credit union, or savings and loan association. These loans include both need-based subsidized loans, for which the government pays the interest while the student is enrolled in school, and non-need-based unsubsidized loans, which accumulate interest while the student is in school. Independent students can borrow more than dependent students, who can borrow a maximum of $5,500 in year one, $6,500 in year two, and $7,500 in subsequent years to finance their undergraduate degree.

Federal Direct Loans. Similar to Stafford loans, but now offered direct from the U.S. Department of Education's William D. Ford Federal Direct Loan Program, these loans are not available on every campus.

Perkins Loans. Low-interest (5%), need-based loans for those students with very low EFCs. A maximum of $4,000 per year is available to students through the colleges, and interest is subsidized while they are in school, with repayment beginning nine months after graduation.

Federal Work-Study (FWS). Work-study funds are allotted to colleges, which then employ students directly in campus jobs in cafeterias, libraries, and other facilities or in local community-service jobs for no more than fifteen hours per week.

Federal Parent Loans for Undergraduate Study (PLUS). For parents, these Direct- or Stafford-administered loans have variable interest rates of up to 9%. They are particularly helpful for parents of dependent students who need extra money to cover college costs over and above other financial aid. Repayment begins sixty days after the loan is disbursed, or six months after the student leaves school.

Via the FAFSA (Free Application for Federal Student Aid), you can request a Student Aid Report from the U.S. Department of Education, telling you whether you and your family qualify for one or more of these programs. For information on receiving this report, see fafsa.ed.gov.

Low-Interest Loans

As part of their financial aid packages, many colleges make low-interest loans available to their students. In addition, there are independent companies that provide various financing plans. These are firms that will prepay the college tuition and arrange a payment schedule to fit the family's financial circumstances. A life insurance rider is available to cover the full cost of the student's education in the event of the parent's death.

State Tuition Savings and Prepayment Plans

In recent years, states have become very creative in offering tuition savings and payment plans to residents. In some cases, families can pay for four years of the state university's tuition at current prices, even if their child has just been born. States have created different forms of savings accounts with tax benefits for families. States also have widely varying requirements for undergraduate students to gain state residency. Such "in-state" status confers the major benefit of decreased tuition. As a rule of thumb, students should expect to have to live in state at least a year, have a driver's license during that time period, and possibly to have filed a state tax return. It is often easier for students to gain in-state residency if they are independent from their parents. Families should contact their state department of education to ask about particular tuition and savings plans for college, as well as requirements to gain residency and any reciprocity the state maintains with other states. Key issues to consider include: tax benefits associated with the plan; ability to withdraw money and under what circumstances; and whether students can apply the money only to that state's public universities, or whether they can use the money outside the state and for private colleges.

While state tuition *prepayment* plans are generally restricted to eventual use at an in-state institution, and guarantee to pay the eventual tuition no matter how inflated, state-supported tuition savings programs are more flexible and often more attractive for middle-income families. Families can use the money from the savings programs at any institution, but are not guaranteed to have enough money accumulated to cover tuition at any particular place. Federal legislative changes in 1996 (Section 529 of the federal tax code) and in 1997 (the Taxpayer Relief Act) made it easier for states to create education savings plans with significant tax and income benefits, particularly for those who can afford to put away significant sums early in their child's life or each year thereafter. The new savings programs allow families to put in significant up-front investments large up-front investments, without a gift tax. The amounts are much more significant than those allowed in IRA investment plans, and while the initial contribution is not federally tax-deductible, earnings in the account are tax-deferred until the student withdraws money from the account for school, at their own, not their parents', tax rate. These plans are known as *Savings Trusts* or *529 Plans* and are variously managed by larger investment banks and other organizations, such as the Teachers Investment and Annuity Association (TIAA). Although one can put in large amounts, one can also find plans that allow individuals to put away only $50 per month.

NEW OPTIONS TO SAVE FOR COLLEGE

Many parents serve as custodians for an account in a minor's name (Uniform Gifts to Minors Account, UGMA, or Transfers to Minors Account, UTMA). Earnings in the account in excess of $1,700 are taxed at the parents' tax rate until the child reaches age eighteen. The "kiddie tax" cutoff age was fourteen until 2006, and the change will likely only further the trend of families choosing to set up

529 savings or 529 prepaid tuition plans and Coverdell Education Savings Accounts instead of custodial accounts. A 529 savings plan allows anyone—a parent, a grandparent, an uncle, or a family friend—to set up an account in a child's name and contribute as much as $12,000 per year without incurring a gift tax. Alternatively, a contributor can in one year donate $60,000 to be treated as an annualized gift over five years, thus avoiding the gift tax while allowing money to grow with compounding interest beginning at an earlier date. Parents' investments are calculated on a per-person basis—each parent can contribute as much as $12,000 a year or $60,000 for five years.

Earnings in 529s grow tax-free, and more than twenty-eight states plus the District of Columbia have state tax incentives associated with these plans. Assets can accumulate in an account to as much as $250,000 to $300,000 in various states. Parents can withdraw 529 funds without penalty to pay for a child's college or graduate school expenses and can transfer them to their own account or to the account of any relative of the beneficiary up to a first cousin if the beneficiary does not need the funds. There is a 10% penalty on earnings in most cases if an account owner withdraws the funds for non-post-secondary educational uses.

Some states maintain a 529 prepaid tuition plan, which allows families to fund a college education at an in-state public university at today's prices. Private colleges and universities have now been authorized by the federal government to begin their own prepaid 529 programs, though the Independent 529 Plan, offered by a consortium of elite schools, is the only one currently available (independent529plan.org). Generally, account holders holding state-sponsored prepaid tuition plans can decide to use their funds to pay for education at a private and/or out-of-state college or university, although there may be a penalty for doing so.

Other benefits of both types of 529 Plans include the following: The funds remain in the control of the account holder, not the beneficiary, so your child will not automatically get control of the funds at a certain age. For financial aid purposes, 529 funds, in either a prepaid account or a savings account, are treated as an asset of the account owner or as not relevant at all on a student's financial aid application. That means the funds will be assessed at a maximum of 5.64% each year as a parental asset available to help fund a student's college education. Older custodial accounts (UGMAs or UTMAs) will be assessed as student assets at 20% to 35%. They can be transferred into a 529 Plan with significant benefits and some restrictions.

The Coverdell Education Savings Account (ESA), formerly known as the Education IRA, has a few significant differences from 529 Plans that make it more and less attractive. Funds from an ESA can be used for elementary and secondary expenses as well as college and graduate expenses, so parents using or considering private K–12 education or who have significant private-education expenses prior to college might want to invest in an ESA. The maximum amount allowable for ESA contributions is now $2,000 per year, and there are income caps and a phase-out for those earning between $95,000 and $110,000 or $190,000 and $220,000 for joint filers.

Adapted selection from our feature article in Consumer's Digest, *May/June 2007.*

Some Issues to Consider in Evaluating Award Packages

All financial aid award packages are not alike, and you must consider federal grants and loans, college scholarships and loans, and outside scholarships and loans in a comprehensive way to see how they work together for you at each college to which you have been accepted.

- Will the college alter its aid package if you have also secured outside scholarship support?

- Have you been offered a full scholarship, or only a partial scholarship?

- What portion of your package is loans, which you must pay back, versus grants, awards, or scholarships, which are free and clear?

- What portion of your loans do you incur, and what portion do your parents take on?

- What would happen to your award if you accepted only part of it, and rejected others (e.g., loans or work-study)?

- If you have work requirements, how many hours will you be required to work, at what rate of pay, and how will you be paid? Are you expected to save additional money from jobs over the summer?

- How many years, exactly, will your aid package cover? Are there certain requirements, such as a high GPA, that you must maintain to keep your awards? What percentage of students graduate in four years?

- What, exactly, will your aid package cover? It may pay only tuition, or include such elements as required fees, books, room and board, a computer, and travel to and from home.

- What is the average loan indebtedness of graduates of the college, and where do they go after graduation?

- Will you be guaranteed on-campus housing for the duration of your degree, or will you potentially have to move off campus? How will your aid package cover such a move?

- Are there special support programs or groups in place for scholarship students? What percentage of students on campus are receiving financial support from the college?

- Are there hidden costs associated with attending the college? High rents or food prices in the area, high travel costs, fees for lab, library, athletic center, or student transportation usage?

- What happens if you lose your scholarship after your first year? What kind of aid could replace it?

- When will you have to begin repaying your loans, and what would happen if you transferred to another college or reduced your enrollment from full-time to part-time status?

- Has the college given you its best offer? Consider appealing your award package, in terms of overall aid as well as the proportion of grants versus loans, due to extenuating personal or family circumstances or because you really want to attend the college but have received aid packages that make it easier for you to go elsewhere.

- If your aid package, plus your and your family's expected contributions, is not enough to meet the costs of the college you want to attend, what other sources can the school recommend that you pursue?

- How important to you is it to attend a particular college, despite the fact that its aid package is not as attractive as other schools'? It may be "worth" your attending a top college with a strong program in your area of interest, more support for you, and a better record of graduate and career placement.

Long-Term Savings and Investment for College

One of the best ways to pay for college, of course, is to have saved the money for tuition in the first place. Now, if that were the case, you would not need to find need-based aid. Nevertheless, for those parents with enough time to plan ahead, and even those with children in high school and college, there are many new investment and tax vehicles available to help save and pay for a child's education. The federal and state governments have been responding to calls from their constituents to make higher education more affordable, and they have used the tax code as a major instrument in their efforts to encourage and facilitate the pursuit of a college degree. Parents can talk with an accountant or investment adviser, and research options with the federal and state departments of education.

Tax credits have become an attractive way for the government to focus attention on education, and to make it easier for middle-class families to save for college. The HOPE Scholarship tax credit allows independent students and parents of dependent students to claim tax credits to pay for a student's college tuition. The Lifetime Learning tax credit assists adult learners going back to school, and upper-level college students who are already enrolled, by allowing them to take a tax credit on tuition and required fees. Another tax-related plus is the ability to deduct interest paid on student loans. For more information on taxes and education, contact the IRS at www.irs.ustreas.gov.

MORE GRANTS FOR STRONG STUDENTS

Need more reasons to study hard? Two grants from the federal government will help. The Academic Competitiveness Grant (ACG) was initiated in 2006–07. It provides $750 in year one and $1,300 in year two for full-time college students who have completed a "rigorous secondary school program of study." The National Science and Mathematics Access to Retain Talent (SMART) Grant is available to college students in years three and four (up to $4,000 per year) who are Pell Grant eligible and who are majoring in physical, life, or computer sciences, math, technology, engineering, or a foreign language critical to national security.

Your Counselor Can Help

Your college counselor will probably not claim to be a financial expert, but counselors are a good source of information on the student aid distributed by your state, and on scholarships in your community or region. You should tell your counselor that you are filing for aid. Information you have on college costs, aid policies, scholarships, and the like will become a resource for others in your school. Your counselor can help you find information by obtaining books and Internet resources through the school, sharing a list of awards that students have won in the past, writing recommendations for you, and filling out appropriate school information on financial aid and scholarship application forms.

Some Creative Ways to Pay for College

- Thank your parents for having invested in mutual funds and Coverdell ESAs, or having prepaid your tuition through the state at 1995 prices.

- Attend the public university in your state, or a state with a "reciprocity agreement" with your state. Look for special merit scholars, honors college, and residential college programs and enticements.

- Attend an in-state two-year public college, do well, and then transfer to the premier four-year public university in your state, or to a highly selective private university. Two inexpensive years, two expensive years, and a degree from a top college.

- Seek out well-endowed Exceedingly Demanding, Very Demanding, and Demanding colleges that offer non-need-based (merit) awards to top students. You can find many of these in *The Hidden Ivies*.

- Apply for a multitude of scholarships that fit your interests, talents, background, and place of residence. You cannot win if you do not play, as they say, so with due diligence search for appropriate scholarships and apply, apply, apply.

- If you are a strong athlete, consider colleges that offer athletic scholarships, and remember that by law, colleges are required to provide scholarship aid to women athletes in proportion to their enrollment.

- Take Advanced Placement and community college courses in high school; take Advanced Placement and SAT Subject Tests in junior year and in May and June of *senior* year. The college credits you earn may reduce the course credits you pay for in college, or even give you sophomore standing.

- Study abroad while in college. You may be able to pay decreased tuition costs while at a foreign university, while earning credits at your home institution. Some colleges have now closed this loophole, however.

- Take advantage of work-study awards. You may not have qualified for grants, but you may be able to gain work-study funds. In other words, you earn money by working at a school-approved job, where the college, individual professor, or department pays part of your salary, and the federal government or state pays the rest. The creative idea here is to try to obtain jobs that contribute to your academic or career goals, including conducting research with faculty, assisting a professor in the classroom, or working in a community service–related field. Such experience will help for graduate school or career placement in the future.

• Participate in the National and Community Service Plan, in which you may work in education, human services, the environment, or public safety and earn a stipend of almost $15,000 per year for living expenses and almost $5,000 per year for two years of college expenses. You can work before, during, or after college and pay for current expenses or accumulated loans.

• Consider those colleges ranked as "best buys," "worth the price," or "best values" by such sources as *Kiplinger's Personal Finance Magazine, U.S. News and World Report,* and *The Fiske Guide.* These rankings take into account such factors as academic reputation, overall tuition and fees, available loans and scholarships, and amount of financial aid awarded to students.

When and How to Apply for Financial Aid

Ideally, planning college finances should begin in your junior year or earlier. Some prudent people begin planning for college while their children are still in the cradle. Yet it is not too late to apply for aid and scholarships to help you continue in college once you are there. The impact of inflation may call for a review of the family financial situation in your junior year. Starting early is necessary, particularly if you are going to need federal grants. Some federal grant money is in such demand that it runs out before all who need it can be satisfied.

It is essential to begin financial planning in your junior year if you are strong enough academically to consider applying for Early Decision/Action in the fall of your senior year. Such candidates typically must file for financial aid by November 1, so that financial aid packages can be announced when the students are admitted in December.

If you are not applying for Early Decision, you will file your financial aid forms early in January. Colleges that require you to file an application for financial aid in addition to the Free Application for Federal

Student Aid (FAFSA) and the College Board's College Scholarship Service's Financial Aid PROFILE have varying deadlines that you should be aware of. Once enrolled, you will be asked to file a shorter form each year you renew your request for financial aid. Unless your academic record is unsatisfactory, or your or your family's financial circumstances change dramatically (a sibling graduates or enters college, a parent is promoted or loses a job), you can expect to receive your aid package each year, with adjustments for inflation. However, it is uncertain how much money the federal government will continue to allot to student aid.

Be aware, if you are not already, that family finances are often a sensitive area among family members. In our experience, most parents prefer not to divulge the particulars of their income, taxes, and so forth to their children. Most of the necessary financial planning will fall to your parents (unless you are personally independent, that is, your parents do not claim you as a dependent on their tax forms, and you file your own taxes). Your parents will rely on professional help from a financial adviser, be it a bank, a lawyer, a tax accountant, or an investment planner. Note that while your parents will take on most of the responsibility for filing for *financial aid,* that is, loans and grants, particularly from the state and federal governments, you can be the driving force in identifying and applying for scholarships, particularly those non-need-based awards given competitively for academic or other distinction.

Financial planning is a sophisticated field, calling for a knowledge of investments, insurance, and taxes. But financial advisers may know less than you do about aid packages, tuition payment plans, and sources of scholarship funds. The information you have been gathering will be extremely helpful to your parents when they talk to bankers, brokers, or investment counselors about your college costs.

We encourage you to form a *family partnership* to realize successfully your college goals. Every family has its own way of doing things. We believe that you should be as involved in planning your college finances as is consistent with family harmony. He who pays the piper calls the tune. Parents are used to being responsible for giving you the best, and they will tend to be senior partners in this expensive college venture of yours. But they will be grateful for your help.

You can provide them with a copy of the *Guide to Getting Financial Aid*, a handbook put out annually by the College Board and available on their Web site, and the U.S. government's *Funding Education Beyond High School: The Guide to Federal Student Aid*, available at studentaid.ed.gov or through the Federal Student Aid Information Center (1-800-4-FED-AID). You should do this during your junior year if possible. It would be well to study it first, go over any questions with your counselor, and then hand it to your parents. This will put you in a position to discuss financial aid knowledgeably.

You can also contribute by providing information about different college costs and tuition payment plans, and other factual material that may already be in your notebook from your campus visits, such as:

- The costs of each college under consideration
- Payment plans available at each college
- What the College Scholarship Service requires on its financial aid form
- What kinds of aid packages are typically worked out at the colleges
- What scholarships you might be able to get
- What loan programs you should consider
- What government programs may offer you

Make out a sheet like the Financial Worksheet below for your parents (there is a copy in the Appendix).

Be mindful of the need to file the FAFSA and possibly the Financial Aid PROFILE early in January of your senior year. If the college requires an application for financial aid in addition to these, send for it. Most colleges publish thorough information on fiancial aid in their admissions brochures and on their Web site. A financial aid office works closely with admissions personnel at each college, and it is quite appropriate for parents and students to contact this office for information and with questions. The colleges understand that many applicants may never enroll, but they value goodwill and are prepared to discuss patiently the complexities of financial aid.

Financial Worksheet

Colleges ____ ____ ____ ____ ____ ____

Tuition ____ ____ ____ ____ ____ ____

Room and board ____ ____ ____ ____ ____ ____

Fees ____ ____ ____ ____ ____ ____

Books and supplies ____ ____ ____ ____ ____ ____

Travel ____ ____ ____ ____ ____ ____

Personal expenses ____ ____ ____ ____ ____ ____

Total one-year budget ____ ____ ____ ____ ____ ____

KINDS OF AID AVAILABLE:

Tuition payment plans
Monthly payments ____ ____ ____ ____ ____ ____

Four years payable
in advance ____ ____ ____ ____ ____ ____

Scholarships ____ ____ ____ ____ ____ ____

Student loans
from the college ____ ____ ____ ____ ____ ____

Government aid
plans administered
by the college ____ ____ ____ ____ ____ ____

Campus jobs
available ____ ____ ____ ____ ____ ____

Hours per week ____ ____ ____ ____ ____ ____

Noncampus jobs
available ____ ____ ____ ____ ____ ____

Summer job leads   _____ _____ _____ _____ _____ _____

Financial counseling _____ _____ _____ _____ _____ _____

ED/EA aid application
due   _____ _____ _____ _____ _____ _____

Regular aid
application due   _____ _____ _____ _____ _____ _____

Completing the Financial Aid Forms

In applying for financial aid from the federal government, you should file the FAFSA. These programs include those mentioned above, such as the Pell Grants, SEOGs, PLUS Loans, and the Federal Direct Loans. You may also need to fill out the College Scholarship Service's Financial Aid PROFILE and the Financial Aid Report of Eligibility (FARE). For some state and private aid programs you will have to fill out other forms. To find out more about which forms you should use, contact your high school counselor, the financial aid office at the colleges of interest to you, or your state scholarship agency, typically housed within the state departments of education. Also visit going to college.org for more information on state financial aid programs.

Selective college applicants who take the ACT will probably use the Family Financial Statement, ACT's financial-need-analysis form, instead of the College Board's Financial Aid PROFILE. Most colleges accept either form. Remember that in either case you may also have to fill out an application for financial aid on the colleges' own forms.

Careful reading of the College Board's financial aid handbook and searching through the materials at www.finaid.org, will answer many questions about financial aid, but the estimated parents' contribution figures could lead to the erroneous conclusion that families with certain levels of assets and income are disqualified for financial aid. This is not necessarily so. We strongly urge no family to draw conclusions about aid eligibility until they have applied for aid.

While there is a fee for each college when filing the PROFILE, an applicant can request a fee waiver based on need. There is no fee for

filing the FAFSA. The FAFSA, PROFILE, and other financial aid
forms call for information on your parents' finances, such as data from
last year's Internal Revenue Service tax return filed by your parents.
Other records you, or your parents, may need to have available in filling out the forms include: your own tax returns or W-2 forms; bank
statements; mortgage records; business records; and your driver's license and social security numbers. Because of the sensitive nature of
family finances, we strongly advise you not to ask your parents about
their finances! Instead, let your parents fill in the financial data after
you have answered all the questions that pertain to you. You will almost certainly avoid hitting a raw nerve if you hand your parents the
forms with the assurance, "I've filled in my part and signed the form.
You can fill in your part—that's your business." Your parents can do so
and mail in the form. If they choose to share financial information with
you, nothing has been lost. Our experience is that the financial aid
forms infuriate many parents with their bureaucratic insensitivity.

Completing Scholarship Applications

Scholarship applications are a separate track from the financial aid
forms, although they may require listing of similar data. Typically, private or public scholarship applications require one or more essays and
short-answer questions connected to the purpose of the scholarship
and your own educational goals and background. You may need official
transcripts from your high school, as well as recommendations from
your guidance counselor and teachers. Your essays may be similar to
those you are writing on the college applications, so you may try to
cover multiple bases with one adaptable personal statement. However,
scholarship applications often require specific explanations of why you
deserve the award and how the criteria of the award apply to you. Take
these essays very seriously, and spend quality time on their completion
(see Step Eight on presentation). Your writing could very well make the
difference between your winning a scholarship and being passed over
for someone who appears to have completed the application more carefully.

In sum, start, complete, and file all necessary financial aid forms
and scholarship applications early. Type them whenever possible, or fill

them out in black ink if necessary or required. Make copies of every application before and after filling it out. While a lot of work, this aspect of your college application process could very well make your college experience not only more obtainable, but more enjoyable as well, by taking off some of the financial stress.

You Can Make Ends Meet

In concluding this discussion of a sensitive issue, we assure you that if you concentrate on doing what you must do to be admitted to a selective college, you will find the necessary money. No selective college wants to lose an applicant because of insufficient funds, and it will go out of its way to work with you and your parents on a reasonable aid package.

Financial aid can influence your choice of college. But you may well wish to persuade your family that it means more to you to attend Columbia than anywhere else that may cost them less; they may be willing to take out a second mortgage and sacrifice several thousand dollars in scholarship money. There are many good reasons to enroll where the out-of-pocket family cost is greater than it is at other colleges. If the most selective colleges were not considered premium institutions, why would anyone be willing to spend what they cost?

Every college will give you a hearing if you are dissatisfied with its offer. You may not get a bigger scholarship, but the loan and job components of your package may be improved. We know this from years of observation. So never say never where money for college is concerned. Plan ahead and ask the selective colleges how you can make ends meet. Approach them with sincerity, openness, and respect. You will be pleasantly surprised by the positive answers you will get.

Step Nine Checklist

✓Plan your college finances as a junior partner with your parents. Start by bringing home the College Board's financial aid handbook in your junior year, if possible.

✓From the colleges, obtain information about their costs and financial aid policies.

✓Look into scholarship opportunities for top students at well-endowed colleges and state universities. Use your school's reference sources for lists of scholarships.

✓Complete and sign your part of the financial aid forms (FAFSA, PROFILE), then let your parents complete theirs and mail them or submit online early in January of your senior year (or before then if you are applying for ED/EA). Remember that you may have to fill out an application for financial aid on the colleges' own forms as well.

✓Do not fail to apply if you need aid, or think you may need aid; do not opt out of the admissions pool. There is no penalty if colleges determine you do not meet aid criteria, and there are other loans and jobs that can help.

✓Never give up on selective colleges because of cost. If you are admitted to a selective college, ways can be found to fund your higher education. Be informed and prepared to negotiate your award offers from competing colleges to which you have been accepted. But be sensitive. Some colleges do not negotiate their aid offers, and your or your parents' approach should not be one of entitlement or aggressiveness.

✓Keep open to good colleges that have admitted you and offered you merit-based awards to entice your entry. It may indeed be worth changing your first choice of college if another appropriate school makes it easier to pay for your college education.

STEP TEN:
Enroll in the Right College for You

]

Admissions Procedures After Admission

You will be reading this before you experience the inevitable elation that occurs upon being notified of admission, so you may wonder why there is a tenth step in our plan to help you enroll in a selective college. It is quite simply because the complex admissions process does not end with admission itself; it ends only after you sign an agreement to enroll in some college. In the case of an Early Decision I or II binding commitment, you have signed this agreement in good faith before hearing whether or not you have been accepted. In the case of regular admissions, you have until May 1, the Common or Candidate Reply Date, to sign a committal form. And even then, as you will see, you can nullify this agreement if you are prepared to sacrifice a not insignificant deposit.

You will, of course, experience great euphoria following receipt of any warm letter of congratulations from a selective college that has admitted you to its upcoming freshman class. Astonishment and excitement may last for days as congratulations pour in. This sense of accomplishment, we almost inevitably observe, is succeeded by nervousness and indecision. Anticipating your options after receiving admissions notifications will allow for smooth planning without the confusion that often reigns at home as the final decisions in the admissions process draw near.

Early Decision Obligations

As Early Decision applications have increased, and more colleges have moved to a binding Early Decision, as opposed to Early Action, program, more students are determining their college choices by a November deadline, and finding out about admissions by the middle of December. Many Exceedingly Demanding , Very Demanding, and Demanding colleges are filling between 10% and 45% of their first-year classes through Early Decision. The acceptance rates for Early Decision candidates range from around 10% at the most selective colleges to 50% at the less demanding institutions. All of you admitted early, whether in round I or round II (when you find out your decision in February or March), have already made a contractual commitment to attend these colleges. We warn you once again that you are bound to submit no applications to any other college, and to withdraw any applications you may already have submitted under non-binding admissions plans. Remember that you are only allowed, ever, to submit one binding Early Decision application at a time. If you are deferred or rejected from an Early Decision round I application, however, you may submit an Early Decision II application. But if you have been accepted through EDI or EDII, you have already given your word, in writing, that you will attend this college.

In other words, if you are tempted to discover what other colleges might have accepted you by filing applications with them, never do this. You can seriously affect your college career. The penalty for breaking this rule is withdrawal of your acceptance. No comparable selective college will admit you, and you will be obliged to enroll somewhere that you probably will feel is beneath your ability.

With your early acceptance comes a financial aid package if you applied for aid. This can be a surprise. It may seem too ungenerous. You should contact the financial aid office and express your feelings. It may be possible to get an improvement in the package, or you may be asked to be patient and wait until spring for a possible increase. At that time the colleges have a clearer picture of the total aid funds to be budgeted for the year. Some applicants promised substantial aid packages may decide to enroll elsewhere, leaving the institution extra money to redistribute. If you are truly unable to attend a college that has admitted you through Early Decision due to financial circumstances, and you have tried to work with the college's financial aid office, then you may break your commitment to attend the college. Apart from a serious change in family circumstances that would prevent a student from enrolling, lack of financial resources is the one reason respected by colleges as just cause for breaking the binding commitment. We emphasize that this circumstance is rare, however, and students should not jump to it lightly.

In practice, Early Decision candidates admitted in December or February face far fewer decisions than those admitted regularly in April. This is one reason why the numbers applying early have been rising at the rate of about 10% a year—and why the competition for early applications is getting stronger year by year.

Early Action

We have explained in Step One the distinction between Early Decision and Early Action. Those of you who have received Early Action admission, or notification that you will probably be admitted, to one or more selective colleges know that you are free to file applications elsewhere. Chances are you will be admitted to a few other colleges. If your Early Action college is truly your first choice, and you can revisit it to ascertain this, you need not apply to other schools. This is not a time for "trophy hunting," as it is crudely referred to in admissions circles. In other words, you should not apply to Princeton or Brown just to see if you would get in if you know that Yale or Georgetown is really your top school and you have been admitted in December. If you are unsure about committing to such an Early Action offer, you can, of course, pursue regular admissions at other colleges. You will in this case typically apply to a short list of only those colleges likely to be more attractive to you than the college already in your pocket.

Choosing Your Preferred College

We have assumed from the start that you will be admitted to at least one selective college, but applicants who follow the Ten-Step Plan are rarely admitted to fewer than two. This is because they apply to some colleges that are an obvious "fit" for them. If, however, you are accepted by only one college, your college career has been determined—unless you have applied to nonselective colleges as "safeties" or because they are less expensive. Nevertheless, if you have only one college choice in April, you can revisit it to determine its appropriateness. If you truly feel you should not attend this college, you can begin discussions with your parents and counselor about alternate options, such as a "gap year," deferred admission, a postgraduate year, and so forth.

Applying to too many colleges can lead to another quandary: too many choices. If you have six acceptances in April to consider, you may have a difficult time narrowing your list. You will need to engage in some of the selection processes we discuss throughout this book (Steps One and Six, for example) to help you focus on what your priorities are, and which colleges best fit your preferences. Factors such as cost, location, athletic opportunities, academic program, size, single-sex versus coed student body, and distance from home may now come to the forefront of your decision making.

Anticipating the choices that lie ahead of you, look in your notebook at your original observations and feelings when you evaluated colleges after campus visits. Then look at the conclusions you drew after studying your pie charts. There is often a conflict between estimating your chances of admission and loving a particular college. You apply to both, expecting to be turned down by the one you love. Then you are admitted to the one you correctly decided would accept you, and you are also wait-listed at the college you really prefer. We discuss the wait-list problem below. For the moment, we want you to be aware of such surprises. In theory, you have only applied to colleges you would be happy to attend. But when the admissions reach your mailbox, you must weigh one college against another, and sometimes you may agonize for days.

We have prepared an Admissions Decision Questionnaire to help you in this process.

Your Admissions Decision Questionnaire

I have been admitted to the following colleges:

1)_____, 2)_____, 3)_____, 4)_____, 5)_____,

6)_____ (list the dates on which the colleges notified you)

Acceptance deadlines are the following: 1)_____, 2)_____,

3)_____, 4)_____, 5)_____, 6)_____

Financial aid packages compared (from Step Nine):

1) $_____, 2) $_____, 3) $_____, 4) $_____,

5) $_____, 6) $_____

Deposits required: 1) $_____, 2) $_____, 3) $_____,

4) $_____, 5) $_____, 6) $_____

I have been wait-listed at: 1)_____, 2)_____, 3)_____,

4)_____, 5)_____, 6)_____

Alumni and/or coach contacts initiated by colleges (names, dates):

1)_____, 2)_____, 3)_____, 4)_____, 5)_____,

6)_____

Alumni and/or coach contacts initiated by me (names, dates):

1)_____, 2)_____, 3)_____, 4)_____, 5)_____,

6)_____

Campuses revisited: 1)_____, 2)_____, 3)_____,

4)_____, 5)_____, 6)_____

I prefer college _____.

I will put a deposit down at _____.

I plan to accept if removed from waiting list at _____.

Do financial considerations require me to attend a public college in my state?
Yes   No

I wish to renegotiate the financial aid package at _____.

I am disappointed in not getting into _____. I want to consider:

1) a 5th year of high school and reapplying to _____, _____;

2) enrolling in another college and transferring to _____

in my _____ college year; 3) putting down a deposit at _____,

but deferring admission there, taking a year off, and possibly reapplying to

_____, _____.

When the Colleges Put on the Pressure

Until now you have been currying favor with the colleges to let you in. Once they have let you in, they have to woo you. This occurs at all levels of selectivity. Alumni groups may invite you to special dinners; colleges may send priority invitations to elaborate on-campus information sessions, including all-expenses-paid travel; the chair of the history department or the dean of the faculty may call you to extol the virtues of their programs. Colleges know and expect that these activities entice many accepted students to enroll, thus raising their overall yield.

You can anticipate being importuned by coaches and even faculty members once you have been admitted. This treatment will make you feel important, loved, and wanted. It may also trouble you and render you momentarily indecisive about two wonderful colleges. That is when it may be necessary to revisit a campus or two.

"VIP" APPLICATIONS

Every college wants you to feel like a VIP (very important person). Many, at all levels of selectivity, from Duke and Drew to Tulane and Vermont, are sending invitations to students early in the admission process whom they feel, based usually on the College Board's Scholarship Search Service, would be a good candidate for admission. A sign you are likely to get in? Not necessarily. But this is likely to be just the beginning of your marketing relationships with colleges.

Revisiting Campuses

In April you will see the buses pulling into New Haven. They carry prospective freshmen. Yale's yield is not 100%; of those who have been admitted, enough enroll someplace else—mostly at Harvard, Princeton, Stanford, Dartmouth, or Amherst—that Yale makes a serious effort to attract the best and the brightest of its admitted class. The buses are one way to revisit the campus, and it is popular because all your expenses are paid by some alumni group. You get a chance to stay overnight and retake "the 10:30 P.M. test" we discussed in Step Six, to reassess the feel of the college late at night and the following morning in a dorm.

From those special alumni dinners and late-night calls, from fabulous campus open houses to high-powered faculty lectures and pre-pre-orientation (marketing) sessions, colleges will put on their best faces to ensure that you, an admitted student, will become an enrolled student. Think about how much work on the college's part went into admitting you. From start to finish, glossy brochures to blogs, online chats to personal calls and letters and e-mails and mugs and hats, colleges have been engaging in an all-out campaign to attract, admit, and enroll you. They do not want to lose you now.

If you are a scholarship student, arrangements will be made for you to make the trip when there is no bus going from your area to a particular college. Even nonscholarship students may get all the expenses of the trip paid by contacting the admissions office and saying that they want to revisit the campus. Alumni in your area are most helpful in this matter. You need not feel obliged to enroll just because the college has gone to the trouble to persuade you of its merits. Be prepared to be impressed. Red carpets are rolled out for prospective freshmen in April—deans and top faculty members or coaches tell you what you can expect during your next four years; student leaders put on a show, and they can be persuasive. You may be invited to an athletic event in the afternoon, or be asked to play tennis or swim in the Olympic pool.

It is not easy to turn down a college after a visit during which you are treated like royalty. However, you need not commit yourself one way or the other. If you possibly can, go to another campus where you have been accepted, and maybe another. Then, with two or more wonderful experiences and a notebook full of fresh impressions, you approach the moment of truth. You talk the problem over with family, counselors, teachers, your peers—and then it is up to you, and you alone. You do not have to explain or apologize to anyone. Go to your room and think about it.

Considering Financial Aid Packages

At the time of your admission you will receive a notice, issued by the financial aid office of each college, of your aid package, consisting of scholarship, loan, and job. From two or more colleges you will receive aid packages that differ in generosity. You may ultimately decide on attending the college that seems to value you the most, and this is fine so long as it is your preferred college. But if you would rather attend a college offering you less, you should make this known to the financial aid office (the admissions committee cannot help you get more aid) of the preferred college.

As we have pointed out, colleges that admit you really want your enrollment. If money is an obstacle, selective colleges will listen to a reasonable argument, especially if new circumstances have developed since you applied for aid—family illness, new obligations, business difficulties. Colleges can, if they have the scholarship money, be more generous than the College Scholarship Service advises them to be. They can raise your scholarship, or increase your loan, or arrange for a loan to your parents, or steer you toward external sources of scholarship or loan support.

So do not quit on a college because of dissatisfaction over their financial aid package. And here is where you, the student, are likely to be more persuasive than your parents. You really are the needy one; your parents, with few exceptions, have more means than you have. Psychologically, their case is bound to be weaker than yours. What can your father say when the question is asked: "Have you considered a second mortgage?" It is a question, however, that can only be asked of you indirectly, since you have no house to mortgage. Be bold and say that you need X thousand dollars, and you want it in the form of an increased scholarship. At the worst, you will be told that there is no scholarship money available, but that a larger loan can be arranged. There is no end of loan money around, although for you to leave college heavily in debt is not a pleasing prospect. (Incidentally, statistics show that selective college students seldom fail to meet their obligations to the federal government.)

The Waiting List

Colleges put candidates on waiting lists to protect themselves from a drop in yield. Yield is the actual enrollment as a ratio of those admitted. If 2,000 are admitted and 1,000 enroll, the yield is 50%. Very few colleges have a yield of greater than 50%, believe it or not, so they must admit twice as many applicants, or more, to reach their enrollment goals for the first-year class. Colleges keep annual yield records, but they can never be sure that the averages will hold, as unpredictably fewer students may decide to enroll in a college this year than last. If the yield drops to 48%, for example, then to make up the 2% (twenty students) that were expected, the college goes to the waiting list. But if 50% or more do enroll, then perhaps no one from the waiting list gets in. When the yield is surprisingly high, some of the freshman class or other classes must be housed off campus. The following year, the college reduces the total number of applicants it admits.

If the college must go to the waiting list for twenty more students, it must still consider how many students it needs to admit from the wait list to assure that twenty additional students will enroll. That is, sending out twenty additional letters of acceptance, or personally calling those students, may only entice ten additional students. The college is still wondering who will be more likely to enroll if accepted.

Colleges are under no obligation to take anyone from the waiting list. If you have been wait-listed, you can congratulate yourself that you are among an elect; you are one who would have been admitted if the class were only a bit larger. But you cannot begin to guess whether or not you will be admitted. You really have no other way to protect yourself than to agree to enroll at another college that has already admitted you.

Meanwhile, in the admissions office where you are wait-listed, the committee is adding up its acceptances and filing them by categories. Let us say there are 100 on the waiting list and finally it is decided that only fifty of these need to be admitted to fill the first-year class. What fifty will be admitted? No one on a waiting list is ranked, any more than anyone in the freshman class is ranked. If you call the admissions office and ask where you stand in relation to others on the list, you will be told that there is no way to answer that question.

Do colleges prioritize their waiting lists to some extent, by region, legacy status, or athletics, for example? To some extent, to be sure. But as uncertainty and unpredictability in the admissions process have increased, more colleges are putting more students on waiting lists so as to have a large, diverse pool of qualified students from which to cherry-pick just the right individuals to balance their freshman class.

The class profile may show, for example, that the number admitted from traditional private schools is already on target; the college wants to admit no more in this category. If you are of this kind, you will not be admitted from the waiting list—and you will not be told why. Or suppose you are an outstanding woman soccer player and were put on the waiting list in the expectation that another woman soccer player would enroll. When she decides to go to another college, you are sent a letter of admission; you have been taken off the waiting list. Or suppose the college is trying to achieve gender parity in its class, and has found that more women than men have enrolled this year. It will give preference to qualified males on the waiting list. Perhaps an overabundance of science majors enrolled; a talented classics scholar will thus be admitted.

Although it would seem that you are completely powerless to do anything if you are wait-listed, this is not the case. Let us assume that you prefer the college that has wait-listed you above any others. You are praying to be the one who is accepted from the list. Here is what you do:

You agree to enroll in the college you like second-best, where you have been admitted.

You then contact the admissions committee at the college where you are wait-listed and tell them you will enroll elsewhere unless you are admitted to their college.

You add, "If you take me off your waiting list, I assure you I will enroll at your college."

Is this acceptable practice? Absolutely. It is not dirty pool to accept one college's offer of admission, and then later withdraw from that freshman class in order to accept another offer as the result of being taken off the waiting list. However, it is costly. You have paid a deposit, usually several hundred dollars, with your agreement to enroll. This you must forfeit as the price of enrolling in the college you like the best. There is nothing morally wrong with this practice. Colleges accept it as a business proposition. None like to lose a freshman, but for a fee, so to speak, the practice is tolerable. For more information on this and other admissions practices, we encourage you to read the National Association for College Admission Counseling's "Statement of Principles of Good Practice" (nacacnet.org). Remember that just as you are hoping to get into one college off the waiting list, and so must forfeit your fee and place at your second-choice college, another student on that college's waiting list will be thrilled to find out they have been accepted, and must now forfeit their fee and place at their second-choice college, and so on.

WEIGHTY WAITING LISTS

Recent wait-list numbers were almost scary, we noted six years ago and even fifteen years ago. They still are. Continuing increases in applications have flooded waiting lists. The use of waiting lists has grown, as has the number of students placed on them, but the number of students taken off waiting lists at the selective colleges remains low. We have also noted the use of waiting lists by some colleges to gauge a student's real level of interest in the college. A student who casually applies to a school with little indication (through visits, interviews, a careful application, and so forth) of strong interest in a college may find him- or herself wait-listed, even though he or she is a strong candidate.

According to NACAC, 41% of colleges now use waiting lists, compared to one-third in the past. In 2007, the average admit rate from wait lists was 29.6% overall, 37.7% at public universities and 27.0% at private institutions. However, the average wait-list admit rate dropped to 13.5% at colleges that accept fewer than half of applicants. It was 29.2% at colleges accepting between 50% and 70% of applicants.

College Bound has reported the following wait-list enrollment numbers for 2008–09: Princeton (about 90 of 1,000 who opted to stay on the list); Penn (90 of 1,000); Yale (45); Amherst (15); Swarthmore (20 of 350); Harvard (200, compared to 50 the prior year); Boston College (250, up from 117); North Carolina (300); Hamilton (36); Georgetown (80); and Wisconsin (375 of 950).

From the point of view of the college that has wait-listed you, your assurance to enroll if admitted is a comfort. The more acceptances a college can be certain of, the less work and worry for the college. It happens that colleges will still be trying to fill all freshman places as late as the end of August. By that time admissions offices are already working on the next freshman class, so they are anxious to put an end to the process, which should have been over by July 1. You, who promise to attend if admitted, become more attractive to the college.

To reinforce your promise, write the college a letter stating your intention, and enclose any new information about yourself that makes you an attractive candidate. Re-market yourself! Send in a copy of your spring varsity letter certificate, or your most recent A+ paper, or a stellar recommendation. Needless to say, if you are hoping to be accepted off a waiting list, excellent spring semester grades can be your greatest asset.

Having taken care of all this, you have done all you can about the waiting list. You may be on two or more waiting lists, and in all cases your procedure is identical. However, you should not promise to several colleges you will enroll if admitted. Be assertive at all of your wait-list colleges, however. Be tough-minded now. If you find yourself in a bind being taken off two waiting lists, smile, accept the college you prefer, and send regrets to the other. You already have reason to cry a little, sacrificing the deposit fee at the college you originally accepted.

And remember, the chances of being taken off any waiting list are very slim. Make up your mind that you will go to the college you have accepted, so if lightning strikes and you are taken off a waiting list, it will be that much more pleasing. Try not to get too down about the fact that you are wait-listed at one place. Rather, allow yourself to get excited about the college you have now committed to.

A GUIDELINE TO THE WAITING-LIST PROCESS

1. Being put on the waiting list (WL) is not the same thing as rejection from a college. If the admissions committee wants to reject a student because he or she is unqualified or there is no chance of his or her being admitted in the competition, they will turn the student down outright.

2. An offer to remain on the WL indicates a genuine and serious interest in an applicant because the student is considered fully qualified for admission. The problem is the combination of a limited number of available spaces and too many qualified candidates.

3. Each college will guess at its traditional yield factor (the percentage of applicants offered admission who will accept the offer). If a smaller percentage than usual commits to a place, the admissions committee will turn to its WL to accept more applicants. If the yield is on target or an underestimate, WL candidates will not be accepted.

MOST COMMONLY ASKED WAIT-LIST QUESTIONS

Q. How do I know where I stand on the WL?

A. Admissions staff do not rank the order in which applicants appear on the WL. They will review only those students who indicated a desire to remain on the WL. Many will decide to enroll elsewhere, thus taking themselves out of the competition for a space.

Q. How do colleges decide whom to admit from the WL?

A. The admissions staff will look for signals of serious interest on the part of the student. They will want to offer admission only to those who are most likely to accept their invitation. They will also take into account the composition of the entering class based on those who have been accepted and add to its mix accordingly.

Q. How do I indicate my serious desire to attend and what else can I do to help my cause?

A. Write a letter to the director of admissions as soon as possible indicating your commitment. Give some specific reasons for wishing to be admitted, e.g., particular programs of study, extracurricular activities that you excel in and will want to continue. Offer to come to campus for a personal interview to explain your interest and your qualifications directly.

Q. What else will help my cause?

A. Have your school counselor send your most recent set of grades and teacher comments where available to the admissions director if they reflect a strong performance. An active counselor will not hesitate to telephone the admissions officer responsible for your high school. Also send new teacher or coach recommendations if you have excelled in that individual's course or sport since submitting your application. This is the strategic point in time to ask a very active alumnus or friend of the college to call or write on your behalf if you know such a person.

Q. What do I do about the other colleges that have accepted me?

A. You must hold a place for yourself at your next-favorite college prior to the May 1 Common Reply Date. Failure to do so can result in a loss of that offer of admission.

Q. When will I know if I will be accepted from the WL and what do I do about the college that I notified of my acceptance?

A. After May 1, the admissions staff will know if it has met or exceeded its target of enrolled students. If this is the case, it will notify WL candidates that the admissions process is over. If, by contrast, the staff wants to offer a number of acceptances, it will notify students immediately by letter, telephone, or facsimile. All colleges abide by this reply-date process and thus understand that a student may now rescind his or her earlier commitment in order to attend his or her first-choice college. The only penalty is the loss of the enrollment deposit. It is possible for a college to maintain an active WL through the entire spring term in order to ensure meeting its enrollment targets. It is legitimate to remain on that college's WL as long as you like if it is truly your first choice. However, make a full and enthusiastic commitment to the college that you are most likely to attend in the coming fall.

Admissions Notification Before April 1

The most selective colleges no longer adhere strictly to the historic common notification date, April 15, which has really been moved up to April 1. Like the less selective colleges, they try to steal a march on their competitors by unofficially admitting a percentage of the stronger candidates around March 15 or even earlier. Dartmouth, for example, has taken to sending out select early-notification-of-future-admission letters to some strong applicants in February.

With a two-week, or two-month, head start, these colleges can put psychological pressure on you to accept their offers of admission, as tentative as they may be.

Be prepared for this situation: You have applied to half a dozen or more selective colleges, four of which adhere to the now common date of April 1; two colleges announce in a letter of March 20 that you have been admitted to their freshman class. These admissions are contingent, the letters say, on your paying a fee (which is supposed to be refundable) prior to the Common Reply Date of May 1, which almost all colleges honor.

Well, now, here is a pleasant surprise. We have told you that you will likely be admitted to at least one selective college, and often two, and this latter goal has been achieved. Is it not a bit greedy to wait to be admitted to one or more of the more selective colleges that will not notify you until later? Why not accept a bird in hand?

For these reasons: (1) It is needlessly costly. (2) You may want to review the financial aid package you receive from every college. (3) If you are rejected by the other four colleges, you can probably enroll at one of the two that admitted you early, since it is obvious that you are an attractive candidate. (4) The late March admissions are a signal that these colleges recognize you as the kind of candidate likely to be accepted by one of their more selective rivals. Therefore, you are not taking a very big risk in waiting a few more weeks; you are in a stronger position than you may think. Early notification, sometimes combined with preferred dormitory or honors program incentives, for example, is an attempt to stampede you into an acceptance at once when you can exercise it later.

Your response to these early notification letters, then, should be a letter that goes something like this:

Dear Dean _____,

Thank you for your notification of admission [or likely admission]. I am deferring my decision to enroll at your college until I hear from several other colleges where I have applied for admission.

[If you are an aid applicant]:

I must also compare financial aid packages from these institutions with yours. It would greatly help me to know as soon as possible what financial aid you plan to offer me.

Please notify me if there is any difficulty in holding a place for me until May 1.

Sincerely,

Now the ball is in the other court. Furthermore, you are not on the hook for a fee of $500 to hold your place. This demand is a bluff, and you have until May 1 to make up your mind responsibly. Ignore it; you will not lose your place. We regret that some selective colleges have been driven to adopt this tactic, long practiced by colleges that must actively campaign to maintain enrollment at a level necessary to fill freshman places and provide the tuition income needed to keep the institution solvent. Needless to say, the practice bothers other selective colleges, which are powerless to fight back without breaking the common notification agreement themselves, which many have. Given another major trend we have discussed, the rise in ED, EDII, and EA admissions, we suspect that, apart from the May 1 Common Reply Date, college notification will continue to become more school-specific and fluid over time.

Blind copies of your letter can go to other colleges, which will notify you of your admission or rejection by their specified date (often April 1). Your counselor, armed with a copy of your letter, can be asked to phone these colleges and say, "Can you tell me how this candidate's prospects look now?" Admissions can say, "Not very good," or "Fair," or "Pretty good." "Pretty good" amounts to admission, since the colleges already know in most cases whom they have admitted.

Deferred Admission

An option some colleges reserve to themselves is to offer you a deferred admission; instead of enrolling in September, you enroll for the winter term in January, or even for the following fall. Duke, Hamilton, Middlebury, Mount Holyoke, and Connecticut College are among those that admit a smaller number of students on a deferred basis. These admissions invariably are given to those on waiting lists, although, as in the case of Middlebury, some students may indicate on their application that they would like to be considered for winter as well as fall admission. Behind the deferred admission is the departure from campus for overseas or special projects of a small number of students, who do not let the college know this until the summer before they are going to leave. To fill their places, the freshman class is expanded. Cornell, Penn, Harvard, and others have been admitting a fair number of students, particularly legacies, for the following fall, either giving specific conditions to fulfill for entry or just encouraging the student to have a productive gap year.

Should you accept deferred admission? Most applicants do. In the case of a midyear entrance, there is the drawback of coming on campus after other freshmen have developed their social arrangements. You will not be able to graduate with your class in the spring. These are minor disadvantages. The colleges are aware of them and do their utmost to make you feel welcome.

In addition to offering deferred admission, many colleges also allow students who have been admitted for the fall to request a deferral of their admission for a semester or a year. You may decide to do this if you travel abroad, have an exciting internship or athletic opportunity, or other reason for wanting to take some time out before enrolling. Usually, you would request this deferral during the summer, after you have sent in your deposit to hold your place. Your letter should discuss why you want to defer admission, what you hope to do during the semester or year off, and why you want to hold your place at the college. These requests are often granted, and students go on to do many exciting things.

Appealing Your Rejection

If you are rejected by a college, that means you will not be considered for admission again until the following academic year. Some students ask us whether they may appeal their admission decision. The answer is, yes, you can, but the decision is almost certain not to change. Very few students appeal their admissions decisions, and those who do usually get a very quick negative response. Unless there were significant extenuating circumstances that the admissions committee did not take into account during its first review of your application, the committee will stand by its initial decision. While there is not much harm in your trying to appeal your rejection letters, groundless or hasty appeals only serve to cause obstruction and bad feelings in admissions offices. Check the college's Web site for guidance on appealing a rejection, if such an appeal is allowed at all.

Statement of Students' Rights and Responsibilities in the College Admission Process

The following statement was drawn up by the National Association for College Admission Counseling (NACAC) in 1997, and last revised in 2006. It has been widely disseminated in school guidance offices. Here is an excerpt:

COLLEGES MUST PROVIDE:

General:
- The cost of attending an institution, including tuition, books and supplies, housing, and related costs and fees.
- Requirements and procedures for withdrawing from an institution, including refund policies.
- Names of associations that accredit, approve, or license the institution.
- Special facilities and services for disabled students.

Academics:
- The academic program of the institution, including degrees, programs of study, and facilities.
- A list of faculty and other instructional personnel.
- A report on completion or graduation rates at the college.
- At schools that typically prepare students for transfer to a four-year college, such as a community college, information about the transfer-out rate.

Financial Aid:
- The types of financial aid, including federal, state, and local government, need-based and non-need based, and private scholarships and awards.
- The methods by which a school determines eligibility for financial aid; how and when the aid is distributed.
- Terms and conditions of campus employment, if financial aid is delivered through a work-study aid program.

Campus Security:
- Procedures and policies for reporting crimes and emergencies on campus, as well as the system of adjudication.
- The number and types of crimes reported on and around campus.
- The school's drug offense policy, as well as descriptions of the school's drug awareness and drug use prevention programs.

To compare campus crime statistics for different colleges, visit http://ope.ed.gov/security.

WHEN YOU APPLY TO COLLEGES AND UNIVERSITIES, YOU HAVE RIGHTS

Before You Apply:
- You have the right to receive factual and comprehensive information from colleges and universities about their admission, financial costs, aid opportunities, practices and packaging policies, and housing policies. If you consider applying under an early admission plan, you have the right to complete information from the college about its process and policies.
- You have the right to be free from high-pressure sales tactics.

When You Are Offered Admission:
- You have the right to wait until May 1 to respond to an offer of admission and/or financial aid.
- Colleges that request commitments to offers of admission and/or financial assistance prior to May 1 must clearly offer you the opportunity to request (in writing) an extension until May 1. They must grant you this extension and your request may not jeopardize your status for admission and/or financial aid.
- Candidates admitted under early decision programs are a recognized exception to the May 1 deadline.

If You Are Placed on a Wait/Alternate List:
- The letter that notifies you of that placement should provide a history that describes the number of students on the wait list, the number offered admission, and the availability of financial aid and housing.

- Colleges may require neither a deposit nor a written commitment as a condition of remaining on a wait list.
- Colleges are expected to notify you of the resolution of your wait-list status by August 1 at the latest.

WHEN YOU APPLY TO COLLEGES AND UNIVERSITIES, YOU HAVE RESPONSIBILITIES

Before You Apply:
- You have a responsibility to research, and to understand and comply with, the policies and procedures of each college or university regarding application fees, financial aid, scholarships, and housing. You should also be sure you understand the policies of each college or university regarding deposits you may be required to make before you enroll.

As You Apply:
- You must complete all material required for application and submit your application on or before the published deadlines. You should be the sole author of your applications.
- You should seek the assistance of your high school counselor early and throughout the application period. Follow the process recommended by your high school for filing college applications.
- It is your responsibility to arrange, if appropriate, for visits to and/or interviews at colleges of your choice.

After You Receive Your Admission Decisions:
- You must notify each college or university that accepts you whether you are accepting or rejecting its offer. You should make these notifications as soon as you have made a final decision as to the college you wish to attend, but no later than May 1. It is understood that May 1 will be the postmark date.
- You may confirm your intention to enroll and, if required, submit a deposit to only one college or university. The exception to this arises if you are put on a wait list by a college or university and are later admitted to that institution. You may accept the offer and send a

deposit. However, you must immediately notify a college or university at which you previously indicated your intention to enroll.

- If you are accepted under an early decision plan, you must promptly withdraw the applications submitted to other colleges and universities and make no additional applications. If you are an early decision candidate and are seeking financial aid, you need not withdraw other applications until you have received notification about financial aid.

An outgrowth of NACAC's Statement of Principles of Good Practice, the students' rights statement makes clear to entering college students those "rights" that are only alluded to by the Principles of Good Practice. It also spells out the responsibilities students have in the admissions process. If you think your rights have been denied, you should contact the college or university immediately to request additional information or the extension of a reply date. In addition, you should ask your counselor to notify the president of the state or regional affiliate of the National Association for College Admission Counseling in your area. If you need further assistance, send a copy of any correspondence you have had with the college or university and a copy of your letter of admission to:

National Association for College Admission Counseling
1050 N. Highland Street, Suite 400
Arlington, VA 22201
Phone: 703-836-2222
          800-822-6285
Fax: 703-243-9375
www.nacacnet.org

The Nonselective College Option

Despite all we have said, we know that some candidates will apply to safety colleges, where they will be accepted without question. Many such colleges are excellent, but the student bodies do not perform at the most challenging level academically. Having considered yourself a selective candidate from the start, you should not, as you near the finish line, decide to drop out of the race. Stay to the end. There is time enough to decide on a nonselective college.

Often the nonselective college is a public institution in your home state, where the cost is as much as a third that of the most selective colleges. Opting for such a college may be unavoidable for financial reasons, although we continue to believe that worthy candidates will be able to make it financially through most selective colleges, private or public. Sometimes the less selective college, public or private, has offered you a substantial merit award that makes it well worth attending. Perhaps this less selective institution will prove a good environment for you in many ways and your education will be what you make of it. You need to look at both sides.

Postgraduate Year

There are two reasons to consider a postgraduate year after high school: One is a realization that an extra year of studying before you go to college will allow you to mature, improve your study habits, possibly improve your test scores, and in general put you in a stronger position for admission to a selective college. The other is rejection by one or more colleges you hoped to attend, and which you can possibly get into after an additional year in high school.

In a postgraduate program you do not repeat a grade. Such programs are demanding and make you stretch. Because you are not in school with your old friends with all their demands and expectations, you tend to make academic work your chief concern. Of course, you will engage in activities and sports, but these will usually be more relaxing than competitive. Some competitive athletes, however, do use their postgraduate year for an extra season of maturing, training, and skill-building that may help them reach for a higher-level program in college. The postgraduate year most typically is taken in a private school.

"We find that our postgraduate year students mature rapidly," one private school headmaster told us. "They are no longer under peer pressure socially. Dating is less on their minds than learning. They improve their SAT and Subject Test scores. When they get to college, they are usually very successful."

Some international students use the postgraduate year to improve their English language skills, to take the SATs, and to pursue a year of advanced course work in an American curriculum. Such a program allows them to show their strengths in a recognizable set of classes for the selective colleges, and to adapt to the American academic and cultural environment.

While many students prefer the experience of "going away" to a boarding school, a postgraduate year at the local high school may allow you to take a part-time job to build savings for college. In a job, you can develop both skills and a deeper sense of responsibility. It is our experience that nothing but good comes of adding a postgraduate year to your secondary education.

SAFETY AND HEALTH CONCERNS ON CAMPUS

Safety. Drugs. Alcohol. Binge drinking. Physical assault. Students and parents are increasingly concerned about reports of the prevalence of these issues on even the most selective college and university campuses. While families should not be frightened to send their high school graduates off to college, they should knowledgeably explore individual campuses and college programs to establish what issues are important on different campuses, and how each school is taking steps to address these major concerns.

Both in the extensive survey and interview research conducted for *Inside the Top Colleges* and *The Hidden Ivies,* and in continuing daily conversations with students and families in our offices, we have found that worries about safety and alcohol abuse are present, and often well-founded. Parents and students familiar with Tom Wolfe's *I Am Charlotte Simmons* and other fictional or factual depictions of life on campus might be tempted to abandon the idea of college altogether. Many students express a desire to attend a college "without a big party atmosphere," a place that is "friendly and secure." There are many such environments out there, and the key is to look for them with open eyes, in addition to learning how to maintain such a climate personally in whichever college or university you choose.

Colleges are now required by the federal government to track crime on campus, and families, by law, have a right to this information. While data are not often absolutely reliable, colleges are increasingly standardizing and more clearly reporting information on alcohol-related crimes, violence, and vandalism. Families can also get data from local police departments if they wish to examine crime around the larger campus context. This is not meant to scare families away from the many excellent schools located in higher-crime (generally urban) environments, but to help them to understand the risks associated with different environments, and to ready themselves for what may be a less safe environment than they are used to.

Many colleges have well-established alcohol and drug education, violence and crime prevention, and personal safety programs. Students and families can inquire as to the nature of these programs, in addition to campus safety and security measures and drinking rules. For example, are there night rides to and from the dorms? Safety phones around campus? Door locks on the outside of dorms? Electronic key cards? Crisis response plans and alert systems in case of a natural disaster, terrorist attack, or campus intruder? Rules about alcohol and parties in the dorms? Universal alcohol and sexual assault education programs? What are the school's policies on medical services for alcohol- or drug-related problems, infractions for drinking or drugs, and enforcement of federal, state, local, and school rules and regulations? One concern often voiced is related to the secondary effects of alcohol abuse, including dorm noise, filth, and trips to the emergency room with passed-out friends. Are there so-called "chem-free" or "substance-free" dorms available on campus, and if so, are all applicants guaranteed a space?

A major issue that must be mentioned is the presence of fraternities and sororities. If they are on campus, what proportion of the student body is associated with them? Do students join in the freshman or sophomore year? What other social outlets are available? Studies have consistently shown that the percentage of students who live in fraternity or sorority houses who are "binge drinkers" is almost twice as high as the overall percentage of binge drinkers on college campuses. Families should be aware of and open about the pros and cons associated with joining a fraternity or sorority, and attending a campus with a large Greek system.

Acknowledgment of alcohol, drug, and safety issues on campus by a university should not necessarily be seen by families as a reason not to apply to or attend a given school, but perhaps as a positive sign that these common issues are being proactively addressed. Particularly when making a final decision about which college to attend or whether to make an Early Decision commitment, students should consider spending a night on campus to get a better idea about the social and environmental climate after dark.

Transferring to Selective Colleges

It is extremely difficult to transfer to the most selective colleges, as we have said. They do not have many extra places, and they prefer to have their students on campus for their full four years of education, though many take off a term along the way. However, the less selective colleges welcome transfers when the applicant has done well at a junior college or state institution. It is not unreasonable for a strong student to plan to attend an in-state public college or a small private institution for a year or two, and then graduate from a selective college. The savings are often substantial. Some estimates indicate that over half of all students in the U.S. who graduate with a bachelor's degree have studied at more than one institution.

As a transfer applicant you will have to arrange for transcripts to be forwarded by both your high school and your college. Since the transfer applicant pool is small, you are competing in a small pie slice and can quickly learn from the admissions committee what your chances are. Your best strategy is to get one or more faculty members interested in having you enroll. Knowing your major can make you a very attractive candidate at a selective college that has encouraged your transfer application.

Transfer applicants are expected to be more mature, focused, direct, and committed. Selective colleges look for them to have at least two full-time semesters' worth of high-quality academic work, with GPAs of at least 3.0, if not 3.5 or higher at the most selective institutions.

CONSIDER TRANSFERRING

We have seen a trend toward the growing possibility of transferring from a less selective college to a more selective one. We have counseled many students disappointed in not being admitted to their first choice not to despair, and to consider applying again for sophomore or junior year as a transfer.

We can cite Duke, Harvard, Dartmouth, Pennsylvania, Stanford, Emory, Georgetown, and many others as colleges that have accepted transfers, from state universities or small colleges. We must add that transfer students should not normally expect a great aid package.

Economics is driving this trend, as well as an awareness of the maturity and motivation of many transfer candidates. Selective colleges must build up their revenues, and a bright transfer student brings more tuition money. Some state universities have become overcrowded and underfunded, and this has meant a diminished educational experience for some students.

On the other hand, some students who have begun their college life at a small college find that they have outgrown the place, socially or academically, after one or two years, and seek a larger, perhaps more urban public or private university to finish their degree. By this time, they typically feel more prepared to take on the challenges of a larger university system.

Overall, then, it is a matter of one size does not fit all, and preferences that may change over time. Sometimes it takes going to college for a year or two to figure out what you want out of college and where you want to be. In such cases, transferring is a good option to consider, and maintaining a strong GPA one's best foundation.

Enrollment at Last

The rule is: Enroll where you will be happy. But how can you know at what college your happiness lies? Have you not always known what pleases you? A wise old headmaster, Francis Boyden of Deerfield Academy, used to say to parents bringing their boys to look over the schools they were considering: "Let the boy decide which is the right school for him. He'll know." He did not want to take any boy who had any reservations about his school.

This is a good dictum for you to follow. Your reservations and uneasy feelings about a college should be respected. They may be quirky and unreasonable to someone else, but you have to live with them. Suppose the students at the college do not appeal to you. You need not feel guilty and tell yourself that they are probably not representative of the whole college. Weighing your reactions to these students and to those of another college where you warmed up to them, you must count one as a negative and the other as a positive. On balance, you ought to spend your four years of college among people you like.

You can be happy at a college with which you are in strong disagreement on a basic issue. William F. Buckley's first book, *God and Man at Yale,* was an attack on what he perceived to be the absence of a religious emphasis on a campus he loved. But you cannot be happy at a place you feel is beneath you. We think of a young man who sincerely believed that he should have been admitted to an Ivy League college. He enrolled in a fine university, but not so highly prestigious as the one he thought he should be attending. The result was a miserable academic performance that finally caused him to drop out. He would have been wiser to stay out of college for a year or two until he got over his disappointment, gained entry to an Ivy school, or came to terms with the fact that he was not suited to the challenge.

So before May 1, you should come to a conclusion as you go through your notes and try to decide among two or more colleges. You have had all the advice you can get from us, from your parents, teachers, friends, and the clergy. The colleges have decided about you. You are a desirable undergraduate in their eyes. Now comes the moment at your desk when you close your laptop, and listen to what your own heart tells you to do.

Some candidates leap before they look. They are so excited about being admitted to a college, especially a prestigious college, that they accept without a second thought. Who would think of not going to Harvard after being accepted? There are those who should. A Harvard administrator told us that every year there are a few students who are emotionally not up to the competition they encounter—or imagine they encounter.

"For example, a freshman will tell me he feels inadequate because his roommate has already written a symphony. In his school orchestra he played first violin. We can change his roommate, but it's not so easy to change his negative opinion of himself," the official said.

Another Harvard administrator calls this the fallen prince or princess syndrome. A tennis star back home finds she is cut from Harvard's freshman squad and goes to pieces. Obviously her expectations outran her capacities, but it does happen. Or the straight-A valedictorian finds himself suddenly struggling to get B- grades in a class full of students as capable as himself and beginning to doubt his own intellectual capacities. Such students would be better musicians, tennis players, and scholars in a less competitive atmosphere, even though academically they can do the work at Harvard, and in their extracurricular lives could be quite content.

Planning Your Transition to College Questionnaire

I plan to take Advanced Placement tests, and/or SAT Subject Tests, in May or June in these subjects: _____, _____, _____.
I have lined up a summer job and will save $_____ toward my college costs.
I am assured of a campus job doing _____ and earning $_____.
I am considering taking the following courses freshman year:

_____, _____, _____, _____, _____,
_____, _____, _____.
My roommate will be chosen by the college _____ or by me _____.
I will be living at _____.
My academic adviser will be _____.
Deadlines for paying tuition _____ and room and board _____.
I will take part in a pre-orientation session or freshman trip on _____.
I will need to report to campus for orientation on _____.

Going to a college to please your parents may be a mistake if the college does not please you. This is often the case if your parents are encouraging you to overreach. A graduate of Amherst, her father's college, wished she had gone to a large university. Such sentiment, of course, does not go over well with her father. It would have been wiser to displease him briefly four years ago than to make him feel guilty now for his enthusiasm for his alma mater. We hear from other students their dismay at being rejected from some of the most Exceedingly Demanding colleges, even though they have been accepted to other excellent schools, because they feel that their parents are unhappy that they have not achieved the ultimate prestige. The students consider themselves failures, despite the amazing accomplishments they have recorded. Better to alert your parents early and throughout the admissions process if you feel their expectations for you are too high, than to apply to the wrong schools and be disappointed and guilty in the spring.

CHOOSING THE RIGHT COLLEGE

Choosing your right college is different from floating on the tide of opinion of your peers and what they consider to be the "in" places to attend. We appreciate the challenge you face as an individual in making the proper choice of a college. We encourage you to set out on your own journey through these choppy waters. What we call "the right fit" in a college is the critical factor in a happy social and academic experience.

"Know thyself" is the time-honored advice of the ancient Greeks if one is to achieve a successful life. Examining as honestly as possible who you are temperamentally, what you believe in, what you are passionate about, what matters to you socially and intellectually, how mature and serious a person and a student you are, where your talents and skills lie, what you need in order to be fulfilled and successful—these are the issues that should be put into play in deciding on your optimum college environment.

Do your personal best to move beyond the ego trip approach to selecting a school. A prestigious name or hot school in the eyes of your friends will not be of much value if you end up stressed out in your studies. You could find that you have to give up the sport you love to play or other activities that have given you pleasure in high school in order to survive as a student. Further, if your goal is to go on to graduate school and a career, you have long dreamed about, you need to perform at a high level academically. We love to hear a student we are advising state that he or she has set a priority of locating a school that will provide a good balance of academic, social, and extracurricular life. Of course, the balance can never be exactly the same for all students, so this is where you need to do the honest and continuing self-assessment to arrive at your right school.

So, as you research and visit campuses this spring, we urge you make the choice yours. Try to pay less attention to the rankings of colleges, an artificial game at best, and your friends. Remember that they will need to do what is best for themselves as well, and this may be quite different from your desires and interests. Not surprisingly, the other individuals who do know you best are your parents. Discuss openly with them what you believe you need, to achieve that happy balance in life. Share your hopes for the future and you will secure their support in identifying that best-fit school. Don't let anyone make a key decision for you, one that you will have to accept the results of and live with for a long time, because you stood back and let it all happen for you. Take charge of the search and the decision process and you will end up with a terrific opportunity that you want.

Before enrolling anywhere, picture yourself at the college as a student and imagine how you will feel there. If you have any doubts, you ought to be guided more by them than by the hope that everything will probably work out all right. Trust your feelings, because they usually stay with you a long time.

Decisions to choose Amherst over Princeton, Berkeley over Stanford, Duke over Rice, or any other college may be based on seemingly irrational considerations. But obeying the dictates of the heart seems to make good sense when it comes to enrolling at a selective college. Here are some explanations for college choices given to us by high school graduates who went on to selective colleges. We should note that the expressions one hears from students often symbolize something deeper and more meaningful that is difficult to verbalize:

NEGATIVES	POSITIVES
Curriculum too limited	Prestige
Don't want foreign language requirement	Campus spirit
	Candlelight dinners
Orientation too literary	Many community-related programs
Lab facilities outmoded	
No environmental studies	No core curriculum
Overemphasis on athletics	Strong Russian studies
Campus too spread out	Great track coach
Fraternities dominate social life	No sexual harassment
Atmosphere is sexist	Excellent sports opportunities for women
Minorities underrepresented	
Lots of drinking	Mother went there
Ivory tower, remote	Better bookstore
Noisy, overcrowded	Math tradition
Preppy	Beautiful buildings
No business courses	Thesis requirement
Too competitive	Year-round tennis
Father went there	Near skiing
No art museum	Safe campus
Too many premed majors	Independent study program
Obligatory remedial writing course	New theater
	Great glee club
Snobbish	Tutorial system
Poor balance of men and women enrolled	Art history collection
	Strong study-abroad program
Campus too hilly	New library
Too much focus on technical studies	Alumni spirit and network
	Friends going there
No town there	Most students have cars
Too alternative a social environment	More dating possibilities
	Great graduate school admission record

CHEATING AND HONOR CODES

"I have always felt that honesty is the most important attribute that a person can have. Far more important than intelligence, honesty shows that a person can take his or her intelligence and use it to make moral and just decisions. . . . [Haverford's Honor Code] is very special to me for I consider personal integrity to be a characteristic of tremendous significance." Thus writes a student on his application to Haverford College, which requires its applicants to discuss the college's honor code and its meaning to them. The message from the college is clear: They take their honor code seriously, and expect their students to do the same. No student enters the college without having considered the college's policy of personal responsibility and integrity, and each student is required to maintain that code once at the school by not cheating or plagiarizing, and by reporting any such activity they witness.

Are we a "nation of cheaters," where "cheating has become endemic"? Yes, according to a number of studies, experts, and students. Students may believe that they are at a disadvantage if they do not cheat: "Well . . . everyone else was doing it!" "If I don't cheat, I'll get a B+, and she'll get an A because she copied that paper . . . or looked over his shoulder . . . or stole the test . . . or . . . ." But what is happening to our education?

If we are cheating, we are not learning. We are just getting by. And if our classmates are cheating, they are stealing our education, and devaluing the same. Honor codes are symptomatic of the reinfusion of values and ethics into our educational system. From the elementary to the graduate level, institutions are putting the responsibility for integrity in the educational process onto the students themselves. At schools like Haverford, Davidson, Vanderbilt, Virginia, Dartmouth, and many others, students are prohibited from cheating, and, more importantly, are required to report it when they see it. And, even more importantly, instructors are barred from monitoring exams, while students are trusted to enforce their own ethical code. With the blossoming of available information on the Internet, the technological wonders of the cut-and-paste, and the heightening of the incentive of competition, cheating may have become easier and more tempting than ever. Many feel that our educational systems must help students to learn to make sound life choices. And our students must take responsibility for helping them to do so.

If integrity and honesty are important values to you, and you would like to learn in an environment where these values are strongly supported by the college and its students, then you should consider the various kinds of honor codes established by many of the selective colleges. For more on honor codes, see *The Hidden Ivies*.

It should be obvious that one student's positive reason to choose a college may be another's negative reason to avoid it, and vice versa, for the same particular college. One way to convince yourself that your "reasons" for choosing one college over another are sound is to poll some students during a second campus visit, asking them to give you some reasons they personally like where they are. If you get "bad vibes," you know this place is not for you.

All selective colleges are happy campuses for most of their students, but because each college is unique, you should make sure that a college's uniqueness and your own personal uniqueness harmonize.

Knowing how many young people every year choose wisely, we know you will, too. Have a wonderful four years in college!

Step Ten Checklist

✓ Become aware of the procedures you must follow after you have received a notification letter (acceptance, wait list, rejection, deferred admission) from the colleges.

✓ Be prepared to spend time comparing the advantages of two or more colleges that admit you. Avoid snap decisions.

✓ Expect pressure to enroll at colleges that admit you. College officials and alumni can be very persuasive. Weigh all their arguments carefully. Consult multiple sources of information.

✓ Being wait-listed can cause disappointment when you are never finally accepted. By enrolling at the college you like second best, you take a positive step. You can always change your mind if you are later admitted from the waiting list. In this case, be prepared to pay a penalty fee to the college you accepted.

✓ Selective college applicants rarely settle for a nonselective "safety" school. Stay with the selectives if you belong in one of them.

✓ As you consider your college choices, be aware of such options as state universities, transfer admissions, and postgraduate study.

✓ Trust your instincts, but verify. Explore your options carefully, revisit campuses, and test your assumptions. You will enroll in the right college for you.

APPLYING FROM ABROAD:]

Follow the Specific Strategies for
International Students

In considering college admissions for the twenty-first century, we have devoted more attention to the needs of selective college applicants from outside the United States, both citizens and non-citizens. This is because so many more U.S. college applications now come from abroad. This is a trend that accelerated through the 1990s and, with brief interludes, kept pace into the 2000s. In 1998–99, 490,933 international students were studying in the U.S., an increase of 2% over the previous year and a record high. Ten years earlier, just 366,354 international students were studying here. We should note that about half of internationals are pursuing graduate degrees. Twenty-nine percent are pursuing bachelor's, and 11.6% associate degrees.

By 2006–07, 582,984 international students were studying in the U.S., up 3.2% from the prior year, according to the Institute of International Education (IIE). Forty-three percent of all internationals came from just four countries: India (14.4%), China (11.6%), South Korea (10.7%), and Japan (6.1%). Taiwan (5.0%), Canada (4.9%), and Mexico (2.4%) were the next biggest sources of students. Only 1.4% came from the U.K., and 1.1% from France. Most students (61.5%) indicated personal and family sources as their primary funds for study, with 26.1% noting a U.S. college or university as their primary source of funds.

We anticipate a continuing rise in international applications. We have helped hundreds of applicants from abroad meet the standards and requirements of America's selective colleges as they followed the application procedures outlined through the chapters of this book. To the applicant from abroad, American admissions procedures often seem puzzling and needlessly individualized and bureaucratic. This is because, unlike most other countries, we have no national education system that establishes a uniform curriculum for secondary schools or standardizes (and limits) admissions procedures throughout the nation. Then again, American universities, private and public, are among the most expensive in the world, especially for non-American citizens or resident aliens (see Step Nine). Our thousands of local high schools are controlled by local communities and school boards, and their standards are determined by the legislatures of the fifty states. Our approximately 2,200 nonprofit four-year colleges and universities, and 1,100 nonprofit two-year colleges are governed by boards of trustees or state regents, which establish higher education admissions policies.

In a national system, the state furnishes the money for operating the universities (a college, in many countries outside the United States, usually is a designation for a private secondary school). Our colleges and universities, both of which offer the postsecondary bachelor's degrees, depend on both public and private sources of money and on the tuition and fees charged to each student. The famous private universities like Harvard, Yale, and MIT have over the years been endowed by private donors, foundations, and corporations with funds invested to provide interest and dividend revenue. Others have small endowments. To complicate the pattern further, some state institutions like the University of Texas have large endowments, and other public universities now raise donations annually from their alumni.

This situation is not unrelated to admissions. Colleges lacking large endowments become dependent on enrollments for tuition money and on government grants to supplement funds from private donations, and they compete almost savagely with other colleges for enrollment. Such enrollment is nonselective. Most high school graduates can enroll in some colleges within a few weeks of filing an application. The open enrollment admissions process at these colleges is little more than a registration function. If you, as an applicant from another country, have read this book, you are aware how different selective admissions procedures are from open enrollment at nonselective colleges. Essentially the difference is that in selective admissions, applicants are screened in order to allow selection of those who qualify under each college's own standards. Again, what is unique about the American system of higher education is its diversity of choices, which allows almost anyone to pursue an advanced degree; its selectivity at the highest public and private levels based on merit and preparation; and its focus on the liberal arts, which allows students to delay their commitment to one or another discipline. We assume that you, by virtue of your strong record, are among the qualified selective college applicants, that your school or family has recommended that you apply to a selective college in the United States, and that you are interested in an American-style liberal arts education or a particular focused degree program, such as engineering or business, at some of the selective colleges.

TOP TEN FIELDS OF STUDY FOR INTERNATIONALS

According to the IIE's "Open Doors 2008" report, these are the top academic areas of focus for the 623,805 international students in 2007–08. Remember, however, that half of internationals are graduate students, who are typically more focused on professional fields of study in business and the sciences.

Business and Management	19.6%
Engineering	17.0%
Physical and Life Sciences	9.3%
Social Sciences	8.7%
Mathematics and Computer Science	8.2%
Fine and Applied Arts	5.6%
Liberal Arts and General Studies	5.2%
Health Professions	5.1%

Intensive English Language	4.6%
Undeclared	3.4%
Education	3.1%
Humanities	3.1%

INTERNATIONAL STUDENT ENROLLMENT AT SELECTED COLLEGES AND UNIVERSITIES BY INSTITUTIONAL TYPE, 2006–07

DOCTORAL/RESEARCH INSTITUTIONS

Rank	Institution	Total Int'l Students	Total Enrollment
1	University of Southern California	7,115	33,389
2	Columbia University	5,937	24,417
3	New York University	5,827	50,917
4	University of Illinois, Urbana-Champaign	5,685	41,342
5	Purdue University	5,581	39,228
6	University of Michigan, Ann Arbor	5,429	40,025
7	University of Texas, Austin	5,303	49,738
8	University of California, Los Angeles	4,704	38,218
9	Harvard University	4,514	20,042
10	Boston University	4,484	31,574
10	University of Pennsylvania	4,484	23,704
20	Stanford University	3,751	15,703
21	Cornell University	3,746	19,639

28	University of California, Berkeley	3,167	33,933
30	Massachusetts Institute of Technology	3,042	11,032
33	Carnegie Mellon University	2,767	10,120
35	Johns Hopkins University	2,635	19,505
40	Northwestern University	2,318	18,506

MASTERS INSTITUTIONS

Rank	Institution	Total Int'l Students	Total Enrollment
1	San Francisco State University	2,496	28,950
2	California State University, Northridge	1,963	34,560
3	San Jose State University	1,889	29,975
4	California State University, Fullerton	1,668	35,921
5	CUNY Baruch College	1,587	15,756
6	California State University, Long Beach	1,585	35,576
7	CUNY Hunter College	1,551	20,679
8	New York Institute of Technology, Old Westbury	1,438	11,681
9	University of Central Oklahoma	1,281	15,953
10	Johnson and Wales University	1,280	10,171

BACCALAUREATE INSTITUTIONS

Rank	Institution	Total Int'l Students	Total Enrollment
1	Brigham Young University, Hawaii	1,201	2,492
2	SUNY Fashion Institute of Technology	1,046	10,010
3	University of Hawaii, Hilo	411	3,507
4	University of Dallas	405	3,050
5	Mount Holyoke College	403	2,100
6	Calvin College	336	4,199
7	Daemen College	332	2,414
8	University of Maine, Fort Kent	328	1,339
9	Middlebury College	289	2,401
10	Wesleyan University	272	3,455
11	Macalester College	255	1,918
16	University of Richmond	211	2,857
17	Wellesley College	210	2,249
18	Smith College	202	3,093
21	Oberlin College	185	2,829
23	Franklin and Marshall College	166	2,068
25	Ohio Wesleyan University	165	1,820
26	Grinnell College	161	1,551
26	Willamette University	161	2,740
28	Drew University	159	2,647
29	Vassar College	155	2,450

30	Morehouse College	150	3,032
31	Bard College	148	1,858
32	Colgate University	147	2,859
33	Lewis and Clark College	146	3,641
35	Berea College	140	1,466
36	Lafayette College	137	2,381
37	Lawrence University	132	1,485
38	Saint Lawrence University	130	2,182
39	College of Wooster	129	1,882
40	Colby College	127	1,865

Involved as the admissions process is at the selective colleges, it is nonetheless reasonable and fair. We urge you as a top student to file applications with several colleges just as if you were applying from an American high school. Be assured that admissions committees of selective colleges will welcome your application. At the same time, you must go beyond the famous names that you already may recognize and, like American applicants, apply to a range of selective colleges.

All the conditions for selective college admissions described in this book must be fulfilled by students who apply from abroad. Nonetheless, an applicant from another country does have one advantage: He or she competes mainly against other applicants who reside outside the United States. You should reread Step Seven—Find Your Place in the Class Pie Charts. Coming from a foreign country, you automatically bring to any college a different perspective, another cultural orientation, another language, and unique experiences that are highly valued. Your slice in any college pie chart will be a small sliver, so that if you qualify as a selective college candidate by virtue of your academic record and your nonacademic interests and achievements, you already have a strong chance for admission to one or more of the colleges we list.

But you still must compete against other interesting applicants, so you must pay particular attention to the presentation of yourself in your application. It is important that you emphasize characteristics that make you distinctive. Merely to be French or Iranian or Argentinean is not sufficient in itself to carry you into an Exceedingly Demanding, Very Demanding, or Demanding college or university; nor are the children of American nationals abroad automatically considered interesting or exotic. You must demonstrate your qualities. How have your experiences abroad shaped your values and educational goals? What do you hope to gain from study in the United States? What will you bring to the American classroom?

Your Academic Résumé

Although your school will be sending colleges your transcript, you should include in your application a detailed academic résumé of your own with the following information: all schools attended from grades one through twelve, with special descriptive emphasis on your high school, especially its programs in eleventh and twelfth grades. Describe your high school, stating whether it is private or public, university preparation or technical. Say in what language(s) instruction is given. Mention graduation requirements—baccalaureate or Advanced Certificate examinations, for example. You will need to discuss the grading system to make clear your level of performance. Your academic concentration in eleventh and twelfth (or what Americans would see as a thirteenth) grade must be spelled out.

When you discuss admissions tests, give the dates on which they were taken. Explain your school's academic calendar: normal school year, graduation, length of courses. Describe the level and degree of difficulty of your courses, since foreign schools vary, and admissions offices simply lack the time to discover their comparable qualities. It is up to you to identify the character of your education as candidly as possible. Your school may help you by having prepared a school profile that it regularly sends to American colleges. Ask to see this if one is available, and clarify any areas that need explanation.

The TOEFL

Your transcript must be in English. If the school does not provide a translation service, you will need to arrange for a translation by a certified agency. Likewise, unless English is your native language, you will have to take one of several English language ability tests, the most common of which is the TOEFL, Test of English as a Foreign Language, administered by the Educational Testing Service, which prepares the College Board tests. Your school will provide you with the most recent TOEFL information and application forms.

The TOEFL is now almost universally administered year-round on a computer at a testing center, at a time scheduled by the candidate. Plan to take the TOEFL at least five weeks earlier than the deadline for submitting your completed application to the colleges. You may take the TOEFL more than once to improve your score, and colleges publish in their materials the minimum TOEFL scores that they suggest for applicants.

Of all the tests of English language for American university admissions, the TOEFL is the preferred test to take. It tests listening comprehension, language structure, writing skills (you must write a short essay), and reading comprehension and vocabulary. It is universally accepted and recognized. The test, of course, is given to avoid enrolling students who are unable to keep up their work in a language foreign to them. Should your score be too low, you can always improve your English and retake the test.

Another English proficiency test now accepted by many institutions abroad and, increasingly, in the U.S. is the International English Language Testing System (IELTS.org). Administered worldwide, a list of U.S. institutions accepting the IELTS and its preferred score level is available online.

English as a Second Language (ESL)

Many American universities and international education programs, such as the Experiment in International Living, the American Language Academies, and ELS, offer intensive English-language training courses during both the academic year and the summer. Enrollment is noncompetitive, since the courses are not part of any university degree program. Accredited ESL programs are authorized to issue the Form I-20 that enables students to receive a student visa for entry into the United States. Be sure to enroll only in an accredited program. American embassies and consulates keep lists of recognized institutions, and the Institute of International Education (www.iie.org) is another source of information.

The Visa

Form I-20 is also obtainable from the college where you plan to enroll. After you have followed the Ten-Step Plan and are accepted by a selective college, the college you choose will send you this form at your request. With the I-20 in hand, you must take it and your passport to an American embassy or consulate in your country in order to apply for a student visa.

Proof will be required that you are in good health and that you have enough money to cover college expenses and living costs in the United States. If you have been given an aid award from an American college to pay for your tuition and expenses, you will need to bring proof of this. Most universities and colleges will ask you to take out health insurance during your stay to cover the cost of major illness.

Your own country's regulations affecting your study abroad must be understood, in order to avoid any delay in your plans. Application for a visa should be made at the same time you apply to American colleges, even though it will not be issued until you have been offered admission to an American institution. Otherwise, you risk arriving late for your first term.

Visas are issued for the length of your degree program, usually four years. Students with advanced standing may graduate in three years. You must indicate on your application the exact length of your planned stay in the United States. Once you are in America, you may apply for extensions of your visa, if, for example, you apply for entrance into American graduate schools. See our Internet Resources list (pages 102–105) for more links to helpful sites for international students.

Financial Considerations

Americans complain of the high cost of higher education. Foreign students at first are stunned to learn that selective private colleges cost so much per year for tuition, room, and board. Public institutions are less expensive but still pricey compared to many countries' university systems. In either case, you must also have money for books, personal expenses, and travel and living expenses when school is closed. There has been a slight trend toward more funding for internationals at elite colleges like Dartmouth, but, unfortunately, you may find yourself rejected from some colleges for which you are very qualified because of financial aid considerations.

As we mentioned in Step Nine, there are few scholarship and loan monies available to foreign students. Nor will you be allowed to earn money in America. For this reason, most colleges to which you apply will include a financial information statement to be completed by your family, giving assurance that you have sufficient funds to complete your study. This must be attested to by a bank officer. If you are sponsored by your home country government or a scholarship agency or foundation, they will help you with this process.

Your Personal Statement

In addition to following the Ten-Step Plan faithfully, as a foreign applicant you should include in your application someplace a statement explaining just why you wish to attend an American college. This means acquainting yourself with the nature of our higher educational style. Most foreign students begin by assuming that our system is like their own, in which specialization begins early and leads to a professional degree. This is typically not the case. Your understanding of the American liberal arts curriculum is critical, and you must let the colleges know you are aware that undergraduate education is broad, even in schools of engineering, business administration, and architecture. We have discussed this characteristic in detail in *The Hidden Ivies*.

In the American system, you will major in one or more academic subject areas. However, true specialization occurs at the graduate level, after you have a bachelor's degree. Whatever you plan to specialize in later, you must first take a number of undergraduate courses in the humanities, social sciences, and the arts. Be at pains to get across to admissions committees what an American liberal arts education means to you personally, how you think it will broaden you and equip you for what you plan to do when you come back to your native country. Speak to the benefits you anticipate from four years in a selective American college. Describe your aspirations for yourself and for your fellow citizens. You can utilize your main personal statement for this purpose, the "additional information" section of the online Common Application, or a college's "Why Us?" supplemental essay question (if there is one) for this purpose, for example.

Experience in counseling foreign applicants leads us to give the same assurances to qualified students abroad that we give to American high school students: If you follow the Ten-Step Plan, you, as an outstanding student, will be able to enroll in a selective American college, and probably will be admitted to more than one. We wish you luck and welcome you to America.

Some International Student Profiles

Here are a few essay excerpts from some foreign applicants to American colleges.

Loretta Coburn, École International, Geneva. Turkish mother, American father. Trilingual. Harvard summer school junior year to improve writing. Modest SAT scores. TOEFL in the 90th percentile (prior to rescaling). Applied to Duke, Union, Trinity, and Bates, as well as Northwestern, where she enrolled.

> "So, where are you from?"
> This simple, straightforward question is probably the one I dread most when I meet someone for the first time. Oddly enough, I am perplexed by the ambiguity of the question and only able to mutter, almost incoherently, "Um . . . well . . . I . . . aah . . ." Where do I begin? Should I tell them where I live, where I go to school, what nationality I am, or something else? How can I answer such a plainspoken question without a tiring recitation of my diverse background? Surprisingly, unlike many, I cannot answer precisely without digression. ". . . Well . . . my family lives in Istanbul, Turkey, and I go to boarding school in Geneva, Switzerland. I am half Turkish, half American. I have lived in Bahrain, Hong Kong, Turkey, Kuwait, and the U.S. and I have attended nine different schools. . . ." (My listener dozes

off as I ramble on discursively.) Although my response seems exhaustive, I find it very difficult to express the mere essence of my experiences without profoundly analyzing them.

Lola Amadan, American School, London. Lebanese. Good SAT scores, high TOEFL. Strong essay and personal interviews led to acceptances at Brown, Connecticut College, Skidmore, Wellesley, and Middlebury. Enrolled at Brown.

Like my ancestors I am a nomad, a wanderer who seeks freedom, happiness, and peace and harmony between myself and the world around me. The whole world is my home because I have no special belonging to any single nation. Both my parents are Lebanese and I was born in Lebanon in 1975. When I was four months old, the civil war started in Lebanon and my family was forced to move from the area of conflict to Saudi Arabia. I have no emotional attachment toward the country where my family was born and lived. I feel awkward when friends around me talk about the great love they have for their native countries and all I can feel is pity for my own country. Saudi Arabia became my home until I was seven years old. As a spectator looking back upon the actions of my past, I can focus on one day in particular which seems to me was a starting point for my search for myself. That day my father took my brother and me to the desert to see how the Saudi Bedouins lived. He took my hand in his and as I looked up I saw the biggest, bluest, and brightest sky ever. Looking back down to the sandy earth, I saw in the distance a black tent that was loosely pegged into the sand. It was so loosely pegged that it could have flown into the air any minute and become free to dance in the wind. I felt inside me so much warmth and excitement as I absorbed the sights around me. Now I look back and realize that what appealed to me most was how unfixed these people were. Any minute they could have gathered their meager possessions and moved on. They really were as free as any man or woman could be. From these people's lifestyle I discovered how vital freedom was to my life. After that visit I felt that all there was to life was being free.

Sarah Chan, Chinese International School, Hong Kong. A and B grades in a strong International General Certificate of Secondary Education (IGCSE) curriculum, SATs in the 1200s. Looked at a broad list of schools that would give her application careful personal attention, which included portions of her art portfolio. Chose to apply ED to Wellesley and was accepted.

For eight straight months in the past year, there was only one thing on my mind, my personal art exhibition. I was encouraged by many to put on a solo exhibition, but there were many factors that both supported and hindered my decision to do so. I needed to prove to myself that I could achieve what I set my mind to accomplish. I decided to see the exhibition through to success. It was one of the most painful yet most rewarding experiences that I have ever had.

The Chinese philosophy preaches humility and modesty, and that is what I believe in. Initially I felt that exhibiting my work would go against the very grain of my character. Therefore, I was apprehensive about the idea of deliberately putting my work on show. Anxiety began to build up as the preparation progressed and escalated to a point where I felt like quitting. However, these feelings of anxiety were a camouflage for other feelings that were dwelling inside me. My insecurities were the source of my distress. Although the reason for putting on the exhibition was a personal one—to prove to myself that I could do it, the notion of public opinion inevitably came into play. My insecurities stemmed from my fear of failure. I was worried that my work would not be appreciated and that it would not effectively communicate what I was trying to convey.

As Pablo Picasso said, "People don't realize what they have when they own a picture by me. Each picture is a phial with my blood. That is what has gone into it." This quote epitomizes the close connection between an artist and her work. I too felt that deep-rooted connection. Feelings of vulnerability that come with putting any work on show are disconcerting. In this instance, it felt as if my entire being was on trial awaiting a verdict. I was insecure because of a fear that my work would not be appreciated, that people would reject it, and unwittingly reject me. After recognizing the source of my anxiety, I made a decision to persevere.

The exhibition turned out to be a success. I gained much satisfaction from the praise and words of encouragement offered. However, my ultimate satisfaction has been knowing that I persevered and achieved what I set my mind to accomplish. I now appreciate the effort and commitment that is required to achieve success. This exhibition is an important milestone in my life. I have become more willing to embrace a challenge and have gained the confidence to grasp opportunities that may present themselves to me. I will not rest on my laurels but as Richard Bach writes, "reach out and touch perfection."

This exhibition turned out to be less about the quality of work of a sixteen year old, but essentially more about a girl in search of something greater within herself and her community.

Karen al Mohammed, Charterhouse School, London. Strong grades in a competitive curriculum, with SATs in the 700s. Applied to Dartmouth, Duke, Harvard, Georgetown, Princeton, and others. Chose Duke over Dartmouth and Georgetown. Several of her essays focused on her unique name and cultural background. Another brought in her perspective on life, art, and literature, accompanying her submission of poems and photographs:

> I constantly question everything: Perhaps I am a natural voyager. I acknowledge there are reasons why certain rules exist, but my mind drives me to dispute many things that we as a society and as individuals accept as absolute. My contribution as an individual is my questing mind that is driven by my firm belief in the value of the artistic consciousness, the validity of the artist's commentary on the world around him or her. I do not want to just exist; I want to make a meaningful statement through the discipline of images and words. . . .
> . . . Through the medium of photography, the pedestrian objects in my environment acquire new significance. A fire escape is no longer just a functional metal device—its elements become beautiful—a progression of refracted light—symbolizing

a parallel journey. Photography has allowed me to see beyond my perceptible frame of reference. . . .

. . . Through the use of a geometrically painted canvas, I have experimented with a third dimension, pushing the parameters of the canvas with my hands and face into a bold frontier of distortion—symbolizing the explorations of restrictions and boundaries that invade our personal lattice of tangled primal instincts—our denial of ourselves because of the demands to conform. . . .

. . . And through my love of literature, I have explored more fully the structure and real meaning of my own life. . . .

A passage that has had a most significant impact on me is the famous quotation in Shakespeare's *As You Like It,* discussing the ages of man: "All the world's a stage, all the men and women merely players: They have their exits and their entrances; and one man in his time plays many parts, his acts being seven ages."

I responded to this profound critique, by attempting to document the tangled web of my own experiences and questions in the following:

The devastating paradox of experience is that you cannot buy back
   innocence

The young simply throw away their experience
to quench their thirst for knowledge
fueled by their belief in their own immortality
The more mature are riddled with regrets
and the wise, well the wise wish to start the cycle all over again
but the truly wise accept their experience as a key to insight
and harbor their regrets as blessings
they lived life in perfect metaphorical time
If you believe the moment is right it always will be
but if you wait for it, and cast all other seconds away as wrong
the right moment will never come and you too will be regretful
Life is what you make it; your destiny is placed in your hands
In a world that forces you to be everyone else
it is hardest to emerge as yourself

Americans Abroad

American applicants living abroad can be guided in many respects by our recommendations to foreign applicants. While, of course, you will not need a visa or have to file proof of financial responsibility, you will need to show admissions committees that you are highly qualified. American colleges are acquainted with a certain number of foreign schools, but not with all. They are therefore on the alert for all indications of your strong academic work and of your uniqueness as a person. If you have the opportunity to visit American colleges, by all means do so.

Like your foreign counterparts, you are of interest to selective colleges because your experience in another culture will add a special dimension to your college class. But you must make it clear just what you have gained from your life abroad, how it makes you stand out, what changes in your outlook and lifestyle have occurred during your foreign schooling. For example, one student educated in an army school in Germany wanted to become an interpreter. Her plan was to spend her college vacations in a German institute that trains interpreters. She was admitted to three selective colleges, attended Georgetown, and after a time working at the U.N. joined a private firm of interpreters in Paris.

Another student was the son of an American expatriate banker in Hong Kong. This student had lived abroad for an extended period, and had used his time in Asia to learn Mandarin and to travel extensively in China, Singapore, and other Asian countries. He took an advanced curriculum at the American School in Hong Kong, and developed an interest in military history and international relations. He was able in his applications to explain the connections between his life abroad and his intellectual interests, and enrolled in the University of Virginia as a military history major.

The Time Factor

Living abroad, you are already aware, no doubt, of how long it takes letters to reach their destinations in the United States. You must allow for delay by factoring the slowness of the mail into your plans. Assume that weeks will pass before you get a response to any query or request.

Naturally you should always use air mail, except in really urgent cases, when you will have to use express service, whatever it costs.

For you abroad, then, the Internet is a real lifesaver. Not only can you tour campuses virtually, download information, and send and receive e-mail to and from the admissions officers, faculty, coaches, and other college representatives, but you can access and submit applications online. For virtually no cost, and with a high degree of security and reliability, the Internet is the fastest and surest way for you to communicate with colleges from abroad.

Summer and Postgraduate Options

Many students abroad, American and non-American, find that taking advantage of summer or postgraduate educational options in the U.S. helps them to learn about and prepare for American college admissions. Summer programs at American boarding schools or on university campuses, including English language study, SAT and TOEFL preparation, and involvement in athletics or in the arts, music, or another academic area of interest, help to supplement a student's academic record and introduce (or reintroduce) them him or her to the American system.

A postgraduate year at an American boarding school (see Step Ten) is another way to make the transition from a school abroad to the American program. Such a year in an American school allows students to take SAT tests, pursue Advanced Placement course work, visit college campuses, and practice their English.

If you are an American or non-American student abroad and are beginning to plan for U.S. college admission, it would be wise for you to consider summer and postgraduate options together with applications to colleges and universities.

A FOUR-YEAR CALENDAR]
FOR YOUR SELECTIVE ADMISSIONS PROCESS

Freshman Year

September

Start planning your high school curriculum with an eye toward selective college admission. Meet with your adviser to talk over your high school's course requirements, and gain a sense of what core courses you will need to take to fulfill the requirements of selective colleges. Don't see high school as just a preparatory step for college, but do consider planning essential to build a strong foundation for your future studies.

What extracurricular activities are you good at or interested in? Would you like to try something new in high school? Now is the time to get involved in new things, and to cut out those activities that you no longer enjoy.

January

You may begin planning for next year's courses. What have you enjoyed the most academically this year? Where are your strengths developing?

Those are the areas in which you will want to continue to push yourself through high school.

February

Start thinking about your summer plans. Will you need to work? Would you like to attend an athletic camp in your strongest sport? What about a writers' workshop, music, or fine arts program? Summers are a time to be with family, but also a time for you to begin to pursue your passions outside of school.

March

Register for SAT Subject Tests in May or June for those courses you are finishing up this year, such as biology, chemistry, or world history. With score choice/withholding, you may even try a Math Level 1 test if you have completed Algebra II already.

May

Take SAT Subject Tests, as appropriate.

June

Take SAT Subject Tests, as appropriate.

Sophomore Year

September

Continue to revise your academic program. Are you happy with your course choices and teachers? Are you being sufficiently challenged? Or overwhelmed? Always be willing to talk with your parents, teachers, and advisers about what is and is not working for you in school. Course changes are usually possible where appropriate.

How are your extracurricular activities shaping up? Do you want to get involved in school or class leadership? Stay with the same sport? Try a new one? Join the band?

Talk with your counselor about the PSAT/NMSQT. You will want to take this test for practice next month. If your school offers the ACT PLAN, mate sure to take that as well.

October
Note the date of the PSAT/NMSQT. Take this test for practice. Take the ACT PLAN.

January
Time again to plan for next year's courses. Have your academic interests and strengths remained constant? Has history grabbed your attention? Or chemistry? How are your foreign language skills developing? It is likely that you will want to take at least one more year of the same foreign language as a junior. Next year is the time to stretch for an Advanced Placement course or two, or a couple of honors/accelerated-level courses, in your best subjects.

February
Summer is again a time to do something exciting, and to explore a major interest. Be a counselor at your old camp. Finish your Scouting badge. Do an Outward Bound program. Bike across America. Go to France. Work full-time. Take a summer class. There are a million and one opportunities out there. Let your interests, within obvious family and financial constraints, drive what you do with your summer.

March
Register for SAT Subject Tests in May or June—chemistry, world history, perhaps a trial Math Level 1.

May
Take SAT Subject Tests, as appropriate.

June
Take SAT Subject Tests, as appropriate.

Consider whether you are ready to start visiting a few colleges this summer. If you want, you can do some tours at some different kinds of colleges to get an early sense of what you like and dislike.

Junior Year

September

Review your curriculum. Start browsing Web sites and thinking about appropriate colleges for you. Begin your initial self-assessment, and get to know the colleges and their requirements (Steps One, Two, and Three).

Review your extracurricular activities again. You may have to make some more choices, within the time constraints of a more advanced curriculum, about what activities you will keep. See Step Five.

Begin reviewing gradually for the PSAT/NMSQT. You will want to work with PSAT prep books, a class, a tutor, and/or online materials, and take at least one practice test before the real thing. Review last year's PSAT results to see where you need to focus your work.

Depending on your readiness level, register for the December or January SAT.

October

Note the date of the PSAT/NMSQT, and take this test. A strong score will qualify you for the National Merit Scholarship competition. Make sure you know your school's College Board/ACT code number, to be used whenever you take tests.

Sign up for the College Board's free Student Search Service (SSS), which matches your background and interests with colleges that are looking for students like you. You will receive information about their programs in the spring.

Plan to attend at least one college fair in your area, and to visit a few model colleges that might be of interest.

November

Begin filling your notebook with preliminary information about colleges that interest you after studying viewbooks, Web sites, and other sources such as college blogs and videos. Talk to recent graduates of your high school about their colleges as well as to alumni (don't forget alumni on your school faculty).

Prep for the December or January SAT.

December

When you get your PSAT/NMSQT scores, review your test booklet in order to continue preparing for the SAT.

Register for the January SAT if you plan to take this test. If your PSAT scores were strong, and you feel you have prepared enough, then take the SAT at this time. However, do not feel pressured to take the SAT this early if you are not ready. Even with the score choice policy, some colleges may ask to see all your scores.

January

Register for the February ACT.

Before taking the SAT, make sure you have reviewed enough to feel confident about your abilities. See Step Four.

Plan your senior-year courses, with a focus on advanced course work in your areas of strength, and on profiling yourself academically for colleges.

Plan your summer accordingly. You will need time for college visits, possibly preparing for fall SATs, and beginning your application writing. See Steps Five and Seven. There may be a key interest, personal quality, or intellectual passion that you would like to pursue or emphasize this summer. Will you need to earn money? Or do you need to take an enrichment course? Make your summer constructive again by thinking it out in advance. Look into special activities that develop your talents and enhance your profile for college admissions.

Using your PSAT scores (and/or SAT scores), as well as your grades and any visits to date, continue to develop an initial list of colleges to visit.

Register for the March SAT.

February

If you took the SAT, you will receive your scores. Use the score report to plan for SAT tests in March and/or May or June, and to consider preparation options you may want to pursue.

Take the ACT.

Take note of admissions procedures of colleges that interest you, paying particular attention to Early Decision requirements.

Consult with your counselor and teachers about taking the Advanced Placement tests in May.

Study the College Board's Index of Majors to help you relate your interests to colleges you plan to visit. You may wish to use a long weekend this month to see some colleges. Take notes on your campus visits, guided by the recommendations in Step Six.

Register for the April ACT.

March

Take the SAT.

Register for SAT Subject Tests in May and/or June. These should be subjects in which you are doing well, especially if they are subjects you won't be taking in your senior year. Check with teachers in each course for their advice. This is especially essential for Early Decision candidates. All of you would like to have at least three strong SAT Subject Test scores by the end of this year.

Use your vacation, weekends, or free days, at least in part, to see some colleges. Try to visit schools when they are in session and you are on break.

Athletes should begin contacting college coaches. Draw up your athletic résumé to send or bring to the coach. Look into special athletic camps. See Step Eight.

April

Schedule campus visits for the rest of the spring, on vacation, on weekends, or during the first couple of weeks in June. You will need to make appointments for late spring, summer, or even fall interviews.

Take the ACT.

Discuss college costs with your parents and draw up a tentative needs budget for use when you visit colleges. Compare the differences in tuition, room, and board expenses as well as aid packages and scholarship opportunities at various colleges.

May

Take AP examinations if advised by your teachers to do so.

List courses and possible majors you might study in college.

Start to identify those people you will ask for letters of recommendation: administrators, counselors, coaches, and others you expect to write glowingly about you.

Start thinking about essay topics.

Take the SAT or SAT Subject Tests (including, for example, U.S. history, chemistry, physics, and Math Level 2).

Register for the June ACT, as necessary.

June

Take the SAT or SAT Subject Tests.

Take the ACT.

Ask two teachers to write recommendation letters.

Make the most of your junior summer!

TEN TIPS FOR MAKING THE MOST OF
YOUR JUNIOR SUMMER

We would like to focus for a moment on all the high school juniors who are wondering what they can do this summer to prepare for the college application process in the fall. We know that many of you will be traveling, working at home, participating in summer programs on prep school and college campuses, playing sports at select camps, and so on. Our list is intended to guide all of you on some important things you can do and start thinking about to make college admissions less stressful and more successful next year.

• *Research colleges.* Read brochures, browse the Web, and talk to teachers and other acquaintances about different schools. As you learn more, you can start to identify which kind of college (small vs. large, urban vs. rural, liberal arts vs. technical, public vs. private, etc.) makes the most sense for you.

• *Visit college campuses.* Particularly use the early and late parts of the summer to see some model campuses when students are around. You can then get a better feel for the kinds of students on campus and what makes the place tick. Touring and attending information sessions are your most likely campus activities. You can interview at schools offering on-campus opportunities.

• *Practice interviewing.* Talk to parents, friends, and advisers about what interests you academically and socially, and what you want out of college. Match your goals and expectations with what you are learning about different colleges. Try to explain why one or another institution makes the most sense for you, given your background, strengths, and interests.

• *Start writing essays.* Note that you will likely need more than one essay, and that you should begin to draft some ideas this summer. Some of you may have papers developed at school that can be adapted to fit college applications, or you may want to write about experiences you will have this summer (so take notes!). You can use last year's Common Application, or many available applications on the Internet, as models.

• *Put together a résumé.* You will want to have this for interviews, and as a model for filling out all those "activities and work experience" lists on the applications. For those with special, well-developed interests (athletes, musicians, and so forth), you may want to have a résumé that is specifically focused on your passion.

• *Contact key college representatives.* For some, this means athletic coaches who might be interested in your background, and who may be able to see you at a summer training camp. For others, this means a music or government professor, for example.

• *Prepare early for fall classes.* If you can get a head start on reading, particularly for some of the AP courses, you will be in better shape in October and November as you continue through your college applications.

• *Consider and contact recommendation writers.* You will need at least two strong academic recommendations for college, and at least one of these should come from a junior year teacher. Perhaps give them your résumé now and ask them, in person, if they are willing to write you a recommendation. They can work on it this summer, and then adapt it for your college applications in the fall.

• *Study for the SATs/ACT.* Most of you will take the SAT, ACT, and/or Subject Tests again in October, November, and even December.

Summer is a great time to build your vocabulary skills, practice grammar, fill gaps in math, and gradually prepare for specific tests.

• *Continue to assess who you are as a person, and what you want out of college.* Avoid focusing on "names" only, and try to consider environments where you will be happy and successful, and able to pursue those activities and ideas that you value. And while this process can be stressful and anxiety-provoking, remember to enjoy the summer and your senior year, to ask for help, and to keep everything in perspective. There is more than one right choice for you out there, and college admissions will work out for you in the right way.

Senior Year

September

Consult your notebook to see where you stand in your college preparations. Have you narrowed your college choices?

Plan to retake the SAT in October or November if you want to improve your score. You may want to use October for the SAT, and November for additional SAT Subject Tests. You may also take the ACT once or twice this fall as a supplement or alternative to the SAT. You still have several opportunities to improve your scores on ACTs, SATs, or SAT Subject Tests. Check which colleges require SAT Subjects and make sure you have enough of them. No school requires more than three. With SATs, schools will typically look at your best math, reading, and writing scores. Put in the time necessary to better your scores: Twenty to thirty minutes every day or so, and a few practice tests on the weekends can make all the difference! Decide which Subject Tests, SAT tests, and/or ACT tests to submit to colleges as you complete your testing through the fall.

Now is the time to complete your writing. Make a copy of the Common Application or the application of your first-choice school or start right on the online form, and use it as a model. Begin filling out the various sections of the application, particularly the essays. An important part of the application is the activities list. Prioritize your activities in order of importance, and also consider the possibility of including a more detailed résumé, and perhaps other supplemental materials, with your application.

Refer to your notes on the various admissions procedures of the colleges you will apply to.

Consider Early Decision, Early Action, and rolling admission possibilities. First-round ED and EA deadlines are generally 11/1 and 11/15. Many schools have added a second round of ED in January. In making an ED (binding commitment) decision, remember that you must be willing to commit to that particular college, and that you must be confident about your grades from last year, and your test scores through October and maybe November.

You should submit rolling admission applications early in the fall, but make sure that if you need them, your October or November test date will be there when the university reviews your application.

If you're applying to any University of California school, remember their online Common Application and 11/30 deadline.

Early Decision candidates should have applications in progress this month, and plans for on-campus interviews and/or a careful second visit to campus. Don't forget the financial aid forms.

Talk to teachers and others about recommendations. Get your recommendation forms to your teachers and guidance counselor early. Let them know about your interests and particular college goals.

October

Conduct additional on-campus interviews and college visits or revisits. Before you visit, consider whether you want to meet with any coaches or teachers from particular departments, and contact them in advance. Focus on your top choices.

Register for the December SAT or SAT Subject Tests or the ACT if you will need these.

Discuss with your counselor the colleges you are going to apply to, and establish deadlines for the mailing of your transcripts. Many high schools ask for three to four weeks' notice in advance of a college application deadline to prepare their materials. Give your guidance counselor appropriate forms to submit to colleges and finalize your list with him or her.

Early Decision candidates should do their self-marketing this month. Do well academically this fall: Strong grades can have a major impact for regular admissions or if you are deferred from Early Decision.

November

Read resource material on scholarships and financial aid, and discuss college costs and financing further with your parents. Get all necessary financial aid forms and explore scholarship opportunities. See Step Nine.

Finish your essays under teacher and counselor supervision.

Study college applications and begin filling one out as a model draft.

Early Decision candidates should be sure not to miss the application deadline this month. Financial aid forms must also be filed. We recommend trying to file your applications at least two weeks before the deadline if possible.

Arrange interviews with alumni of selected colleges over the next several months. Typically colleges or their alumni representatives will contact you once you have submitted all or part of your application.

December

SAT and SAT Subject Tests are given again this month, as is the ACT.

Give your counselor, principal, or designated school official the Secondary School Report section of your college application forms early this month if you have it already.

Register for the January SAT or SAT Subject Tests if you plan to take them.

If you have not done so already, give recommendation forms for each college to appropriate teachers and others. See Step Eight.

Be sure you give your parents the appropriate financial aid forms (FAFSA, etc.) to begin filling out. Form a partnership with them so you all complete the forms and the aid process correctly. Write a family letter to financial aid offices if you need to explain any extenuating circumstances affecting your ability to pay for college.

Use vacation to do any extra study needed to do well on your fall school examinations.

Early Decision applicants who have been admitted must withdraw any other applications.

Early Decision applicants who have been deferred or rejected and non–Early Decision Round I applicants should consider Early Decision Round II opportunities at their first-choice school, if they have one and are ready to make a binding commitment.

Preferably, all applications should be completed and sent out prior to the holiday vacation. That means forms to your counselor and teachers, requests made for official transcripts, requests made for official SAT or ACT scores to be sent to the colleges, financial aid forms completed, essays and activities lists polished and done, and checks made out to the colleges.

January

Take the SAT or SAT Subject Tests if you are scheduled to.

Applications for admission and financial aid forms must be mailed or filed electronically to meet deadlines (usually 1/1 or 1/15). Make copies of everything, and check all details before sealing your envelopes or sending electronically.

Make sure recommendations and transcripts are being mailed.

Alumni interviewing will be available from most schools over the next couple of months, once you have submitted your applications.

If you have been deferred from a first-choice school, there is still hope! Write a letter to the admissions office bringing them up to date on your classes, activities, and continuing interest in the college. Send in any new materials or information worthy of inclusion in your application, possibly an additional recommendation from a senior-year teacher, and new grades.

Speaking of new grades, keep them up! Good grades this winter and spring can make a significant difference for deferred applications, regular applications, and, perhaps, a waiting-list situation in May/ June.

February

Ask your counselor to submit midterm grades to the colleges you have applied to.

Arrange now to take Advanced Placement tests and SAT Subject Tests in May, and possibly more SAT tests in June.

This is a good month to do self-marketing with faculty members and coaches at colleges.

Early Decision II applicants who have been accepted must withdraw other applications.

If you have not finished your college applications, time is running out, so wrap up final colleges now. This includes rolling admissions schools with March or April deadlines.

Take advantage of any alumni interviews that a college may offer you. This is a good chance to further enhance your application, and to find out more about particular colleges.

March

This is a good month to nail down sources of financial aid.

Continue to work hard academically and keep colleges informed of your progress and of extracurricular achievements or other awards.

Stay in touch with your counselor to see if there is anything else you should be doing, or to fill him or her in on any new developments.

You may begin hearing from colleges toward the end of this month.

April

This month you will receive your letters of admission. Follow the procedures described in Step Ten.

Visit one or more campuses if necessary to help decide what college to accept.

Make sure that you are getting the best possible financial aid package, and let the financial aid office know of any dissatisfaction or questions you have. Aid packages can be revised.

If you still want to attend a college that has wait-listed you, let the admissions office know your desire, following Step Ten procedures. Send admissions officers any news, such as high grades or awards.

Don't forget the deposit deadline.

May

Notification-of-acceptance deadline is May 1, known as the Common or Candidate Reply Date. You should also notify colleges you regretfully do not plan to attend, thanking them for accepting you.

Take AP examinations.

Take SAT Subject Tests, as appropriate. This may help you gain extra credits and advanced course placement in college.

June

Take additional SAT Subject Tests, as appropriate.

Respond promptly to all requests from your college regarding housing preferences and preliminary selection of courses for first semester.

Notify your school to which college it should send your final grades, class rank, and proof of graduation.

Plan to earn money this summer, or to get a head start on courses you will be taking. Some colleges have a required summer reading book.

Make plans for any pre-orientation or freshman trip programs at the college.

Drop a note of appreciation to your counselor, teachers, or others who have helped you in the admissions process.

APPENDIX:

Your Worksheets for
Making the Ten Steps Work for You

College Requirements Worksheet

Name of college ___ ___ ___ ___ ___ ___ ___

Level of selectivity
(Demanding,
Very Demanding,
Exceedingly
Demanding) ___ ___ ___ ___ ___ ___ ___

Units of high school
courses required
(1 unit = 1 year):

English ___ ___ ___ ___ ___ ___ ___

Mathematics ___ ___ ___ ___ ___ ___ ___

Science ___ ___ ___ ___ ___ ___ ___

Languages ___ ___ ___ ___ ___ ___ ___

History or

Social studies ___ ___ ___ ___ ___ ___ ___

Electives advised ___ ___ ___ ___ ___ ___ ___

Total units required ___ ___ ___ ___ ___ ___ ___

Is SAT or ACT
required? ___ ___ ___ ___ ___ ___ ___

How many SAT
Subject Tests
required? ___ ___ ___ ___ ___ ___ ___

Tests recommended ___ ___ ___ ___ ___ ___ ___

Early Decision or
Early Action policy? ___ ___ ___ ___ ___ ___ ___

ED or EA deadlines ___ ___ ___ ___ ___ ___ ___

Notification dates ___ ___ ___ ___ ___ ___ ___

Regular admission
deadline ___ ___ ___ ___ ___ ___ ___

Notification dates ___ ___ ___ ___ ___ ___ ___

College Visit Summary Sheet

Before visiting a college be sure to review carefully the information in the school brochure or Web site. Upon completion of your visit, write in your responses to the issues contained here. Do this for each college visited and then compare your summaries for each.

COLLEGE OR UNIVERSITY: _____ LOCATION: _____

Date of visit:_____ Interviewer:_____

STUDENT BODY
(Impression of student body in terms of appearance, style, friendliness, degree of interest and enthusiasm, diversity of social, religious, ethnic background.)

ACADEMIC FACTORS
(How serious about academics is the college and its students; how good are the facilities for academic pursuits; how varied is the curriculum; how strict or flexible are the requirements; how appropriate is the college for your interests?)

CAMPUS FACILITIES AND SOCIAL LIFE
(How complete and modern are the facilities, such as dorms, library, Internet system, student center, athletic complex; how active is the social life, how diverse is it; is it a suitcase or commuter campus?)

OVERALL IMPRESSIONS
(What you liked least and most; what seemed different or special. What type of student do you feel would be happiest there? Are you the type?)

RATING
(On a scale of 1 to 5, with 1 being the top grade, rate the college on the basis of your interest in it.)

College Visit Summary Sheet

Before visiting a college be sure to review carefully the information in the school brochure or Web site. Upon completion of your visit, write in your responses to the issues contained here. Do this for each college visited and then compare your summaries for each.

COLLEGE OR UNIVERSITY: _____ LOCATION: _____

Date of visit:_____ Interviewer:_____

STUDENT BODY
(Impression of student body in terms of appearance, style, friendliness, degree of interest and enthusiasm, diversity of social, religious, ethnic background.)

ACADEMIC FACTORS
(How serious about academics is the college and its students; how good are the facilities for academic pursuits; how varied is the curriculum; how strict or flexible are the requirements; how appropriate is the college for your interests?)

CAMPUS FACILITIES AND SOCIAL LIFE
(How complete and modern are the facilities, such as dorms, library, Internet system, student center, athletic complex; how active is the social life, how diverse is it; is it a suitcase or commuter campus?)

OVERALL IMPRESSIONS
(What you liked least and most; what seemed different or special. What type of student do you feel would be happiest there? Are you the type?)

RATING
(On a scale of 1 to 5, with 1 being the top grade, rate the college on the basis of your interest in it.)

College Visit Summary Sheet

Before visiting a college be sure to review carefully the information in the school brochure or Web site. Upon completion of your visit, write in your responses to the issues contained here. Do this for each college visited and then compare your summaries for each.

COLLEGE OR UNIVERSITY: _____ LOCATION: _____

Date of visit:_____ Interviewer:_____

STUDENT BODY
(Impression of student body in terms of appearance, style, friendliness, degree of interest and enthusiasm, diversity of social, religious, ethnic background.)

ACADEMIC FACTORS
(How serious about academics is the college and its students; how good are the facilities for academic pursuits; how varied is the curriculum; how strict or flexible are the requirements; how appropriate is the college for your interests?)

CAMPUS FACILITIES AND SOCIAL LIFE
(How complete and modern are the facilities, such as dorms, library, Internet system, student center, athletic complex; how active is the social life, how diverse is it; is it a suitcase or commuter campus?)

OVERALL IMPRESSIONS
(What you liked least and most; what seemed different or special. What type of student do you feel would be happiest there? Are you the type?)

RATING
(On a scale of 1 to 5, with 1 being the top grade, rate the college on the basis of your interest in it.)

College Visit Summary Sheet

Before visiting a college be sure to review carefully the information in the school brochure or Web site. Upon completion of your visit, write in your responses to the issues contained here. Do this for each college visited and then compare your summaries for each.

COLLEGE OR UNIVERSITY: _____ LOCATION: _____

Date of visit:_____ Interviewer:_____

STUDENT BODY
(Impression of student body in terms of appearance, style, friendliness, degree of interest and enthusiasm, diversity of social, religious, ethnic background.)

ACADEMIC FACTORS
(How serious about academics is the college and its students; how good are the facilities for academic pursuits; how varied is the curriculum; how strict or flexible are the requirements; how appropriate is the college for your interests?)

CAMPUS FACILITIES AND SOCIAL LIFE
(How complete and modern are the facilities, such as dorms, library, Internet system, student center, athletic complex; how active is the social life, how diverse is it; is it a suitcase or commuter campus?)

OVERALL IMPRESSIONS
(What you liked least and most; what seemed different or special. What type of student do you feel would be happiest there? Are you the type?)

RATING
(On a scale of 1 to 5, with 1 being the top grade, rate the college on the basis of your interest in it.)

College Visit Summary Sheet

Before visiting a college be sure to review carefully the information in the school brochure or Web site. Upon completion of your visit, write in your responses to the issues contained here. Do this for each college visited and then compare your summaries for each.

COLLEGE OR UNIVERSITY: _____ LOCATION: _____

Date of visit:_____ Interviewer:_____

STUDENT BODY
(Impression of student body in terms of appearance, style, friendliness, degree of interest and enthusiasm, diversity of social, religious, ethnic background.)

ACADEMIC FACTORS
(How serious about academics is the college and its students; how good are the facilities for academic pursuits; how varied is the curriculum; how strict or flexible are the requirements; how appropriate is the college for your interests?)

CAMPUS FACILITIES AND SOCIAL LIFE
(How complete and modern are the facilities, such as dorms, library, Internet system, student center, athletic complex; how active is the social life, how diverse is it; is it a suitcase or commuter campus?)

OVERALL IMPRESSIONS
(What you liked least and most; what seemed different or special. What type of student do you feel would be happiest there? Are you the type?)

RATING
(On a scale of 1 to 5, with 1 being the top grade, rate the college on the basis of your interest in it.)

College Visit Summary Sheet

Before visiting a college be sure to review carefully the information in the school brochure or Web site. Upon completion of your visit, write in your responses to the issues contained here. Do this for each college visited and then compare your summaries for each.

COLLEGE OR UNIVERSITY: _____ LOCATION: _____

Date of visit:_____ Interviewer:_____

STUDENT BODY
(Impression of student body in terms of appearance, style, friendliness, degree of interest and enthusiasm, diversity of social, religious, ethnic background.)

ACADEMIC FACTORS
(How serious about academics is the college and its students; how good are the facilities for academic pursuits; how varied is the curriculum; how strict or flexible are the requirements; how appropriate is the college for your interests?)

CAMPUS FACILITIES AND SOCIAL LIFE
(How complete and modern are the facilities, such as dorms, library, Internet system, student center, athletic complex; how active is the social life, how diverse is it; is it a suitcase or commuter campus?)

OVERALL IMPRESSIONS
(What you liked least and most; what seemed different or special. What type of student do you feel would be happiest there? Are you the type?)

RATING
(On a scale of 1 to 5, with 1 being the top grade, rate the college on the basis of your interest in it.)

College Visit Summary Sheet

Before visiting a college be sure to review carefully the information in the school brochure or Web site. Upon completion of your visit, write in your responses to the issues contained here. Do this for each college visited and then compare your summaries for each.

COLLEGE OR UNIVERSITY: _____ LOCATION: _____

Date of visit:_____ Interviewer:_____

STUDENT BODY

(Impression of student body in terms of appearance, style, friendliness, degree of interest and enthusiasm, diversity of social, religious, ethnic background.)

ACADEMIC FACTORS

(How serious about academics is the college and its students; how good are the facilities for academic pursuits; how varied is the curriculum; how strict or flexible are the requirements; how appropriate is the college for your interests?)

CAMPUS FACILITIES AND SOCIAL LIFE

(How complete and modern are the facilities, such as dorms, library, Internet system, student center, athletic complex; how active is the social life, how diverse is it; is it a suitcase or commuter campus?)

OVERALL IMPRESSIONS

(What you liked least and most; what seemed different or special. What type of student do you feel would be happiest there? Are you the type?)

RATING

(On a scale of 1 to 5, with 1 being the top grade, rate the college on the basis of your interest in it.)

College Visit Summary Sheet

Before visiting a college be sure to review carefully the information in the school brochure or Web site. Upon completion of your visit, write in your responses to the issues contained here. Do this for each college visited and then compare your summaries for each.

COLLEGE OR UNIVERSITY: _____ LOCATION: _____

Date of visit:_____ Interviewer:_____

STUDENT BODY

(Impression of student body in terms of appearance, style, friendliness, degree of interest and enthusiasm, diversity of social, religious, ethnic background.)

ACADEMIC FACTORS

(How serious about academics is the college and its students; how good are the facilities for academic pursuits; how varied is the curriculum; how strict or flexible are the requirements; how appropriate is the college for your interests?)

CAMPUS FACILITIES AND SOCIAL LIFE

(How complete and modern are the facilities, such as dorms, library, Internet system, student center, athletic complex; how active is the social life, how diverse is it; is it a suitcase or commuter campus?)

OVERALL IMPRESSIONS

(What you liked least and most; what seemed different or special. What type of student do you feel would be happiest there? Are you the type?)

RATING

(On a scale of 1 to 5, with 1 being the top grade, rate the college on the basis of your interest in it.)

Financial Worksheet

College ____ ____ ____ ____ ____ ____

Tuition ____ ____ ____ ____ ____ ____

Room and board ____ ____ ____ ____ ____ ____

Fees ____ ____ ____ ____ ____ ____

Books and supplies ____ ____ ____ ____ ____ ____

Travel ____ ____ ____ ____ ____ ____

Personal expenses ____ ____ ____ ____ ____ ____

Total one-year budget ____ ____ ____ ____ ____ ____

KINDS OF AID AVAILABLE:

Tuition payment plans

Monthly payments ____ ____ ____ ____ ____ ____

Four years payable in
advance ____ ____ ____ ____ ____ ____

Scholarships ____ ____ ____ ____ ____ ____

Student loans from
the college ____ ____ ____ ____ ____ ____

Government aid plans administered by the college ____ ____ ____ ____ ____ ____

Campus jobs available ____ ____ ____ ____ ____ ____

Hours per week ____ ____ ____ ____ ____ ____

Noncampus jobs available ____ ____ ____ ____ ____ ____

Summer job leads ____ ____ ____ ____ ____ ____

Financial counseling ____ ____ ____ ____ ____ ____

ED/EA aid application due ____ ____ ____ ____ ____ ____

Regular aid application due ____ ____ ____ ____ ____ ____

Financial Worksheet

College ____ ____ ____ ____ ____ ____

Tuition ____ ____ ____ ____ ____ ____

Room and board ____ ____ ____ ____ ____ ____

Fees ____ ____ ____ ____ ____ ____

Books and supplies ____ ____ ____ ____ ____ ____

Travel ____ ____ ____ ____ ____ ____

Personal expenses ____ ____ ____ ____ ____ ____

Total one-year budget ____ ____ ____ ____ ____ ____

KINDS OF AID AVAILABLE:

Tuition payment plans

Monthly payments ____ ____ ____ ____ ____ ____

Four years payable in
advance ____ ____ ____ ____ ____ ____

Scholarships ____ ____ ____ ____ ____ ____

Student loans from
the college ____ ____ ____ ____ ____ ____

Government aid plans admin-
istered by the college ____ ____ ____ ____ ____ ____

Campus jobs available ____ ____ ____ ____ ____ ____

Hours per week ____ ____ ____ ____ ____ ____

Noncampus jobs available ____ ____ ____ ____ ____ ____

Summer job leads ____ ____ ____ ____ ____ ____

Financial counseling ____ ____ ____ ____ ____ ____

ED/EA aid application due ____ ____ ____ ____ ____ ____

Regular aid application due ____ ____ ____ ____ ____ ____

COLLEGE APPLICATION ORGANIZER	COLLEGES					
KEEP A COPY OF EVERYTHING!						
1 Request application and catalogue from college admissions office by phone or e-mail on their Web site.						
2 Schedule a visit, tour, and/or interview at colleges of genuine interest. If an interview is planned, practice your interviewing skills.						
3 Send a thank-you note to your interviewer.						
4 Contact coaches, professors, and music/art instructors, as appropriate.						
5 Note both early and regular decision deadlines.						
6 Complete essays and activities list.						
7 If college uses a Preliminary Application, or Part I Form, complete and send in early.						
8 Complete applications. Proofread and spell check. Make draft copy first. Add résumé, portfolio, other materials, if appropriate.						
9 Request (from ETS or ACT) that SAT, Subject Test, AP, and/or ACT scores be sent to each college to which you will apply.						

10 Give teachers formal recommendation form and a stamped, addressed envelope to the college. Request additional recommendations from teachers, coaches, activity adviser, or employer, if desirable.						
11 Give the Secondary Report section of the college application to your college adviser or guidance counselor.						
12 Complete FAFSA and any other required financial aid forms if applying for aid or scholarships.						
13 Send thank-you notes to all teachers, coaches, and others who wrote recommendations for you.						
14 Consider EDI or EA options. Are you ready to commit to one college? If so, deadlines are usually 11/1, 11/15. Sign ED form.						
15 While waiting for answer from an ED, EA, or rolling admission application, prepare other regular decision applications.						
16 In case of an ED/EA deferral, send note to the college in January, updating on grades, activities, level of continuing interest.						
17 Send applications (Overnight, or Reg. Return Receipt, electronic, e.g.), preferably one week prior to deadlines, best before 12/15.						
18 Consider EDII options: Perhaps you are now ready to commit to a top choice college with a January/February EDII deadline.						
19 Note receipt of college's card or e-mail saying your application is "complete," or call college to make sure.						
20 Take advantage of alumni interviews.						
21 Revisit schools of interest to which you are accepted.						
22 Send card to stay on waiting list of schools of interest.						
23 Send form/deposit to commit to one college by 5/1. Send letters of regret to those colleges you will not attend.						

NOTES

NOTES

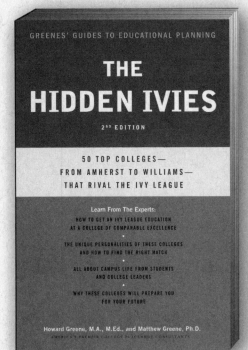
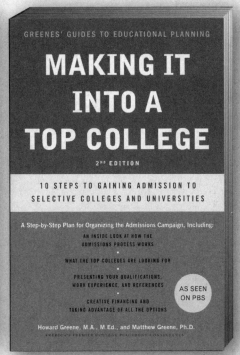